EXTREME BRITAIN

ELIZABETH PEARSON

Extreme Britain

Gender, Masculinity and Radicalisation

OXFORD
UNIVERSITY PRESS

Oxford University Press is a department of the
University of Oxford. It furthers the University's objective
of excellence in research, scholarship, and education
by publishing worldwide.

Oxford New York

Auckland   Cape Town   Dar es Salaam   Hong Kong   Karachi
Kuala Lumpur   Madrid   Melbourne   Mexico City   Nairobi
New Delhi   Shanghai   Taipei   Toronto

With offices in

Argentina   Austria   Brazil   Chile   Czech Republic   France   Greece
Guatemala   Hungary   Italy   Japan   Poland   Portugal   Singapore
South Korea   Switzerland   Thailand   Turkey   Ukraine   Vietnam

Oxford is a registered trade mark of Oxford University Press
in the UK and certain other countries.

Published in the United States of America by
Oxford University Press
198 Madison Avenue, New York, NY 10016

Library of Congress Cataloging-in-Publication Data is available

ISBN: 97801977720721

Printed in the United Kingdom

CONTENTS

v

ACKNOWLEDGMENTS

This book would not exist without those 'extremists' who gave their time to talk to me, some briefly, some at length. I am grateful to everyone who shared their story with me. We are never likely to agree, but I hope you find yourselves fairly represented within these pages. I have been incredibly lucky since I started out in academia, first with a Master's, then with the PhD from which this book grew. Special thanks are due to Katherine Brown, Jelke Boesten, John Bew and War Studies and Defence Studies at King's College London; and to the ESRC, without which this research would not have been possible. Also, to Michael Dwyer and Lara Weisweiller-Wu at Hurst for being patient while life took unexpected turns. And to Laura Sjoberg and the anonymous reviewers–David Duriesmith and Leonie Jackson–whose comments helped improve earlier drafts of this work. Nonetheless, all errors remain my own.

Many people have supported me in the research and writing stages of this book and I will always try to pay that forward. This list is not exhaustive but includes: teams at RUSI, IISS and RAN and Hurst; Christine Cheng, Doug Weeks, Brooke Rogers, Wyn Bowen, Susanne Krieg, Jackie Gower, Alexander Meleagrou-Hitchens, Maura Conway, Lisa McInerney, Marysia Zalewski, Laura Shepherd, Marsha Henry, Paul Higate, Paul Gill, Hilary Pilkington, Gavin Bailey, Jacob Zenn, Atta Barkindo, Adebiyi Kayode, Raff Pantucci, Emily Winterbotham, Andrew Glazzard, Saqeb Mueen, Sabrina Downey, Michael Clarke, Michael Kenney, Brett Kubicek, Sara

Zeiger, Naureen Chowdhury Fink, Bruce Hoffman, Andrew Silke, Jonathan Bright, Jennifer Eggert, Virginia Comolli, Nelly Lahoud, Jayne Huckerby, Stuart Macdonald, Alastair Reed, J. M. Berger, Joe Whittaker, Victoria Williams, Alison Perry, Rebecca Lewis, the SALT team, Annie Mullins, Richard Graham, Suraj Lakhani, Will Baldett, Shereen Williams, Aleksander Dier, Alex Phelan, Michael Nwankpa, Chitra Nagarajan, Joana Cook, James Forest, Thomas Renard, Devorah Margolin, Rachel Bryson, Gina Vale, Innes Bowen, John Morrison, Emily Glorney, Nick Hardwick, Rosie Meeks, Akil Awan, Rob Jago, Ravinder Barn, Matthew Humphreys, Anthony Richards, Kaat Smets, Katy Vaughan, Ashley Mattheis, Joel Busher, Shiraz Maher, Vivienne Jabri, Jamie Bartlett, Carl Miller and Zeynep Sütalan, Daisy Leitch, and the copy-editing team at Hurst involved in creating this text. Also, Elizabeth Hurren, who knew I was bored.

There are many friends to thank too, including some of those listed above. You came with me to meet Anjem, listened to me talk endlessly about extremism, which probably wasn't fun, distracted and entertained me, got me extra work when I was broke, and kept me going when I was giving up. Thank you.

Finally, my family, who always made sure we had books: hand-me-down, bought and borrowed. You are no longer all with me to see this book in print. I hope you would have been proud.

LIST OF ABBREVIATIONS

AfD	*Alternative für Deutschland* Alternative for Germany
ALM	Al-Muhajiroun
AQ	Al-Qaeda
ASBO	Anti-Social Behaviour Order
BBC	British Broadcasting Corporation
BFP	British Freedom Party
BF	Britain First
BNP	British National Party
CCE	The Commission for Countering Extremism
CE	Cumulative Extremism, also known as reciprocal radicalisation
CNN	Cable News Network
CPS	Crown Prosecution Service
CSE	Child Sexual Exploitation
CSMM	Critical Studies on Men and Masculinities
CT	Counter-Terrorism
CVE	Countering Violent Extremism
DFLA	Democratic Football Lads Alliance
DV	Domestic Violence
EDL	English Defence League
FA	Football Association

LIST OF ABBREVIATIONS

FB	For Britain
FGM	Female Genital Mutilation
FLA	Football Lads Alliance
GBV	Gender-Based Violence
HM	Hegemonic Masculinity
HT	Hizb ut-Tahrir
IDF	Israeli Defence Force
IED	Improvised Explosive Device
IR	International Relations
IS	Islamic State
ISIS	Islamic State of Iraq and Syria
JAS	Jamaat Ahlus Sunna Lidawati Wal Jihad/Boko Haram
LGBTQ+	Lesbian Gay Bisexual Trans Queer + identities
MAC	Muslims Against Crusades
MAPPAs	Multi-Agency Public Protection Arrangements
MUU	Mixed, Unclear and Unstable
NA	National Action
PBIED	Person-Borne Improvised Explosive Device
Pegida	*Patriotische Europäer gegen die Islamisierung des Abendlandes*
	Patriotic Europeans Against the Islamification of the West
PTSD	Post-Traumatic Stress Disorder
Q	Question
SAS	Special Air Service
SMT	Social Movement Theory
TPIM	Terrorism Prevention and Investigation Measure
TS	Terrorism Studies
UKIP	United Kingdom Independence Party
UNSCR	United Nations Security Council Resolution
UP	United Patriots
WLM	White Lives Matter
WOT	War on Terror
WPS	Women, Peace and Security

LIST OF ILLUSTRATIONS

Author note: This book covers both the radical right and Islamists networked to al-Muhajiroun. However, only the radical right are featured in the illustrations; Al-Muhajiroun–linked events are not represented for legal reasons and the preservation of participant anonymity.

1. EDL demonstration, Telford, 5 November 2016. Courtesy of *Express & Star* newspaper.

2. 'Working Class Hero' sign at a 'Free Tommy Robinson' protest, London, 9 June 2018. Photo by Daniel Leal/AFP via Getty Images.

3. Protestor in a homemade Robinson T-shirt, Britain First demonstration, Rochdale, 22 July 2017. Photo by Elizabeth Pearson.

4. White Lives Matter demonstration, Margate, 22 October 2016. Penelope Barritt/Alamy Stock Photo.

5. Britain First demonstration, Telford, 25 February 2017. Photo by Elizabeth Pearson.

6. Women leading a Britain First demonstration, Rochdale, 22 July 2017. Photo by Elizabeth Pearson.

7. Anne Marie Waters leading an "Islam Kills Women" event, London, 20 August 2016. Vickie Flores/Shutterstock.

INTRODUCTION

Robert is maybe 60, in a blue fleece. He did six years in the air force, he says, but they don't make the planes anymore. All the cuts, it's totally depleted. He's also worried about the schools—the Trojan Horse cases. The media is sweeping it all under the carpet, he says. Another guy comes over, more aggressive. Who are you, he asks, are you Antifa? He's tall, bent over, in my face. Gavin, he's called. Gavin from Gateshead. No, I say. So, do I agree with it all, what Britain First are doing? No, I say. By now the crowd is transformed into waving Union Jacks. The main banner is brought to the front and Jayda calls for 'the ladies' to come forward.[1] They start to march. A big angry guy in a Nike top is shouting at Asian families watching from their doorsteps.[2] They give him the finger. The marchers chant, "Keep St George in my heart, keep me English…!", "There's only one Lee Rigby!", and the core anthem, "Britain First! Fighting Back!".

Notes from my field diary, Rochdale, 22 July 2017

What masculinities are evident here, on the streets of Rochdale, England, in July 2017? And what does gender have to tell us about extremism in Britain today? A recent report on extremism in the UK suggests far-right street protest is on the rise again.[3] However, initial research on this book began in markedly different times. Leaders of the key groups considered, including Tommy Robinson, Anjem Choudary and Jayda Fransen, have now all served time in prison; indeed Choudary faces possible further prison time after being charged with three terror offences in July 2023. Fransen has left

1

Britain First and spoken publicly of the domestic violence she alleges she suffered from Leader Paul Golding during her time there. Social media platforms removed some of these figures, then allowed them back, then removed some of them again. Since 2014 and the outset of the study, Islamic State has been defeated in Syria and Iraq. The so-called *hijrah* of British, or any other, jihadis to these countries has ended, and there is little political interest in and much public hostility towards bringing them back.

Additionally, both Brexit and COVID-19 have arguably disrupted the UK's political landscape with a shift to the populist right, mirroring similar shifts across Europe and beyond.[4] Lockdown legislation produced more distrust in, and contestation of, the state. Mistrust of statistics combined with deliberate disinformation by bad-faith actors has amplified conspiracy theorists. Lines between extreme or not, threat or not, are blurred. In July 2023, Elon Musk, the billionaire owner of Twitter—now rebranded 'X'—caused consternation when he 'liked' tweets on immigration by Golding.[5] It was reminiscent of 2017, when then President Trump retweeted Fransen, then Deputy Leader of Britain First, leading her to gain 45,000 new followers. Twitter expelled her some weeks later, while the President, whose views on Islam appeared not dissimilar, remained.[6] Whether American voters re-elect Trump, whose activities are followed with avid interest by the British radical right, remains to be seen at the time of writing in 2023. Given hostile British Government policies towards immigration, interviews cited in this book reveal a radical right whose views increasingly resemble dominant discourse; and, furthermore, a movement that frequently rejects its characterisation in political terms of left- or right-wing at all. The situation is not better than it was when I ended the research, and dealing with it is ever more urgent.

What is extremism? The term is no easier to define at the time of writing than when I began research for the book in 2014. And yet this book is all about extremists. It is not easy to interview them— they are not keen on academics—but protests are a good place to start. I attended sixteen events—radical-right and Islamist—and interviewed some thirty-one extreme activists in depth during my research for this book, some of whom I got to know well. If people talked to me, it was because we had a rapport, or they were bored, or curious, or perhaps saw me as a useful mouthpiece. We engaged with each other as people. I disagreed with them on everything, but there were people whom I liked. When police raided one Islamist participant and ultimately charged him with terrorism offences, it was me he turned to for help. Nobody I interviewed expected I would understand them, and I make no claims here that I do.

This book is based on those interviews. I use analysis of them to make an argument: that radicalisation, the process towards extremism, is a project of masculinity. As I write, there is a great deal of popular as well as academic interest in how misogyny and masculinities factor into extremism. This is progress. For too long, both have been ignored. However, while it is often argued that the same misogyny and toxic masculinity are at the heart of the far right and jihadism alike, here I explore the complexities of gender and masculinities (plural) in forging different types of extreme activism. Yes, there is extreme misogyny—understood as the policing and punishment of women who fail to conform to norms supporting patriarchy[7]—and it is important to recognise and combat this; extreme women are often subordinate within their own groups. However, there is also room for extreme women to set the agenda, to lead and mobilise other women, albeit with pushback from patriarchy. Women are also often the victims of extremist groups.

In this world of culture wars, some people are gender sceptics. They think gender studies is harmful, perhaps. Or they wonder, what can thinking about masculinities tell us about extremism that we don't already know? Can gender really matter that much in understanding Britain's radicalisation? The answer is an emphatic yes. This book argues for the importance of gender in understanding the masculinity project that is radicalisation. Additionally, it argues that misogyny matters in radicalisation to both movements discussed, the radical right and ALM. However, the misogyny evident in both movements is not easily distinguishable from misogynies in wider society, or the social norms and backgrounds from which the extreme actors emerge. Extreme identities are not distinct. Extremists have more in common with us than we would like to think.

What this book is about

It goes without saying that this book is about extremists. My focus was also on masculinities, and what they would tell me about misogyny in the groups studied. However, the central research question asked was, how does gender matter in extremism? This led me to a more fundamental question: how would I know what extremism is, and therefore who extremists are? The 2015 UK government's Prevent duty guidance refers back to the 2011 Prevent Strategy for a definition of extremism, which is "the vocal or active opposition to our fundamental values, including democracy, the rule of law, individual liberty and the mutual respect and tolerance of different faiths and beliefs." The government "also regard calls for the death of members of our armed forces as extremist."[8] It is jihadist terrorism that successive CONTEST counter-terrorism strategies have identified as the principal threat to the UK, with the far right secondary.[9] The extremism definition was crafted explicitly to reference actors across Britain's radical-right and Islamist movements. In turn, radicalisation is understood by the UK government as the "process by which people become involved in terrorism or extremism leading to terrorism".[10] It is widely acknowledged in the academic literature, however, that there is no one radicalisation process; radicalisation is not scientific, and can hardly even be labelled a 'process' at all.[11] Furthermore, the terms 'extremism' and 'radicalisation' themselves are contentious and politicised, as will be explored in Chapter One.

Understanding extremism matters, given that counter-terrorism discourse increasingly relies on the above definition. Anthony Richards, a key scholar of definitions of terrorism, has identified a vogue for discourses of extremism over radicalisation and a concomitant muddying of the waters.[12] What is more there is no consensus over extremism as a relative or objectively measurable state. The 2009 UK counter-terrorism strategy CONTEST equates extremism with the undermining of "shared values".[13] In his 2013 review of the literature, Alex P. Schmid concurs, regarding extremism as inherently relational, defined relative to mainstream societal views as well as the rule of law.[14] He suggests that extremism concerns ideology, behaviours and connectedness. However, since

Schmid's work was published, the key contribution to defining extremism has come from American academic J. M. Berger in his book *Extremism*.[15] He disagrees with Schmid on the relational definition. Berger addresses a clear problem: if society's core values undergo an apparent shift—as arguably has been witnessed in both Europe and the United States since the election of several right-wing populist leaders—this impacts the continued framing of only minority groups as extreme. Berger borrows from Henri Tajfel's Social Identity Theory, which posits the idea of the in-group (our own) and the out-group (the other, irredeemably different from ourselves).[16] Berger's definition is focused on the denigration of out-groups. He defines extremism as:

> the belief that an in-group's success or survival can never be separated from the need for hostile action against an out-group. The hostile action must be part of the in-group's definition of success. Hostile acts can range from verbal attacks and diminishment to discriminatory behavior, violence, and even genocide.[17]

This definition has become a new benchmark for policymakers and academics in understanding extremism. Perhaps it is not a surprise that it does not reference gender. Gender theorists have persistently highlighted the security studies landscape's historic neglect of gender.[18] This has been particularly true in the subfields of terrorism, extremism and radicalisation.[19] The situation is, however, changing. One might even say that the field has become obsessed with the function of gender, particularly anti-feminist movements and misogyny, in terrorism since the identification of the incel movement as a contemporary threat. Greater focus on misogyny is urgently needed; we know that jihadist groups such as Islamic State, or Jamaat Ahlus Sunna Lidawati Wal Jihad (Boko Haram), specifically target women in their hostile actions against out-groups, and in certain ways, because they are women.[20] Think of Islamic State's bartering and rape of Yezidi women, or of jihadist abductions of young women students in Nigeria. Yet despite mention of genocide, Berger's definition does not highlight sexual and gender-based violence as a 'hostile act'.

A further important definition therefore comes from the
Commission for Countering Extremism (CCE) in a 2019 report
under lead Commissioner Sara Khan, which prefaces the term
'extremism' with the word 'hateful'. It defines "hateful extremism"
as:[21]

> Activity or materials directed at an out-group who are perceived
> as a threat to an in-group, who are motivated by or intending
> to advance a political, religious or racial supremacist ideology:
> a. To create a climate conducive to hate crime, terrorism or
> other violence; or b. Attempt to erode or destroy the fundamental
> rights and freedoms of our democratic society as protected
> under Article 17 of Schedule 1 to the Human Rights Act 1998.[22]

Gender is still not explicit in this definition. However, Khan's
foreword to the report notes of her research into extremism, "Some
of the stories have left me heartbroken. People, young and old, have
cried as they described how extremists targeted them because of
their sexuality, their gender, their race or religious identity."[23] Both
Khan's response and her new suggested definition remind us of the
affective outcomes of extremism: pain, hate, suffering.

Who this book is about

This book is a study of gender in two of the most significant
extremist movements in the United Kingdom in recent times:
the radical right, an umbrella term for activists opposed to the
perceived 'Islamisation' of Britain and Europe, and therefore Islam;
and the Islamist movement linked to the now-proscribed group al-
Muhajiroun (ALM) (meaning 'the emigrants' and referring to those
who originally followed the Prophet to Mecca). Both movements
have links to the current extremist scene. ALM is a Salafist–Islamist
organisation, and the UK Government has long considered it and its
Leader Anjem Choudary a key threat. Although officially the group
named al-Muhajiroun no longer exists, I interviewed Choudary and
actors following him, some since ALM days, and therefore refer to this
network in the book as ALM. This reflects ALM's understanding that
names do not matter; the call (to the group) matters.[24] Much of the

terminology in discussion of al-Muhajiroun and the actors connected to it is contested. Salafi–jihadi extremism and Islamism have been complex and controversial terms for some years.[25] Scholars using the term 'Islamism' generally define this as political Islamic activism, distinguishing it from Islam as a faith. Salafi jihadism is the violent struggle to establish an Islamic Caliphate,[26] and can be differentiated from other non-violent strands of Salafism.[27] I use the term 'jihad' in this book in place of the phrase 'violent jihad', and for clarity, because that is how the participants used it. In Islam, the 'greater jihad' represents the personal spiritual struggle to live as a good Muslim. The 'lesser jihad' refers to the violent struggle for the faith. Some do not like the term 'Islamism'. Islamism is a diverse ideology, frequently divided into those groups who reject participation in democratic systems and those who do not.[28] Rejectionists include Anjem Choudary and his followers, who advocate violence to achieve the establishment of Shariah law, with the caveat that this must take place only outside of the country of residence—their so-called 'Covenant of Security'. Other groups, such as Hizb ut-Tahrir (HT), support democratic participation. While a number of authors make the distinction between political Islamism and purely religious Islam, this distinction is not made by any of the participants in this research.

While the book focuses on the interviews given by men—women were harder to interview, as Chapter Two explores—I also consider women's navigation of extremism's homosociality, and how they both adopt and resist masculinist norms and misogynies, as well as being constrained by them.

The key radical-right groups studied were the English Defence League (EDL), Britain First (BF) and For Britain (FB). There have been times in the years prior to the publication of this book when Tommy Robinson, a co-founder of the EDL, was barely out of the news. Nonetheless, since I conducted my research, many of the offline activities that once made the headlines hardly appear in the news at all. Free speech protests in 2018 saw thousands march to support him when he was jailed for contempt of court. At the time of writing, banned from mainstream social media platforms, Robinson is less visible, but no less active.[29] Hope Not Hate's 2022 report suggested that he had 180,000 followers on the alternative social media site GETTR and was making a "return", exercising an anti-vaccine, anti-Boris agenda.[30] By mid-2023 Robinson's GETTR followership had increased to almost 235,000, and he was speaking out in support of online influencer and misogynist Andrew Tate and seemingly teaming up with Britain First's Paul Golding, who remains on Twitter while Robinson does not. While anti-far right extremism charity Hope Not Hate notes an increase in far-right street activism, the EDL has all but disappeared.[31] From 2016 to 2018, when I attended demonstrations, pressure on activists was intense. The police filmed events; meanwhile far-left and Antifa activists used social media to shame and 'out' those at protests, hoping to see them lose their jobs.[32] During my field research, perhaps only those with little to lose remained committed to street protest.

At the time of writing in mid-2023, Anjem Choudary has been rearrested and charged with three terrorism offences related to a proscribed organisation.[33] However, like the radical right, ALM has largely been quiet. Anjem Choudary (also known as 'the Sheikh') was at one point almost the go-to media spokesperson for fringe Islamism, to the anger of most British Muslims. He was jailed in September 2016 alongside his younger colleague Mizanur Rahman (also known as Abu Baraa) for support of Islamic State (IS), the violent Islamist group that between 2014 and 2017 claimed and held territories in Syria and Iraq. Choudary has hardly been heard from publicly since, even though stringent release restrictions ended in July 2021.[34] Terrorism Prevention and Investigation Measures (TPIMs), Anti-Social Behaviour Orders (ASBOs) and post-conviction Multi-Agency Public Protection Arrangements (MAPPAs) have been employed in the past to prevent activities such as Islamist congregation in public space and to restrict the employment, living arrangements, activities and associates of activists.[35] In fact, writing in 2018, Michael Kenney suggested that measures against ALM meant the network was "just barely" surviving.[36]

There is no room for complacency. Islamic State may be militarily defeated, but its jihadist ideology remains a key security concern. And while we might not see activists on mainstream social media or in public spaces as much as in the past, it does not mean that they are no longer committed. Indeed, for jihadist groups a period of preparation and inactivity in violence is an important part of the fight. Both ALM and the radical right have proved resilient despite past external pressures. In fact, I chose these movements for this book not simply because they are resilient, or because their homosocial nature lends them to a gender analysis, but because they were for a long time understood to be linked through the phenomenon of Cumulative Extremism (CE), otherwise known as reciprocal radicalisation.[37] However, while gendered constructions of Islam emerged in the study as a key motivator to radical-right activists, to Islamists the radical right or wider far right was largely irrelevant, except as a vehicle for publicity via, for instance, public confrontations. Essentially I was not able to evidence reciprocity in radicalisation between the two movements discursively, or in terms of violence.[38]

Why gender, why masculinities?

The starting point of masculinities theory is an epistemological position that understands gender as socially constructed and is reliant on Judith Butler's concept of performativity. Building on Simone de Beauvoir's assertion that one "becomes" a woman, Butler asserts that gender is a verb: "gender proves to be performative—that is, constituting the identity it is purported to be. In this sense, gender is always a doing".[39] Gender is a normative concept, and can be read in different ways. The most basic reading—typically seen in security studies and policy—is a simple consideration of gender as pertaining to women.[40] However, 'women' and 'gender' are not synonyms. As Laura Sjoberg, Grace D. Cooke and Stacy Reiter Neal note, gender "describes the socially constituted behavioural expectations, stereotypes and rules that construct masculinity and femininity".[41] Gender is malleable, socially constructed and context-dependent.[42] Raewyn Connell, the most influential scholar of masculinities, considered in more detail in the next chapter, first defined masculinity as "a place in gender relations".[43] Kimberly Hutchings notes that this relationality comprises two logics: contrast (with other masculinities) and contradiction (between masculinities

9

and femininities).[44] Historian Joan W. Scott suggests that gender organises relationships in both symbolic and concrete ways.[45] Gender is also about power, because it is a means of creating hierarchies between people. In patriarchal societies, even within groups seeking to control power, masculinities matter.

Building on this, there are four core theoretical reasons why gender and in particular masculinities are crucial tools for understanding contemporary British extremism:

Contemporary British extreme groups are homosocial

The first reason for a gendered approach to Britain's extremism lies in the demographics of contemporary extremists: far-right extremists and violent and non-violent jihadists are mostly men, although by no means exclusively.[46] Sex is one of the only predictive variables in understanding terrorist violence. Edwin Bakker, for example, conducted a study of twenty-eight European jihadi networks from 2001 to 2006 and recorded 237 male convictions, while only five were of women.[47] Studies by terrorism experts Marc Sageman, Daveed Gartenstein-Ross and Laura Grossman made similar findings.[48] The same is true of the far right and the anti-Muslim radical right. Matthew J. Goodwin and Robert Ford, for example, suggest that in its early days the EDL attracted members who were "mainly young, working-class and poorly educated men".[49] The group has always been predominantly male, although women have attended street demonstrations, albeit in smaller numbers.[50] The male dominance in EDL activism mirrors that of previous nationalist groups in the UK, such as the BNP.[51] It also mirrors political parties on the extreme right, as well as non-extreme conservative parties more broadly.[52]

ALM, too, is led by and largely composed of men involved in several formal activities to spread their message. They carry out street *Dawah*, manning stalls, engaging passers-by and giving out leaflets, and created a publishing house (*al-Khilfa*) with the same purpose. Both Choudary and ALM founder Omar Bakri Mohammed led regular classroom sessions for UK members. These were attended by a variety of people, including some later convicted of terrorism. Such activities had multiple aims and multiple audiences:

provocation (for moderate Muslims, non-Muslims and the 'right'), publicity (for the media) and differentiation from other creeds in Islam (for non-Islamist Muslims as well as 'like-minds'). ALM is not just composed of men, however. In his 2005 study of the group, Quintan Wiktorowicz noted that a distinguishing feature of ALM was its inclusive attitude towards women, who were welcome at classes and on *Dawah*—if on separate stalls—and encouraged to participate actively in the group, although not in leadership roles.[53] Ethnographers Doug Weeks and Michael Kenney, despite spending extensive time with ALM, do not reference women in the group in their work beyond noting that they have taken part in protest, and women are not amongst their interviewees.[54] Indeed, in a British context as elsewhere, the majority of violent jihadist incidents have overwhelmingly involved men.[55]

Gender is a fundamental organising principle of contemporary violent groups

Consideration of extreme ideologies further emphasises the significance of gender. Gendered oppositions and binaries constitute the organising principle of the contemporary terrorism and extremism prioritised by Western states—jihadist and far-right—as the backbone of both their beliefs and their actions. Both jihadist and far-right organisations, particularly those advocating violence, tend to position men's and women's roles as complementary and oppositional.[56] Masculinities are an important feature of their narratives. Jihadist groups such as Islamic State present themselves as the only place for "real men", who demonstrate a "rightful masculinity" when contrasted with supposedly "emasculated" Westerners.[57] Feminist scholars have long emphasised the importance of states in the production of masculinities, and the enabling of war.[58] For nationalist and far-right movements, particular forms of manhood—often violent or hypermasculine—are associated with nationhood and the protection of the white race, particularly women.[59] Motherhood is exalted and symbolic, with mothers crucial as the "biological reproducers of 'the nation'".[60] The radical right does not wholly cohere to this ideology, as will be evident in the findings of this book. However, its proximity to far-right groups that do means a gendered analysis is important.

Misogyny and masculinities are poorly understood

As journalism and academia increasingly recognise misogyny and gender-based violence as central to extreme groups, it has become more difficult to ignore gender. Some authors have framed contemporary extremism as being about male supremacy and misogyny; it is.[61] However, current understandings remain simplistic, and lacking in empirical evidence. Kathleen M. Blee, who has spent a lifetime talking to America's far right in order to understand them, has suggested that researchers of far-right extremism know that gender matters but are less clear on the detail of how.[62] This book addresses a gap in existing knowledge of the precise mechanisms of gender in extremism, considering masculinities and anti-feminism. In doing so it answers a call by masculinities scholar Michael Kimmel, who emphasises that gender should be understood as a means of mediating between structures and extreme individuals, and exploring masculinities and femininities.[63] He echoes Jean Bethke Elshtain's demand for work on masculinities to focus beyond men and on gender.[64] This means that misogyny and masculinities are simply aspects of gender's function in the organisation of contemporary extreme groups. Incel men ('incel' is a shorthand for 'involuntary celibate'), for instance, understand themselves as subordinate to men who have women sexual partners.[65] Incel men embody male entitlement and objectify women as rewards which they are angry they have not received.[66] Incels do not, however, just express misogyny; their animus is also directed towards men they see as (more) sexually successful, who are held to be exemplars of hegemonic masculinity and therefore 'other'. Sexuality is also important in extremism, although a detailed analysis is beyond the scope of this book. Far-right and jihadist groups have frequently stigmatised homosexuality and trans identities as deviant forms of masculinity or femininity outside of the established gender binary and the reproductive purpose of the group or race. One result has been the persecution and execution by Islamic State of homosexual individuals;[67] another the pursual of an anti trans agenda by far-right groups.

International norms entail the consideration of gender

Another good reason to consider gender in extremism is that international security norms and legal statutes point to the importance of gendered approaches in understanding and countering terrorism. The United Nations Security Council has by now produced ten resolutions to address the global problem of terrorist violence and extremism, and in 2015 UNSCR 2242 identified the importance of a gender perspective in dealing with terrorism. Part of the Women, Peace and Security (WPS) agenda, it recommended the inclusion of gender as a "cross-cutting issue" in CT activities.[68] Despite this, gender is still often absent in analysis of terrorism and extremism. If thinking about countering terrorism and radicalisation entails a consideration of gender, thinking about terrorism and radicalisation themselves must also. Gender organises the expression of societal power, producing hierarchies through masculinities and femininities.[69] Terrorism and radicalisation also concern power and violence; one definition of terrorism is the use of violence against symbolic targets in order to send a message and achieve an ideological goal.[70] Terrorism aims at change to the status quo, whether by states to further cement power or by non-state actors who perceive themselves as disenfranchised. Gender analysis is therefore relevant to understanding how power operates within radicalisation to masculinist groups practising terrorism. Indeed, recent feminist critiques have outlined how radicalisation is itself gendered.[71]

Methodology: why use interviews?

This book is theoretical, in grappling with how to understand and 'see' gender and masculinities; for terrorism and security studies scholars this gender analysis might be new, and I hope that they see its importance. The book is also empirical. For gender scholars, the empirical chapters will provide an important source of analysis and information. Contemporary gender scholars are trying to understand the apparent global shift towards right-wing populist and far-right politics. For those working on backlash politics and the far right, these chapters will make an important empirical contribution. Here the comparative focus is of particular significance, given that this adds depth to the analysis of each group, which encompasses leadership and grassroots figures alike.

Talking to people engaged in extreme behaviours and groups enables us to use gender to better understand their actions, motivations and interiorities. It also permits space for participants themselves to contest state labels applied to them, challenging security discourses. The analysis emphasises primary source material, and the voices and experiences of participants as those with "a privileged window into their motivations";[72] as Kenney writes, activists "understand better than most ... why they do what they do."[73] The centrality of the participants does not, however, obviate the need for a critical analysis. The research does not take participant narratives at face value. There is further detailed discussion of the ethics of this research in Chapter Two.

Radicalisation as masculinity project: findings and core argument

This book explores the making of extreme men and women, and the centrality of gender to radicalisation. It uncovers how both men and women 'do' masculinities, and the different masculinities evident in contemporary British extremism. It contains a comparative analysis of two extreme movements, and I suggest important differences between them in gendered terms. Indeed, one of my main conclusions is that much separates these ideologies, despite current scholarship's attention to supposed similarities in their gendered practices, particularly misogyny. I emphasise that while gender recurs, genderings differ.

There are five key findings:

Radicalisation

The book argues that radicalisation is a project of masculinity. Gender is fundamental to defining the extremism of the radical right and ALM. Both radicalisation and extremism are produced through masculinities and around gender binaries.

14

Misogyny

Misogyny is apparent in both movements, yet its expressions are not straightforward or evenly distributed, given that anti-misogynistic ideology is also incorporated into the radical right.

Women

Women are enthusiastic participants in these masculinity projects, yet frequently find themselves navigating the exclusion and misogyny that masculinist groups entail. Even when they employ agency and actively choose to accept the gender inequalities within activism, they find those used against them.

Systems

Masculinities function in systems, and are lived as chords, not notes. They are heterarchical, with different masculinities often simultaneously experienced.

Difference

The gender dynamics and masculinities of the radical right and ALM differ. Additionally, different groups within the radical right embody different masculine cultures to distinguish identities and invoke distinct cultural practices, and gender is a point of fragmentation.

If radicalisation is a masculinity project, as the first finding contends, then the aim of this book is to elucidate the specific ways different masculinities are produced in support of that project. The book uses gender analysis to show the 'messy' and complex nature of radicalisation: from exposure to extreme ideology, to mobilisation to the extreme movement and in some cases to violence; also, with respect to the daily maintenance of extreme identities. The gendered analysis additionally problematises current understandings of radicalisation as a primarily transformative process, both in terms of thought (cognitive) and of action (behavioural).[74] The book instead emphasises the ways in which masculinities and misogyny within extreme groups remain to a large degree consistent with masculinities and misogyny before and outside of them, and are contiguous with masculinity norms in wider society.

Core argument

Significantly, the comparative empirical analysis supports the core argument and theoretical analysis of Chapter One: that despite increasing emphasis in contemporary discourse, misogyny and toxic masculinity are not differentiating attributes or even always appropriate descriptors for the movements studied.

Men and women interviewees from both movements reveal a continuity of gendered behaviour into the group. This certainly includes misogyny, but misogyny is rarely the reason for mobilisation towards the group. This misogyny is often part of the wider culture from which the radical right and ALM emerge. The misogyny apparent in the EDL, for instance, is the same misogyny directed towards Muslim women and towards white working-class women that is evident elsewhere in society. It relies on shared tropes: that white working-class women are promiscuous or 'disgusting', for instance, or that Muslim women are meek, submissive and oppressed. Similarly, empirical analysis of ALM participants reveals a continuity of gendered beliefs and misogyny from before the group into the group. Differences in misogynies are evident, however. ALM had more control over women's activism within the group. Also, the possibilities for women's leadership across the movements were not the same. Neither movement had a straightforward relationship with misogyny, given that both made space for women's rights and inclusion within their activism, yet this occurred in different ways and to different degrees.

Regarding toxic masculinity, what the movements share is that the men within them are reviled as toxic by wider society. Men's behaviours in the movements studied are harmful; yet, again, many of these behaviours, particularly within the radical right, are consistent with life before the group. Extreme masculinities are forged in the intersections of place, sex, race and faith, and in wider discourses. However, gender and masculinities function in different ways in the two movements. The masculinity project of each movement is not the same, in that different masculinities are at the fore. The findings chapters support the argument that each movement functions around a different system of numerous hegemonic masculinities.

These systems are not the same, in terms of either moral value to participants—for example, Islamist participants regard their Islamo-cultural masculinity system to embody values superior to those of secular society; symbolic value to participants—for example, radical-right participants believe that a masculinity system in which men and women have distinct roles has longstanding links to both Britishness and Christianity; or authenticity, with both sets of participants seeking gendered roles and values that have affective worth, producing a feeling of fit. There is no one system of masculinities I could describe as toxic, given that all incorporate masculinities with positive as well as negative outcomes (and intentions).

Considering the book's finding about systems, that masculinities can be simultaneously experienced, ALM interviewees describe a constant reflexive engagement with what they suggest is the gendered compromise of assimilation. It is this that they locate at the heart of their definition of in-group and out-group, and the move to ALM and Choudary's network. This problematises understandings of masculinities as hierarchical, suggesting they function as heterarchies. Masculinities are not just multiple; they are, as Eve Kosofsky Sedgwick has suggested, *n*-dimensional and can be multiply held.[75]

The central findings suggest a gendered definition of extremism as an alternative to the one we are used to, as formulated by Schmid or Berger, for example, or the British government. These findings show that it is the perception of gendered difference that enables the in- and out-group formation that is central to Berger's definition of extremism: gendered difference forms the backbone of group ideologies, separating male and female roles; it dictates male and female identity and agency within groups; and it underpins the different cultures of group activism, at times causing fractures between them. A feminist engagement with radicalisation must define it not simply as a process towards an end point of support for violent extremism, but also as a project of masculinity, in support of patriarchal domination. This is as true for radical women in Britain's extreme groups as it is for radical men.

How this book is structured

This Introduction has set out the research question I commenced with when I began the fieldwork for this book: to what extent does gender matter in extremism in the UK? It has also covered why it is important to address gender, how I set out to ask questions of extremists about gender, and, briefly, what I found. The next chapter considers the existing literature on gender in radicalisation and why the presence of men has been taken for granted: a 'boys will be boys' approach. In particular, it looks critically at how the field has engaged gender in understanding radicalisation, drawing on models and theory from a range of disciplines, but primarily terrorism and security studies. While wide-ranging, the literature explored is fundamental to understanding both current narratives about radicalisation and extremism and the ways gender is already present and absent within them. The chapter details the need for the book and the importance of the holistic framework employed.

Chapter One also argues that the current academic literature on radicalisation and extremism within the two movements tends to reduce the role of gender to either 'deviant women' or 'toxic men'. Neither approach is enough to understand adequately the role gender and masculinities play in radicalisation. It contends that a new framework is required to holistically analyse the complex function of gender and masculinities within the movements, understanding gendered identity as situated in space. This is the starting point for the research, and much of the argument will be familiar to gender scholars.

Chapter Two focuses on methodology, asking: Is it ethical to interview extremists? The question is central to the findings chapters and explores the moral, as well as practical, challenges of research that relies on the stories of people involved in extreme groups. It argues for an empathetic feminist approach to research with extremists, situated within a framework of care. The chapter also considers power, race and my positionality as a woman researcher in interviews with both movements.

I have endeavoured to make discussion of the two movements as straightforward as possible, introducing the radical right in the first findings chapters (Chapters Three, Four and Five) and turning to ALM in Chapters Six and Seven. The empirical material in these chapters makes a clear and compelling case for comparative work in this field and powerfully demonstrates how gender functions to shape the movements.

Chapter Three begins with analysis of the radical right, situating masculinities that are later mobilised into activism. It introduces the participants and the wider far-right scene, noting key named leadership figures alongside other, anonymised, grassroots activists. It then engages with the pathways interviewees outlined into the radical-right groups researched—Britain First, the English Defence League and For Britain—beginning with the period prior to activism. Here, masculinities are produced in the intersections of race, gender and faith. The chapter also finds that perceptions of gendered difference within local spaces are fundamental to the production of in-group and out-group boundaries that underlie Berger's definition of extremism.

Chapter Four explores how the masculinities considered in Chapter Three are mobilised into activism. The chapter focuses on the mobilisation of activism around diverse gendered symbolic cultures, permitting the expression of specific masculinities and femininities to produce specific affects. The argument across these chapters is that continuity, not transformation, is the key to understanding radicalisation to the radical right. However, gender analysis reveals how groups seek differentiation, thus fragmenting the wider movement. The radical right is characterised by different groups, united in countering Islam, but differing in masculine approach.

Chapter Five draws on in-depth interviews with two women leaders, Jayda Fransen (BF) and Anne Marie Waters (FB), as well as grassroots activists, to explore the tensions of women's activism in the radical right. The chapter finds that women employ different gendered strategies, making patriarchal bargains to negotiate the masculinism of the wider movement. Women 'do' masculinities as well as femininities to fit in. This chapter explores the implications for female agency and inclusion, noting the costs to both men and women of women's activism in a masculinist scene. It also examines the ideal of gender equality against the reality of anti-Islam protest for women.

In Chapter Six the book turns to al-Muhajiroun, introducing the group and the participants, including Anjem Choudary, and situating group masculinities in place and discourse. Echoing the narratives of the radical right, interviewees describe the centrality of perceptions of gendered difference in radicalisation to the group, and, in particular, the importance of meta-reflexivity in the rejection of their own gendered assimilation. This chapter details the role of gender and masculinities in so-called 'identity crisis', a foundational concept in radicalisation theory.

Chapter Seven explores how the masculinities of Chapter Six are mobilised. Both chapters consider the multiple masculinities valorised by participants, and how they combine them to validate one another. The chapters suggest the importance of systems of multiple masculinities that can be simultaneously inhabited by different participants. As with the radical right, the emphasis is on continuity over transformation. In Chapter Seven there is discussion of misogyny within the movement and the policing of women; also of the mechanisms of adherence to ideology for the women participants.

Comparisons between the two movements are made in the final conclusions chapter, which draws together themes for broader research and considers the implications of the research in this book for policy in Britain now: different leaders may wield power, but the same extreme ideologies pose risks. The chapter notes parallels between the two movements: the importance of place in the production of extremism, and the marginalisation of women in what are essentially masculinist movements. Both movements also make claims to representation of an authentic masculinity system which they regard as absent in contemporary society. However, there are key differences. The radical-right participants in this research emphasise the significance of local spaces and gender within these, while Islamists embrace the wider transnational context; Islamists echo narratives of liberation struggles in their own families, while those on the radical right recall struggles for domination; the radical right holds space for women in public leadership roles, while al-

Muhajiroun does not; the radical right embraces progressive politics including gay and women's rights to some degree, and not entirely cynically, in their agendas, while Islamists do not; and, finally, the radical right believes that its actions stand in for a neglectful state, while the Islamists reject the state.

Summary

This book is about the people who make up Extreme Britain, and it uses a gender analysis to fill a gap in the current knowledge of radicalisation processes, which, despite much research, are still not well understood. It concludes that radicalisation is a project of masculinity, towards an end goal of domination. However, although misogyny is apparent in both the radical right and the Islamist network linked to Anjem Choudary, the function of gender goes beyond the narrow confines of this goal. Each movement represents the realisation of conflicting visions of masculinity and femininity, vying for domination, although over different sets of actors. The book makes an important contribution given its reliance on first-person narratives derived from semi-ethnographic research with Islamist actors who support the now-banned ALM; and with the broader anti-Islam(ist) radical right, with emphasis on the English Defence League, Britain First and For Britain. It answers calls for a multi-disciplinary approach to terrorism studies (TS) from Magnus Ranstorp;[76] for creativity in theoretical frameworks in gender work from Maria Stern;[77] and for normatively neutral insight from Cas Mudde.[78] It also engages in an 'un-disciplining', echoing Foucault's belief in the futility of discipline due to the limitations and ontological omissions it can produce.[79]

The next chapter turns to gender in both historical and contemporary understandings of radicalisation, underlining why a gender analysis matters, how it has been missing, and why focus on misogyny and masculinity can be theoretically problematic.

1

THEORY
MASCULINITIES AND EXTREMISM

Introduction

My research on British Islamist extremism began with a meeting in East London, with Anjem Choudary during a break in his 2016 trial for support of Islamic State. We had dessert in a café at the end of his street. A friend who had barely heard of Choudary acted as my *mahram*, listening in polite disbelief as he explained why adultery is rightly punishable by death, as I took notes.[1] Two months later, I sat with a group of his male supporters in the public gallery at the Old Bailey. Women supporters were not permitted to attend. In September 2016 a judge sentenced Choudary and fellow preacher Mizanur Rahman to 5.5 years in prison; they served 2.[2]

For many in UK counter-terrorism, Choudary's imprisonment was long overdue. Born and educated in the UK, Choudary has provoked much criticism over the years with outspoken attacks on democracy and calls—often in British media—for a Caliphate in the UK, run according to Shariah law.[3] Choudary was originally involved in al-Muhajiroun under Omar Bakri Mohammed, taking on the leadership role when Bakri Mohammed was deported in 2005.[4] In the same year, al-Muhajiroun officially disbanded in order to escape being banned, and it remains a legally proscribed group.[5] Although proscribed, discussion of ALM as an entity remains valid, as the protagonists continued under new banners with Choudary's leadership, and there is a network of individuals around the group who share its outlook but are not members. Subsequent offshoots have also been banned several times for support of the violent institution of a global Caliphate.[6] The government's 2018 CONTEST strategy suggested that ALM had been "reenergised" as a result of ISIS's declaration of a Caliphate.[7] Numerous authors have linked ALM to transnational terror plots. After his release from prison in 2018, however, Choudary largely avoided the headlines, until his arrest and charge in July 2023.

Another extreme movement in the UK are the radical right, a nebulous collection of mainly white actors, groups and street movements mobilising around 'second-class citizen' identities, and against liberal elites. Much of their campaigning has focused on issues of immigration and the alleged threat of Islam, if not explicitly race. Some of the key groups include those discussed in this book: the English Defence League, Britain First and For Britain.

The EDL emerged in 2009 as the first radical-right populist movement in the UK. Robinson has written of the origins of the EDL, via an earlier group named the 'United People of Luton', as fulfilling three aims: a response to Choudary's deliberately provocative poppy-burning protests;[8] a defence of the military; and a local reaction to demographic changes in Luton.[9] It proclaimed itself a working-class protest movement—predominantly, if not nominally, white working-class—with a "single-issue" focus on opposing "global Islamification".[10] Its website, inactive from April 2021, stated, "We arose as a street movement from the English working class to become the forefront of the counter-jihad."[11]

Britain First, meanwhile, was founded in 2011 as a registered political party with a formal membership list. Jayda Fransen was the party's Deputy Leader until January 2019, when she announced her departure from the group.[12] This followed a jail term for religiously aggravated harassment. The head of the party is Paul Golding, and on 8 May 2018 he was released from prison, where he had been serving a sentence on the same charge.[13] Their imprisonment related to the pursuance and harassment of a group of men charged and later jailed in a Kent case of child sexual exploitation.[14]

Britain First does not oppose unity with other, more far-right and racist groups. Golding is a former BNP activist, and there is a high degree of crossover from the BNP to Britain First. Ideologically, Britain First identifies as a "loyalist" movement with "King and country" its priorities. A 2016 BF newspaper article, "BRITAIN FIRST AND 'RACISM' – THE TRUTH!", reads, "Britain First is not 'racist' in any way and we do not hate other ethnic groups. ... We want to see a world filled with nations, cultures and peoples, all living together in peace within our respective countries."[15] However, this is clearly a direct challenge to British multiculturalism. Fransen, for instance, describes herself as an "ethno-nationalist".[16] BF has an explicitly Christian identity and has aggressively promoted its faith.[17] Fransen has carried a white cross while leading demonstrations, and she and Golding also carried out a series of so-called 'Mosque Invasions', entering mosques uninvited to hand out Bibles. Such practices led to Britain First's reputation as "the far-right mirror image of al-Muhajiroun".[18] In 2016, Bedfordshire Police won a High Court bid to prevent Fransen and Golding from entering any British mosque for 3 years.

I also talked to Anne Marie Waters, who led the radical-right party For Britain, which she disbanded in July 2022.[19] This followed failed attempts by Robinson to rally support for the group.[20] Waters had come from a mainstream political route (the Labour Party) to the radical right. She joined Tommy Robinson in—unsuccessful— steps to establish the German anti-Islam street movement *Pegida* in the UK, and she then set up the group For Britain in 2017 following her failure to become UKIP Party Leader.[21]

This book is about Britain's extremism, and radicalisation to the movements and groups outlined above. It argues that radicalisation is in essence a project of masculinity, enacted by both women and men. Gender scholar Katherine E. Brown notes that, despite years of feminist interest in violent extremism and terrorism, there is as yet no feminist theory of radicalisation.[22] This book addresses that gap, beginning in this chapter with an account of how radicalisation theory has neglected gender, and why it can no longer continue to do so. This chapter is about extremism and masculinities, and how they are related theoretically. It gives some context to the discussion of gender and radicalisation to come in the findings, by exploring what is past. It charts a historical absence of gender in security studies; a period in which the mainstream literature neglected women, except as victims, and took for granted men's violence. This period was followed by pushback from feminist scholars, writing to assert the importance of women's agency. In this period, gender was largely read as a synonym for women. There is now much greater focus on gender, including deviant, toxic masculinities and misogyny. However, this risks returning to narratives of extremism as men's deviance and women's victimisation. This chapter is an argument for gendered analysis in the field, and a connecting of the gender dots—women, masculinity, misogyny—present in the literature to date.

An age of misogyny and toxic masculinity?

There is perhaps a greater focus on masculinities in the understanding of radicalisation and extremism at the time of writing than at any other time. Masculinities have long been a subject of feminist international relations.[23] Yet despite the dominance of men in both criminal convictions for terrorism and participation in contemporary extreme groups, discussion of masculinities was oddly absent for some time from the literature on terrorism, extremism and radicalisation. This was the case even as authors recognised that men mattered, with scholar of jihadism Marc Sageman even producing a seminal "bunch of guys" theory of radicalisation.[24] Ten years ago, security studies hardly recognised the significance of gender; now guardians of the field such as Bruce Hoffman have turned attention to the misogynist online movement formed by 'incels' (involuntary celibates).[25] Something has shifted. At the same time, authors are highlighting the importance of 'toxic masculinity' as a causal factor in extremism, and 'political masculinity' and 'strongman politics' in the rise of authoritarian populist politicians who exploit themes of victim masculinities in their recruitment propaganda.[26] These two concepts—misogyny and toxic masculinity—are not unrelated.

The key discourse at the centre of much writing and thinking on contemporary gender and extremism suggests that extremism is an issue of problem or toxic men, who are focused on the fear, hatred and abuse of women: in other words, misogyny.[27]

The problem is not recognition of toxicity or misogyny. I have argued for their importance since writing on Boko Haram's gender-based violence in 2014, and in other work on masculinities in UK extremism.[28] The issue is when misogyny and the associated 'toxic masculinity' become simplistic explainers for the extremism of diverse ideologies, seen to share a common root cause. Growing numbers of authors have catalogued how misogyny appears in the different expressions of extremism.[29] Misogyny is even understood as predictive of violent extremism and terrorism. In her work on preventing violent extremism, Sanam Naraghi-Anderlini suggests:

> The violence that extremist groups and individuals condone and perpetrate against women and marginalised communities but gets little attention or is framed as 'cultural' is the same phenomenon that metastasises and spreads to become the high profile 'terrorism' or 'violent extremism' that gains attention.[30]

It is the key point Naraghi-Anderlini makes—that misogyny is ideological, not cultural—that Caron E. Gentry returns to in a 2022 paper on terrorism and misogyny. Misogyny is political; it is a strategy, as well as a belief system, and it has been present as such in terrorist groups for years, well before movements such as the incels drew the attention of contemporary malestream scholars.[31] In fact, Joshua M. Roose et al. note that misogyny is "flagged as an early warning sign in recent studies of both Islamist and far-right groups".[32] Writing on UK terrorist actors, Joan Smith has advocated actively profiling domestic violence cases, stating that "a history of domestic violence should be one of the highest risk factors" for later terrorist offences.[33] Misogyny, a widespread social harm, is securitised as a problem of extreme men.

There is, of course, good reason for a focus on misogyny. The contemporary groups that have posed the core terrorist threats have enacted brutal and systematic violence against women. The jihadist group Islamic State explicitly abused Yezidi women, enslaving them, raping them and selling them as part of a wider genocide of Yezidi people.[34] The Nigerian jihadist group Jamaat Ahlus Sunna Lidawati Wal Jihad (JAS, locally and informally known as Boko Haram) also became notorious for its abduction and 'enslavement' of women, the kidnapping of some 276 young women from a school in Chibok in 2014 making headlines around the world.[35] Both terrorist organisations sought to justify their abuses of women through recourse to jihadist ideology; nonetheless, there is no consensus on the theological validity of acts such as the abduction of Muslim women, or the employing of young women to carry person-borne improvised explosive devices (PBIEDs, also known as suicide bombs), another JAS tactic. Far-right actors, too, have employed violence against women, instituting it within their ideologies, even where such ideologies are ostensibly focused on other identity groups: Muslims, Jews, immigrants. When Anders Breivik killed seventy-seven people in Norway in 2011, he left a manifesto to explain why. Within its pages, he blamed not just Muslims, along with weak governments and the left, but women and feminism, which he claimed had caused the creeping emasculation of the Norwegian state.[36] In the intervening period, violence and hatred of women has been evident in attacks carried out by actors including Elliot Rodger and Scott Beierle, who explicitly targeted women due to their incel ideology.

Such was the scale of the exploitation and gender-based violence by designated terrorist groups against women that the United Nations in 2019 introduced Security Council Resolution 2467. This was part of the Women, Peace and Security agenda, and had the explicit aim of ensuring the recognition of gender-based violence as a "weapon of terror".[37] Asante et al. note that "UNSCR 2467 positions the link between WPS and CT/CVE at the locus of sexual violence crimes".[38] The resolution can, however, do little to address the key structures producing these crimes.[39]

All this is to say that misogyny clearly matters. However, there are problems with accounts of extremism focusing predominantly on misogyny. The first is the enabling of counter-extremism practices based on agendas of 'empowering' those oppressed women suffering misogyny: these are usually women of colour and, most recently in Western counter-terrorism, Muslim women.[40] Feminists have critiqued such practices for their reliance on Orientalist stereotypes of the oppression of such women by non-white men, and for their assimilatory intentions.

A second issue is that misogyny narratives homogenise diverse gender strategies within extremist groups, when understanding differentiation is vital to understanding practice. For instance, Abubakar Shekau, the leader of JAS, became renowned for gender-based violence through tactics of women carrying PBIEDs and the abduction of women. These tactics were, however, by no means widely supported by other JAS leaders. Reliance on abuses of Muslim women caused organisational dissent that would ultimately lead to jihadist factionalism and Shekau's death, brought about by his rivals.[41] This is to say that ideologically, while jihadist groups recognise women as different and not equal to men, they deem violence against women acceptable only in some situations, against some women, and leaders do not always agree on which.

Third, it is not uniformly the case that misogyny tells the whole story of extreme gender-based violence. Extreme groups similarly victimise men, and sexuality is also important. Both far-right and jihadist groups have stigmatised homosexuality and trans identities as deviant forms of masculinity or femininity. They do this because these identities do not conform to the established and distinct roles of men and women, or, as they see it, the reproductive survival of the group or race. However, they do this in different ways. IS has persecuted and executed LGBTI individuals, with propaganda showing gay men pushed from high buildings.[42] Incel attacks, on the other hand, have also targeted men understood as more sexually successful. These victims are absent in accounts of extremism that focus solely on misogyny.

Fourth, misogyny is not simply the preserve of extreme groups. It is everywhere, as demonstrated by its prevalence online—whether in the so-called Manosphere, where women are denigrated in ever-evolving terms, or in everyday abuse on mainstream platforms by 'ordinary' people.[43] The targeting of women goes beyond the terrorist groups that make the international headlines. Women politicians and journalists are vilified in abusive and sexualised terms online; they are threatened and attacked. The daily abuse of women and girls, online and off, is an unhappy feature of contemporary society.

Toxic masculinity

A concomitant narrative is that of toxic masculinity. The problem with men, it is said, is that they are suffering from a 'crisis of masculinity'.[44] The result is toxicity, and narratives of toxicity have always been implicit in those concerning extremism. Toxic masculinity can be broadly understood as a form of masculinity that is unhealthy, embodying the worst stereotypes of male behaviour and producing harms for men themselves and those around them.[45] In a study of prison masculinities, Terry A. Kupers defines toxic masculinity in relation to male bodies, as well as violence, deviance and the marginalisation of other groups. Toxic masculinity, he writes, is "the constellation of socially regressive male traits that serve to foster domination, the devaluation of women, homophobia, and wanton violence".[46] Misogyny and toxic masculinity are therefore intrinsically and semantically linked.

While policy focus on the far right and online hate from movements such as the incels is new, the narrative of masculinity in crisis is not. Political discussion of extremism increasingly features debates on the 'toxicity' of men who are often marginalised through class or race, or both.[47] When al-Qaeda carried out its coordinated attacks on the United States on 9/11 in 2001, this heralded not just what some scholars called an age of 'new terrorism',[48] global in scope and without restraint in terms of casualties, but a new counter-terrorism. Zillah Eisenstein suggested that both 9/11 and President Bush's 'War on Terror' (WOT) demonstrated the "manly moment" of the new millennium.[49] The United States took on the persona of 'global protector' against apparently 'dangerous' Muslim men. It would claim to 'come to the rescue' of Afghan women, and mobilised gendered and racialised narratives to do so.

The effects of 9/11 evident in the international system meant that other national counter-terrorism responses across the globe replicated these gendered logics. Post the War on Terror, Western security policy characterised Muslim men through familiar Orientalist discourse: they were cast as a hypermasculine, over-sexed threat, from whom Western societies and Muslim women alike needed protection.[50] The UK created its counter-terrorism strategy CONTEST in 2003 in response to 9/11,[51] and the state counter-radicalisation programme Prevent followed soon after in 2006/7.[52] As in the War on Terror, Muslim men were framed as a threat both to Muslim women and to national security and stability, a 'suspect' and 'risky' community. Policymakers and analysts alike discussed extremist violence in the context of a 'crisis of masculinity' and 'toxic masculinity'.[53] Labour politician Diane Abbott, for instance, linked extremism to this crisis and "a culture of hyper-masculinity —a culture that exaggerates masculinity in the face of a perceived threat to it".[54] In essence, the identity crisis of radicalisation theory became a crisis of exaggerated masculinity, affecting marginal men and producing an "aggrieved entitlement".[55]

Brown has observed that the counter-radicalisation strategy Prevent betrayed both maternalist and paternalist logics: the state protects its citizens from Muslim male 'others', whilst inviting Muslim women to join it in an allied project of empowerment, focused on surveillance through motherhood. Prevent, Brown suggested, read Muslim women according to "their expected gender and racialized role as mothers."[56] Prevent resembles other counter-terrorism policies in the Global North, which have broadly stigmatised and even criminalised men in Muslim communities while positioning Muslim women as oppressed potential allies.[57] Such policies have become an instrument of neo-colonialism in the Global South.[58] Prevent and other deradicalisation schemes suggested they were partnering with 'vulnerable' Muslim communities whose men were at risk of radicalisation, framed as a transformative process, towards a dangerous and undesirable masculinity.

It would not be fair to suggest that academic discussion of masculinity and extremism entirely ignored the socio-structural drivers or the discursive production of masculinities, yet it is clear, as Paul Amar notes, that discussion of radicalisation as it applied to Muslim men invoked inevitably racialised discussions of 'toxic' masculinity and deviancy.[59] This had the effect of labelling the radicalisation process as a matter of problem Muslim men, and neglecting the specific structural conditions producing 'radicalised' identities and behaviours.

Such gendered discourses prevail, and incorporate class as well as racial biases. Since 2011 the UK Prevent strategy has engaged with the far right as well as Islamist groups. Its vision of those likely to be radicalised to either movement has been of men from low socio-economic groups and lacking education. Prevent envisaged radical actors as "usually male, poorly educated (although there are some cases of high-achieving individuals) and often unemployed".[60] It posited a particular type of deviant underclass male as the common theme in radicalisation to two diverse extreme groups and ideologies. Policymakers equated extremism with low achievement; there were no explanations of radical men's violence without dysfunction. The effect was to resort to a discourse of toxicity around men active in communities understood as 'extreme', whatever the ideology. The conversation is not about gender and men per se; it is about specific, problem men and irredeemable deviance, even though this is not broadly evidenced in the literature. Far-right and jihadist actors as a transnational group come from a range of backgrounds.

Amar's critiques of masculinities industries notwithstanding, nuance is possible when considerations of masculinities transcend "binarist approaches".[61] This is the aim of this book: to challenge what David Duriesmith terms the "monolithic picture" of extreme masculinity.[62] Through interviews with extreme actors, it explores the diverse masculinities evident in extreme movements, how these are situated in space and place, and how they are contiguous with wider societal values.

Radicalisation and extremism theory and the absence of gender

Much of the reliance on toxic masculinity and misogyny as explainers for extremism is in part a response to the radicalisation literature's historic lack of engagement with gender, whether understood as pertaining to women, masculinities or gendered ideology. This is despite the fact that radicalisation theory has the necessary tools to see gender. Since 9/11 there has been a huge expansion in what we can term the 'mainstream' literature on radicalisation and the models seeking to explain it.[63] By mainstream, I mean those approaches relied on by policymakers tasked with tackling radicalisation and produced by predominantly male authors ensconced within the academic-security nexus.[64] There is no one theory of radicalisation in the mainstream literature, and, as already outlined in this chapter and the Introduction, the term is contested and politicised in gendered ways.[65] Despite the proliferation of models, radicalisation is generally under-theorised; the mechanisms of radicalisation are as numerous as the accounts of those radicalised.[66]

Nonetheless, many authors have attempted to understand the processes behind people's journeys into violent and extreme groups, and have drawn on a variety of disciplines and methodologies and a range of empirical data to do so. What is described as radicalisation 'theory' is no more than a series of models, engaging different approaches.[67] All of them have omitted gender.[68] This is curious, as radicalisation models share common themes which should point to the importance of gender. The first is the physical space in which radicalisation occurs. Feminist authors have long pointed to the gender dynamics of everyday spaces as telling stories about national and regional security. Cynthia Enloe, for instance, has traced the chronology of shifting politics and, later, the war in Iraq in the use of a beauty salon.[69] In the aftermath of 9/11, the radicalisation literature also emphasised everyday spaces as locations of 'vulnerability' to radicalisation; places where 'grievances' were exploited by radical influencers, preachers and ideologues. Amongst these were spaces with specific gender dynamics, accessible only to one sex, or segregated: mosques or gyms or prisons.[70] There were also locations where the gender dynamics were less obvious but still important, such as universities or the internet.[71]

Related to this is the social space of radicalisation, important because radicalisation itself is regarded foremost as a social process. Radicalisation models have emphasised the importance of the people around the radicalised individual, the "specific, immediate social environment", which Stefan Malthaner and Peter Waldmann term the "radical milieu", but gender is rarely considered a significant feature.[72] Social movement theory (SMT) has also provided key concepts to radicalisation models:[73] the need for extreme group messaging to resonate with an intended audience, and for violent actors to emerge from a wider social milieu. Radicalisation models have used metaphors including the pyramid, the conveyor belt and the staircase to represent ideological progression alongside a narrowing demographic group, and a temporal aspect to radicalisation.[74] In her review of the radicalisation literature in the early 2010s, Anja Dalgaard-Nielsen noted that this social aspect of radicalisation processes was key, and appeared in interdisciplinary models: sociological, social network/movement and empiricist.[75] Both friendship and kinship groups are highlighted by numerous authors.[76]

Yet the literature did not explore the gender dynamics of the all-important collective. This is especially peculiar given its explicit reference to the prevalence of men in extreme groups. As noted above, one of the more seminal theories on radicalisation is even termed the "bunch of guys" theory; Sageman suggested that friendship group formation was a fundamental precursor to the adoption of radical ideology and made the explicit observation that such radical groups were generally male.[77] He also referenced the macho "rock stars" of jihad, and pointed to a "masculine conception of heroism among these terrorists".[78] Sageman did not employ gender theory, but he at least recognised its potential importance. The same is true of other authors. Arabist scholar Thomas Hegghammer has discussed the performance of a range of masculinities in jihadi culture, from the scholar to the emotional, weeping fighter and the warrior.[79] Others, including Akil Awan, have insightfully discussed manhood in jihadist work. Yet they have neglected analysis employing the term 'masculinities', or reference to the gender literature.[80]

Another key author on radicalisation, Olivier Roy, notes that the macho culture of violent jihad enables male "losers" to become the "avenging hero".[81] Yet he does not make the next analytical step, linking emasculation to an understanding of masculinities, hierarchies of power or structural systems, or to existing masculinities work. Without reference to the wider gender literature such observations dangle, and the role of gender in constituting homosocial socialisation to radicalisation is left unprobed. Other researchers have gathered empirical data that is almost entirely homosocial, for instance from datasets of convictions for violent terrorist incidents, and yet have not reflected on this.[82]

There is a tension here because, despite the obvious significance of the social, discussion of radicalisation processes can often focus on the individual. In discussion of jihadist radicalisation this individual has been assumed to be a male youth. Although understood as rational and having agency, such youths are also 'vulnerable' to the transformation towards violence that characterises radicalisation.[83] Roy, for instance, writes of "unmoored youth", a "lost generation" whose radicalism is Islamised by jihadist groups.[84] Vulnerability is explicitly linked to the so-called 'identity crisis' which appears in numerous models of radicalisation. This crisis is so vague as to be meaningless, given that it includes anything unexpected or challenging, including parental divorce, bereavement or moving to university. The crisis precipitates a "cognitive opening", which lays the individual open to resonance with extreme ideology delivered by charismatic—male—extreme leaders.[85] One key aim of this book is to explore the mechanisms behind the so-called crisis.

There have been inconsistencies and omissions in the key theories: the people these theories discuss tend to be men; they are rational, and radicalisation is social; yet the individual radicalised youth is vulnerable and in crisis. The radicalisation process takes this vulnerable youth and transforms him along a path that resembles a conveyor belt or staircase, until violence is the only solution. In all of this, men were often mentioned; gender, whether in the consideration of why men dominate contemporary radical groups or in any mention of women, was largely absent. Where the mainstream literature did discuss women as extreme or terrorist actors, the assumption was again of deviance, given that women are stereotypically understood to support peace, to embody maternalistic qualities and to oppose violence. They were wives of men who had influence over them; they were failed mothers; they were victims of rape; they were singularly lacking in agency and rational thought. Such women were described according to their prettiness, or otherwise, or their relationships with men. Gender was the preserve of violent women, exceptionalised and read as deviant in the literature.[86]

Whilst the numbers have always shown terrorism and extremism to be homosocial pursuits, it is not the numbers that have seen women's violence exceptionalised; it is the gendered assumptions about the nature of women themselves. Consistent with international relations (IR) more broadly, men's violence in radicalisation studies was not framed as a function of gender, and women's participation and violence were exceptionalised or not seen at all.[87]

Adding women, seeing masculinities

It took the travel of some 5,000 women from Western Europe to join the so-called Islamic State for many mainstream scholars to take seriously either the question of women or that of gender.[88] This exodus, or *hijrah*,[89] as IS termed it, took mainstream IR academics and radicalisation theorists, as well as policymakers, by surprise. Radicalisation theory had made no attempt to explain or account for this. It was the moment for decades of feminist scholarship on women in terrorism to shine. Feminist scholarship predates theory on radicalisation, yet has often occupied a position in the margins of the mainstream security studies literature, separated from and by implication irrelevant to the wider field considering men. Yet looking to understand gender in radicalisation processes has meant turning to the literature on women, predominantly authored by women. Theorists have drawn on feminist scholarship in international relations to address the lack of attention to women, their experiences, their voices and their violence, as well as their victimisation in war and through extremism. It is one of two bodies of academic work that reference gender, the other being the critical studies on men and masculinities literature (CSMM), which I come to later.

Inevitably, given the systematic neglect of women as actors in conflict, much scholarship on women in terrorism has engaged with gender as a synonym for women, rather than adopting a gendered approach. As Sjoberg has noted, "women are perceived to have gender while men are not".[90] In particular, the literature on female terrorism has focused on women's agency. Security studies literature has routinely neglected women as agents of violence, or, where they do appear, has framed them as victims subject to external forces; appendages to male actors; wives or girlfriends, ignored and minimised.[91] In their 2009 review of the literature on women as terrorist actors, Karen Jacques and Paul J. Taylor note two key approaches: the first foregrounds women's lack of agency within patriarchal structures; the second seeks to redress a wrong, emphasising the importance of women's "missing agency".[92] This is evident in work focused on particular case studies, such as Miranda Alison's studies of women as violent actors in the Liberation Tigers of Tamil Eelam,[93] or making a broader point about the political nature of women's historically ignored engagement, as considered by Sjoberg and Gentry in their book on women's representations in global politics including terrorism, *Mothers, Monsters, Whores*.[94] The recruitment of women to IS, as noted, had revealed an international blind spot concerning women's violence in work to counter jihadist groups.[95]

Scholars of women and terrorism drew attention to what mainstream theory minimised and ignored: the reality of women's activism, and their participation in and support for violent Salafi–jihadi groups or the far right, for instance.[96] Authors have presented detailed accounts, often based on interviews, of how women mobilise and what motivates them; they have shown their importance to wider groups or movements in fundraising and propagandising; or they have highlighted how mothers matter ideologically, in furthering and continuing conflict and grievance by raising children within jihadist ideologies or those committed to the supremacy of the white race.[97]

While research on women's participation in extreme and terrorist organisations adds much to an understanding of terrorism, it cannot, alone, progress a gendered analysis of radicalisation pathways; such an analysis would have to engage with gender as relevant to both women and men. From an epistemological perspective, work on women resembles that dealing solely with men, as it interprets gender as a question of sex. It is the cousin of the mainstream literature, which is only capable of seeing men as toxic or vulnerable or both. The women's literature adds women to the gender-blind field of radicalisation studies. However, this means understanding gender, and specifically 'violent women', empirically, as a new category of biological sex.[98]

For feminist international relations scholars, this issue was not new. They had tried to shift the conversation post-9/11, recognising this as a moment of increased global political 'virility' to seize upon and interrogate. Into this arena, Marysia Zalewski and Jane Parpart posed a question about men. Gender scholars focused on feminist theory, this was their second attempt to pose the '"Man" question' in IR, the first having come 10 years before. Their objective was to problematise men, fixing the question of gender on them, rather than on the ongoing struggle to centre women and render them visible. The Man question had in its sights an assertion of the importance of recognising gendered relations, of seeing gender as power, and of destabilising a masculinist field. IR theory had been intransigent. International relations, politics, security studies and radicalisation theorists—all were slow to engage with the question of gender. The reposing of the Man question was a new way to challenge a wider academic field that had stubbornly resisted engagement with women, or their agency, or the importance of gender as a framework through which to theorise international politics and the role of the men within it.[99] By shifting the focus to men, the Man question also challenged the notion that academic study of women constituted a holistic approach to gender.

In fact, authors within CSMM, rooting their work in feminist theory, had for some years tried to address the Man question, engaging with the subject of men, violence, terrorism and extremism. Yet this literature was distinct from the literature on gender and women. Scholarship on men, masculinities and violence has flourished since the 1950s,[100] but owes the biggest theoretical debt to work by Carrigan et al.,[101] and in particular Raewyn Connell. She approaches masculinities through a socio-structural lens, first formulating masculinity as hierarchical, "a place in gender relations, the practices through which men and women engage that place in gender, and the effects of these practices in bodily experiences, personality and culture", refining the concept over later years.[102] Where masculinity was initially conceived of singularly, Connell later emphasised the plurality of masculinities.[103] This was a response to recognition of positionality and the diversity of men's experiences, constructed through race, class, earning power and location, with emphasis on disparities between the Global North and South.[104] A multiplicity of masculinities is evident, however, not just across but within locations,[105] and the same cultural setting can produce different masculinities.[106] Additionally, different masculinities function as hegemonic across time,[107] varying according to men's life-stages, historical contexts and cultures.[108] Connell also proposed that gender operates on multiple levels: the macro level of gender orders; the meso level, evident in organisations and networks, of gender regimes; and the micro level of gender relations and individual interactions. It is at this level that normative expectations around masculinities are embodied and actualised. Gender functions as a "mechanism whereby situated social action contributes to the reproduction of social structure".[109]

Importantly, Connell provides four foundational concepts that masculinities authors have employed in their work on men, violence and extremism: hegemonic masculinity, subordinate masculinity, complicity and marginalised masculinity.[110] None of the attributes of these categories are fixed. It is perhaps the concept of hegemonic masculinity, the highest-status masculinity, that has had the biggest influence in the understanding of which masculinities dominate, or produce aspiration, and what masculinity means.[111] As Kimmel notes, "all masculinities are not created equal".[112] Broadly speaking, however, hegemonic masculinity (HM) is frequently constructed as heterosexual and associated with the maximisation of power.[113] Connell notes that hegemonic masculinity is "constructed in relation to various subordinated masculinities as well as in relation to women".[114] HM legitimises unequal gender relations;[115] it concerns systems of masculine domination, and the ideology that reproduces those systems.[116] Some masculinities and corresponding femininities are the "legitimating rationale" for embodied actions and the regulation of social practice. This is their hegemony.[117]

Masculinities are hierarchical and relational; they are constructed in distinction to one another, and to qualities associated with femininity.[118] Hegemonic masculinity is agreed upon and understood by social groups and used to enforce acceptable scripts, prescribing and proscribing particular behaviours. Kupers clearly relies on these concepts to distinguish as 'toxic' a masculinity aimed at men's subordination of other men, as well as women. Criminologists engaged with the study of 'problem' violent and criminal men have often employed the lens of "subordinate masculinities".[119] Within the post-9/11 extremism discourse, 'toxic' Muslim men were frequently, however, also marginalised and subordinate, when we consider class, race, or both.[120]

Critics of Connell have suggested that women are too absent from her formulation of masculinities; they are important actors in the social processes constructing masculinities and are also able to embody masculinities, which are not solely accessible to male bodies.[121] Women are, however, addressed in later work by Connell and James W. Messerschmidt.[122] They, too, can 'do' masculinities,[123] although this refusal to submit to a "relation of subordination" can threaten male dominance, which pushes back.[124] To 'do' gender is in effect to accomplish gender in a given situation, through interactions with other individuals, interactions with institutions and embodying "normative gender expectations".[125] Both masculinities and femininities are therefore open to expression within male and female bodies. Additionally, Connell has proposed the category of "emphasized femininity", focused on enabling the needs of hegemonic masculinity.[126]

Connell does not explore the term 'toxic masculinity' in her ground-breaking book *Masculinities*. In fact, although now hard to escape, the concept did not gain traction in criminology until the 2000s, and has only been widely employed in the past 10 years in relation to extremism. However, Connell has elsewhere said that its use is "worthwhile".[127] She has also considered the issue of extremism and political violence. In parallel with scholars such as David Rapoport, who regard trends in global terrorism as 'waves' enduring decades,[128] Connell has pointed to violent political phenomena such as Islamist violence as having "crisis tendencies".[129] In fact, there is little evidence of a crisis of masculinity, although analysts have held this responsible for both far-right and jihadist radicalisation.[130] Yet the 'crisis' discourse has problematically and repeatedly arisen as an explanation for social ills for more than 100 years.[131] The theory of a 'crisis in masculinity' as the cause of toxic or other problem masculinities, including extreme masculinities, is universalising. It conflates different masculinities and gendered experiences. In doing so, it suggests that men and women occupy distinct positions, and are at loggerheads. Men in crisis become, as masculinities author Rebecca Asher suggests, a "homogeneous mass … posited in relation to equally theoretical self-assured females".[132] The crisis also positions particular men—those 'toxic' men most susceptible to crisis effects—as deviant from a normative 'healthy' masculinity,[133] even though misogyny and masculinist values are not limited to extreme groups.[134] 'Toxic masculinity' has become a vessel into which is packed extremism, and other male crime and violence, as a specific manifestation of contemporary male crisis.

Crime, extremism and masculinities

Scholars of the radical right have sought to interview male activists in an effort to recognise the importance of gender in individuals' experiences. In their work on the English Defence League, criminologists James Treadwell and Jon Garland emphasise the interiority of their interviewees, dwelling on the personal and the subjective.[135] They suggest that socio-structural approaches can serve to pathologise particular men, including extremists. Given critiques of Connell's early work as too one-dimensional and too monocultural, later criminologists have sought to evidence the multiple dynamic masculinities that constitute criminal behaviour. Hypermasculinity cannot be understood as something monolithic, a "static background" to draw on when committing crime.[136] Additionally, just as gender has historically, and wrongly, been understood as a quality of women rather than men,[137] hypermasculinity, read as 'excessive' masculinity—perhaps in the current terminology, 'toxic' masculinity—has been understood as a quality of particular deviant or racialised men.[138]

Amar notes that the early disciplines of police sciences and criminology distinguished between 'manliness', as hegemonic, upper class and authoritative, and 'masculinity', which was subordinate and concerned excess.[139] Scholarship in the 1950s and 60s on 'working-class' criminality, for instance, was subject to critiques that it reified the working class as sharing criminal masculine norms, and neglected middle- and upper-class crime.[140] Working with masculinities to understand criminality has long risked replicating narratives of deviance and stigmatising particular groups.

Masculinities authors within criminology employed both Butler's foundational insights on gender as performativity and Connell's on the importance of masculine performances as starting points from which better to analyse the complex function of masculinities in crime, including terrorism and extremism. Whatever the theoretical difficulties of the terms 'hegemonic masculinity' and 'hypermasculinity'—understood as violent, power-projecting manhood[141]—researchers of criminal subcultures note that masculinities have a clear function in both men and women's identity construction. Work by Connell and Messerschmidt has emphasised the importance of masculine capital, which compensates for a lack of access to other forms of capital: social and cultural.[142] As well as Connell, Kimmel has pointed to the role of transnational phenomena such as globalisation or changing gender norms in prompting wide-scale emasculation and the production of compensatory 'protest' masculinities, male power manifested in terrorism, and collective violence.[143] Such violence is implicated in contexts outside of terrorist crime—for instance, men's use of violence against women in response to changing gender roles in Puerto Rico.[144]

Extremism is about collectives, and the collective is important in any study of the relationship between particular forms of crime and masculinities. Influential here is philosopher and ethnographer Pierre Bourdieu, for whom empirical research is fundamental to theorising masculinities and their relationship to social capital. His work utilises concepts of masculinity, status, everyday practice and place. For Bourdieu, practices and identities are manifested and demonstrated through 'habitus', which constitutes those practices shared by a group. It is through the use of shared symbols and shared habitus that members of the same social field connect and recognise their actions as having precise meaning to one another, a concept mobilised in the findings chapters of this book. For Bourdieu, masculinity is about domination: power over subordinate others.

The peer group features in recent criminological work on masculinities in multiple ways: as a group that vies for prestige through "gendered power",[145] as the means through which masculinities are policed[146] and as a source from which challenges to masculinity can occur. It is through 'masculinity challenges' against antagonists that masculinity is proved to the group and dominance is asserted amongst peers.[147] Masculinity challenges entail projecting or using violence to "create street reputation through either establishing masculinity by challenging someone else or defending against the challenges of another".[148] Confrontation enables the production of collective masculine identities.[149] The masculinity challenge reveals masculine honour as something that has the permanent possibility of being increased, unlike feminine virtue, which can only be lost.[150]

Empiric investigation, such as that undertaken to produce this book, is the ideal site for work on masculinities, as it reveals what it means to 'do gender' as situated social action. For instance, Tea Torbenfeldt Bengtsson's work on masculinities in a prisons context suggests that hypermasculinity functions as an interpretive and symbolic frame, through which prisoners construct value, status and meaning. While cautious about the limitations of the term 'hypermasculinity', often used to denigrate working-class or racially other men within "deviant subcultures", Bengtsson notes that in a prison context, the term does have power.[151] This is in part because its meaning mirrors the familiar hypermasculinity of street culture outside prison.[152] Working with Erving Goffman's theory of the presentation of self,[153] in this context hypermasculinity functions as a frame which constrains the identity choices of incarcerated youth. Additionally, Bengtsson builds on the work of both Goffman and Chris Brickell to emphasise the dynamic nature of gender as performativity, rejecting the idea of masculinities being drawn upon as if a "static" resource.[154]

The continuity of masculinities performed by extremists in this book is notable. They bring pre-group masculinities into extreme activism. But masculinities are fluid, changing through people, through time and through place. Indeed, in his work on Muslim masculinities, Peter Hopkins suggests that the dynamic nature of masculinities means that hypermasculinity may be the goal, but the problem for men is that they suffer disruptions to attaining this.[155] Discussing affect, James M. Jasper similarly notes that these interruptions to men's practices matter, as interruptions "can provoke violent emotional responses."[156] Relating identity to time, Christoffer Carlsson employs life-history criminology to emphasise the importance of particular masculinities at particular points in life.[157] In contemporary society, milestones historically associated with adulthood or manhood, such as marriage or becoming a father, are less rigidly recognised. Nonetheless, to some extent, they endure. Class, race and gender construct masculinities, Carlsson notes, and this enables—or not—a transition into and between social institutions. Crime in particular is more compatible with acceptable youthful roles.[158]

Feminist methodologies, and particularly those of black feminists, have emphasised the importance of intersectionality;[159] to follow Sandra Harding, we are all hyphenated.[160] It is the social facts of a man's life that exert pressure on masculinities.[161] Indeed, hypermasculinity is only one of many possible frames that both men and women might use to understand their identity choices.[162] Hypermasculinity as a frame has no permanence: it serves a purpose within a particular social group, at a particular time. Brickell asserts that this is apparent only through a process of self-reflection; reflexivity gives men the means to consider the choices they have available to them, revealing the hypermasculine lens.[163] For Brickell, this is the core of understanding criminal masculinities. They are dynamically co-constituted through (social) space: "socially constituted masculine selves act in the social world and are acted on simultaneously".[164] Examining masculinities is therefore a matter of considering the specific conditions of their production. This is what this book sets out to do.

A holistic framework

Theorising masculinities is foundational to understanding how multiculturalism is lived and resisted by both the Islamist and the radical-right participants in this research. The totality of these masculinities authors' scholarship offers a framework for a more complete analysis that considers how different identities in this study are constituted within a particular social field, through particular symbolic frames. Such identities are socially constructed according to a gendered symbolic practice and require personal investment, with emotional cost as well as benefit to the performer.[165]

The previous sections have also revealed gender as a blind spot in mainstream radicalisation models. Women's radicalisation has been relegated to a sub-category, with gender a synonym for sex, further read as women's sex: an outlier variable in the radicalisation equation.[166] Men are generally regarded as gender-neutral, their masculinity unconsidered. When gender is applied to men, they are exceptionalised and seen as deviant and toxic. However, as the field has evolved since 9/11, alternative approaches have emerged based in feminism and critical studies on men and masculinities (CSMM), and in criminology emergent in the same period, theoretically integrating gender and race. Reading gender not as sex but as a "meaning system",[167] they demonstrate the co-construction of group and individual—men and women understood together—through gendered norms, values and beliefs. This meaning system shapes radical masculinities and femininities, their actions and thoughts, and is in return shaped by them. Additionally, it is situated, embedding gender in context and space.[168] Importantly, recent studies of male deviance in criminology and sociology emphasise masculinities as dynamic, and hypermasculinity as a symbolic framework constraining action.

The complete story of radicalisation, then, is not told within radicalisation theory, which has neglected gender; nor is it told in the literature on women's engagement with violent groups, which has often focused on women's agency above structural issues and read gender as a synonym for sex; nor is it told in the literature on extremism as a factor of 'crisis', which puts too much emphasis on the structural and elides the local; and nor is it told in the story of toxic masculinity and misogyny, which occludes men's agency and subjectivities, and the importance of women outside of their role as victims. I noted earlier in this chapter that discourses of men's toxicity and misogyny in extremism were semantically linked; both also have the effect of obscuring the role of women in extremism. The wealth of feminist literature tells us that this is not justifiable:

women are active and present in terrorism and extremism in contemporary groups, even homosocial ones employing gender-based violence, whether far-right or jihadist.[169]

I do not hope to tell the complete story of radicalisation in this book. What matters for understanding extremism is to integrate the approaches outlined in this chapter in order to produce a more holistic account of radicalisation as gendered than has been offered so far. This account should incorporate women as actors, but also men; the social as well as the personal; and masculinities, without pathologising the men and women who perform them. It should balance the agential and the structural. Indeed, Sune Qvotrup Jensen and Jeppe Fuglsang Larsen suggest that a gendered framework is ideally placed to achieve this.[170] Criminological and sociological approaches to extremism and terrorism have frequently employed a gendered lens and, building on the work of CSMM scholars, have explicitly engaged with men's violence, as men.[171] Work engaging gender, not sex, need not be complex. It involves gathering the same data and analysing the same materials. Its starting point is however an epistemological position that understands gender as socially constructed, regulating social organisation. Such an approach sees men and women not as distinct objects of radicalisation, but as situated within shared "hierarchies of structural position".[172]

Such research must also concern real people, their bodies and their practices, as well as their gendered subjectivities. Connell regards bodies as fundamental to 'doing' gender, and, indeed, this understanding drives her methodological approach: the life-history interview. This will be considered in further detail in the next chapter. Bourdieu, like Butler, understands male and female bodies as socially constructed, principally in order to confirm "what is normal, natural, to the point of being inevitable".[173] Such inevitability, echoing Connell, constitutes patriarchy and masculine domination. This idea is central to the findings presented in later chapters. Importantly for this book, gender is situated in practices by bodies, in space.[174] Analysis of gender, bodies and space is central to understanding the extremism of Islamist and radical-right participants I encountered in my research. Each set of actors invests in a particular symbolic practice, associated with a particular identity. Such performances require personal investment, with emotional costs as well as benefits to the performer.[175] It is through the use of shared symbols and shared practices that members of the same social milieu connect and recognise their actions as having precise meaning to one another. 'Natives' of particular cultures constantly negotiate rules, which are to some degree innate and deep-rooted in bodies.[176] And they negotiate these rules through their bodies.

To think about radicalisation from this gendered and embodied perspective provides fresh insights into existing work, contributing the next analytical step in theorising radicalisation, and a solution to the bifurcation of the literature. As gendered approaches are situated, they enable ethnomethodological insights gained from a practical engagement with those affected by radicalisation. Protest masculinities, peaceful or violent, appear in literature on the misogynist incel movement and jihadist groups, as well as the far right and others, and authors including Duriesmith, Kimmel, Messerschmidt and Noor Huda Ismail have produced detailed analyses to evidence this, through interviews and case studies.[177] These case studies reveal a multiplicity of situated masculinities, not simply one 'terrorist masculinity'.[178] This gendered ethnography is also the kind of first-hand, empirical work emphasised as both lacking and important in the terrorism studies field research literature.[179] Such situated work emphasises that 'terrorist masculinities' cannot be universalised.

Summary

It is impossible for anyone working on gender to lament mainstream, policymaker and media interest in gender, misogyny and masculinity and their relation to extremism: this has been a long time coming.[180] It is possible, however, to sound a note of caution around discussion of masculinity when this is read as monolithic: the same 'toxic' masculinity understood as a key shared feature of contemporary extreme groups.[181] Misogyny, gender-based violence and patriarchy: all are concerns to me, and all are evident within the extreme groups that appear to pose the greatest current threat to Western societal stability: the far-right and jihadist. Nonetheless, the argument this book presents is that masculinities, not masculinity singular, are key. It is the complexities of gender that should prompt more research, not a focus on simplistic explanations: misogyny, masculinism, toxic masculinity or an apparent 'crisis' of masculine values. Radicalisation is, my findings will show, a project of masculinities, plural.

The chapter is also an appeal to those engaged in studying radicalisation, whether in academia or in policy. I have outlined how radicalisation studies have, historically, been gender-blind, but to some degree they have also been sexist, and complacent. They are not alone. Security studies and the wider international relations field have historically failed to engage explicitly with feminist theory, women or gendered narratives. Yet no field can escape gender. The fields lacking gender, that have been constructed by men for men, of a particular race and with particular power, are gendered. When these fields of study share gendered characteristics—patriarchy, male dominance—with the masculinist terror groups they seek to understand, their blindness to gender is a limitation for all of us. The failure is one of epistemological and ontological position: how we decide to understand the field and what counts as worthy of study within it. But it is a question of choice. As Gentry has suggested, misogyny has always been there; for academia and policy to recognise this only when incels emerge shows complacency and cynicism. The evidence of the importance of gender within terrorism has been there for decades, even if this evidence has largely been divided into two subfields: women's literature on terrorism, and work on masculinities.

A failure to see gender in terrorism and extremism is a missed opportunity to counter it. Yet, as theoretical analysis in this chapter shows, simplistic narratives that homogenise extreme men as 'toxic' and focus on misogyny when this is just one axis of an abuse of power might not help. Gender is fundamental. But it is not the only principle around which political violence is organised: race, religion, sexuality, ethnicity are also factors. Women are not simply the victims of extreme groups; the picture, as the findings of this book indicate, is more complex than that. Nor are they absent from extreme activism, as many narratives would suggest. Gendered approaches provide a framework for thinking about radicalisation that neither ignores women nor takes men's violence for granted. It understands these shortfalls as linked. Such approaches are not mysterious: they concern subjecting the data gathered to a different kind of analysis. The next chapter considers the ethics of how that data should be collected.

2

METHODOLOGY
IS IT OK TO TALK TO EXTREMISTS?

Introduction

The point of this book is better to understand masculinities and extremism in Britain, but what is the best way to access them? Masculinities are active, dynamic; for Connell and other scholars of masculinities within criminology, ethnography is the means to understanding the function of masculinities in particular subcultures.[1] Indeed, Bourdieu sees no other way to research masculinities and Goffman, in his work on the presentation of self, argues that it is only in "concrete situations" that the limits of what is socially acceptable become visible.[2] While my research is not truly ethnographic, it is based on talking to extremists. This follows methodological exhortations from within terrorism studies and feminist theory to use empathy in order to better understand their motivations. Radicalisation, terrorism and extremism have people at their heart. These are people who can be hateful and harmful, but who nonetheless have multiple and complex identities, and sometimes victim identities.

The ethnographer Harmonie Toros reminds us that to challenge extremism we have to remember that extremists also deserve empathy.[3] International security in fact relies on empathy through skills such as diplomacy, even in conflict situations, and the best way to create this is through meaningful first-person encounters.[4] There is, though, in using empathy in extremism cases, a significant risk: the legitimisation of harmful beliefs, and harmful actors. This is nothing new. Konrad Kellen addresses the dilemma in his work on the German left-wing terrorist group the Rote Armee Fraktion, active in the 1970s and 80s, asking, "Am I an apologist for the West German terrorists? ... I only try to understand, and I do not support the French saying *Tout comprendre, c'est tout pardoner*".[5] As Bourdieu suggests, showing things as they are is to face accusations of supporting how they are.[6] Researchers operate under the foundational principle of research ethics, 'do no harm', or perhaps, as John Morrison, Andrew Silke and Eke Bont suggest in relation to terrorism studies (TS), "do no undue harm".[7] The terrorism researcher has a responsibility to report criminal activity, or information such as details of an impending attack. Many of the moral risks of terrorism and extremism research are longstanding. But contemporary researchers face a new challenge. In an age of far-right terrorism and extremism, is close-up research seeking empathy with the extreme in itself a form of harm?[8]

This chapter is about how to avoid harm in doing research: to the interviewee, to society and to oneself. It is about the difficulties— ethical, moral, emotional and practical—of doing 'close-up' research with extremists. Yet it also argues for the necessity of empathetic research, within a feminist framework of care. Radicalised people are frequently constructed as (an appropriate) 'other', the out-group; as ideologically and behaviourally distinct from the 'non-radicalised': everyone else in society. This book challenges that view, evidencing the continuities and contiguities of the practice and belief of both jihadist and radical-right actors with the mainstream. Society often demonises and dehumanises radicalised people. This monstering can function as a re-othering, given that alienation, stigmatisation and structural inequalities were already part of radicalisation processes for some, according to models outlined in the previous chapter. This book does not condone the views or actions of any of the interviewees; they have all caused harm to others. However, it is about forging an ethical understanding through an empathetic path and directly engaging with extremists. This chapter explains why, and how.

Empathy as methodology

Empathy was a natural path for the research presented in this book to take. Before academia, I had worked in radio journalism, one aim of which is to present people narrating their own stories. However, academia is not journalism. Within terrorism studies and critical terrorism studies, authors recommend empathy as a method and have for years bemoaned how few researchers attempt to talk directly to terrorists or extremists. Terrorism studies has therefore emphasised the importance of primary sources, with first-hand stories seen as a vital window into the minds of the radicalised.[9] Within the terrorism studies literature, empathy is recommended as a methodological approach, but for pragmatic rather than humanising reasons.[10] That is to say, the approach does little to prevent the 'othering' of extremists. The most significant aspects of empathy discussed in the literature are enabling access, the possibility of gaining the trust of research interviewees, and creating the right context in which to produce meaningful and authentic interview material. Without empathy, there is—baldly put—no interview data. Yet trust is far from a given.[11] Academics may have little familiarity with extremist communities, even in their own countries.[12] Empathy essentially becomes a method through which to build rapport and facilitate an in.

But what is empathy? Writing on research ethics, Toros explains empathy as recognition of self in other, writing of terrorists, "To understand them and their violence, we need to recognise their humanity—how they are 'like us.'"[13] It is about putting oneself into another's skin.[14] Such an approach is primarily concerned, therefore, with a "principle of non-dehumanisation", as ethnographer Joel Busher terms it.[15] Indeed, I engaged with interviewees not just as 'sources of data', but as people. They were people I had relationships with throughout the research and who could be emotionally affected—proud, hurt, angered or let down—by what I said, or what

I wrote.[16] The principle of non-dehumanisation is key to the study of extremism and terrorism; indeed, much of the recent history of critical terrorism studies has been concerned with the rehumanising of terrorist and extreme actors, given their othering and monstering in both policy and the media.[17] Terrorism studies scholarship is also implicated in these narratives. TS was itself concerned—for years—with the search for the 'terrorist personality' and the terrorist psychopathology;[18] scholars, governments and the public struggled to believe that terrorists, by definition authors of fear and brutal attack, could be psychologically normal. While the overwhelming evidence after decades of research is that most people convicted of terrorism are as mentally healthy as most members of society,[19] the myth of abnormality and deviance remains. The toxicity framing, as discussed in Chapter One, is applied not just to terrorism but also to extremism and radicalisation, to monstrous women and deviant men.

For feminist scholars asking gender questions, empathetic methods are important as part of an ethic of researcher care for the interviewee and responsibility in research.[20] Empathy requires personal emotional labour, but it is also political.[21] Feminist author Christine Sylvester suggests that empathy is the ability to take on the struggles of others with whom we do not agree, by listening in a "subjectivity-moving way".[22] This understanding is of empathy as dialogic, an exchange; it recognises that exercising empathy has the potential to change both those researched and the researcher.[23] This is political, because, as Margaret R. Somers notes, it admits "the previously excluded subjects and suppressed subjectivities into theories of action".[24] What is more, empathy becomes the only choice when talking to the disengaged. Empathetic methodologies constitute a form of political inclusion, which Somers suggests is an epistemologically appropriate tool for gaining knowledge of those—marginalised—groups for whom identity politics has replaced alternative politics as a force of action.[25] To take a minority perspective—even one that is reviled, and contested—is to reveal how dominant structures exclude and discriminate.[26] Such an approach essentially brings the marginal to bear on collective knowledge from a distinct epistemological position, and creates new knowledge.[27] It also necessitates a focus on the 'everyday', the 'trivial', as a site of meaning and politicisation.

Understanding gender, extremism and radicalisation explicitly concerns hearing stories from subjects excluded—arguably self-excluded—from the mainstream, because of their beliefs and actions.[28] An empathetic engagement is important in the expression of interviewee subjectivity and agency, and the presentation of a complex identity. In consideration of masculinities, it is an approach that permits interviewees to express masculinities beyond and outside of those presupposed by radicalisation narratives of toxicity and deviance. The rest of the book explores how complex masculinities are a central part of the arc of radicalisation stories.

Harm as a consequence of empathy?

There is, however, a 'but', and it is a significant one: feminist theory was not designed for talking to extremists. It is politically antithetical to many of the views espoused in this book. Some scholars do not believe it is 'ok', moral or ethically permissible to talk to extremists, or at least extremists of every ideology. Some believe that if a researcher does engage in dialogue, this should not be reproduced in related academic publications, for fear it could legitimise extreme views. The researcher has a moral responsibility that frames every research decision.[29] 'Terrorism' and 'extremism' are pejorative terms.[30] To engage in the practices they signify creates harm and leads to social stigma. If empathy is a political choice, giving voice to the marginalised with whom we do not agree, who are demonised and in this case radicalised, what are the consequences of empathy?

The casual reproduction of harm should not be a consequence of empathetic research; empathy with extreme activists is something that to many is possibly beyond comprehension. The radical-right and jihadist communities engaged in this book are radical, but in different ways. Even if social disadvantage is part of the stories of some participants in this research, radical-right activists can fall back on structures of white privilege, structures I share. These were not available to most of the jihadist participants discussed here, although jihadists come from all ethnicities. Busher suggests that a test of his own methods for study of the radical right was to ask himself if he would treat hypothetical jihadists in the same way as he was treating the English Defence League.[31] In my work this was not hypothetical; I was always engaging with both sets of actors. But should a (white) researcher treat the radical right in the same way as jihadist actors? Furthermore, is it ethical for a white, middle-class, 'English' researcher, who is not Muslim, to treat these two groups similarly?

Race and power have frequently been overlooked within terrorism studies,[32] and critical terrorism studies, which can act as the conscience of TS, has repeatedly highlighted their absence. Stephen D. Ashe suggests that terrorism studies experts researching the far right have been slow to recognise the importance of race in their work, or to use critical race theory. Terrorism studies has, instead, privileged the impossible objective of an approach free of bias, and has failed to draw on critical race or gender studies, which reveal the futility of such a goal. This is a particular failing given that both higher education and terrorism studies specifically are implicated in the structural production of racism, and the reproduction of whiteness.[33] Terrorism studies has historically been linked with government departments seeking to challenge terrorism, in both funding and objectives; as such, it is implicated in the Orientalist effects of the War on Terror in stigmatising Muslims.[34] Whiteness has also shaped the language used to construct both terrorism and extremism.[35] What is more, Rae Jereza argues that empathy as method "upholds white supremacist methods within the social sciences" and, in a sense, lets the far right off the hook, understanding radicalisation as "flowing from legitimate political and economic grievances".[36] Drawing from Elaine Castillo's work, Jereza suggests that empathy allows the white researcher to understand herself as distinct from those being researched, while sharing structures of power. Instead, Castillo's concept of inheritance is recommended: this shifts the perspective from researcher-and-other to 'our', and enables us to understand far-right activism as part of a collective inheritance. Jereza emphasises the centrality of relationality to the logic of inheritance, which involves "knowing ourselves as fundamentally made possible by—and fundamentally reliant upon—other people, both living and dead."[37]

Research relationships with the radical right are particularly problematic at this point in time, when far-right views are being both mainstreamed and normalised;[38] especially if the researcher is white and shares racial privileges with far-right extremists. Without awareness of these complexities, the researcher perspective can fail to 'do no harm'.[39] The populist right has seen a resurgence in recent years, with elected leaders including Donald Trump in the US and Jair Bolsonaro in Brazil, and with Marine Le Pen in France and Alternative for Germany (AfD) in Germany enjoying electoral success based on agendas that are anti-immigration and anti-multiculturalism, and which push back on women's rights.[40] Studying the radical right in a Western context is to study a dynamic phenomenon with a close relationship to structures and institutions of historically white power, even as populism challenges elites.

As a white researcher, I was very concerned that interviews with the radical-right interviewees would enable different forms of discourse to those with Anjem Choudary's circle. The worst-case scenario was that they would promote racism, cause harm and enable 'white privilege', an idea much mocked by the far right. Peggy McIntosh first coined the term,[41] and defined it as "an invisible package of unearned assets" benefitting white people, who largely "remain oblivious".[42] In a white-majority society such as Britain, whiteness is invisible. Race, as a discourse, has largely been used to refer to people of colour.

The possibility of ethical empathy

Empathy does not exclude the recognition of shared structural privilege, particularly when a researcher takes a reflexive approach with an awareness of positionality. Exisiting research with the far right in particular demonstrates the possibility of ethical empathy. Hilary Pilkington, who has conducted much ethnography with the radical right, and Gavin Bailey, a researcher of both British far-right and Islamist groups, assert the necessity of recognising the legitimacy of the interviewee viewpoint, even where the view crosses the *cordon sanitaire* of acceptability. Those who have researched terrorism and extremism remind us that extremists perceive their own behaviour as moral, and an absence of researcher empathy would neglect this.[43] Virinder S. Kalra and Nisha Kapoor note the frequently uncontested categorisation of Britain's white working class (Britain's working class is a diverse group) and Muslims as two 'problem' groups, within which issues of extremism are—exclusively—rooted.[44] Bailey highlights the prevalence of racism and Islamophobia across all layers of society, demonstrating that they are by no means exclusively attributable to—already marginalised—white working-class subgroups often uniquely understood as racist 'knuckledraggers'.[45] He also notes that in some cases, researchers can seek to avoid the legitimisation of politically challenging views at the expense of the core task of (social) scientific research, which he suggests would be a mistake.[46] Furthermore, to seek to interview people widely understood to hold racist or otherwise exclusionary views is to acknowledge the possibility that racism is not intransmutable. People can change.

I actively sought to avoid raced harms in this research, but it was hard to know how my whiteness impacted the conversations produced during research encounters. White interviewees, whether radical-right or jihadist, did not regard me as sharing their whiteness; they saw me as different, by virtue of education and class. Busher has described his own work with the EDL by saying that "in some ways the 'culture shock' … was more profound than that which I had experienced while carrying out my doctoral research on the Namibia–Angola border."[47] His reference to an African research context, where he is the raced 'Other', is interesting. It implies, perhaps, an experience of whiteness back in Britain that was not shared with the EDL. This does not mean that invisible structures of white power did not form a thread linking the radical right to me, or to other white researchers, and to power itself.

The extreme interviewees are the subjects of cognitive but also affective responses, including disgust and revulsion. Such responses are raced, sexed, gendered and classed.[48] Affect is part of the construction of social order, according to which extreme actors are, normatively, at or near the bottom. It is important in producing stigma, and maintaining the *cordon sanitaire* that prevents the normalisation of extreme views.[49] Interviewees reported how perceived lack of empathy in those around them hurt, and became a source of frustration or pain. Kate, the mother of a convicted al-Qaeda-related terrorist, described a typical exchange with a taxi driver taking her to the prison to see her son. Ignorant of her son's crime, he told Kate, "Paedos, rapists and terrorists, I think they should kill the whole fucking lot of them."[50] This was hard for her to hear, and contributed to her already strong feelings of isolation and distress, she said.

Mudde, an expert on the far right, advocates researcher avoidance of a normative position.[51] Too often, the views of those in extreme, but also marginalised groups are judged against a white middle-class liberalist normativity (my own background); too often, their views are regarded as exceptional, rather than a manifestation of discourses shared with other, more mainstream groups in positions of power. In the contemporary UK context, both Bailey and Pilkington have also emphasised the need to avert a normative approach which either homogenises or condemns the experiences of those who hold 'radical' political positions, whether far-right or Islamist.[52] However, not to condemn can risk censure for the researcher from other parts of the research community, or from wider society. Blee, a seasoned researcher of the American far right, notes the fear of being tainted by the unpalatable views of research interviewees.[53] As Busher recognises, one risk of any work on extreme groups is that the researcher is seen as publicising or sympathising, or simply naive.[54] He advises that such dangers are outweighed by the good of producing important insights into the extreme position.[55]

How to talk to extremists

This book is based on university research that was subject to ethical parameters, set by the institution. This imposed some limitations on the scope of the questions I could ask, and on how the research was carried out. For instance, I could not ask interviewees questions that might lead them to implicate themselves legally—for example, "Do you support Islamic State?", given that this is a criminal offence in the UK. I would have a moral, legal and ethical obligation to report this, or any illegal activity. I could not ask if they had participated in violence. In practical terms, this meant truncated discussion of some themes. Ultimately, this was not such a severe restriction, as interviewees were themselves keenly aware of the legal risks in speaking to me, including criminalisation. None would knowingly implicate themselves. However, this renders this book's discussion of jihadist beliefs and ideology at best a partial account. I also did not ask interviewees questions about issues—funding, for example—where I expected they would not be truthful, or might suspect my motives.

Universities seek to give research interviewees protections. This meant that I explained the aims of the research to all interviewees at the outset, along with any possible benefits of participation, such as the chance to tell their story. I also explained protections such as anonymity. This was given to all interviewees, except well-known figures whose names will be familiar, and who have influence. These figures included Anjem Choudary; Jayda Fransen, who left Britain First in 2019 to found the British Freedom Party;[56] Anne Marie Waters, who founded For Britain in 2017 and five years later disbanded it; John Meighan, who founded the Football Lads Alliance (FLA); Hel Gower, Tommy Robinson's Personal Assistant; and Tommy Robinson. Pseudonyms are used throughout for grassroots activists. Indeed, I did not always ask interviewees for their names and do not know some of them.

How to meet extremists

From May 2016 to February 2018, I travelled around Britain by train and car, trying to talk to extremists. I also travelled online through extreme websites, looking for hashtags for the EDL and Islamic State, which at that time were easy to find. I went to lots of different towns, some for the first time.[57] Sometimes I went to unfamiliar areas of places I thought I knew well. It is a well-worn cliché for right-leaning extremism commentators that the radical right concerns the so-called 'left behind'. The broader far right comes from a diverse class base; so, too, do jihadists. The far-right supporters I talked to are a small sample, from a specific demographic: anti-Muslim radical-right groups associated with lower socio-economic backgrounds. Perceptions of being left behind infused radical-right interviews. In truth, the towns they and some of the jihadist interviewees lived in did feel left behind. I walked out of train stations past pound shops and sex shops, along high streets of charity shops and boarded-up frontages. Britain is not an equal society; relative deprivation, grievances and socio-economic issues are part of the extremism story. And yes, at times I heard stories rooted in political grievances linked to social deprivation and the widely acknowledged inequality and division in Britain today. Nothing I heard, however, legitimised responses that harmed others.

For people to talk to you, they need a point of reference. People working in countering extremism projects, who I initially thought might help me as gatekeepers, didn't or couldn't. So, instead, I met key respected leadership figures within movements in an attempt to access their circles and gain a sort of legitimacy. These included Tommy Robinson, the former EDL leader, and Anjem Choudary, former leader of al-Muhajiroun and associated groups, both of whom seek out publicity and interviews. The trust of interviewees remained hard-won, however. While meeting Choudary was rarely enough to convince his associates to meet with me, the contact with Robinson proved crucial.

Interviewees did not know what I meant by gender; they all believed this meant that I was interested in learning about women, and eyes inevitably glazed over when I explained. Feminist theorising begins with recognition of women's experiences. This entails revealing the unheard narratives of women, but also contextualising women within the patriarchal systems of power from which they are excluded. Indeed, an empathetic and explicitly gendered approach makes clear the patriarchal structures that the radical right, as well as ALM, shared with the rest of us. It was, however, harder to talk to women in both movements, for reasons that are not clear.[58] Islamist women were not present at the Dawah stalls I visited, and nor did they attend trials. Additionally, male Islamists told me that they were concerned to introduce me to women members of their circle, as this might put them at risk. They were particularly afraid of the potential removal of children by social services, they said.[59] Meanwhile, women of the radical right were often suspicious and hostile, perhaps indicating—as a colleague suggested—female competition for male attention within groups.

But both gender and extremism also concern men.[60] Studying masculinities, Connell advocates a biographic "life-history" approach.[61] This is also a common interview approach with extreme groups, as it allows interviewees to talk freely around semi-structured questions. For Connell, the approach is consistent with the theoretical understanding of masculinities and gender as dynamic and collective; requiring insight into subjectivities and place, "the making of social life through time".[62] The visibility and humanity of the interviewees was a central focus of my research project; so, too, was the recognition of men and women's subjectivities, as well as the structural influences they both resisted and constructed.

The application of feminist thinking to the study of extremism meant accepting extreme actors as what anthropologist Kirin Narayan describes as "subjects with voices, views, and dilemmas—people to whom we are bonded through ties of reciprocity".[63] In practice this could raise questions about how much to reveal, and misunderstandings. Some interviewees repeatedly referred to me as 'the journalist', although I told them, truthfully, that my work for the BBC was in the past. Interviewees were also interested in my life and identity, asking questions that paralleled those posed at the start of a friendship. Radical-right interviewees wanted to hear about my family. Islamists were curious that I had travelled in Egypt and was familiar with Islam as practised in a majority Muslim country. Yet curiosity did not mean trust. To encourage trust, I was always honest. Sometimes I felt uncomfortable, yet I engaged in full disclosure where my security was not put at risk by doing so (for instance, I was careful not to disclose where I lived, or too much about my private life). I never practised deception, and I do not believe that this is either desirable or necessary in talking to people in extreme groups. Plenty of researchers have been entirely honest about their identities and succeeded in talking to extremists and to terrorist groups.[64]

I also often used humour. For instance, I admitted to radical-right interviewees that I had cried at Brexit and was a Labour voter. This made for banter, and (playful?) mocking from them. Honesty about my identity, alongside my year-long persistence in seeking an interview, were, then Britain First Deputy Leader Jayda Fransen told me, the reasons she allowed me into the initial Britain First meeting I attended in December 2016. Some of the language people used in interviews, or their own humour, was offensive. Sometimes, I simply did not know what people meant, or how to read them. Language is an 'adopted position', and John Myles suggests care in attending to linguistic difference, as "the evaluation of any discourse is the result of the structuring of social perception and evaluation of the legitimacy of individuals of a particular class to speak on certain topics".[65] Interviewees supporting the radical right were suspicious of my goals and tried to use language that would avoid my censure. Iain, a 19-year-old EDL activist, for example, corrected his friend Daniel's repeated use of the offensive word 'Paki' to 'Muslim' as he listened to our conversation, aware that I was making notes, and explicitly keen not to appear racist. Both Daniel and Iain told me that they had Muslim friends, and that white people were "not better" than non-whites, likely in order to avoid being labelled white supremacist, or racist. There was a great deal of slippage in terms, as Pilkington has noted in her work with the radical right.

My presence at events and my interview technique sometimes made interviewees self-conscious. How would I view them? How would their actions and language reflect on them? Other interviewees considered their use of language, and mine, as we talked, treating me as a form of authority, which they resisted. Jane, in her fifties, sometimes stopped and reflected on her interviews, which I was transcribing by hand, leaving comments like "That's probably the racist side of me" hanging in the air. Or she might explicitly invite me to comment, asking "Is it racist?" of questions including whether 'Britishness' as a nationality should be accessible to immigrants.[66] She had suggested that 'Britishness' might apply in a different way due to the emphasis she lays on birthplace: "If you have come here from other countries then obviously you can apply for British citizenship, but it doesn't make you 'British', because you weren't born within Britain."[67] Such conversations led to discussion of identity and the relevance of place, and how these were connected to racism. Although the discussion seemed genuine, and Jane was interested in my perspective, I did not believe that she wanted to alter her view as a result of our conversation, or that she was likely to. Radical-right interviewees also talked a lot about the 'working class', by which they meant a narrow—reviled—subsection of people of mostly low socio-economic status sharing their views, as well as a broader milieu that they claimed to represent. I use the term in this book not in acceptance of their meaning of it, but to illustrate that it meant something to interviewees.

As will be clear from Chapter Six on, Islamist interviewees used interviews to interrogate some of the same issues of identity and race. They, too, demonstrated a slippage between terms that, to me, denote different categories, such as 'English', 'white' and 'non-Muslim'. When Rifat, a member of Choudary's circle in his thirties, discussed different generational attitudes to marriage and the degradation of moral standards, he said, for example, "Mothers aren't as strong in this day and age. Even Muslim mothers. In English families, divorce wasn't so common [in the past] either. They always made it work."[68] He references 'English' families as something distinct from 'Muslim' families, although many English people are of course Muslim. Others also used the term 'English' as a synonym for white and non-Muslim. Differences in interviewees' use of language was expected, as part of differences in community practice, and interviewees across the research clearly perceived differences between my use of language and theirs. They were also aware that their use of language was one way in which they would be delegitimised and condemned, by me and by wider society.

Being a woman researcher: gender, power and reciprocity

Gender and power matter in research into extremism, and I want to reflect briefly on this before moving to the findings. Research ethics naturally seek to insulate interviewees and researchers from contact beyond the researcher–interviewee relationship. This proved more difficult in practice than I had anticipated. I spent hours with some interviewees and shared a rapport with them; I went to their houses and on trips with them to demos, had lunch with them and met their friends and families. Others I spoke to only once, and some I did not meet in person at all. The research for this book was not a matter of judgment, but nor was it a matter of sympathy or seeking friendship, and nor should it have been.[69] However, it did not mean rejecting personal encounters with interviewees either, and it entailed experiencing them as rounded human beings with a full range of emotions—not just, as Busher has observed, witnessing their anger or rage or hate.[70]

Researchers as well as research interviewees need protections, and there are specific risks for women in a masculinist field. Being a woman researcher can be advantageous, with interviewees perhaps more likely to trust the "naïve little lady", as Enloe puts it.[71] What Marta Bolognani terms the "reciprocal exposure" of the empathetic approach also revealed the gendered power dynamics of activism,[72] and exposed my lack of power and vulnerability in the field. My presence as a woman at radical-right protests or at Islamist *Dawah* stalls, or in interactions with interviewees, exposed the masculinist norms structuring behaviour and enabling interviewees to read my presence. This was not without its challenges. Interviewees needed to situate me within the gendered norms of their landscape. Men therefore often asked intrusive questions about my marital status and living arrangements. A typical question was "What does your husband think about you doing this research?".

While all interactions provide important data, this occasionally made me feel uncomfortable. One Shariah-supporting interviewee suggested I become his second wife, my unmarried status representing to him a form of transgression of my duties and expected role. A second Islamist with whom I had communicated mainly through text messages asked me to dinner when his marriage broke down. A Britain First member who suggested he would give me an interview, meanwhile, repeatedly texted me suggesting we meet "for fun". When I did not reply he responded, "You are one ignorant bitch". Another repeatedly asked me to go out with him. At radical-right demonstrations, men grabbed and hugged me, or otherwise touched me in familiar ways—for instance, putting their hat on my head or pulling me towards them by the belt loop of my jeans. They did this without seeking permission and without warning. I am not unassertive; however, I needed interviews and did not want to 'make a fuss', even if at times I felt both ambushed and compromised, particularly given the ubiquity of cameras at demonstrations and my own negative feelings about such intrusions. I was reminded of other moments I had felt a similar loss of power, in different circumstances. I tried to politely assert my physical boundaries. Yet I believed—rightly or wrongly—that to carry out the work, and gain trust, I would need to endure practices I would otherwise vocally contest. The power dynamic was not always in my favour.

Initially, I found it easier to have empathy for the jihadist activists, arguably more reviled by wider society. This was despite the fact that their views are damaging and offensive to most Muslims, as well as non-Muslims, whom they regard as inferior.[73] Perhaps, given the literature discussed in Chapter One, I assumed that racism would be the mobilising factor in their radicalisation journeys (something that they all denied, although the Islamist interviewees of colour all discussed experiences of racism). There were moments with interviewees from both the radical-right and Islamist movements where I had a choice: to offer help or not. One involved responding to an injured interviewee; another, helping someone following a police raid and subsequent arrest. In both cases I did what I could to help, within what I believed were the parameters of the research and framework of care. Both instances of help changed my relationship with those interviewees; I was somehow more involved. Ultimately, neither interviewee I assisted wanted further contact with me and I was unsure of the long-term consequences of my actions. These are the practical dilemmas of research with extremists.

It was important to admit my own limitations and my views; to be willing to become visible in personal engagements with interviewees, "exposing the research persona".[74] The researcher may at times hold the reins of power;[75] however, power may equally reside with the interviewee.[76] Interviewees in contentious research, such as on extremism, more often view the researcher as the 'vulnerable' party, not themselves.[77] Not all of this power concerned my gender. Giving up researcher power can be a sign that the project is not one of spying or domination, as interviewees often feared.[78] I did not always know if I could trust them. Authenticity is not a given. However, interviews always had value, if not verifiable truth.[79] I tried to anticipate the fluctuating dynamics of the researcher—

interviewee relationship, and the impossibility of producing a single truth.[80] I experienced hostility frequently, but at other times warmth. Some interviewees asked me whether I liked them. They felt, understandably, that a level of friendship was necessary to the experience of confiding in the researcher, an experience which becomes part of the subject narrative.[81] As discussed above, others sought my help, as someone in a position of relative authority. When Islamist Adam was arrested in connection with terrorism offences, for instance, it was me he called as soon as police had left. He asked what he should do. All the interviewees knew that I did not agree with them, even as I saw their point of view. Nonetheless, it was a research aim to adhere to the standpoint philosophy of recognition and empowerment of the subject and their perspective, if not their views. This entailed respect for the interviewee's ability to tell their own story, but not through endorsing their views or allowing them to spread open propaganda.[82] Interviewees likely would not have perceived this as empowerment at all.

Once my personal political convictions were discussed, conversations sometimes took on a surreal tone, acknowledging the difficulties of dialogue and our lack of familiarity with one another. Jason, who said he was linked to the neo-Nazi group National Action, not proscribed at the time of our meeting, was an avowed white supremacist. He told me:

> It feels weird talking to you. ... Generally, I only talk to the converted. ... Liberals are the most closed-minded. They dismiss you. You're a racist straight away, they just judge you. ... I think, how dare you write me off! Now, I can't be bothered trying and begging for their attention. ... I feel weird preaching to you because you are a brick wall.[83]

Interviewees from both movements were acutely aware that talking to me potentially ceded control of their narratives, and those on the radical right repeatedly expressed fears that they would be 'stitched up' and that my book would intentionally focus on the portrayal of their movements as racist. Both Bonzer and Glynn suggested they had been deliberately misunderstood in the past.

EDL supporter Glynn voiced reservations about the possibility of my academic objectivity:

> The idea that your research will be ground-breaking—it's just jumping through a hoop. I am sure that [another researcher who, he believes, 'stitched up' his interviewees] came under pressure to say, "frame it this way". I think it's fundamentally flawed and it's become slanted so that it supports the existing narratives. You can make a name by being slightly controversial, but not [very].

The assumption expressed here is perhaps not unreasonable, given both mainstream discourses and Mudde's warnings about the dominance of normative narratives in research on the 'extreme right' (although Mudde himself is active in opposing the far right). Interactions meant a constant dynamic engagement with my own position, and how this potentially impacted dialogue. While, as outlined, I believed interviewees frequently felt conscious of my possible condemnation of their language and sought to avoid this, at times I felt that there was some attempt to shock deliberately through the use of offensive, including racist, language. For example, this is an extract from an interview with Hel Gower, informal Personal Assistant to Tommy Robinson until 2017 and in her sixties when I met her:

> Hel: Some of them [the EDL] that came were retards.
> Me [laughing]: You can't say that Hel…!
> Hel [laughing]: I can!

Later in this conversation she told me, "I come from the East End originally … so, I'm used to immigrants moving in. Blacks or coloureds, or whatever you call them now … Chinese. But they did come in, and no problem, they assimilated. But Muslims don't do that, and so the problems started."[84] Problematic language was wielded to demonstrate a lack of respect for, or conformity to, my perceived world of liberal values, and—from their perspective— adherence to left-wing dogma, all of which they understood as inauthentic and not based in interactions in real—read as 'working-class'—life.

Summary

It is doubtless clear from this chapter that I believe not just that it is 'ok' to talk to extremists, but that to do so, with an empathetic approach situated in feminist ethics of care, is vital to understanding them. If we are really to decentre the power of the academy and social structures more generally, we cannot only apply power-disruptive protocols and practices with communities we like or care for, or agree are worthy. The research was an education for me in engaging, with an ethical research practice as an objective, with people whom I sometimes struggled with, personally and politically. This chapter is about how I tried to make that work.

It should also be clear from this chapter that responsible research involving talking to extremists must engage with power, with race, with class and with gender, within academia as well as society. The empathetic approach is one that opens the possibility of a difficult and perhaps indefinable relationship with the research interviewee. It is friendly, without entailing friendship; it shows a level of trust, and at times mutual disclosure. Yet it is bounded by the awareness that the research relationship is ultimately a transactional one, in that it is deliberately produced by the researcher in pursuit of a product: knowledge. I adopted an empathetic approach with the awareness that to enable another person to tell their story can mean unintentionally entering that story.[85] Historically, the assumption is that researchers must do no harm, as they hold all the power. Yet the balance of power is not always in the favour of the researcher of terrorism and extremism. My own identity was clearly important in producing the knowledge in this book. Interviewees' responses to and perceptions of me communicate something about the field, how it works, and the gender relations within it. This chapter presented how I carried out the research, recognising that research is always imperfect and was in this case, as outlined, complex and sometimes emotionally charged.

The key aim of this book is to understand the function of gender in radicalisation from the inside out; this necessitates recognition of the political subjectivities of actors often seen as the products of 'evil ideologies', or simply hatred itself. The research findings presented in the following chapters are based on the theory and methods set out here. They explore how practices of masculinity and femininity are institutionalised, collectivised, individualised, resisted and permitted. Fundamentally, the following chapters reveal radicalisation to be a project of masculinity, better understood by thinking through power and gender. The next chapter begins with an introduction to the radical right, before moving on to the interviewees, and then a gendered analysis of their narratives. It discusses what influenced them before they ever found the movement, and how they situate themselves, their social field and the practices that give their later activism meaning.

3

THE RADICAL RIGHT
SITUATING MASCULINITIES

Introduction

Tommy Robinson, Jayda Fransen, Anne Marie Waters. These are key names in British extremism, and therefore in the battle to stop it. This chapter introduces these leaders alongside fourteen other radical-right participants to explore how masculinities functioned in their radicalisation to radical-right activism, with specific reference to the English Defence League (EDL), Britain First (BF) and For Britain (FB). It seeks to understand the relationship between place, gender and masculinities in the time before their activism. Space was of both practical and mythic meaning, consistent with nationalist tropes. The way in which gender was understood within local space was also important in both establishing and recognising community, and in constructing in-group and out-group. If, as Berger suggests, extremism is the belief that in-group success depends on hostile action towards an out-group,[1] then this chapter demonstrates the importance of gender, masculinities and sexual norms in producing perceptions of group difference, the basis of in- and out-group creation. Gender plays a central role in the perception of boundaries between communities.

The chapter follows criminological theory that points to the importance of everyday interactions and "daily behaviours" in local spaces in the formation of masculine identity in both men and women on the radical right.[2] Participants construct agency and frame actions through a hypermasculine lens, predicated on the potential for violence. Their gendered interactions in local spaces with symbolic meaning produce particular racialised masculinities, which they will later mobilise towards group activism. Drawing on the existing literature, this chapter engages with the—often offensive—transcripts of the radical-right interviewees. What is clear here is that the first steps on the path to extremism are steps that also construct particular masculinities, situated in social and physical space.

Existing literature: masculinities on the radical right

Before discussing masculinities on the radical right, it is useful to consider the terminology of the 'far right', as this is diverse and problematic.[3] Who am I talking about when I talk about the radical right, and why do I not use the label 'far right'? The term 'far right' is—confusingly—used in different ways by the media, academics and policymakers, among others, to encompass a variety of ideological positions and, as this book makes clear, different gender positions elevating different masculinities. This is the 'far right' as an umbrella term. Wider discourse often uses labels such as 'extreme', 'far-right', 'alt-right' and 'populist right' interchangeably, applying them all to the radical right groups in this book. To some degree the diversity of labels represents the fluidity of actors, whose allegiances can shift between ideological positions.[4] The use of 'far right' is also contingent on the political context, with several authors arguing that the far right has been mainstreamed in the UK and USA and, following Brexit and the Presidency in the United States of Donald Trump, to some extent normalised.

Use of the term 'far right' also says something about the political position of the researcher;[5] for instance, some researchers do not recognise a meaningful distinction between neo-Nazi ideology and the ideologies of more recent groups focused on contesting

Islam.[6] Current British government policy understands the anti-Islam radical right as both 'far-right' and 'extreme'. Some scholars term the radical right the 'counter-jihad', a term sometimes used by groups themselves. 'Counter-jihad' describes an anti-Islam(ist) movement, located within a broader (transnational) networked scene of frequently shifting groups and allegiances. It reflects what Joe Mulhall suggested even in 2018 was a "post-organisational", nebulous arena.[7] Leadership and grassroots figures from different movements are familiar with one another and might identify with one another's aims, even if they do not share tactics or ideology, or even dislike one another. Other authors understand counter-jihad or radical-right groups as inherently fascist. Different experts use different labels for the key groups studied here, the EDL and Britain First. Busher uses the term "anti-Muslim" to describe the EDL.[8] Pilkington terms the EDL "anti-Islamist" and regards it as part of a populist radical right rather than a traditional extreme-right or far-right movement.[9] Terminology is not consistent.

Some authors analyse the emergence of the counter-jihad through the ideological prism of 'new fascism'. In 1995, Tore Bjørgo identified the growth of new fascism in a fresh fascination with ideas of "people, blood and soil".[10] Around the same time, scholar of the far right Roger Griffin also suggested that fascism was experiencing a resurgence through "such forces as militarism, racism, charismatic leadership, populist nationalism, fears that the nation or civilization as a whole was being undermined by the forces of decadence, deep anxiety about the modern age and longings for a new era to begin."[11] A section of the literature suggests that anti-Islam politics is simply fascism repackaged. Matthew Feldman, for example, describes the EDL as "old wine in new bottles", with the 'old' racism of skin colour replaced with the 'new' cultural racism of faith.[12] Authors including Feldman, Martin Barker and Paul Jackson use the label 'new' to suggest its opposite—a rebranding, rather than an ideological shift.[13] Donald Holbrook and Max Taylor suggest that formerly racialised targets have simply evolved to encompass faith: Jews, Muslims, and even governments and their agents, the police, and liberal activists, among others.[14] John Meadowcroft and Elizabeth A. Morrow agree that the EDL is an "Islamophobic, right-wing extremist group",[15] while Pietro Castelli

Gattinara, in an overview of the literature, also suggests that assertions of cultural 'incompatibility' merely represent a narrative development from assertions of racial 'inferiority'.[16] This strand of analysis regards groups such as the EDL as members of the same political family as the explicitly racist British National Party (BNP) led by Nick Griffin, or the 2010-2012 British Freedom Party (BFP).[17]

My own position is that the groups studied in this book differ ideologically from neo-Nazi and traditional far-right groups. I employ the term 'radical right' for this extreme movement. It contests multiculturalism and religious diversity; is populist and socially divisive; and numerically, involves a minority of society.

The British radical right, consisting of those who first and foremost oppose Islam, does not uniformly fulfil core features that Mudde suggests are required to count as 'extreme-right' (which includes neo-Nazi groups): nationalism, racism, xenophobia, an anti-democratic stance and a belief in the need for a strong state.[18] Contrary to both this and Schmid's definition of extremism, the EDL, Britain First and For Britain have all supported democracy. Indeed, Mudde has more recently noted the key difference between the extreme right and populist radical right: the latter challenges aspects of liberal democracy, while the extreme right opposes democracy in its very essence.[19] Britain First is a political party. Anne Marie Waters repeatedly stood in elections representing For Britain, and the EDL's core activity was legal street protest, although there was also street violence. While BF have organised so-called 'Mosque Invasions' and harassed individuals, when considered both ideologically and tactically, there is a difference between most activists I talked to for this book and those engaged with neo-Nazi groups such as Stormfront or National Action. There is also a difference in the public visibility of their tactics. What unites the leaders and the grassroots of the groups considered is that at the time of research, they prioritised and mobilised around opposition to Islam(ism), and in gendered terms.

While I consider the British context, the radical right is a transnational movement. In 2010, Tommy Robinson, then Leader of the EDL, announced in a speech in Amsterdam that the movement stood together with counter-jihad groups across Europe.[20] The (now defunct) EDL website claimed that the group had an "international outlook".[21] Alexander Meleagrou-Hitchens and Hans Brun have suggested that the EDL and associated European Defence Leagues form a "European Counter-Jihad Movement", providing a broad ideological milieu from which lone actors such as Breivik have emerged.[22] As well as Meleagrou-Hitchens and Brun, Nigel Copsey notes ideological connections between the EDL and American influencers, such as Pamela Geller and Robert Spencer of 'Stop Islamization of America'.[23] Counter-jihad activists broadly, although not in this book, come from all social classes, ranging from middle-class activists and pundits such as the former *Apprentice* contestant Katie Hopkins to self-proclaimed working-class leaders of street movements such as Robinson or Fransen. Perhaps the most infamous transnational connection was President Trump, who in 2017 retweeted Fransen, leading to her removal from Twitter and Facebook.[24]

As noted in the Introduction, within the wider literature on the far right specifically, masculinities scholar Kimmel has called for a holistic approach to gender as an analytic framework. He is an expert on masculinity on the far right in the United States and in Europe, and has drawn analytic attention to how the all-male nature of such groups is taken for granted.[25] Since Kimmel has made this call, more authors are applying masculinities studies to the emergent incel movement; however, this is due to the explicitly anti-feminist nature of incel rhetoric and attacks.[26] It is less common for masculinities studies to be routinely engaged in analysis of Islamist and far-right extremism, given that mainstream authors have historically considered maleness (and, until recently, misogyny) within these groups as secondary to other objectives, as discussed in the previous chapter.

In the UK context, several authors have challenged the taking for granted of men's activism that Kimmel highlights. In their criminological studies, Treadwell and Garland suggest that feelings of marginalisation and disadvantage prompt anger and disillusionment, which are expressed in violent masculinity in the EDL.[27] The EDL previously "tapped into the frustrations of a disenfranchised section of the white working class," they note.[28] They emphasise that individual psychological perspectives matter as much in understanding the EDL as broader cultural and socio-economic change.[29] The narrative is of marginalised men of reduced status accessing a violent masculinity to compensate for this loss, and working against those they seek to blame for it. In such accounts, masculinity expressed in racism operates as a form of social capital.[30]

In three case studies of young male EDL supporters, Treadwell and Garland identify factors familiar from the criminological literature which are also evident in this chapter. These include the importance of violence as performance in front of male peers; status-gaining behaviour, such as retaliation after victimisation; resentment of Asians as having more, and so of relative deprivation; and the construction of the Muslim man as a worthy rival and target (of which there is less evidence in this chapter). In essence, the authors associate anger, marginalisation, alienation and frustration with male EDL violence, alongside a lack of access to 'legitimate' expression.[31]

Busher, however, cautions that masculinity in the counter-jihad and the far right can often be reduced to pathologising accounts, depicting men as "angry, white, damaged and vulnerable ... seeking to protect their social status and reassert their compromised masculinity".[32] Busher admits there is a "kernel of truth" to this account, consistent with wider notions of toxic masculinity. However, he asserts that it contributes little to understanding how gender functions as what Sjoberg terms an "organising principle",[33] which explicitly constitutes their "angry, white, damaged" activism.

Other scholars link far-right masculinity to specific subcultures, including football hooliganism. Here it becomes part of the almost ritual display of achieving manhood. Eric Dunning suggests that this milieu tends to "stress ability to fight, 'hardness' and ability to 'hold one's ale' as marks of being a 'man'."[34] His research also suggests the importance of masculinity in enabling status-gain and re-masculation. In similar analysis, but of violent white supremacist skinheads in the United States, Mark Hamm identifies the affective contribution of ideology, style and expression within a particular subculture towards group aims:

> All of this—ideology, music, weaponry and white male bonding—comes together to trigger the vitality, the emotions and the excitement necessary for skinheads to 'go berserk'

on their perceived enemies (blacks, gays, foreigners, Jewish institutions, etc.).[35]

Additionally, Hamm notes the importance of celebrity and masculinity, recommending that terrorism studies learn from criminology's emphasis on subculture and symbolism. This emphasises the meaning created by groups for themselves.[36] Anoop Nayak, for instance, explains that skinhead style articulates "multiple masculine fantasies of existence related to manual labor, militarism, prison identity and 'hardness'".[37] Scholar of the far right Cynthia Miller-Idriss has similarly outlined how, in a European context, "far right style links masculinity and nationalism by articulating shared aspirations for ideal national traits and ideal masculine ones, clearly identifying what it means to be a 'real man' in any given nation."[38] Such analyses show how gender shapes and enables violent cultures within movements. They have formed the basis for using masculinities to understand other forms of extremism—for instance, the lone actor.[39] Criminological work on subcultures is influential in this book; it is through an interdisciplinary approach engaging gender and masculinities that the radical right can best be understood.

Introducing the participants: radical right

This part of the book introduces the radical-right participants, men and women, before exploring the narratives of their pathways into activism, and the roles gender and masculinities play within this. I talked in depth to a total of seventeen core radical-right interviewees, who came from different parts of Britain. There were six women, some of whom will be familiar to followers of past years' headlines covering the radical right and others for whom I use pseudonyms. They were, with ages at time of interview: Anne Marie Waters (forties), Georgey (thirties), Hel Gower (sixties), Jane (fifties), Jayda Fransen (thirties) and Lydia (fifties). There were also eleven men who were core interviewees: Alex (twenties), Bonzer (forties), Daniel (twenties), Darren (forties), Glynn (age unknown), Henryk (sixties), Iain (nineteen), Jacek (thirties), Jason (thirties), John Meighan (thirties) and Tommy Robinson (thirties).[40]

In addition to these interviewees, I spoke informally to others, some repeatedly, without their contributing a formal interview. Britain First and the EDL were the two main radical-right groups supported by participants in the research. However, and despite some mutual antagonism between supporters of these groups,[41] participants moved between protests, organisations and movements. This means the whole scene has a stability that individual groups, which might disappear, do not. While people no longer take part in EDL street protest, for instance, they may not have changed their views, but are simply expressing them elsewhere, in different ways.

Of the seventeen interviewees, four are named leaders: Tommy Robinson, who founded the EDL, was active in *Pegida*, was an 'independent online activist–journalist' with the Canadian alt-right Rebel News and is now a radical-right influencer; Britain First's then Deputy Leader Jayda Fransen; the founder of the now obsolete For Britain, Anne Marie Waters; and John Meighan, who set up the Football Lads Alliance in 2017 and resigned in 2018.[42] Waters came from a mainstream political route, the Labour Party, to the radical right. She joined Tommy Robinson in—unsuccessful—steps to establish the German anti-Islam street movement *Pegida* in the UK and she then set up the group For Britain in 2017, following her failure to become UKIP party leader. The For Britain website stated that it was neither a "left" nor a "right" but a "common-sense" party for the "forgotten majority".[43] Its manifesto did not focus on Islam, mentioning the religion only in the context of education, where it called to "[r]emove Islamic indoctrination from the classroom",[44] and saying that the stance on Islam would be left to members to decide.[45] In January 2019 one of its eight campaign priorities was to "[e]nd the Islamisation of the UK", which was linked with crimes against women.[46] Waters disbanded For Britain in 2022 and since April 2023 has again been active for UKIP.[47]

Two interviewees were close to leadership: Hel Gower, who ran the women's movement in the EDL, the EDL Angels, also acted as Tommy Robinson's Personal Assistant; and Henryk was close to those running Britain First. Others were grassroots activists without leadership roles. Ten had been active in the EDL. Three were active in Britain First. Two were associated with *Pegida* and two were independent. Other groups' or movements' participants mentioned as relevant to their activism at times were (various) Infidel groups, the United Patriots, White Lives Matter[48] and the English Democrats. One participant (Jason) said he had links to the neo-Nazi group National Action (NA), which was founded in 2013 and proscribed in December 2016 following anti-Semitic protest, stickering and propagandising, as well as plots.[49] However, Jason did not identify as an NA member, and I could not verify any connection.

I saw very few people of colour at protests; however, I did not succeed in speaking to them. The sample informing this book is exclusively white, although not all British. All identified either as English, British or Polish. Lydia was British–American, with dual nationality. Two of the interviewees, Henryk and Jacek, were Polish, and had settled in the UK in the past 10 years. Both said that ideally they would not stay here: Henryk because of 'British injustice'; Jacek because he regards Britain as a 'totalitarian state'. The 2018 Hope Not Hate report noted the presence in the UK far right of many Poles, and a particular connection with Britain First.[50] A significant number of the other respondents also had immigrant heritage. The most common second heritage was Irish, a finding consistent with a previous study on the EDL by Busher.[51] Anne Marie Waters was the only fully Irish—now British—interviewee. Jason described himself as having Irish heritage, and three had one Irish parent: John Meighan was Irish–Welsh, Darren Irish–Mediterranean and Tommy Robinson Irish–English. Iain claimed he had distant West Indian heritage. Broadly speaking, the sample included eight people (47 per cent) who said that they had an immigrant background. Clearly mine is a small sample, but it is demographically similar to the radical-right and far-right scenes noted in the wider literature.[52]

Whose streets, our streets: gender, masculinities and place

Even if far-right street protest is growing, it is some time since the English Defence League, Tommy Robinson or the Football Lads Alliance drew supporters to the streets in the thousands. For Britain and Britain First never have. Fundamental to protest for all these causes is the street: not simply presence on it, but ownership of it. Local space mattered to all the participants. It was where they lived and worked, where they grew up. It was local—not national—issues that prompted most interviewees to become involved in activism. Indeed, Iain, a 19-year-old activist, told me that the EDL's increasingly national scope in its later days was a reason why he no longer felt the movement was for him: "I won't slag the EDL. But [for me] it's more about local issues. ... The EDL wasn't doing it. It's [become] a national movement. So—I dunno."[53] For Iain, it is his local area that constitutes his life, peer group and identity.

The masculinities discussed in this chapter are produced in the intersections of gender with race, narratives of socio-economic deprivation and class. For interviewees, location as a source of identity was laden with meaning, much of this gendered. Consistent with existing scholarship on criminality and street culture,[54] the ability to gain and maintain status on the streets of the place considered home was important and linked to the performance of particular masculinities and femininities, with different expectations of each. Participants' emphasis on place was also consistent with a change that Selina Todd, writing on the history of the British working class, associates with 1980s working-class identity, in which class becomes associated with lack.[55] Both men and women I spoke to described their local neighbourhood as 'working-class', an identity that was important to them. They understood working-class culture as productive of (my phrasing) a particular set of locally circulating gendered practices, regarded as hegemonic and enabling status in their communities. I understand this as a 'masculinity system', a normative gender framework within which multiple masculinities and femininities have status and conjoin to produce a system. In naming this a masculinity system I emphasise that multiple masculinities, not solely hypermasculinity, function as hegemonic, alongside complementary femininities. As Mimi Schippers notes, "any conceptualization of hegemonic masculinity must also be defined by how it articulates a complementary and hierarchical relationship to femininity";[56] masculinity is, in fact, part of a gendered system.

Participants believed that dominant culture denigrated local practices, and the places and masculinities producing them. Local hegemonic masculinities offered local social capital, and were produced through what interviewees identified as class-associated norms. These gendered norms regulated violence and aggression, with high-value hegemonic masculinities predicated on expectations of aggression, the ability to defend oneself and a performative hypermasculinity that verged at times on toxicity in its effects (understood as the assertion of misogyny, homophobia and violence).

These norms shaped both men's and women's identities, attitudes to the performance of violence or the threat of violence, and actions. Tommy Robinson's former personal assistant Hel Gower, in her sixties, explained what place meant to her identity as working class:

> That was what was bred into me. You're working class. … My dad worked for the post office, he loaded the cargo ships at what used to be Canary Wharf, and my mum was a book-keeper. … [Q: What did it mean to be working class?] It was political— it was always, you vote Labour and nothing else and you know you're working-class stock—you're not one of those snotty people. … They were very proud of where they came from, the fact that they were Londoners. … Proud of being English! … I'm very blunt and say what I think. People don't like it. … But I grew up in Bow. … It was rough and ready. I don't think growing up in the East End you can be anything else.[57]

Gower invokes gendered notions of race, nation and the inevitability of her identity with the word "stock", and her emphasis on how this is "bred" into her. Class in this sense echoes historic visions of nationality: something bred through kinship, not chosen, and embedded in ideas of space. States have long mobilised militarised nationalism and relied on gendered arguments to produce violence. Nationalist violence relies on a gender binary and constructed dichotomies of insider/outsider and masculine/feminine, with the masculine/men always read as superior to and protective of the feminine/women.[58] Nationalists require that the protected female and male protector originate in the same discursive space of the mythical 'homeland', founded on 'natural ties' and the ideology of kinship.[59] However, while nationalist ideologies tend to limit men and women to separate physical spaces—the feminine home versus the masculine public realm—here Gower asserts her ability as a

81

woman to assume particular masculine traits defined by the social landscape. Both Hel Gower and Georgey, an EDL supporter in her thirties, told me they had been involved in aggressive but non-violent confrontation with Muslim men in their local space. They perceived such encounters as particularly forceful displays of emasculation, based on their belief that it is humiliating for Muslim men to be publicly confronted by women.

The neighbourhood itself entails a particular socialisation within the "rough and ready" environment—within which, Gower suggests, agency is absent. There is no possibility of anything else. Yet her identification with this identity is in fact a choice, as she told me her family had moved from Bow when she was ten.

There was little contestation of norms in which violent masculinities were hegemonic, even where those norms appeared, or were described by participants as harmful to them. Interviewees embraced them. Hel and other interviewees both idealised and mythologised a—white—working-class past, its values and its (sometimes lost) physical terrain. Darren, in his forties, described the area he grew up in in similar terms. He was introduced to the EDL and, later, Infidel groups through football violence and the British National Party (BNP), which is an anti-immigration and explicitly racist political party. He had a strong attachment to the inner-city area in which he grew up. Nonetheless, the attachment to place is fraught with potential violence and victimisation:

> When you're growing up in [X], you walk over them, before they walk over you. You become a face—a face who is known on the street—or you become a target. You have to become someone that people think, don't fuck with him, that's Darren. … Then that reputation spreads and keeps you out of trouble for life.[60]

Darren presents a binary understanding of masculinities: physical aggressor (a hegemonic hypermasculinity) or target (subordinate). Any performative masculinity that enables victimisation is subordinate; any masculinity that projects a capacity for violence gains status. He does not mention 'men', but he implicitly describes a community in which men are socialised from an early age into this binary. What is more, it is important to establish an aggressive hypermasculinity that endures through time, and across the community by word of mouth. As Christopher Mullins notes, "Gendered power on the streets is not as simple as men's dominance over women; men vie with one another for prestige and street influence".[61] Projecting the potential for violence is one important mechanism to achieve this. This is the hegemony that masculinities scholar Demetrakis Z. Demetriou divides into external, over women, and internal, over men.[62] The interviewees did at times explicitly discuss sexuality and violence over women in these accounts. As I will discuss later, in this book's examination of ideology, participants also referenced the protection of rights for gay men and women. Given participants' binary understanding of the roles of men and women (explored in Chapter Five), this hegemonic masculinity can be described as heterosexual, with gay men requiring the same heterosexual protection from Islam as women.

Peers mattered in the policing of both men's and women's behaviours.[63] They also provided the audience to which violent masculinities are performed and proved.[64] The risk of non-conformity appeared to be the risk of being forever bullied; not by Muslim men, but by all and any men. Connell wrote that masculinity is expressed in "certain postures and ways of moving … to distinctly occupy space, to have a physical presence in the world".[65] In the formative world of the radical-right participants, size becomes an indicator of strength, with perceived hypermasculinity fixed in physicality and bodily presence.[66] Others also described pressure on young men to conform to masculine norms requiring them to appear physically able to defend themselves. Robinson, for instance, told me that it had been important always to walk with his head up, to own the space, particularly as he is neither big nor tall.

Football, identity and violence

Men and women interviewees equated their class identity with threatening spaces and physical insecurity—what some termed a 'rough' area, for instance. They described how the permanent threat of low-level violence meant people faced a choice: performing violence or becoming a victim of it. Violent masculinities were not the only route to status. Football was another marker of masculinity in this—self-proclaimed working-class white—culture, and a way of distinguishing men who deserved respect from men who did not. Support for football teams was historically about place. Consistent with Nicola Ingram's findings, men's participation in football is both a positive expression of culture and a route towards masculine status, predicated on positive aspects of (working-class) masculinity, including belonging, community and friendship.[67] Darren told me, "Football, it's like, when you meet a man, you ask what football team they support, and if they're not into football then you totally lose respect for them."[68] Football has the ability to connect men across social divisions, through shared emotion and an environment permitting the expression of that emotion. This is something participants could share with any other football fan.

However, football had another meaning for participants, one that separated them from most British football fans. For some of the interviewees, football was inseparable from hypermasculinity predicated on both class and violence. For Darren, football was again about the performance of violence, and hooliganism. He engaged an affectionate tone as he discussed both the younger men coming up and those still active in their fifties:

> When it's in your blood, it's in your blood. I'm forty-three now, and in front of me you have the younger ones. Then the old-school, proper old-school hooligans. …You have your cat-A old-school for a big match, they all come out of the woodwork. I haven't done that for 10 years or more though. But in certain games, the passion comes back. … A lot of them have been to jail and they only come out for these high-end games. They sit under the cameras, where they can't be seen and they're on their phones all through the game, controlling everything in the stadium. They're fifty-five or sixty now, old boys. … They were talking about running amok in the world cup in Russia,[69] I'm thinking, you're talking like a 30-year-old, not 55. I wouldn't be doing that at that age. Not at my age, even.[70]

Darren perceives a masculine life cycle to violence; one he is at the older end of. Youth are socialised into violence, and yet, echoing

Hel Gower, this socialisation is inevitable, lacking agency: "in your blood".

Although football violence is clearly criminal, interviewees described a moral code guiding how violence is conducted. The code suggested that violence, like going to football matches, constitutes a valid pastime, with associated rules. Ramón Spaaij found that football hooliganism has six key features: "excitement and pleasurable emotional arousal, hard masculinity, territorial identifications, individual and collective management of reputation, a sense of solidarity and belonging, and representations of sovereignty and autonomy".[71] Interviewees suggested that gaining reputation meant adhering to a moral code: not seriously injuring others; not targeting women; only attacking those who visibly communicate that they are seeking violence—for instance, through clothes. Hypermasculinity entails the protection of some (women), and violence to others. Miller-Idriss has outlined how, in a European context, "far right style links masculinity and nationalism by articulating shared aspirations for ideal national traits and ideal masculine ones, clearly identifying what it means to be a 'real man' in any given nation."[72] For Alex, who is in his twenties and a former football hooligan, clothing was an important identifier of those you could fight, and this had to be respected:

> When I was young, I went to the football with my family. There was violence. At first—well, I didn't like it. But then, you kind of get used to it. It was people that were dressed a certain way. They would never attack people like that was wearing [football] kit; it was only people that were wearing a certain kind of clothes, Stone Island, Burberry. When I first started getting into [the violence] I was 16 years old, and I was told to change how I dressed.[73]

While Darren only implied the harm of being socialised into an environment in which violence was less choice, more sole means to protect oneself, Alex admits that as a child he did not like violence. It was not innate to him as a male child; he became socialised into violence. Eventually he became a willing participant, and this led him to later EDL activism.

Masculinities are constituted through casual violence throughout the broader social milieu. Several of the male interviewees in the research—both ALM and radical-right—described casual violence as not just normative, but tantamount to a form of communication and bonding. I asked Robinson if violence was normal to him. He replied, "Yes, it was fucking normal. If there's a disagreement— if people disagree, they fight!"[74] To Robinson, casual violence functioned as a means of discovering which men have high status; a male bonding experience; even a way of making friends. He told me, for example, that the best man at his wedding was someone he met in a fight outside a nightclub.

Interviewees described how they used the rules and practices of violence—the habitus of violence—to establish gendered divisions between Muslims and their own self-identified peer group. It was around such division that later activism manifested. Robinson suggested that the rules and practices of male aggression differed between Muslim and non-Muslim communities, in ways he believed again defined and divided them. He used as an example a group fight that he experienced in his twenties, involving a Muslim friend whom Robinson perceived as changing sides:

> There was a massive fight, guy comes out of a club, there was about six Muslim lads waiting to kick his head in—so I've gone over and helped him, pull him out. … [T]hen three of their friends then attacked me and M---- is one of my friends [who is Muslim], he's fighting on their side, yeah—on their side! … [H]e said the next day, "Man, when it goes like that, I've got to be on my brothers' side." And we were mates![75]

Violence, but also the rules of violence, mattered to interviewees. When others were perceived not to 'play fair', or practise the same rules, participants understood this as evidence of an identity boundary, a life lived according to a different masculinity system.

What is important in these narratives around violence norms is that interviewees regarded their norms as indicative of a particularly masculinised working-class tradition, associated with an identity they perceived as itself under threat. This masculinity is also performed by women, although in a more limited form (and I will say more about this in Chapter Five). The narratives suggest that casual and football violence are not just permissible but normative, a means to perform hegemonic masculinities and achieve status in front of one's peers. They demonstrate how interviewees perceive gender differences—differences in what counts as hegemonic masculinity— in the violence rules of their community, when contrasted with local Muslims. This perception served as confirmation for the radical right that their communities fundamentally differed from those of the Muslims they encountered in ways that they believed were harmful to them.

Nonetheless, the boundaries participants set for perceived integration by working-class Muslims living locally appeared insurmountably high. Both Daniel and his friend Iain, long-term radical-right activists, told me they did have Muslim friends, but perceived the very fact of their friendship as evidence these associates were not 'proper Muslims'. Iain said, "I don't think they are very good Muslims, to be honest. They come to the pub with us. But if their parents found out, they would be in big shit. ... They ain't integrated. [Q: Why, if they're in the pub?] Because they would be in the shit, they would be in trouble."[76] Young Muslims' efforts at a masculine assimilation into activities with non-Muslim young men, such as drinking alcohol, were therefore undermined. Daniel and Iain refused to accept Muslim drinking friends as individuals with agency independent of their faith, instead persisting in regarding them as members of a generally 'unintegrated' collective. In a sense, assimilated Muslims no longer counted as Muslim to the radical right. It was a lose-lose situation for them.

Not only do both radical-right men and radical-right women gain self-respect through reference to a locally produced hyper-aggressive hegemonic masculinity, but they also regard the absence of it in others—particularly white elites, amongst whom casual violence can be understood as a failure to resolve conflict through dialogue, or a moral failure—as evidence of inauthenticity and inexperience, lack of credibility and respect. Any masculinity that does not project possible violence is regarded as inauthentic. I say inauthentic rather than subordinate, as liberal masculinities are recognised as less meaningful, but also more powerful in the milieus outside of the local area.[77] Part of this inauthenticity is linked to an inability to hold one's own in the local milieu in which violence is normative; part is linked to mainstream liberal attitudes to multiculturalism, and an acceptance—or, in fact, perceived celebration—of Muslim gendered difference, and the disruption to gender norms represented, for instance, in support for trans rights. Radical-right men construct masculinity as linked to heterosexual men's bodies.

Gendered difference and identity boundaries

Gender was central to the narratives participants told about their affinity with space, and practices within that space. Interviewees resisted change; in particular, they challenged gendered change. In 2016, the year of the Brexit referendum to decide whether the UK should leave the European Union, and in which I began field research, Louise Casey's government-commissioned review into opportunity and integration in the UK reported on findings within 'white communities'. It found that immigration was not fundamentally threatening to those consulted; it was rather the perceived pace of change that had apparently created a sense of disempowerment. The report read, "As some communities have become more segregated, the increased pace of immigration has added new pressures, leaving long-standing communities struggling to adjust to the changes around them."[78] In particular, it highlights gender inequalities in "some communities" and notes that the "prevalence and tolerance of regressive and harmful practices has been exploited by extremists, both 'Islamists' and those on the far right, who highlight these differences and use them to further their shared narrative of hate and division."[79]

Otherwise put, perceptions of gendered difference, including the sexual practices of Muslim Others, as well as masculinity practices such as violence, are key in producing in- and out-group boundaries, and later extremism. The Casey report's findings resonated with narratives told to me of change in participants' communities. This was negatively associated with immigration, particularly Muslim immigration, even when participants' own families were immigrants, or they themselves were immigrants. For some, Britishness went back only one generation; as in the case of the Polish interviewees, others were not British. Here race and whiteness are the salient aspect of claims to, and expectations of, community ownership of public space. Additionally, race appeared to be perceived, as Todd suggests, as "the only legitimate way" for people from low socio-economic backgrounds to discuss inequality in an increasingly immigration-focused political climate.[80] However, it was not just the pace of change but the perceived nature of that change that participants judged negatively. Race was a factor in perceptions of "disruptive public sexualities":[81] how they disrupted, and whom. Importantly, this judgment preceded participants' later entry into extreme activism and was a factor in why this activism made sense.

Within this research, masculinity systems, gender relations and regimes—practices, routines, rules—that were situated in place were most clearly differentiated through values associated with that space. Radical-right interviewees expressed frequent slippage between boundaries of physical and symbolic space. Interviewees strongly linked geography and, in particular, local town affiliation to their gendered identity. Far-right actors come from all social demographics; however, the radical-right interviewees I spoke to all identified as belonging to a particular section of the working class whose struggles were deliberately minimised by white liberals. Ingram is among the authors who have noted that working-class identity is often linked to working-class locality,[82] partly because, for many working-class youth, local neighbourhoods shape both horizons and identities.[83] Although not all participants had engaged in criminal behaviour, this has resonance with work by Rod Earle on male juvenile offenders for whom "postcode pride" is about "the salience of 'the local' in the young men's accounts of themselves".[84]

This pride was evident in women participants' narratives too. Georgey, for instance, was a long-term EDL demonstrator, her involvement prompted by what she felt were challenges to 'British' gender values in her local space. In her thirties and living in an inner-city environment, Georgey described experiences of gendered change in everyday encounters in her community which she regarded as "regressive" and believed should be resisted:

We've had a big influx of Somali Muslims in this area. ... My mum got sent on a course ... to a talk on FGM [female genital mutilation]. And I see a lot of girls in prams here with a *hijab* on; they are just 2 or 3 years old. I just despair at the reaction of our society—we fought hard, tooth and nail, people died, the suffragettes—and praying, that crap, was brought into the twenty-first century in Britain. We are allowing society to regress right in front of our eyes and are not doing anything about it.[85]

Georgey's observations resonate with Orientalist discourses on the dualism of West and East, particularly the narrative positioning Western sexual norms as a civilising instrument of modernity.[86] She cites an institutional response to FGM—the course her mother went on—in her response to the presence of Somali women in her area and describes their practices as indicative of wider social regression. Other interviewees described how a liberal multiculturalism predicated on the 'live-and-let-live' sharing of space with people from different cultures had disturbed the 'natural' ways in which community formed; participants believed that different cultures naturally choose to live separately. Lydia, in her fifties, told me, for instance, "It's a natural phenomenon; if you think about animals, animals stick to the same type. Like lions with lions, zebras with zebras, bees with bees—they stick with their own breed because they are similar."[87] Interviewees experienced change as the disruption of communities of shared values and essentialised racial types. Islam in particular was seen as a threat to societal gender norms. Participants' expectations of gendered ownership of space and the continuity of their values within it meant that any perceived discontinuity rendered their sense of community fundamentally altered, even eradicated.

As feminist scholars have noted, nationalist groups—and indeed nations—have long understood differences in women's behaviour as marking group difference. Moral difference in particular has been judged, and used to mark group boundaries.[88] What is more, and to contextualise some of the views expressed here, it should be noted that the position of various interviewees on gendered difference and Islam differs little from various European government stances on Islam and gender equality. Since the London transport attacks of 7 July 2005, and the introduction of the Prevent counter-radicalisation strategy, the gender practices of Muslim immigrant others have constituted a litmus test of integration into British culture for the British government.[89] Britain is not the only country in which the gendered behaviours of immigrants are judged as proof of assimilation. In France, images of a Muslim woman surrounded by male police officers demanding she disrobe on the beach were met with outrage by many. The burkini (full-body swimsuit) was not deemed suitable beachwear; French Muslim women's swimwear was therefore literally policed.[90] In my research, interviewees were aware of these wider media discussions, and felt bolstered by them when they discussed gendered practices such as conformity of dress as important for acceptance into British culture. All radical-right interviewees also understood British norms (understood as separate from and not inclusive of Islamo-cultural norms) as 'progressive' when contrasted with Islamic norms, or cultural norms prevalent in Muslim-majority countries.

Not all radical-right interviewees were personally familiar with high levels of community change in the time predating their activism. Some views appeared to be the result of exposure to far-right narratives. Some had clearly appropriated ideas of Islam—both ideology and culture—as incompatible with 'British values', without either direct experience or evidence. Jane, in her fifties, had recently become active in both radical- and far-right demonstration when I met her. For Jane, the threat is to an imagined community bounded, she suggested, not by race, but by faith: "I've never lived in a predominantly Muslim area. It's what I see and hear. There are the Sikhs who let anyone in. Doesn't matter what your religion is, they help you … I don't think Muslim communities would do that."[91] Praise of Sikhs, as a religious group generally consisting of people of colour, was used to deflect accusations of racism emerging from critique of another group: Muslims. When challenged, Jane admitted she had only once attempted to talk to women in Muslim communities or to go to a mosque. Jane herself was not a Christian; however, she strongly believed that Islam was dominant to the exclusion of the traditional Christian values that she associated with 'community' and Britishness.

Gender and the liberal Other

It was around gendered norms associated with different sexual practices and encountered in everyday interactions before they turned to radical-right groups that interviewees seemed first to mobilise. It was here that they most obviously perceived boundaries of difference between themselves and Muslims, and themselves and liberal white political elites. Given that space is a source of identity which interviewees relate to gender, income and class, differing responses to changes in that space are regarded by interviewees as markers of class identity. Additionally, if space is associated symbolically with nation, and nation is about the protection of one's own women, the arrival of Other women in a local space disrupts the relationship with nation: the women within the space are no longer those who should be protected. This leaves men unable to fulfil the masculine role of protector so fundamental to gendered ideas of nationalism.

Even though some of the so-called 'British Values' originally articulated by successive Conservative governments are shared by radical-right supporters, they perceive governments to have supported long-term change that has destroyed communities and their norms, and undermined traditional roles. Worse, they believe governments have broadly supported a Muslim Other they regard as a gendered threat. All the interviewees saw Muslims as the absolute Other, and cited sexual and gender norms surrounding dress and practices such as FGM or cousin marriage, not to mention child sexual exploitation (CSE) by so-called 'grooming gangs', as fundamental differences, and therefore crucial in defining and maintaining boundaries between Muslim and non-Muslim groups. Gender, then, is fundamental to the constitution of perceived identity boundaries between in-group and out-group that is intrinsic to extremism.

Interviewees discussed community change as something that produced a negative affective response to the perceived intrusion of the unfamiliar, and an alienation from space; also, a concomitant loss of power and identity. This was expressed by all the interviewees, but articulated most clearly by those with leadership roles. Anne Marie Waters is Irish but now has British citizenship. Formerly a Labour

Party activist, she set up the For Britain party because she believed it could better represent the "British white working class" (her words), who were pushing back against the values of multiculturalism. This was rooted not simply in beliefs and feelings about multiculturalism, but in resistance to normative liberal narratives:

> A friend of mine ... she's grown up in a housing estate ... all her life. ... Suddenly it became full of Somali immigrants. [She says,] "They won't look at us; they won't say hello." ... This alien dress—and it is alien to people—[white British people] are expected not just to put up with it, but celebrate it. This was their spot—and it's gone.[92]

What Waters references as different is both practice and dress. Public debates around Muslim women's dress have been central to Muslims' experiences of Islamophobia across Western contexts, with focus in particular on the *hijab* (scarf), *niqab* (face veil) and *burqa* (full-body covering).[93] A number of women participants in particular drew on narratives around Muslim women's dress to justify their radical-right activism.

There is another way that gender is apparent in Waters' references to affective responses to change: the tension between 'elite' outsider perceptions of change, multiculturalism and immigration as positive, and 'insider' perceptions of loss, particularly in everyday interactions, such as greetings rituals. However, it is clear that the white British people she believes she represents feel entitlement: ownership of 'their spot', and have an expectation that this means it will remain the same in terms of cultural practices (white British).

Participant responses to liberal outsiders indicate the difference between values, norms and masculinities. Like Waters, former EDL Leader Tommy Robinson also suggests that contrasting emotional responses to demographic change constitute a fundamental difference between elite outsiders and insiders. The negative meaning Robinson attributed to population changes in Luton is accessible only to insiders, who perceive change through the prism of affective response he suggests. This emotional proximity to change gives insiders greater authenticity, Robinson believes. He characterises outsiders who celebrate multiculturalism as occupying a position of distance; of rationalism, 'decisions' and 'judgments':

> [A]ll you politicians who treat Luton like a fucking zoo. ...Yeah, [impersonates] "Oh look! We walk through Luton, and oh isn't it lovely! Look! Look at all these different ... oh it's great!" And then they fuck off back to fucking—where they live. No. ...You can't have a clue what it's like! But yet you're making judgments, you're making decisions, you're making policy decisions ... all these fucking decisions, and actually just slandering and slagging anyone off who ... speaks out against it.[94]

The interviewees' relationship to power and cultural capital was imbued with ideas about masculinities: what is authentic and hegemonic and what is not, and where. Formal higher education was understood as an important distinction between in- and out-group. As Goodwin, Jamie Bartlett and Mark Littler point out, stereotypes about a lack of educational attainment in the radical right and EDL can be inaccurate.[95] In Bartlett and Littler's 2011 research, 30 per cent of EDL supporters were found to be educated to university or college level, with a further 15 per cent attaining a professional qualification.[96] However, educational achievement in the research sample for this book was mainly low. Two of the sample went to university (Jacek and Anne Marie Waters), a clear minority. Tommy Robinson completed a 5-year aircraft engineering apprenticeship. Aside from those with degrees, no others had completed A-levels. Two male participants did not complete school to age sixteen.

Interviewees did not trust white liberals with an advanced education, and white liberal men and masculinities were understood as locally subordinate yet nationally hegemonic. While university education and book-learning were understood as incompatible with local hegemonic masculinity and projecting violence, a certain form of subversive masculinity expressed in cleverness aimed at rule-breaking and the undermining of institutional power did have status. For instance, Iain, nineteen, whose father and older brother were EDL supporters, said he had been excluded from school and then could not find another place because of his attendance at EDL demonstrations and open hostility to deradicalisation efforts. Iain was at this point living with his grandmother due to the relationship breakdown between his parents. His negative childhood experiences with multiple state agencies had shaped his current mistrust of state institutions. He described what had happened, though, with a degree of pride. He had only had to make one basic point, he suggested, to defeat the imam sent to deradicalise him:

> I left school at Year 9—I was fourteen or fifteen. ... Through the links with the EDL and that, no other school would accept me. ... I was sat in meetings with the counter-terrorism police at thirteen—through my involvement with the EDL. ... They were trying to get me away from it. ... Education-wise, I couldn't do nothing. They wouldn't have me. [Q: What did your parents do to help?] Mum was trying hard to try and get me into education. Nothing worked. We had meetings and meetings—we had meetings with the council. No one helped. [Q: How did that affect you?] I don't think I was bothered because I was at a young age. When you need it [education], you don't think it's a big thing. But when you haven't got it... [Q: Which agencies were involved in helping? What did they do?] The social workers, and then the police was involved. ... Different organisations were involved. They sat me down with the Muslim leaders, they tried to help me. The bloke who came, he was called Mohammed. I said, "Wasn't it the case that Mohammed was a paedophile? Because Mohammed married a 6-year-old." So, he didn't like that. He walked out of the room.[97]

It was Iain's mother who attempted to keep him from the EDL; his brother and father were active in the movement. There was no competition: being able to prove masculinity through the exchange with the imam was what mattered to Iain, in part, as he notes, because he was too young to understand what a lack of education would later mean. Iain did not regard his reference to paedophilia as either rude or abusive. His reflections on his failed education end with his perceived demonstration of cleverness, which essentially defeated the imam in debate.

Participants were keenly aware of the reputation of the radical right as racist 'knuckle-draggers', an accusation, for example, levelled at Tommy Robinson on social media by *Guardian* journalist and commentator Owen Jones.[98] They were angry at liberal attempts to delegitimise them, and eager to refute claims that they were unintelligent. A number of participants explicitly referred to their lack of formal education as a source of marginalisation. Darren and Jason emphasised that this did not make them 'stupid'. Jason, in his thirties, for example, highlighted his self-education on genetics and eugenics as part of his decision to take part in my research, telling me:

> We have 1,300 years of history of Irish, Welsh, English here. ... They come from a genetic group, the haplogroup, it has the gene R1b. ... You'll realise talking to me, I am an intelligent person. And I think that if you [as a researcher] are a channel to put through my educated view on this matter, then I'm more than happy to take part.[99]

For the participants, hegemonic masculinities did not incorporate formal education, associated with an inaccessible middle class, but a more streetwise form of 'cleverness'. Darren blamed his lack of success at school in part on his intelligence, saying, "I was a clever fucker, but I was easily distracted. I finished the work early and got bored, then I'd start disturbing everyone else. So, I didn't like school."[100] He was eventually expelled, which he saw as "the turning point in a wrong direction", linking this to his later involvement in football violence and violence with the far-right Infidels.[101] Still, he believes his intelligence has both kept him out of jail so far and ensured previous leadership roles within the EDL. He said of a good friend, also in the EDL, "He's a stereotypical far-right thug really, but yeah, he's my mate. He hasn't got the brains to run a division. When I ran stuff I never got arrested. I've never been to jail, and I never want to either."[102] Georgey, who was in her late thirties and worked in childcare, also referenced her intelligence in refutation of stereotypes about the EDL. She challenged notions of what constitutes 'education', suggesting that book education was simply a marker of class at a certain point in time. This is how Georgey defined being working-class:

Not going to private school. Never going to university. Uni was never even mentioned to me as an option. My sister is 3 years younger, and she went to uni. ... It was more of a thing for the working class [by] then. Uni wasn't on the horizon for me, though I was intelligent. ... I'm proud of being working-class.[103]

Georgey and others were therefore proud of not going to university, regarding this as incompatible with a particular class performance and masculinity. To Iain it was particularly important, for example, that I visited him in his local area, so that I—the middle-class researcher from whom he initially withdrew his interviews—could see where he lived and understand his reality. He told me that the middle class are "snotty arrogant bastards", but this is primarily because he feels they do not acknowledge people like him, and do not listen. At school, nobody listened, he said, and little has changed: "[P]eople are struggling. I don't know. People ain't got a voice. Nobody listens to no-one. I don't know. Politicians don't listen, councillors don't listen." On one occasion we talked in his local Wetherspoons pub, and he told me how important it was that I had travelled to meet him, "very important, because you've come here—to my pub, in my area. You can't see things from a perspective unless you take part—things like that. It's like Telford [the demo], when you came to Telford, you took it from our perspective, from why we was there."[104]

Telford was an opportunity to express anger over the sexual exploitation of local young women (see fig. 1), and against Islam and the 'liberal left'. It was CSE by apparently Muslim-heritage grooming gangs that participants viewed as the most egregious crime, and as evidence of incompatible sexual norms.[105] Iain told me that his area had experienced CSE, and he believed that the issue was more common across the Muslim community, as he noted in the association of family and community: "Over 500 girls ... was targeted, all victims. ... One driver was arrested; it was a family-run taxi rank though, they were all in it together."[106] On another occasion he told me he had other concerns about his town, and felt the police were not doing enough:

Islam is a massive problem, massive, massive problem. Links with terrorism in the town. Massive links with Syria and ISIS. Twelve people was arrested for Syria-related terrorism. All were linked to the *Dawah* stall. ... We confronted the table and they just said, "racists". But it's not a race, it's not a religion, it's an ideology. ... There still is actively people here who support ISIS. [Q: But aren't the police doing something if there have been arrests?] The police was more bothered about coming here today to stop us [demonstrating].[107]

Iain wanted more local events and demonstrations aimed at addressing local issues. While seemingly glad to talk to me about his grievances, he was also conscious that he would only be listened to by the 'Middle England' that Robinson had told me was the EDL's original target audience if the message was conveyed in the right way:

Who's going to listen to 300 football hooligans? If you turn up with 300 lads trying to kick off at an EDL demo, who will listen? With reasons, they will listen. ... [Q: Why do you think people won't listen to them?] ... You would rather listen to people who show concern than chant, "Mohammed is a paedo". I would rather walk in silence than with people chanting "Mohammed is a paedo". There's things that should be allowed and things that shouldn't. We should be allowed to chant. But we shouldn't be allowed to chant provocative chants. It makes you look uneducated.[108]

Talking to me, Iain distanced himself from the crude and emotive—authentic—masculinity of the EDL and emphasised the rational. Believing that journalists and researchers seek to 'stitch up' the EDL, he was keen to portray the group in a way I would not censure. He understood that the frame I used to understand his masculinities was 'inauthentic'; the masculinities that are hegemonic in my world are predicated on rationality, learning, rule-abiding. I enjoyed speaking to Iain. He is young and I feel there is a life for him beyond the radical right. And just as our meeting encouraged me to see the situation from his perspective—in which I was no doubt clueless and condescending—I want to believe he also saw himself through my eyes. This was clearly uncomfortable for him, as he believed that he was being judged not for his views, but for his class. However, despite the opinions he expresses in the above excerpt, I have witnessed Iain taking part—seemingly enthusiastically—in provocative and offensive chants at demonstrations with his friends.

Masculinity challenges

As noted in Chapter One, masculinity challenges involve the projection or use of violence to foster street reputation in active confrontation with, or successful defence against, other men. Interviewees described the importance of aggressive hegemonic masculinity and the threat of violence, understood as fundamental to working-class identity, in their socialisation to the radical right. They also recognised football as another route to status, particularly when combined with casual violence. They described using perceived differences in the characteristics of hegemonic masculinity, and violence norms, to demarcate the in- and out-groups that would determine the targets of their later activism within radical-right groups. Violent interactions were produced by a culture in which violence is a normative practice, rooted in both class and place and associated with particular values (defending your friends, not giving in) which prove high masculine status. This violence, enacted through a series of contestations between men, was also productive of new racialised masculinities through everyday interactions in local space. Daniel described a relationship of spatial proximity to Muslim neighbours, characterised by tension and the permanent possibility of male violence. He was in his twenties and a veteran of Iraq, but it was in his hometown, he said, that he experienced his worst injury:

I was attacked by ten Muslims. I had my left cartilage chopped off and I was stabbed in the back. [Q: What happened?] They were fiddling with my neighbours' van, and I saw what they were doing and went out and chased them. They called me a white bastard, and ... I confronted them—I had a pipe in my hand. [Q: A pipe?] I thought I needed a weapon, because they all had weapons. They ran into the pizza shop on [X] Street, hiding behind the counter, calling me a white bastard. They said, "It's our town; we will do what we want." So, they chopped me ear and stabbed me in the back.[109]

For Daniel, this experience had several consequences: it reified his racialised identity through an insulting label ("white bastard"); it confirmed radical- and far-right rhetoric of racialised others with excessive masculinity;[110] and it evoked violence as an appropriate and masculinised response to Muslims in his area. Daniel now believes that violence is demanded as a necessary aspect of competition for 'ownership' of the town that he feels should uncontestably be his. To defend it, he suffered an injury that he suggested was worse than anything he had encountered in Iraq. He indicated that his own community is experienced as a warzone, a site of conflict and contested identity.

Whiteness, place and liberal masculinities

Daniel's story is indicative. Participants described how violence that fell outside of the accepted norms and racialised expectations of their community could prove productive of new racialised masculinities. The white masculinity experienced and performed by Daniel, however, is not consistent with the hegemonic white masculinity projected by middle-class society. Predicated on the ability to exercise power through violence, Daniel's habitus and masculinity system has little in common with mainstream norms, which cede violent responses to the state. He and other interviewees associated violent white masculinity with a particular working-class and multicultural space. For Daniel, authority and authenticity are not accessible to those from outside this space and group, or to anyone who could not perform his kind of masculinity or understand it. Daniel does not experience his white masculinity in this incident as privilege. He recognises his whiteness only in those moments where it becomes a means to insult, exploit and denigrate him. He perceives this denigration from all Muslims sharing his geographic space, not just his attackers.

While Robinson and Darren both suggested they were successful in projecting a violent masculinity that resulted in status, Jason, in his thirties, believed he had failed in his efforts towards the hegemonic masculinity circulating in his community:

> Yeah, it was a rough area where I grew up. It was working-class, chavs. ... It was all white working class. [Q: So what gave boys respect in that environment?] Being able to fight. There was a lot of fighting and I'm not good and didn't want to—I always wished that I could be, but I wasn't confident in my ability to hurt other people.[111]

Here Jason's class is, to him, already synonymous with underclass stigma (the pejorative 'chavs'), something which Todd suggests has been a common association since the 1980s.[112] Unlike other interviewees, Jason framed his inability to fight in terms of masculinities, suggesting that the hegemonic, violent masculinity was that of the "alpha male": "I wanted to be friends with the bullies, but they wouldn't have me. ... I wanted to be an alpha male like they were. ... It's sad, isn't it? It's sad. ... I should be an alpha male—and I'm not."[113]

Jason explicitly racialised hegemonic heterosexuality as white. He recalled an experience of perceived racial emasculation as formative: "There was a situation where a black lad snatched a tennis racket from my sister. So I said, 'Give it back.' And he said, 'No, make me.' And I didn't, and I wasn't confident enough. To a guy—pride means everything."[114] Emasculation at the hands of a person of colour, in a physical space over which he felt ownership and in front of peers, was what Jason identified as pivotal in his initial interest in far-right politics: "I just kind of became resentful of more ethnic migrants appearing in my community."[115] Jason began to perceive his personal micro-emasculation on a macro scale, believing that Muslims were similarly humiliating 'the English': "We are trying to be peaceful to these people. And what do they do? They molest our children; they run us over with lorries; they rape our women; they stab our people."[116]

The gendered norms—a masculinity system—of the white working-class space interviewees described divided men into either the weak/emasculated or the strong/violent/masculine. Jason was also rare among interviewees in that he said he had links to the banned National Action and was explicitly racist; he regarded white masculinities as innately superior and therefore perceived a double emasculation in being physically intimidated by a black youth. Jason framed the purpose of hegemonic masculinity not simply as protecting himself, but also as protecting his female relations. It is a narrative recognisable from both nationalist and ultra-nationalist tropes. He was one of the few interviewees who appeared to reflect on my potential perception of his failures, suggesting that his masculinity deserved to be regarded as subordinate: pathetic and 'sad'. Indeed, his story was depressingly familiar from the literature. It contained the key elements of emasculation and backlash masculinity identified by Kimmel and Messerschmidt, also associated with the incel movement, which has been emergent since I carried out this research. Extreme masculinities offered Jason a resource to compensate for his perceived inadequacy as a man, unable to defend himself or the women in his family from a racialised Other.

For Jason, racial separation, sexual norms and procreation are necessarily entwined to ensure the survival of a particular racial type. Jason is in his thirties and one of two people in this research who self-identified as a 'liberal racist'. He remembered his shock when he first saw black men with white women: "I just thought black would be with black, and Asians with Asians. I just thought people stuck with their own, and that was normal."[117] This shock was accompanied by a sense of injustice; a feeling that it was not fair or right that black men, whom he regarded as inferior, should have sexual access to white women. He also believed that those women were reduced through their association with black men. To better understand this, William Ian Miller's work on affect is useful. The affect of 'disgust' is transferred from the black men to these white women.[118] Other interviewees, like Lydia, who used animal metaphors to naturalise racial difference, referenced what they saw as people's instinctive preference for those recognised as 'their own'. Interviewees believed that those who looked like them would be likely to share practices, rules and norms, and sexual partners.

Only a minority of interviewees explicitly described these issues as racialised, as Jason did. Mostly, participants distanced themselves from accusations of racism, suggesting either that racism did not exist or that it was a problem of more ideologically motivated 'others' (discussed in more detail in Chapter Four). Such distancing is a feature of whiteness broadly, which is often treated by majority-white populaces as a norm, and therefore without race.[119] Nonetheless, race is not simply a question of skin pigmentation,[120] and race and whiteness were present in the gendered assumptions and narratives of all the participants. Race, whiteness and racial difference are socially constructed, with social racial categorisations contributing to the production of individual and group racial identity. It is through systems and institutions that both race and racism are discursively constructed.[121]

As ground-breaking whiteness studies scholar Judith Frankenberg has noted, "white people and people of color live racially structured lives. ... White people are 'raced', just as men are 'gendered'".[122] In her influential tract on the American experience of the "diversity rationale", "White Like Me", law professor Osamudia James explores how race and colour are often elided, with the white experience held as 'transparent'.[123] White identity, unlike black identity, is valorised as the 'standard' in the US, she explains, and, because of the power inherent in this, becomes taken for granted. She suggests that white identity is "grounded in a sense of entitlement and victimhood relative to people of color"; communities of colour, however, construct identity around shared practices and experiences, which means positive representations of a shared culture, as well as experiences of disadvantage.[124]

Connell suggests multiple masculinities within shared race and class categories. Similarly, James suggests that there are white people—the so-called "marginal white"—who do not experience "full" white privilege.[125] This suggests varied experiences of whiteness and the privileges it affords. Law and sociology professor Camille Gear Rich has suggested that the term 'marginal whites' might describe social groups who have only lately acquired what is termed 'full whiteness'; in the American context she suggests this includes identity groups including Jews, Hispanics or the Irish, who have all historically experienced racial discrimination.[126] James emphasises, therefore, the need to incorporate class into understandings of racial privilege. She suggests in turn that the term 'marginal whiteness' does no more than draw attention to the impact of class on identity and the importance of an intersectional and nuanced approach to understanding marginality,[127] with the aim of tackling racism and social inequality.

Similarly, but from a UK perspective, Roger Hewitt has written of the "white backlash" to British multiculturalism as a "socially disparate set of responses to equalities discourses".[128] Intersectionality and identity studies now infuse the debate. Cliff Leek and Kimmel suggest that, just as masculinities studies has learned to pluralise, recognising multiple possible masculinities, "studies of race and class are missing parallel notions of 'whitenesses and elites' in their consideration of the superordinate".[129] Indeed, the analysis in this book takes an intersectional approach in order to explore white participants' narratives; they frequently engage with class, attempting to weaponise what they perceive as 'white marginalisation' to advance their arguments. Whiteness, like maleness, is not uniformly experienced. This also appeared to be the contention of the participants. Rejecting shared commonalities with white liberal others, their interviews demonstrated a rejection of racism as a structural issue, and any responsibility for it.

The white interviewees with immigrant heritage came from backgrounds that Rich suggests might have incompletely attained 'full whiteness' in a US context: Irish, Eastern European, working-class.[130] For them, assimilation is interpreted in two ways: pressure on Muslim Others to adhere to their understanding of 'British culture' pre-multiculturalism; and a feeling that they, too, are being asked to assimilate, in their case to dominant white middle-class norms. Their sense of grievance at both the perceived inability of Muslim Others to assimilate and the perceived pressure on them to adopt values they do not believe in can be acute. Additionally, they equated claims by immigrants of special identity with victimhood and weakness, and therefore read these as signs of emasculation. For example, Anne Marie Waters told me that she "never identified as 'the Irish one'". To her, although she now perpetuates narratives of the Muslim victimisation of non-Muslims, this would involve adopting a disempowered victimhood she has sought to escape:

The Irish are miserable and negative and self-pitying. The Irish identity is founded on being the victim of England. The underdog. The "poor us" shit is still there. I haven't lived there in 20-odd years. Victims of England! [Scoffs.] Ireland is dominated by British culture. Working-class suburbs, you hear the *Coronation Street* theme from the neighbours ... my brother has a Manchester United tattoo. A lot of men in Dublin have English football teams on their arms.[131]

Waters describes the shared norms of Irish–British masculinity—norms of football support and tattoos. Robinson also strongly identified with his Irish mother's family. However, he rejected the republicanism of other Irish immigrant groups in Luton,[132] in order to, in a sense, over-assimilate towards an English identity he confessed he did not entirely understand. Indeed, he told me that he was brought up "the Irish way", which to him represented close ties, loyalty and frequent family contact. In fact, ironically, he told me that he did not know what English family life even was.[133]

The interviewees in the sample appear to regard their whiteness as no more 'invisible' than the races of the people of colour around them. Experiences in which they are confronted with the fact of their race, which they feel should be transparent, engage them in a constant reflexivity, with race at the centre of this. Everyday hostile confrontations with Muslim Others reinforce a sense of racial and cultural difference, which when associated with violence produces a particular form of white identity rooted in victimhood and the need for a hypervigilant, aggressive masculinity. Daniel's earlier narrative of his assault emphasised the low status he believed his attackers placed on his whiteness: to them he was simply a "white bastard". Georgey gave an account of being called a racist by a woman wearing a *burqa*, after she crossed herself for luck on a bus. The interviewees do not perceive their whiteness as a given. In the stories they tell, they suggest that they are reminded of it on an everyday basis, not in feelings of privilege, but in perceptions of abuse and discrimination. It is these perceptions on which they focus their narratives. Here gender is an important mechanism of situated social action, and, with race, it contributes to the reproduction of particular social structures.[134]

Whether interviewees' experiences constituted any real disadvantage or simply the loss of a power which they took for granted by virtue of being white was difficult to discern. The interviewees were mostly—but not uniformly, as some lived in leafy suburbs—from socio-economically deprived areas and lacked educational opportunities. Many of the towns they lived in or grew up in were suffering from economic disadvantage (in the cases of Darren, Jason, Iain, Daniel, Jane, Georgey and Tommy Robinson). Although they did not articulate these circumstances as the 'grievances' of radicalisation theory, some were also victims of sexual or domestic abuse (Jane, Lydia and Tommy Robinson), violence (Tommy Robinson and Daniel), school exclusion (Iain) or rejection by their family (Jason), or they were Polish immigrants who saw themselves as victims of Western liberalism and stigmatised in the UK (Henryk and Jacek). This is not to accept any such factors as excuses for harmful or hateful behaviours. However, analysis of their narratives suggests they feel justified in asserting their race and culture as something positive because this is permitted and encouraged for people of colour. Equally, they are conscious that mainstream media and political discourses can frame assertions of whiteness as innately racist. This leads to a double sense of marginalisation: by people of colour who share their class; and by white middle-class elites who share their whiteness.

Summary

Following a number of authors, including Wiktorowicz, Busher, Mitchell D. Silber and Arvin Bhatt,[135] this chapter has explored the importance of the period prior to joining the radical right. This period sees the production of masculinities that will be mobilised and maintained into group activism. Masculinities are produced through material practices situated in the local spaces that matter to participants, and for social cohesion.[136] The modes of violence that become evident in the next chapter on participant activism are clearly ingrained here, in behaviours that are everyday.[137] The social dynamics of local space play a key role in ascribing legitimate masculinity scripts and expectations of their masculinity systems;

these are framed through a hypermasculine lens, with the ability to project physicality and the potential for violence as key. Importantly, masculinities appear to function as chords, not discrete notes within a scale; it is possible for men simultaneously to use different and contradictory frames to understand their own behaviour, placing them in tension with one another and therefore unsettling identities. They recognise hypermasculinities' lack of currency within wider society, where they believe liberal masculinities have power. Violence is a practice with rules and multiple meanings: ritual, communication, pastime, a means to achieve masculine status before peers, a means to lose status with outsiders. There is therefore a tension for them in how to 'do' masculinity.

The chapter has also shown that perceptions of gendered difference are fundamental to the construction of the in-group and out-group boundaries that enable later extremism. Men and women interviewees use gendered difference in justifications that posit Islam as an exception to the success of British multiculturalism, which they otherwise profess to accept. Interviewees identify a process of socialisation into the extreme group. Through a series of everyday encounters and practices in local spaces, interviewees construct Muslim Others as an unassimilable presence. It is not, as Ted Cantle, Derek McGhee and others suggest, that people have little meaningful contact with others who are not like them, but that the contact is too laden with meaning.[138] Everyday interactions that expose seemingly trivial differences in practices, such as greetings rituals, are woven into a narrative of negative affective change prompted by immigration. This is not simply the shame and anger that Treadwell and Garland identify as crucial in catalysing racially motivated masculine violence or EDL activism;[139] it is, rather, a narrative of reckoning with perceptions of a changed landscape. The ownership of this landscape is based on assumptions of white masculinity and its privileges and rewards. Whiteness matters to the participants; their race is far from invisible in their narratives. It is problematic to them, as it does not connote the 'white privilege' they expect and feel that their families have been working towards. The relative deprivation, familiar from radicalisation literature, is here not indexed against socio-economic advantage, but social and masculine racial capital.

4

THE RADICAL RIGHT
MOBILISING MASCULINITIES

The lads are angry, their blood is up, and this is how we express ourselves.
Ian Crossland, EDL Spokesman, Telford 2016

Introduction

Masculinities matter in understanding the lives of activists before they began to participate in radical-right protest. The last chapter explored interviewee narratives to show how violence was part of a habitus of masculine practice associated with self-claimed working-class identities. This masculinity system was inhabited by both men and women. Chapter Four now explores how the masculinities discussed in Chapter Three are mobilised into radical-right activism, in both recruitment and participation. It develops the themes of the previous chapter, observing that mobilisation centres less around ideology and more on the development and continuation of pre-existing masculinities and gendered relationships, norms and behaviours.

Masculinities are important because they are embodied in a constructed world of social meaning—what Connell terms "body-reflexive practice". Actions, she proposes, "involve social relations and symbolism; they may well involve large-scale social institutions. Particular versions of masculinity are constituted in their circuits as meaningful bodies and embodied meanings."[1] In this chapter, which explores gender and protest, the concept of affect is important. Affect is central to body-reflexive practice and emphasises how sexed and gendered bodies interact. It is emotion generated in interactions, and can be read as a physical state of being, enabling us to engage with others,[2] as well as the outward expression of an inner psychoanalytic drive.[3] Affect is transmissible; it provokes change, in interpersonal or collective arenas.[4] It is, for instance, the feeling or mood when you walk into a room. The understanding of gender in this chapter also echoes Bourdieu's concept of the "symbolic violence" of masculine domination, constituted in symbols, cognition and feeling.[5] This symbolic violence is evident in the protest outlined in the chapter.

The chapter considers the role of different masculinities within the various discourses active in the movement, each constructing different expressions of each group's activism: the English Defence League (EDL), Britain First (BF) and For Britain (FB). There are three key expressions around which activism mobilises: the idealised muscular, self-proclaimed (white) working-class and authentic masculinity typified within the EDL and by Tommy Robinson, incorporating subcultures of football and football violence; the militarised Christian masculinity of Britain First and Jayda Fransen; and—the odd one out—the explicit assertion of women's and gay rights, as typified by Anne Marie Waters. This latter activism will be addressed in more detail in the next chapter on misogyny, women and the radical right. The chapter also explores masculinities in mobilisation to the radical right, and begins with a discussion of masculinities and participant understanding of radical-right ideology. It should be noted that the chapter contains language some readers might find offensive throughout.

Does ideology matter to the radical right?

Given radicalisation theory, it might be assumed that ideology is a significant feature of mobilisation to the radical right. Certainly, the symbolic gendered frameworks shaping radical-right activism are important in understanding ideological commitment. However, if ideology is regarded as strict adherence to a coherent system, or a single explanatory 'premise', as Arendt suggests,[6] few of the radical-right participants in this book could accurately be described as ideological.

Later in the book I will explore how ideology, scholarship and knowledge are status-enhancers and provide social capital for those involved in ALM; however, the opposite can be true for those on the radical right. The radical right, unlike a far-right movement such as neo-Nazism, for instance, has no clear ideologues, although some figures are revered. Indeed, radical-right participants frequently distanced themselves from explicitly ideological positions; these were regarded as inauthentic and feminised due to their perceived emergence from book-learning (second-hand knowledge), rather than lived (first-hand) engagement with the issues at hand. The more pragmatic approach to ideology advocated by Joseph Schull is therefore adopted in this chapter. Members of the same movement, he suggests:

> need not share the same belief system in order to share the same ideology. An ideology should rather be understood as a form of discourse or a political language—a body of linguistic propositions expressed as speech-acts and united by the conventions governing them. Its adherents will have varied beliefs about its conventions, yet all will be constrained by them in order to be recognized as competent speakers of their discourse. Ideology's power lies at the level of communicative action and cannot be reduced to its role in constituting beliefs.[7]

This definition, centred on communicative action, means that a lack of book-learning is less important than the ability to utilise a particular discourse in order to be recognised by others as like-minded. Ideology consists of symbolic practices that communicate membership of a shared community. Later in this chapter, I explore how participants in this research created a shared culture based around a native habitus they felt was under threat. However, ideology is not simply a matter of symbolic practice, but also of the shared emotion, the affect, created through that practice.

111

The theoretical writing on affect suggests that to understand emotion is to understand the social function it serves.[8] Emotion has been described as the 'glue' of solidarity. The collective emotion of groups can have both negative and positive outcomes; it is both "what holds a society together ... and what mobilizes conflict."[9] Indeed, it was Émile Durkheim who originally suggested that shared emotion generated within a group also generates the requirement to defend it.[10] Shared emotion is therefore inherently politicising, whether it is shared anger, pain, grief or love.[11]

For Sara Ahmed, a leading scholar of affect, there are two important consequences: the need to reconsider the public manifestation of sentiment assumed to belong to the private sphere; and the contestation of the assumed dichotomy of emotion versus rationality.[12] Gradually the—false—dichotomies between emotion (historically gendered female) and rationality (historically gendered male) are being broken down.[13] In this alternative framework, which might appeal to radical-right participants, affect and emotion are not subordinate to cognition or reason; instead, the two follow a parallel course. Feelings are recognised as inherent to thinking.[14] As James M. Jasper writes, "To categorize [emotions] as rational or irrational (much less to dismiss them all as interferences with rationality) is deeply wrongheaded."[15] A reappraisal of concepts routinely accepted as 'rational' is advocated: for example, 'values', which Randall Collins suggests can better be understood as cognitions endowed with emotion.[16] Value-driven behaviour can rationally optimise what is best for the collective.[17] The two are not necessarily distinct.

In this chapter, this means that participants' actions can be read as ideological, despite the fact that they would not accept this, in that ideology is produced through action—in this case, collective masculine action. The shared beliefs and masculine practices of protest and the priorities outlined constitute a broadly nationalist ideological agenda. Ideas of nation feature in group names (English, Britain), and in the production of group identity, while group and participant aspirations frequently reflect the gendered ideologies of nationalism. The chapter first explores how participants understood and rejected the idea of ideology itself, and its role in their culture. It then considers the diverse masculinities evident in protest culture and affect, and how this constitutes an ideological position through reference to existing masculine cultures, despite participants' understanding of what ideology is.

Ideology as stigma: masculinities of the weak

Radical-right leaders are able to articulate reasons for their activism, and are often called upon to do so. For all but a minority of grassroots activists, however, ideology is a descriptor they do not identify with, and the term is understood to stigmatise and delegitimise radical-right action. Authentic action was instead predicated on a robust masculine response to issues in communities: perceptions of harms caused by Muslim immigration, gendered difference and, on a national scale, child sexual exploitation (CSE) by grooming gangs and terror attacks by sympathisers of jihadist groups such as al-Qaeda and so-called Islamic State. This coincides with Busher's findings on EDL activism specifically—that participants focused on issues and emotion in mobilisation, rather than belief.[18]

The concept of ideology meant little to radical-right interviewees in terms of a formal set of belief systems. When asked about ideology, the most common response was for participants to refer not to themselves, but to Islam and Muslims. All activists regarded Islam not as a religion—and certainly not as a race—but as an ideology that threatens Britain and the 'Western world'. This response offered two means of rebutting accusations of racism: first, they associated racism with ideology, explicitly Nazi beliefs, and learned doctrine, which they denied; second, if Islam is not a racial grouping, then they suggested that anti-Islam sentiment could not be racism. For instance, despite past EDL assertions that the group did not oppose Muslim people, or Islam, but Islamist ideology,[19] Tommy Robinson's focus when we spoke was opposition to "the ideology of Islam" itself. The conflation of Islam with political Islamism and jihadism is evident in his co-authored chronological version of the Quran, titled *Mohammed's Koran: Why Muslims Kill for Islam*, in which he writes "Islam = Islamism = Violent Islamism".[20] Robinson believed that this rendering simply emphasised an Islamic necessity for both Shariah law and jihad to impose it.[21] Robinson is self-educated on

Islam, having read the Quran in English, he told me, while in solitary confinement in prison.

Ideology represented something learned and therefore inauthentic, as discussed in the previous chapter. Robinson, for instance, did not regard his activism as essentially ideological or political. To him it was instinctive, which is to say emotional and masculine. Robinson—and other participants—did not accept the possibility of cultural racism. Through de-emphasising the ideological aspects of radical-right activism, he believed he was able to reject accusations of being far-right or racist, instead projecting a narrative of the movement's common-sense authenticity. His view on his own activism was that he was fulfilling a much-needed public role at great risk to himself—extending to persecution by the state. Given the stakes, he regarded his activism as an expression of courage and moral purpose devoid of the inauthenticity of emasculated liberals on 'the left' (essentially those condemning the EDL). For Robinson, it was important to see the EDL as politicising without being political or ideological. He ascribed this to its self-proclaimed working-class origins. He told me:

> [W]hat the EDL managed to do was sort of politicise a working-class generation. It brought them involved. ... I didn't know what left-wing and right-wing was when I started the EDL. I didn't know a fucking thing. Labour, Conservatives, I didn't. Know. Anything. And I wouldn't have given a shit either. ... That's why I didn't know anything. And that's how our kids are being brought up, to not know, understand or have any interest in the political system. Any of it, any of it at all. So, what we managed to do, all these kids who wouldn't have had any interest, they started to be brought into it. Open their eyes to it.[22]

This is questionable, as Robinson had British National Party (BNP) membership for a year as a youth, but he has since denied he knew this was a racist group. Inequality in parliamentary representation—in terms of ethnicity, sex, sexuality and educational level—is well-documented, and increasing.[23] However, and despite the prominence of some working-class politicians in parliament, Robinson understands mainstream politics as accessible only to a certain type of middle-class person who demonstrates weak masculinity.

Most research participants said they did not hold racist beliefs; however, nor did they necessarily accept the validity of the term 'racism'. They believed that 'racist' was an easy insult, levelled by the left to delegitimise not just radical-right beliefs, but white working-class experiences of difference. Additionally, some participants, and others encountered at demonstrations, referenced their own families to justify their claimed position as non-racist, citing affection for mixed-race relatives—including, for some people, their own children. Conversation around such relatives tended towards arguments of exceptionalism, however: that although these relations were mixed-race, they were 'not like the others'.

Participants implied that the term 'ideology' was a derogatory label. Activist and leader John Meighan described the burden of the designation 'far-right' when I spoke to him ahead of his first organised FLA march in 2017. He was debating whether to allow Tommy Robinson to attend, and his strategy was to avoid the criticism and attention of the left:

> I'm focused on extremism, and that includes attacks against British people or foreign people or the Finsbury Park Mosque.[24] All forms of extremism. ... I'm going to get Buddhists, Sikhs, Jews, British people to speak. People from all faiths. No race issues. We are centre, in the middle, we don't want to be left or right. [Q: What about Tommy Robinson? Will you let him march with you?] I had some chats with Tommy Robinson recently. It's not that I'm not a fan of him. It's just that I want to do it differently. ... [P]eople say, you need to respect Tommy. I do have respect, but his downfall is the EDL days—I don't want the stigma. I don't want to be labelled far-right, because then I will have left-wing groups attaching to me. I want them to stay away.[25]

In the event, it was primarily white men who attended the march, and they were focused on opposition to Islamist extremism. Robinson was not at the first demonstration in 2017 in London. However, after a splinter movement formed, the Democratic Football Lads Alliance

(DFLA), Robinson joined up to 2,000 marchers in Birmingham in March 2018.[26] Meighan resigned from the FLA leadership the following month, a move linked to a row over charitable donations and his leadership style.[27]

Few outside the leadership group I interviewed (Fransen, Robinson and Waters) told me they had engaged with literature on Islam, although some had read at least parts of the Quran. They were, though, avid consumers of the non-mainstream media and social media and obsessively followed current affairs regarding immigration and what is now—but was not at the time of research—commonly referred to as the 'culture wars'. Participants fervently resisted the label 'far-right', believing that it did not reflect their views and was a class-based insult. In fact, a commonly heard EDL slogan is 'not far-right, just "right"'. Few interviewees self-identified as either right-wing or far-/extreme-right, or identified with any characterisation as either 'left' or 'right'. There were exceptions, though; Darren (a former Infidel) was one. Perhaps Darren was less fearful of being labelled 'extreme-right' than others, given that he regarded 'stigma' as a badge of honour and a marker of his potential for violence.[28]

Indeed, those few interviewees who openly and explicitly advocated racist views, such as the idea that different races should not intermarry, were also the most likely to justify their position ideologically. Jason, who is proudly racist and regards racism as good for Britain, cited reading on the subject to justify this. However, he appeared to be not entirely convinced of his position. Reflecting on how I might read his assertion that "non-North-Western" people should be deported from Britain, he said, "the problem is that this sounds a very bigoted view."[29] Beyond the participant group, I also encountered perhaps two or three other openly racist people at Britain First demonstrations who told me, for instance, that people of colour or 'non-white races' were genetically inferior. They cited controversial pseudo-scientific racism such as *The Bell Curve* as proof of, for example, black—as well as female—intellectual inferiority.[30] Jason, too, had read books on eugenics and genetics, he told me—reading he used to justify claims of white superiority. Both Jason and Jacek, a professional Polish graduate in his thirties, took an explicitly ideological stance, and openly endorsed their position as 'racialists'.

116

Ideology and masculinity challenges by the state

At grassroots level, it was the Polish participants, Henryk and Jacek, along with Jason, who represented the most ideologically astute of the sample. Jacek and Henryk shared an inherently political outlook, and one in which the state itself was understood as presenting the biggest masculinity challenge. During one interview, Jacek cited Hans-Hermann Hoppe, author of *Democracy: The God That Failed*, and Bill Warner, author of *Sharia Law for Non-Muslims*, as authors he had engaged with. He frequently referenced his childhood reading in pre-democracy Poland, which appeared extensive and similarly subversive, including banned authors, introduced to him by his father. Henryk, in his sixties, discussed contemporary British politics in the context of European politics and communism. Both Henryk and Jacek rooted their positions within ideology and appeared conversant with ideological discussion, which they attributed to coming from a Polish background.

Both men told me that they were ideologically opposed to Western European 'liberal' democracy and the way in which it has flattened relations between the sexes. They regarded this as debasing, unnatural and emasculating. They located their view of the liberal state as an enabler of emasculation in the recent history of Poland and its perceived decline and effective political castration following the end—or to them, loss—of communism. Henryk was named after an uncle who was shot by the Nazis in the Second World War, he proudly told me. He therefore did not support national socialism or fascism, he said. However, he regarded liberal democracy as the antithesis of freedom, using nationalist justifications that the state was unable to protect women. He believed that security should be a key function of the state, and contrasted current crime and insecurity under democracy unfavourably with his life in communist Poland:

> When we had communism, it was better. ... [W]e had order, structure. No crime against women ... there was a lot more security. [Q: I'd rather have a bit of insecurity than live in a police state, wouldn't you?] But for women it's dangerous, even shopping for example. Now democracy is just for Muslims. [Q: But the UK is not like Poland. You seem to want to return to

Poland circa 1975. Freedom is a good thing, isn't it?] Freedom. 'Freedom'! What did 1989 [the year communism ended in Poland] mean to us? What did freedom mean to us?? It destroyed our society and our industry. That was 'freedom'.[31]

All participants felt they were at war with Islam, but their activism necessitated another battle—with a liberal class of politicians who they believed were determined to protect Muslims and their faith. Participants rarely used the term 'liberal elite'. However, they frequently and sarcastically referenced liberals, generally meaning those who, they believed, seek to limit the freedom of speech and actions of the (white) working class. These 'liberals' included Labour Party politicians, media institutions such as the BBC and public figures who spoke out against Tommy Robinson, including Gary Lineker, former footballer turned BBC presenter. Lineker's former footballing status perhaps engendered a more pronounced sense of betrayal. Participants held liberals responsible for the betrayal of the working class and 'indigenous' British people, and liberal values were understood to have disempowered the state through a disruption, again, of a natural and anticipated order which included gender (explored more in Chapter Five).

Contemporary gender debates were therefore central to the mistrust of liberals, and again symbolic of participants' feelings of emasculation. Referencing discussion of trans rights, for example, at a speech at a march in Telford, the then National Spokesman for the EDL, Ian Crossland, used humour and an appeal to the authenticity of common sense to ridicule the debate. I noted in my field diary: "Ian says, 'The left is now telling us that genitalia does not dictate gender', a look of disbelief on his face. 'Yes, it does!' he shouts. 'How do you know what a man is? I'll tell you how—if it's got a cock, it's a man!' The crowd bursts into infectious laughter."[32] He then immediately invited Antifa to address the demonstration and explain the beliefs of the left. It was the left who were held responsible for the weakness and inadequacy of state responses on any number of issues. In fact, the Telford demonstration was held in front of Telford's police station in order to protest institutional failure to deal with CSE. While Crossland's response was primarily emotional and, to other activists, authentic in terms of masculinity, he was clearly invoking an ideological and gendered position in which manhood and masculinity are constituted through the male body. Participants were contributing to national discourse on gender, amongst other issues, whether they accepted that their messaging and activism were ideological or not.

Weak masculinities and inauthentic liberalism

Given perceptions of the state as an antagonist and an author of masculinity challenges to activists, much of the radical-right protest I attended was anti-state as well as anti-Islam. While countering Islam is the primary motivation of the radical right, the state and 'the left' constituted equally dangerous ideological enemies for activists across groups.[33] Focus on so-called 'anti-government extremism' is a new strand of radicalisation studies. However, radical-right opposition to the state is not new. Both state and left embodied for participants a masculinity that neglected working-class bodies, and the lived experience of disenfranchised communities. They positioned this perceived bourgeois–rational masculinity, one of four archetypes in the Western tradition,[34] as subordinate, despite its wider societal acceptance and hegemony. Participants believed that this was evident in liberal discounting of their white working-class experience through the prioritisation of Islam and people of colour. For some, the feeling of betrayal was personal. I met several older protestors at Britain First demonstrations—outside of the formal interviewees—who had previously been Labour Party members, a group Busher terms "Swervers" in his study of the EDL.[35] They said they had become disillusioned by Labour's stance on issues affecting working-class (their term—indicating white) people, particularly in the north. Others I encountered in BF, however, came from a background of explicitly racist politics and parties such as the BNP or the National Front. Some told me they still retained membership of these groups.

For all three leaders—Fransen, Robinson and Waters—grievances over the media as a promulgator of weak masculine values and group emasculation were important. As the longest-standing national broadcaster, the BBC in particular was seen as ignoring white working-class concerns, and bearing a special responsibility for misreporting on gendered issues such as child sexual exploitation rings—so-called 'grooming gangs'. There was little trust in the BBC. However, texting me about the BBC drama series *Three Girls*, which was based on the Rochdale grooming scandal and used real court transcripts, Fransen told me, "I was genuinely amazed at how honest *Three Girls* was. Is probably the only time I've ever plugged the BBC!"[36] For Robinson, the BBC's perceived bias motivated his own 'journalism'. Robinson was, at the time of research, working for Canadian radical-right broadcaster Rebel News. He perhaps not inaccurately predicted, "Over the next 5 years I think the BBC, CNN will be completely irrelevant—no-one's going to watch their outfits, they want to watch videos on their phones, and this is the future of news [he shows me his phone and a Rebel News video he has made on rape by migrants to Sweden]. I see this as the future."[37] Soon after this meeting, Robinson left Rebel News and then found himself removed from Twitter, becoming reliant on his webpage and various alternative so-called 'free speech platforms' such as Gab, Parler and GETTR to disseminate information online. The BBC, meanwhile, in the period since I spoke to Robinson for this book, has seen increased pressure, with detractors claiming it is 'woke' and 'unpatriotic' and calling for it to be defunded.[38] Sensing a gap in the market, GB News launched in 2021 as an alternative to the so-called 'mainstream media', with magazine items including 'Wokewatch' and 'Free Speech Nation'.[39]

Emasculation: from self to group

Male participants aspired to a valorous nationalist masculinity, in which violence may be necessary to defend oneself and one's people. This was also compensatory. Such behaviour became necessary, participants believed, to compensate for the failure of the state or other authorities, which did not protect them and instead caused their emasculation. State failure was evident in two stages: first, the refusal to combat what were regarded as Islamic predators; second, the persistent punishment of those who, seeing the state's neglect of its duty, stepped in to fill the gap. All believed that the state had neglected and abandoned them and distinguished state (negative) from nation (positive). Patriots were left to protect women (narrowly defined) from Islam, activists believed, but they would be the ones punished by the liberal state for their actions:

> I feel that white nationalism is the 'new Jew'. ... Do you get my drift? ... If I don't have money in this country and you don't have the right credentials to get a decent job or you can't get on the housing ladder. ... A lot of the situation is built on liberalism, feminism and capitalism. I cannot stand all three of them [Jason, thirties].[40]

> If Islam people or Antifa attack me—I don't care about dying—it's not a problem for me. Because I will be the victim. ... I want to be a martyr, a victim of the British system. I went to an employment tribunal, you know, against a trade union. It went as far as Strasbourg. No chance, no chance! There is no justice. It's better in Poland than here [Henryk, sixties].[41]

> Anything classed as racist is clobbered. If you're in the far right, you'll get slaughtered for it. If you're a lefty, then you just seem to get away with it. We did major demos. ... Patriots were in court and there were thirty-five of the other side in court, can't remember if they were lefties or Muslims. All of those for the far right got prison. No one on the left or Muslims got prison; it was all just small fines or community service. That's why we say there's a two-tiered justice system [Darren, forties].[42]

Darren's comment shows how he equated the threat from Islam with that from 'lefties'. This was a common theme, and is familiar in the literature. However, what is important here is not simply that activists understand themselves as the victims of a two-tier system, but that this perceived victimisation is predicated on the central notion that the state only rewards one masculinity performance, and that this is not the—authentic—masculinity that is normative in their social group. The state is understood as emasculated, and it is up to patriot men to exert a more robust masculinity both to substitute and to compensate for this. Jason's story, for instance, was particularly apt. He described at length his estrangement from his

121

biological family, at the same time as he became active in the broader far-right scene. He explicitly articulated a vision of the state as a new mythic racial family.

Mobilising masculinities

If ideology was not the key mobilising factor for involvement in radical-right activism identified by interviewees, what was? Of the men, aside from those noted above who did discuss ideology, one cited friends, two cited family (Iain and Tommy Robinson), and two seemed to be drawn in online. Three were unclear. Of the women, Anne Marie Waters' activism was a direct ideological development of her mainstream politics, two said that experimentation with protest was their way into the scene (Georgey and Jayda), one became active online (Jane), and two again were unclear. In this section I consider the role of masculinities in participants' mobilisation to activism, with more exploration of women in particular in Chapter Five.

Authentic masculinity and the everyman

As noted in the previous chapter, formative masculinity experiences within local communities mattered. Participants recognised a tension between the masculinity norms enabling status in their own social groups and spaces (understood as working-class), and the masculinity norms of what they understood as middle-class liberal society. To see someone who apparently embodied their masculinity values and yet had high status—often in the news, on social media with thousands of followers and a high-profile target of the police—was important. Tommy Robinson appeared to project a high-status masculinity read as authentic by other men seeking validation of their own experiences. Darren, for example, told me, "The EDL, when Tommy Robinson came out—he was like a hero to me when I first got involved. ... I thought, they are doing something that other people aren't doing."[43] Robinson remained a male role model across the participant sample, although he was no longer involved with the EDL and had moved to other forms of activism.

Veneration of Robinson suggested he was regarded as representative of the robust authentic masculinity he seeks to portray, which refuses to cede to elite attempts to silence him.[44] When he was removed from Twitter, to the derision of many on social media, supporters of Robinson demonstrated how strongly they identified with him, tweeting under the hashtag #IAmTommy. In May 2018, Robinson was arrested while live-streaming around Leeds Crown Court, including images of people involved in the trial. In breach of a 3-month suspended sentence relating to a similar offence in 2017, he received 13 months in jail for contempt of court within hours of the arrest. The arrest, quick conviction and imprisonment were accompanied with a reporting ban on these details, to avoid further prejudice to the ongoing grooming trial. This created a furore among Robinson's supporters, who mobilised to protest at Whitehall in their hundreds, and thousands signed a petition for his release. They believed the arrest was an attempt to stymy free speech.[45] Even when the reporting ban was lifted and he pled guilty, many still refused to accept that Robinson's actions were in contempt of court. They were, in fact, a clear breach.

Such encounters with the state were read as masculinity challenges, performed—thanks to social media—for a collective peer group of thousands. When he was jailed, Robinson appeared as a semi-folk hero and masculine icon to large numbers of disenfranchised men. Indeed, a "Working Class Hero" poster was evident in one image of a protest over his arrest (see fig. 2). "He's a figurehead what many looked up to," Iain told me.[46] This does not mean that activists did not criticise Robinson: they referred in interviews to his abandoning the EDL, and to his paid collaboration with the now defunct counter-radicalisation thinktank Quilliam, run by former Islamist extremist Maajid Nawaz.[47] However, it appeared that radical-right perceptions of an unjust institutional assault on Robinson's right to speak—and therefore his masculinity—made activists less willing to denigrate him, at least to me.[18] Even when criticising Robinson for behaviour such as drug use, violence or leaving the EDL, the sample were careful to frame with praise any remarks that might be interpreted as hostile to him.

In my research, Robinson, as a male influencer, emerged as an important mobiliser into radical-right activism. According to Hope Not Hate's 2019 report, 55 per cent of British people had heard of

Robinson; of those, 37 per cent had seen or heard one of his videos on social media, a figure rising to 57 per cent of 18–24-year-olds.[49] However, only 6 per cent of British people had a positive view of him. By the time of the Hope Not Hate Report 2023, this figure was higher, at 9 per cent, and 13 per cent for men only. The Hope Not Hate 2023 report states that he remains "the single most well-known far right activist even though his influence is in decline".[50] For participants, he possessed a uniquely high status as a male role model who would not refrain from speaking the 'truth' or from protecting white working-class women. This meant that he was able to mobilise both men and women—as the next chapter will explore—into activism, and appeared more important in doing so than what could be described as ideological motivations.

While other figures, including Jayda Fransen, were symbolically important within their specific milieu, Robinson's appeal as an everyman figure appeared to transcend group boundaries. At a Britain First demonstration, for instance, I saw organisers tell a protestor to remove his homemade T-shirt, which bore a photo of Robinson's face. He took it off, but proudly held it up for my photograph (see fig. 3), telling me he loved Robinson but, in an assertion of support for the norms of patriarchy, "not in a gay way". Fransen later suggested that such orders were prompted by BF Leader Paul Golding's jealousy of Robinson's status.[51]

Masculinity challenges

In the last chapter I noted Daniel's experience of an attack in his local area and its mobilising impact on him. Masculinity challenges, however, did not need to be either violent or personal in order to mobilise. Iain became regularly involved in EDL activism aged fifteen. He described a formative experience that factored into his participation:

> What it was—I was at school and a lad was watching a video, and there were maybe thirteen or fifteen Muslim lads in [a suburb of his town], this highly Muslim-dominated place. They were claiming [this suburb] to be Pakistani. This is at 12 years old, when I'm full of testosterone. I thought, why ain't no one

doing anything? As I was watching I was thinking of the EDL. They were confronting people like that, like Anjem Choudary. So, when they came to [a major nearby city] to do a demo in 2012 or 2013, that's when I got involved.[52]

The collective male experience of watching the video at school with other boys ensured that the taunts, centred on the ownership of local space, were read as a masculinity challenge. Iain immediately thought of the EDL, perhaps as men he believed would be able to challenge back, no doubt also because men in his own family were involved. Iain's language suggests he regarded Muslims as dominant at the expense of what he understood to be British, given the claims of ownership over the suburb. His sense of outrage, which was affective, combined with male role models in his family and a male peer group at school, indicates the need to counter with a confrontational masculinity through protest. Additionally, Iain himself noted that he was "full of testosterone". This reference implies that he saw a biological masculine inevitability to later activism. Iain's own link between his activism, the EDL as role model and his maleness echoes the narratives of the past chapter: particular masculinities are 'in the blood', a given. There is a sense of inevitability—a lack of agency and therefore responsibility—around some behaviours that appear to me, the interviewer, as choices.

Football, purpose and getting involved

Football hooliganism is recognised as a path to the EDL in particular, and Treadwell and Garland go so far as to suggest that the EDL and Casuals United (a hooligan network) were almost synonymous in the EDL's early years of 2009–10.[53] Of the radical-right men interviewed for this book, four cited football as their pathway into the movement (Tommy Robinson, Darren, Alex and John Meighan), in particular the subculture of criminal networks and football hooliganism discussed in Chapter Three. I asked Darren when his football hooligan violence became political. He said, "When I decided that I didn't want to fight for football no more. … I'd been out of the country a lot for some time. Then I came back, and there was like this big void, with no one around me. [I needed a] sense of belonging."[54] Darren implied that he would always have been fighting; it was simply a question of who and what for. Later in the interview, he cited concerns about the economy as a political motivation to his move to the EDL and then the Infidels. He worked in the building trade and said he felt that the recession in that industry was due to an immigrant labour force willing to take lower wages. However, this theme was presented as an aside, and his own emphasis was on how his life with the far right represented a continuation of the violent hypermasculinities of his football days, now simply 'repurposed'. These masculinities remained stigmatised as far as mainstream norms were concerned, and criminal, as they were associated with the same behaviours.

A sense of moral purpose within the radical right was important to men as a way of reframing masculine behaviours continued from a criminal past. Alex, in his late twenties, had a similar trajectory to Darren. He linked status, appearance and hypermasculine violence with his transition from football hooliganism to the EDL. He told me that EDL activism was about "fashion, politics and violence", although he was quick to add "that [violence] doesn't happen anymore".[55] This is not a new finding. Rajan Basra, Peter R. Neumann and Claudia Brunner, amongst others, have noted a redemption narrative amongst men involved in crime who then turn to jihadism because of a cognitive opening, to borrow the radicalisation terminology: "a shocking event or personal crisis [that] prompted them to re-assess their lives and become open to a radical change of values and behaviour".[56] Yet what Basra, Neumann and Brunner describe is not truly a radical change of values or behaviour; it is, as they after all note, a continuation of criminality—and, which they do not note, the same subversive masculine behaviours. What changes is the masculine lens used to frame this behaviour. Amongst the radical-right participants, for whom, as discussed, ideology—and faith— are largely absent (there is more on this in Chapter Five), there was nonetheless an emergent narrative of fulfilling a higher purpose through political activism. Darren and Alex continued to engage in risky and adrenalising hypermasculine violent behaviours—at least for a time—but repurposed them into a more morally justifiable cause consistent with a reassessed masculine identity, due to age or change in circumstance: the protection of nation, women and children.

Changing life circumstances, and 'life stages' such as becoming a father and having a family, are understood to be important in desistance from crime; the activities that provide masculine status in youth are not the same as those in older age.[57] For some participants, radical-right activism was framed as a form of desistance. Indeed, since becoming a father and recognising his responsibility of care towards younger generations, Alex had tried to recruit other football hooligans into the EDL. He regarded this as a means of helping them, and others:

> I thought it could be different. You could have footy lads stop fighting pointlessly and have voices here where needed. I look at all that now [football violence], and I think it's stupid. I—now—think it's pointless. I mean, I could do things that will channel it into something productive.[58]

Alex's new role—fatherhood—forced him into a confrontation with his football violence. Yet instead of recognising the possibility of relinquishing this behaviour, he simply reframed it to cohere more closely with his new perception of himself: as a morally responsible carer. John Meighan, founder of the 'anti-extremism' street organisation Football Lads Alliance (FLA), is another activist who is a former football hooligan.[59] When, in June 2017, Meighan staged the first FLA march in London, it was aimed at protesting the London Bridge attack earlier that month.[60] In this attack, three jihadists drove a van into pedestrians in the busy area of London Bridge and then jumped from the vehicle to attack other passers-by at random with knives. Eleven people were killed, including the attackers, whom police shot dead at the scene.[61] Just as Henryk justified his involvement with Britain First as a positive way of helping British teenagers betrayed by the state, Meighan and Alex regarded their activism as the manifestation of a social conscience, channelling football into 'good', and in particular reframing their own past football violence as a form of desistance, providing protection for the community while continuing much of the same behaviour.

Alex also cited an Islamist attack as a key factor in his mobilisation. He told me that his change of focus was prompted by the murder of off-duty soldier Lee Rigby by two Islamists in 2013. Working to combat Islam, the perceived cause of Lee Rigby's death, offered Alex a form of redemption, alongside the familiar buzz of the protest and scuffles he knew from football hooliganism:

> I've been active on the right wing now for 4 years. When Lee Rigby got killed, I started to make a difference with charity work raising money. Now I try to do this kind of thing [the protest we were attending]. I used to hold meet-and-greets to educate people. ... That's key. We tell people verses out of the Quran, facts about Shariah law and the population like the community and the ratios for crime. Where I'm from there are 64,000 Muslims, that's [just] 0.04 per cent, and already we have had a terrorist conviction.[62]

I first met Alex as he and other men manned a stall in the centre of a small city some hours from London. They were near the local council offices, protesting refugee status given to Muslim men and attempting to give passers-by negative information about Islam. This need to apparently 'educate' others, mentioned above by Alex, was shared by other participants. After the first White Lives Matter demonstration in this country, in Margate, one man I talked to informally told me, "even if we enlightened a few people, we did our job."[63] Men reframed their violent and subversive activities to cohere with shifts in their identities, caused as they grew older and achieved milestones of manhood such as fatherhood, or reappraised their priorities after time abroad. They sought purpose; usefulness. What they did not do was give up violence, subversion or widely stigmatised behaviour. This was too ingrained, too much a part of a masculine endeavour shared with too many men who were integral to their sense of both community and self.

Patriot men, protest masculinities

So far in this chapter I have considered the narratives men tell about their mobilisation to activism, and how the formative masculinities outlined in the previous chapter enabled this. I want now to turn to discussion of the culture of protest and its relationship to ideology. I have already suggested, as other authors have noted before, that most participants had not read far-right ideologues and rejected the notion that ideology was foremost in their mobilisation to the radical right, or was an appropriate way to describe their involvement. However, as Hegghammer notes, ideology is more than a belief system: it is "doctrine and aesthetics", the symbolic practices which indicate to others that you belong to a shared community.[64] Political parties through the ages have employed collective ritual—the practices and communicative meaning of ideology—to politicise and mobilise.[65] Here, shared emotion, shared practice and ideology are not distinct. Rationality and emotion are entwined. Margaret Wetherell uses the term "affective practice" to encapsulate the essence of affect within collectives as "meaning-making"; it can be entered into, it is created, and it therefore must be sustained.[66] This section of the chapter explores the symbolic practices of the distinct shared communities I encountered when I attended radical-right protests, and how they link to the masculinities of Chapter Three.

The section details how the protests I attended represented different expressions of masculinities: the authentic working-class masculinity which cannot be disciplined (Robinson and the EDL); a militarised disciplinary masculinity also expressed by women (Fransen and Britain First); and an explicitly political position in which masculinity was not prioritised and women's rights and visibility were key (Waters and For Britain). There will be more on Fransen and Waters' activism in the next chapter. To some degree these three stances constructed the ideological aesthetics by which the grassroots could identify to which strand and group they belonged, and what masculinity they understood as normative. They also represented the varying positions of the influencers leading each movement, and their different visions of the role of men and women in relation to each other.

I want now to consider in more detail two key masculine subcultures utilised at protests: football and football violence (the EDL); and the military (Britain First primarily, but also the EDL and White Lives Matter). The subcultures mirror similar findings by Fabian Virchow and Miller-Idriss about European far-right youth groups, in which military symbols are used as a form of hegemonic masculinity and to assert the association of a strong nation, with men ready for violence.[67] The radical-right cultures represented through symbol and ritual are hypermasculine and predicated on strong in-group/out-group binaries, antagonism (non-physical) and aggression (violent) towards the Other. They also endow participants with social capital via the assumption of particular masculinities with high status among the wider milieu, and enable both reciprocal and shared emotion, alongside group aggression. This aggression is directed variously at Muslims or Islamists, the police, Antifa, the unsympathetic public and 'the left' generally. Radical-right cultures are also subcultures of meaning which, as Ahmed suggests, position particular Others emotionally as well as politically.[68] This politicisation, which references subcultures with ideological symbolism, belies the participants' own contention that their activism is distinct from politics or ideology.

Football culture, affect and the EDL

While any form of collective action can enable bond-making,[69] the roots of EDL symbolism in football enabled the movement to draw on the threads of men's pre-existing affective bonds, and to weave fresh political and ideological meaning from them. Demonstration could conjure the camaraderie of the football match, or the adrenaline rush of football hooliganism.[70] This is not an accident. Hope Not Hate's Nick Lowles suggests that football fans were once the target audience of EDL financial backer Alan Lake, who was determined to make a pseudo-army of them.[71] Whether this is true or not,[72] the core constituency of EDL support was self-identifying working-class men who also enjoy football, and the fusion of EDL politics and football culture enabled the mobilisation of familiar affective antagonisms, as well as geographic affiliations, in a new direction.

Participants anticipated events with sometimes childlike excitement. Demonstration involves a natural sharing of emotion; however, activists also invest emotional labour in creating this emotion. Before an EDL demonstration in Telford, 19-year-old Iain posted on social media, "buzzing like a kid at Christmas – My return to the English Defence League is here." The importance of this emotion was not just that it was felt, but that it was shared. Robinson earlier noted that the EDL was about politicising people, yet also claimed that he knew nothing about politics and was not political. Nonetheless, emotion collectively experienced is political; it positions subjects, and is able to create or reproduce power relationships between them.[73] As Ahmed notes, nobody "arrive[s] in neutral".[74] Our affective responses are predicated on our habitus, the judgments and values we bring into a collective space, and the emotional meaning they carry. In particular, marches and protests serve as an emotional meeting point, or what Virchow calls an "emotional collective".[75] James M. Jasper further distinguishes the affective friendship ties he names "reciprocal emotions" from the "shared emotions" aimed at the Other—for example, anger at grooming gangs or public immorality.[76] Both directions of emotion (intra-group and inter-group) are part of the 'libidinal constitution' of a movement, the 'love-based' emotions that are generated either to facilitate or to hinder collective action.

Iain's social media excitement about the protest continued: "Demo day 🏴 🍻 🍻 🍻" and "Woke up this morning feeling fine, Got the EDL on my mind - some thing tells me I'm in to something gooood oh yeahhh"—words that recollect songs from the football stands. Iain and Daniel have a friendship which has been strengthened through active demonstration at EDL and other radical-right protests across the country for some years. Iain fondly remembered his first demo as a teenager, alongside Daniel. Daniel is a former soldier in his late twenties who said he suffered PTSD after serving in Operation Telic, the UK's military operations in Iraq in the 2000s. He is also the activist whose mobilisation was linked to an alleged attack by men telling him he was a "white bastard", described in the last chapter. Iain and Daniel's conversation referenced football, shared emotion and identity. They also emphasised belief:

> Iain [nineteen]: The first one I went to was with [town] Youth
> Division. There were five of us, and I knew them, but they
> weren't like my best friends though. But they were all right.
> It's like—anyone is made welcome, cos it's one more person to

stand. … My family are very big on it, they say, "You believe in something, stand up for it!" So that's what I did. There was a good 800 or 1,000 people there. Easily. 800 to 1,000! It was quality—felt like at a football match. The adrenaline, and people believing in the same thing. [Q: Was it mainly men?] It was mixed—men, women…

Daniel [twenties]: Maybe sixty–forty men–women…

Iain: It's just a working-class movement. It represents the working-class community. No one else represents them.

Daniel: The atmosphere…

Iain: The singing, the chanting—it's quality![77]

As Pilkington has noted,[78] and former EDL leader Tommy Robinson remembers, "It was the culture. Like a football culture. When you meet up in the morning you'd go on the piss, have a few beers, back to the coach, all drinking, all partying, all singing. It's the culture that made it successful as well."[79] This culture was the football culture explicitly invoked as emblematic of a particular working-class masculinity. It empowered activists, produced affect and proved politicising. It also provided an enabling environment for violence. In its early days, the EDL commissioned songs by Alex and the Bandits, a group popular with football hooligans. At the time of research, the Bandits' Facebook page alluded to post-protest violence, citing interests including, "Football… playing, watching and all the fun after! Politics-ICHORTRUST.com Travelling and doing gigs. Playing live to the masses! Being in sureal and lary situations! Ave it!!!"[80] ICHOR stands for (I)nfinite (C)ovenant on (H)uman Rights, (O)bligations and (R)eparation, and the ICHOR Trust both opposes Islam and represents "Ænglish" values.[81] The band's music merges football, nationalism and violence as subcultures which become indistinguishable from one another.

The active referencing of football subcultures in the EDL had a powerful effect.[82] Iain already had a frame through which to understand the excitement of his first EDL demonstration, because it replicated the buzz of the football match. Matches see spectators united by the shared emotion of investment in their team, engaging a symbolic culture which represents a particular habitus and set of rules.[83] EDL protests used this, mobilising affects derived from an existing cultural landscape and its associated values: the particular working-class hypermasculinity explored in the previous chapter.[84] The football subculture is rich with norms and values drawn on at EDL protests, for example, where the 'team' is now the group, representing not just place but what place stands for: community and culture. The football stand is an important affective resource to the radical right, as it provides one of the few acceptable locations and atmospheres in which it is justified for men actively to show a range of strong emotions, including love, sadness, anger and grief.[85] Groups on the radical right such as the EDL used football symbolism to reinstitute familiar working-class masculine subcultures involving drinking, football and fighting, but now in the context of political protest.[86] In so doing, they reignited the affective bonds of the pub, terrace and street.

Within the EDL, which had no official membership system, online communities, demonstrations and marches constituted the key means of expressing—and fostering—EDL identities. The cultures of football and football hooliganism in EDL protest are hard to disentangle. Robinson's name is borrowed from a notorious Luton football hooligan;[87] his real name is Stephen Yaxley-Lennon, and he was involved in football violence before the EDL. Consistent with understanding violence as akin to a pastime, as outlined in the previous chapter, he told me he believed football violence could be usefully planned, citing Russian organised fights as a precedent. Darren, the former football hooligan who was active with an Infidels group until 2016, emphasised that for him, demonstration was always about both violence and fun. Of protest, he said, "It's the adrenaline. I'm an adrenaline junky. Like kite-boarding, or snowboarding or rock-climbing, wake-boarding—anything. You put a board under my feet and I'm at home."[88] He similarly described his participation in the EDL and Infidels as "like a hobby … in my spare time",[89] although it is clear from what he told me that his activism has dominated and often disrupted his life.

Dunning suggests that "football hooligan fighting is basically about masculinity, territorial struggle and excitement".[90] This might also be said of EDL participants for whom football violence was the route in; political violence provides a parallel outlet for emotion and a continuation of masculine practice, and this is key in nourishing the reciprocal emotions evident in the EDL. Darren suggested that the fun and adrenaline of protest confrontation and violence were crucial in increasing affective bonds with a core circle of male friends. He considered this group a form of army corps, telling me there were "fourteen people, fourteen of us trusted people. You don't go to war with someone you don't trust, and at the time we were fighting a war."[91] The anecdotes of this "war" were remembered with animation, and an (uncomfortably) infectious macho humour. He described a post-demonstration encounter with a group of Muslims who saw him and other protestors in a pub near to a mosque:

> We were in the red-and-white, we were banging on the window at them from inside the pub, with the flags. Suddenly, two young Muslims came into the boozer, like they wanted to give us some. So I grabbed a flag and said, "What? Do you want to have a go, do you? Wanna go?" I was right in their face. Then this old guy said, "Why you do this?" That was quite cool! So, after that, that was my name. "Darren-why-you-do-this".[92]

The mobilisation of football hooligan cultures within EDL protest created a permissive environment for particular masculine behaviours, only one of which was violence. Football endows masculine status, as noted in Chapter Three. It also enables playful and hostile antagonisms rooted in location, directed against an Other defined by origin, affiliation and clothing. Clothing norms outlined by Alex in that chapter, in which those seeking violence wear certain brands, were replicated at protest. Clothing is used to distinguish 'patriots' from anti-fascists, who wear all black.[93] The EDL co-opted items from Burberry and Stone Island, along with C. P. Company and Aquascutum.[94]

Spaaij notes that "symbolic opposition and ritualized aggression" are key companions to violence in the football scene, and consist of such actions as taunts, "parading" as an assertion of space, graffiti and "eyeing" in order to subdue a rival.[95] Pilkington suggests that EDL chants have three purposes: opposing Islam, expressing patriotism and affirming identity.[96] Busher notes that EDL events reveal activists' shared "project of collective world-making".[97] This world is produced through raised flags, beer bottles and banners proclaiming a town affiliation, or an anti-Shariah or anti-Islamist slogan. There is also noise. No radical-right protest is quiet. Protestors sing from a repertoire of well-known and deliberately provocative verses, including "Muslim paedos! Off our streets!". Chants also express a provocative patriotism, such as "Keep St George in my heart, keep me English! Keep St George in my heart, I pray! Keep St George in my heart, keep me English! Keep me English till my dying day!". This is sung to the tune of the hymn "Give Me Joy in My Heart". Other chants include "No surrender! No surrender! No surrender to the Tal-i-ban!" and "We're the IN-FI-DELS of the E-D-L! And we're com-ing dowwwwn the road!". This latter chant asserts an identity that is the antithesis of Islam, and is often heard alongside, "E-E-EDL!", which serves as a base-chant and may segue into longer renditions.

There is a fourth purpose to the chants, however, and that is masculine ownership. As discussed in Chapter Three, space is not devoid of meaning. EDL activists, some drinking, continuously sang and chanted as they proceeded from their police-designated meeting point to their rally destination, along a route generally heavily policed, often with as many officers as protestors. Katz describes the purpose of parading as a way of controlling public space, with groups marching "in apparent unison ... while displaying insignia of membership".[98] Space is a—gendered—way of ordering and understanding ourselves and others, and certain protest spaces therefore have particular significance.[99] Radical-right protest frequently takes place in towns affected by widescale cases of grooming and sexual exploitation involving British–Asian men, or in predominantly Muslim areas, where provocative chants include the phrase "Mohammed is a paedo", bacon has been thrown on mosques and protestors have worn pig costumes, invoking an animal offensive to Muslims.[100]

If radical-right groups frame these events and the towns in which they take place as areas of English emasculation, the chant "Whose streets? Our streets! Whose fucking streets? Our fucking streets!" signifies active defiance and empowerment. When chanted in public, particularly in a Muslim area, by groups of predominantly men, the songs pose a direct masculinity challenge. Pilkington, Garland and Treadwell note that such chants draw explicitly on football culture and the hooligan scene.[101] They construct a masculinist space in a site of perceived in-group sexual emasculation.

The hooligan culture within EDL protest also opened up the recruitment pool. Football violence is not uniquely English. The norms of football violence, situated around team and working-class identity, are to some degree shared transnationally.[102] They may also cross boundaries of class.[103] Radical-right protestors from outside the UK who belong to a particular cultural milieu can also access this culture. For example, Jacek, the Polish professional in his thirties, had lived in the UK for 11 years and was a regular attendee of radical-right demonstrations under different banners. He was introduced to nationalist protest in his native Poland, where football hooligans were also active in joining white supremacists in clashes with police. He remembers of his first demonstration, "[I]t was a mess. The police was beating everybody, because they didn't see the differences [between them]. Most of the people were showing their views and affiliation ... football supporters, others ... Nazi skinheads. ... Many football supporters were local patriots only."[104]

Many participants at demonstrations in fact disapproved of violence. For several participants, in a continuation of the masculine practice of their lives before activism, casual violence—as long as it adhered to certain rules—was a positive expression of emotion and male working-class culture. Football violence conforms to the moral rules of a habitus commonly shared by EDL participants in this research, and explored in Chapter Three, although these 'rules' may not always be either understood or respected.

Masculinity challenges and subversive cleverness

Another key means of producing and consolidating reciprocal emotion at events was through masculinity challenges and cat-and-mouse interaction with the authorities. This form of challenge is not violent, involving humour and, as Jeffrey S. Juris suggests, "play".[105] At the EDL demonstration in Telford in November 2016, for example, some 150 marchers were channelled along a heavily policed route, past a group of masked demonstrators. The groups were kept apart by both barricades and police horses. Protestors reached the Telford police station car park, where speeches were made. The car park sloped down around 8 feet to the road below, with a view across it. Protestors instigated a game with the police, to the accompaniment of loud music blasted from the PA system, as my field notes recall:

> Ian [Crossland] points to the crowd across the road, separated from the EDL by a cordon of more police, several on horseback. "You see them over there," he says. "They're our boys. Don't be scared of them, they are Pie and Mash and they're on our side, but the police won't let them join us."[106] … He suggests demonstrators make a dash to join them instead. It's all a bit half-hearted, but some people do descend the grassy slope and give it a try. It's clear they will never get across, as the horses are big and the police nervous. But the escapade invokes a sense of mischievous rebellion. People are laughing and joking, even as they fail. I am reminded of a giant game of British Bulldog, the police playing 'it' in the middle, waiting to catch those who chance their arm at making it across.[107]

Reciprocal emotion, Jasper's term for the affective ties of friendship that are vital in creating intra-group bonds, was clearly evident in the collective protest at radical-right demonstrations, as well as participants' accounts of past events. Most important in affective terms were the friendships fostered at events, which participants described as a form of 'family'. Indeed, for some activists, this was literal, not metaphorical. Earlier I described Iain's narrative of his path into the EDL as a young teenager. However, this was influenced by his older brother and father, who were active and had status in the movement. He told me that his mother and grandmother were ambivalent: "My nan was worried—she would ring me up on demos and ask if I was ok. But none of them tried stopping me. But I would have still went [if they did]. I had no role models—well, probably my big brother. … He was big in the EDL. Most of my dad's side of the family, we was all involved."[108] Indeed, Britain First seemed to be entirely a family affair at the leadership and administrative level. Paul Golding's mother Chris ran the office;

she told me that her other son was one of the Britain First security team. A nephew was responsible for media productions. However, as Iain emphasised, the importance of family in the radical right is not simply as a blood connection enabling a simple pathway in through kinship links, but as a feeling developed with strangers through involvement together in group activities and events.

The greater the numbers, the greater the reciprocal emotion. This bond was strengthened through the shared experience of active opposition from outsiders (the left, hostile locals, Muslims or police) within the protest space, large attendance numbers, communal rituals and practices, and masculinised activities such as chanting or—for some—fighting. Male and female protestors relied not just on each other, but on reciprocal emotion generated with (a minority of) sympathetic outsiders. For example, Lydia was delighted when at one point an elderly white man passing the protest stopped to tell her that Britain First were doing the right thing, as "there are too many Muslims".[109]

The purpose of radical-right collective action was ultimately an appeal to class-based action as an expression of subjectivities. If there is a crisis of masculinity, Steve Hall suggests that this is unevenly distributed, and that class is an important consideration.[110] Considering the radical right, while traditional white working-class masculinity is often talked of as 'toxic', 'in crisis' or subordinate,[111] their particular activism is constructed as part of a working-class movement that male participants explicitly reference and believe offers them many positives. Working-class culture is often regarded by those on the outside as "a hurdle that needs to be overcome."[112] From the inside of this subculture, however, aggressive masculine behaviours, rituals and practices that might appear threatening to others are positive and serve as an important resource—part of a cultural repertoire. This is their patriarchal dividend. For example, my field notes from the EDL's 5 November 2016 Telford demonstration read:

> I am struck by the contrast of the offensive chants ("Mohammed is a paedo"), and the content of the key message (child sexual abuse by grooming gangs is wrong), as well as Ian Crossland's

more moderated interviews afterwards with the press. We walk to the car park together and discuss my impressions of the event. He says, we always get bad press. I'm not surprised, I say. The chants are really crude and offensive. It's not exactly the sort of protest you'd want your kids to see; and yet people might have sympathy for aspects of your message, if you communicated it differently. Nobody after all thinks grooming gangs should be allowed to continue. Yeah, he says, but it's who we are. The lads are angry, their blood is up, and this is how we express ourselves.[113]

Drawing again on Ahmed's discussion of the role of emotion in the formation of feminist politics along intersectional lines,[114] Crossland can be seen to assert the right to self-expression in terms familiar to a marginalised male working-class demographic, and consistent with his habitus. He also invokes the right to have the "lads'" anger read as a political performance, whatever its cultural associations, and therefore not dismissed;[115] and the need to express negative emotion en masse as progressive.[116] This is not, of course, to imply that Crossland or the EDL are representative of working-class culture, or that working-class culture is homogenous (it is not); nor is it to judge these invocations as justified or reasonable. It is to suggest that the collective demonstration was an attempt at expression of a particular masculine identity.

Radical-right participants expressed much nostalgia for the EDL's 'heyday' of mass protest and confrontation, and a sense of disappointment that protests—during the research period of 2016–18—did not attract more people. At the Telford EDL demonstration in November 2016, Iain shook his head as he looked at the group of around fifty gathering there and told me, "It's nothing like what it used to be."[117] Others remembered the early days of EDL mass demonstration with nostalgia. Georgey, the EDL supporter who works in childcare, had fond memories of years gone by: "Peterborough. I'll always remember that. It was one of the better ones, there was 4,000 there at that one ... a good atmosphere."[118] She told me that this atmosphere had contributed to the making of lasting relationships that have outlived her involvement in street activism.

Georgey no longer attended demonstrations because "the EDL served its purpose", which, she said, was to focus public attention on so-called grooming gangs and force prosecutions.[119] She was still active for the cause, but told me, "I can do more tweeting now."[120] Others shared this view. Before being removed from social media, Tommy Robinson also told me that online activism was the future of protest:

> I don't see street protest any more—it's pointless. ... [Q: So you're trying to become a new media outlet?] Well, yeah. ... Become a source, like when people hear something on the news, they'll say—well, let's see what he's saying. Cos I'll give them the truth. ... if they're not going to give people a platform, then they will create their own platform. Which is what's happened with online—I've only just cottoned on to all this the last few months, and I thought, shit. ... This is what we should have been doing all along.[121]

Nonetheless, online activism was no substitute for the intense emotion of street protest. Iain told me why he looked forward to protests so much: "Everyone there is doing the same thing and is up for the same thing. It's more like a family social gathering than a protest, once you've been doing it for years."[122] As noted earlier, Iain's father and brother had also been active in the EDL, so for him this was literally true. For other participants, the family is created—Hel Gower, for instance, described Tommy Robinson as "like a son".[123] This echoes Pilkington's findings on the importance of envisaging the EDL as a strong community, with ties that go beyond protest friendship.[124]

Military masculinities and protest culture

At all the demonstrations I attended, activists waved flags, sang songs and marched. However, differences in the culture of protest represented normative masculinities that varied between groups. Britain First demonstration entailed a code of conduct for protestors, with rules on what to chant and instructions not to drink.[125] Then Deputy Leader of Britain First Jayda Fransen supported a militarised, disciplinary vision of activism which she contrasted with the pub-going, football-watching masculinity of the EDL. She associated this with indiscipline, inaction and ignorance, and the eventual triumph of Islam. In fact, Fransen blamed such masculinity for the 'rise of Islam':

> People are too ignorant to pick up the Quran. Lee Rigby was killed, and I got it out and read it back to front. Four different translations. I just thought, let me double-check. ... [But] they can't be bothered, they would rather watch football, or go to the pub, or watch *The X Factor*, or go to Legoland. What happens if you're at Legoland and your children get blown up? It's laziness and ignorance.[126]

For Fransen, patriot men are not in the pub, or on the football stands—they are on the streets leading the fight against Islam. Fransen had attended EDL protests, and told me that she quickly realised they were not for her. While she did not criticise Tommy Robinson, who personifies a less disciplined approach, she did not support this informal EDL approach either. Affect politicises, but if the core protest values are not ideological, focus can be lost. Robinson, in fact, suggested this was accurate, telling me that the EDL culture ultimately became a distraction from the main purpose of the EDL: to combat Islamism and Islam. This he believed, contributed to the movement's eventual demise.

Unlike Robinson, Fransen continued to prioritise street protest, believing that online activism was no substitute. She addressed the issue of low attendance in a 2017 video 'rant', saying, "I am sick to death of what's happening to our country—and worst of all, I'm sick of watching hundreds of so-called 'patriots' mouth off on social media, but never actually attend a protest or get involved in anything that might make a change."[127] For Fransen, change comes from offline behaviour, not online. If offline protest matters, as Fransen suggests, it is perhaps because of the importance of shared emotion and affect in binding groups together, particularly in times of stress and pressure. Wetherell suggests that affect is generated through shared "meaning-making".[128] This is evident at demonstrations. Britain First marches include chants, some shared with the EDL (for example, "Mohammed is a paedo"), and loud traditional anthems played via speakers. Both songs and flags can also, in the climate of decreasing demonstration numbers, give the impression of higher attendance.[129] At the inaugural White Lives Matter rally in 2016, the culture of wider radical-right protest was evident, a drummer providing the beat for marching feet (see fig. 4).

Nationalist symbols in protest invoke affect through hypermasculine identities which favour a defensive stance and suggest nationalist ideology. These emphasise both reciprocal and shared emotion, with 'patriot' protestors uniting through the performance of a masculinity deemed appropriate to the defence of the flag. All the radical-right demonstrations I attended employed a variety of national markers with military associations. These included national songs (Britain First), drums (White Lives Matter), 'uniforms' (Britain First security wear branded clothes), use of the poppy (Britain First) and flags (all demonstrations), which create an atmosphere of militarised parade, characterised by reference to both current and past 'warrior masculinities'. Through the appropriation of army/warrior masculinities, the predominantly working-class/underclass protestors are able to assume an identity prized by mainstream society, alongside a working-class masculinity which they feel has been consistently denigrated.[130] In particular, Britain First's use of military symbolism—in conjunction with the symbol of the cross and rules on orderly conduct, such as not being drunk—contributes to the construction of a more disciplined protest environment, a substitute for the state.

Use of military symbolism makes military masculinities accessible to the self-identifying working-class men on the radical right. Some male research participants and various others I encountered at demonstrations had served in the military. For others it was aspirational. Darren, who referred to his time in the Infidels as "war" and his associates as "foot-soldiers", has always worked in construction. However, he had childhood dreams of joining the Marines. Meanwhile, Daniel had served in Iraq and subsequently had PTSD. He told me, "I lost two mates once when on patrol. This person comes out, says 'Allah Akbar', and it's an IED and he were blown up. ... I'm the one who picked him up."[131] He felt that few other groups actively supported veterans. Radical-right rhetoric, however, adopts issues including the poor treatment of veterans and the right to commemorate war heroes. For Daniel's friend Iain, local commemoration of Armistice Day was crucial to the wider cause: "Remembrance Sunday, let's go together and show respect together. I set up a local patriots' page, then got national support for that. Now we have 30,000 likes on our page."[132] The radical-right scene also mobilised narratives of Second World War victory. Polish demonstrator Jacek told me that he had never experienced hostility from others in the radical right, "only the opposite. I met people from the EDL, and we were drinking beer and they were slapping me on the arm and remembered the Polish pilots who defended the British in the War."[133] Narratives predicated on the hypermasculine role of 'war hero' created bonds that could transcend nationality and class.

Military symbolism inevitably also enables masculine antagonisms. At EDL demonstrations the St George's flag was dominant, a flag with direct reference to the Crusades.[134] Britain First's constitution supports the greater involvement of the military in schools. At Britain First demonstrations the Union Flag was also on display, alongside flags bearing the Welsh dragon, the St Andrew's Cross for Scotland and the Royal Standard (see fig. 5). Flags have several meanings. They can signify belonging, but also mobilisation towards war—future, present and past. Britain First explicitly reference the Crusades,[135] and their use of nationalist flags has religious symbolic significance. Fransen frequently carried a cross at protests. Given that she explicitly regards Islam as Satanic,[136] this becomes an aggressive act that poses a direct challenge to Muslims to fight. This was particularly apparent in the Britain First practice, now outlawed, of 'Mosque Invasions', in which the cross was taken into mosques and worshippers challenged.

What is also important here is that the two cultures through which radical-right masculinities are constructed—football, including football hooliganism, and military actors—have important structural connections to nation, race and whiteness in a UK context.[137] The British military has historically acted as the tool of colonial dominance over people of colour through Empire; football hooliganism was for some time linked to racist groups, and football itself has suffered from manifestations of racism, particularly from supporters against black players. As noted in the previous chapter, participants contested accusations of racism. They did not recognise the construction of racism through structures of white privilege, and they rejected any implication of themselves in such structures, because they framed their own collective whiteness as 'working-class' and therefore disadvantaged.

This move is consistent with wider UK discourse in which racism has only recently been understood as structurally constructed, and is more frequently positioned as a problem of individual people.[138] Participants normalised their activism, much as far-right extremism itself has for years been normalised in wider British society as a "normal male [youth] issue",[139] or through media narratives which have linked it to the personal—mental health issues, for instance.[140] Meanwhile, wider societal discourses framed jihadist violence as organised and exceptional. Similarly, participants discussed both jihadist violence and Islam itself as ideological, structural and unacceptable in modern Britain.

Summary

Mobilisation into activism, as well as activism itself, in the radical right is dependent on the range of masculine performances discussed in Chapter Three. Activism is an "exaggeration of the existing patriarchal logics" evidenced in the previous chapter.[141] Miller-Idriss notes of European far-right style that "nationalism and masculinity become mutually self-reinforcing",[142] and this chapter goes some way to exploring how this is also the case in a British context. Protest across the radical right is constructed through reference to the cultural symbols of familiar gendered subcultures, which for interviewees have an association with place. It also draws on the situated masculinities outlined in the last chapter from interviewees' pre-activism period. Football and football violence cultures do not just constitute an emotional resource in which particular actions endow status; they also enable the designation of others as an out-group or 'enemies' and, in the hooligan culture, as targets of attack. Participants are aware that others view this subversive subculture as criminal and dangerous. Military masculine symbolism similarly provides a positive resource at Britain First demonstrations and a way of identifying with and as a part of the state. The radical-right movement reproduces symbols with familiar shared values, drawn upon as a resource to enable particular responses from the—mainly—men involved in protest. One of these responses is violence, confrontation and antagonism. However, it is only one. The act of protest, using these symbols, involves the generation of reciprocal emotion: collective groups of men enable violence, but also excitement; a form of bonding that is akin to the love felt within a family; anger and the ability to challenge institutions understood as emasculated through subversive play.

Still, it is hard to escape violence. If masculinities are constituted through violence, as outlined in Chapter Three, then this is "the mode by which one asserts one's masculinity".[143] The hypermasculine protest subcultures mobilise people familiar with these cultures to action; however, they also render the message inaccessible and even repugnant to outsiders. EDL founder Tommy Robinson, for example, told me his original intended audience was "Middle England". He later realised, however, that the EDL culture could never appeal to them: "Every demonstration's a cry for help; that's how I used to describe it. It's a cry for help—so fucking listen. ... But the way we talked and the way I acted—I'm only really appealing to my sort of people."[144] He told me that he was therefore delighted with the class diversity at 'Day For Freedom' marches held in 2018, and the feeling that people were gathered around a positive (support of free speech), rather than a negative (anti-Islam(ism)).[145] Participation in so-called 'positive' events also reduced the risk of activists being outed on social media and losing work, Robinson said. He alluded to the considerable extra emotional risk and labour required to maintain levels of commitment to EDL demonstration given these challenges. Demonstration was the site at which the emotion was paid back.

It is also apparent that men are mobilising to different groups, whether White Lives Matter, the EDL or Britain First, because they represent particular hegemonic masculinities. Robinson's robust and violent masculinity is widely understood as authentic, and it is revered. For those for whom football or hooligan culture is already part of a cultural practice, EDL demonstration, which draws heavily on this, is a natural movement to join. Britain First—and White Lives Matter, at the one demonstration I attended—offered something different, privileging military masculinities. For Britain First, this is consistent with a more disciplined organisation: they are a political party, in contrast to the EDL, which is a street movement. BF has a uniform, a newspaper, patrols and security guards; the EDL did not. BF remains a political party; the EDL collapsed under its own fluidity and disorganisation. The culture reflects the practices, and the practices are continuations of a pre-activist life; they are masculine practices that are not just part of extreme movements, but part of society writ large.

What also emerges in this chapter is radical-right resistance to being understood as ideological. However, the radical right has an ideology: that it is the obligation of 'patriots' to defend the country from Islam, understood as sexually predatory, and seeking to conquer and dominate. Leaders emphasised different masculinities in their specific movements: a 'passionate' working-class masculinity which cannot be disciplined (Robinson); and a militarised disciplinary masculinity (Fransen). To some degree, these stances construct the ideological aesthetics by which the grassroots can identify to which strand they belong. Although interviewees reject ideology, both for strategic reasons and because they do not consider themselves ideologically informed, an affective reading of their protest—as politicising—confirms that whatever they might say, their activism is ideological. Ideology is, as defined by Hegghammer earlier in this chapter, "doctrine and aesthetics", not just belief.[146] Participants are contributing to national discourses on gender, whether they accept that their messaging and activism are ideological or not.

In the next chapter I explore another key issue in the radical right: misogyny, the role of women and gendered fragmentation in the movement.

1. EDL demonstration, Telford, 5 November 2016.

2. 'Working Class Hero' sign at a 'Free Tommy Robinson' protest, London, 9 June 2018.

3. Protestor in a homemade Robinson T-shirt, Britain First demonstration, Rochdale, 22 July 2017.

4. Flags, branded T-shirts and drums: White Lives Matter demonstration, Margate, 22 October 2016.

5. Britain First demonstration, Telford, 25 February 2017.

6. Women leading a Britain First demonstration, Rochdale,
   22 July 2017.

7. Anne Marie Waters leading an "Islam Kills Women" event, London,
   20 August 2016.

5

THE RADICAL RIGHT: MISOGYNY, MASCULINITIES AND WOMEN'S LEADERSHIP

I'm not here as a misogynist, like, hating on women. But I am a traditional woman—and I'm a hypocrite, by the way ... because I am a woman in a position I shouldn't be in. Feminism is responsible for all of this. All of the downfall—the trans, all of the agendas, the immigration—all of it.[1]
Jayda Fransen, former Britain First Deputy Leader,
on her forthcoming book on the evils of feminism

Introduction

A short train ride from London on a scorching day and I am sitting at Jane's living room table while she makes me a cup of tea. I'm distracted. The TV is big and loud. The current affairs programme *Victoria Derbyshire* is on, and the topic is extremism. Even though it's on the BBC, much hated by the radical right, Jane watches the programme often. Derbyshire is one of the only people discussing all this, "Islamist extremism, grooming, rape, and now all these Muslim migrants", Jane tells me. Jane, a slight, blonde woman in her fifties, doesn't really know any Muslims—it's mainly Sikhs round here, she says. But she knows male abuse. For years, her partner beat and controlled her. Her escape was the internet—the EDL on

147

Facebook, and the friends she made there. Her ex, a white traveller, never learned to read. When Jane was online, he had no idea what she was doing. He left her alone. Years later she left him, and that's when she found her voice. She is using that voice to speak out against grooming and against Islam, she tells me. Finally, she says, she feels fulfilled.

A question often posed of the radical right is: If the movement is so hostile to women, why do they get involved? Jane was one of the six women activists across the movement whom I talked to in depth for this research, alongside other women outside of official interviews, to get an answer to that question. The accounts of radical-right activism in the previous chapters have highlighted the role of masculinities and the homosocial nature of the movement. Men dominate. However, women have always been present, even if "overlooked or considered unimportant" by mainstream scholars of the far right.[2] So far, this book has depicted a patriarchal movement. Men's numeric domination at protests both enables and is enabled by existing cultures that privilege varied performances of hypermasculinity, in front of male peers and focused on men's bodies and projection of physical power. And yet, women are also found in the 'masculine spaces' of these demonstrations. Writing on men and the state, Hooper has asserted that:

> Masculine spaces are precisely the places where such [masculine qualities] are cemented and naturalized. Therefore, even the marginal appearance of women ... together with feminist ideas, and/or other self-conscious references to gender issues, may sufficiently alter the overall ambivalence of such spaces that their masculine associations become weakened.[3]

In the case of the radical right, however, this chapter explores how women's participation enables the strengthening of masculinities. Sjoberg has suggested that masculinist movements into which women intrude have a choice: either to strengthen the masculinities that constitute activism, or to transform fundamentally.[4] There was no evidence of transformation in my research. Rather, as Joshua S. Goldstein suggests of war, women's supportive presence reinforces displays of men's power when women themselves validate dominant norms.[5] This occurs in part through performance of the "emphasized femininities" that Connell notes women exercise in support of patriarchy, and in part through a series of what Deniz Kandiyoti terms "patriarchal bargains". Kandiyoti observes that within the asymmetry of patriarchy, varied "forms of patriarchy present women with distinct 'rules of the game' and call for different strategies to maximise security and optimise life options with varying potential for active or passive resistance in the face of oppression".[6] While patriarchy requires masculinity performances by men to oppress women, the role of women and female masculinities in this oppression is rarely explored. As this chapter examines, the tensions inherent in the production of female masculinities result in the constant policing of radical-right gender relations, and of the position of women overall, by both men and women.

Female masculinities, misogyny and the far right: the literature

In earlier chapters of this book, I discussed the increasing scholarly focus on misogyny as a central element of extremist ideology. Misogyny is a tool of patriarchy. Kate Manne, in her book *Down Girl: The Logic of Misogyny*, asserts that misogyny is widely misunderstood to mean the hatred of all women. Manne, however, argues that it would be impossible to find someone who hates all women: misogynists "need not hate women universally, or even very generally".[7] Instead, misogyny is about dividing women; it is a mechanism of control over the women who challenge patriarchy specifically. Misogyny is "a social-political phenomenon ... a system of hostile forces that by and large makes sense from the perspective of patriarchal ideology, since it works to police and enforce patriarchal order".[8] This order is both "oppressive and irrational", a logic supporting patriarchy to punish women. Misogyny does not, however, punish all women equally. It separates women into conformists, who support patriarchy, and antagonists, who do not. Men are distinct from women and ultimately have power as a group overall. Of course, women can be misogynists too, and that does not rely on masculinities, even as it relies on patriarchy.

Discussing the far right, Gentry has asserted that "there is no far-right terrorism without misogyny".[9] If misogyny supports patriarchy, and extremism is a precursor to terrorism, what is the relationship of the radical right to misogyny? As previous chapters have made clear, patriarchal norms encompassing a range of masculinities are an important part of radical-right radicalisation stories. How those masculinities are aligned towards women, and uphold patriarchy, is important. For Connell, writing in 1995, patriarchy is the "main axis of power in the European/American gender order", subordinating women to men.[10] Writing around the same time, violence scholar Sylvia Walby defined patriarchy as "a system of social structures and practices in which men dominate, oppress and exploit women",[11] across structures including the mode of production, paid work, the state, violence, sexuality and cultural institutions. Patriarchy has certain requirements. It requires men and women to be understood as distinct, and with distinct roles as well as bodies. Given its gender binarism, patriarchy is also heteronormative.[12] It is a system of power, constructed by men with the most power and maintained in their interest.[13]

Female masculinities, patriarchal bargaining

How does that power impact women in the radical right? How do women in the far right 'do' masculinities? How are those masculinities produced and what are their effects? While, as Jack Halberstam writes, "masculinity and maleness are profoundly difficult to pry apart",[14] masculinities are not owned by men or male bodies, and Connell did not envisage them as such.[15] Women both consume and can produce masculinities;[16] we have already seen in Chapters Three and Four that women in the radical right understand working-class masculinities as an important aspect of their own identity formation. While Connell positions hegemonic masculinity as the partner to a compliant "emphasized femininity", women also 'do' masculinities, and this alters how their performance is read.

If, as Connell asserts, masculinity is hegemonic, not all "masculine forms of femaleness" elevate status.[17] When women do masculinity it is transgressive; gender binaries and conformity is challenged. Female masculinities can, however, gain esteem, from both men and women. Amar cites the example of the women factory workers vital to the success of the Arab Spring and 2011 Egyptian Revolution—women who were understood as 'macho' and 'masterful' by the men around them.[18] Alternatively, in attempting to gain esteem, female masculinities can embody the worst forms of violence, as was evident in women's enthusiastic participation in gendered abuses of Iraqi men at the American prison Abu Ghraib.[19] Importantly, Schippers engages with Connell's assertion that all femininity is subordinate to masculinity. She considers Karen D. Pyke and Denise L. Johnson's 2003 study of Asian American women, which noted that, in parallel to hegemonic masculinity as white and heterosexual, hegemonic femininity could be similarly understood in the American context.[20] However, given that race, not gender, is the determinant factor in this hegemony, Schippers concludes that hegemonic, or emphasized, femininity is the complementary enabling counterpart to hegemonic masculinity. A corollary to this is femininity that challenges men's hegemony and cannot be tolerated within patriarchal systems. "These are characteristics that", Schippers writes, "when embodied by women, constitute a refusal to complement hegemonic masculinity in a relation of subordination and therefore are threatening to male dominance. For this reason, they must be contained." She names these "pariah femininities".[21]

Female masculinities in the far right can prove elusive. The far right is historically patriarchal, predicated on men's domination. Within far-right ideologies, bodies are essentialised as an articulation of men's power, and the relationship between masculinity and male bodies is naturalised.[22] Men and women are a binary construction, and the heteronormative family is the core unit of nation. Sexual reproduction is a fundamental aspect of far-right ideology, expressed, for instance, in US white supremacist David Lane's infamous Fourteen Words.[23] To return to Mudde's forensic categorisation of the far right from Chapter Three, the extreme right represents extreme nationalism, incorporating nationalism's gendered structures. Nationalist ideologies limit men and women to separate physical spaces. Elshtain, in *Women and War*, clarified the historic association of women with *oikos*, the domestic realm, and men with *polis*, the state.[24] Feminist scholars have emphasised how states have mobilised such binaries in order to go to war.[25] They have juxtaposed the privileged masculinity of man, constructed as the 'Just Warrior'—for whom the greatest honour is to die for the Homeland—with the 'Beautiful Soul' of the female citizen. This vulnerable woman homekeeper requires man's protection; her role is to enable his status as protector.

The gendered formulation of nationalism is of manhood in support of nationhood; women are understood as mothers, and motherhood has symbolic power. Floya Anthias and Nira Yuval-Davis suggest five models according to which women have been permitted participation in nationalist processes. First, as was evidenced in Chapter Three, groups use women's behaviour to delineate the in-group from the out-group, with only in-group women judged to be morally upstanding. Women's moral behaviour is used to define and maintain group boundaries. Second, women must participate in and propagate group ideology. Third, women are symbolic of ethnic or national difference, and fourth, they must support military struggle. Finally, they are exalted as mothers, tasked with the biological reproduction of the nation, frequently racially defined.[26]

There would seem to be little room for female masculinities here. Instead, nationalist ideology is predicated on an internal misogyny, directed at in-group women through claims of both care and control; nationalist womanhood is rather about emphasised/ hegemonic femininity, in support of patriarchy. In a US context, Blee, for instance, has found women actively recruited to far-right groups to promote men's involvement and stabilise their activism.[27] Women bargain with patriarchy for what power it affords them. Motherhood becomes an important feminine role which women often willingly valorise, given that it is one means of achieving status within patriarchal systems.[28] In fascist groups, mothers have proved an active constituency, mobilising around maternalism, not in spite of it.[29] Blee has explored how women willingly accept limitations on their behaviour because they actively endorse the production of far-right hierarchy through the gendered ideology of patriarchy. Women willingly become involved in anti-feminist support roles, something Jean Hardisty has termed "kitchen table activism".[30] Indeed, the role of the 'tradwife' has been an important element of women's declared motivation to support the alt-right, an online-based branch of the far right that emerged in the late 2000s in the United States.[31] This apparent structural subordination does not obligate a lack of agency. Far-right women clearly ascribe value to roles liberal feminists might understand as being subordinated to men and masculinities. What is more, it is not the case that far-right women lack power. This power is wielded to the extent that women's opposition to men's activities can even effectively prevent male commitment to them.[32] However, typically, such power has not been expressed in leadership positions, which are reserved for men.[33]

New far right, new approach to female masculinities?

In Chapter Three I discussed how to describe the anti-Islam groups explored in this book and suggested they are best examined as belonging to the radical right. This is a strand of nationalism that does not straightforwardly replicate the binary ideology of bygone fascist groups. Radical-right groups do not always ascribe to clear-cut militaristic protector masculinities and the relegation of women, as was evidenced in the diversity of subcultural symbolism in the last chapter. In a Western context, they mobilise around gender and sexual equality as evidence of cultural superiority over Islam.[34] Niels Spierings and Andrej Zaslove have discussed the EDL, for instance, as incorporating two contradictory gendered ideologies: the traditional nationalist gender narratives of the far right, which site the nation's honour in its protected women; and a new approach, claiming Western gender equality and freedoms, including for gay people. Sarah L. de Lange and Liza M. Mügge distinguish between these two positions, labelling the first straightforwardly "national[ist]" and the latter "neoliberal", although they note overlap between the two.[35] Here the traditional far right's internal misogyny, directed at the control of in-group women, is less evident; it is externally-directed misogyny against out-group (Muslim) women that is mobilised in narratives against, for instance, the *burqa* or headscarf. Indeed, elements of the radical right in the UK, while embracing some aspects of traditional far-right gender norms, counter others. The EDL, for example, was officially supportive of elements of a sexually progressive agenda, in that it promoted defence of homosexuality and (non-Muslim) women's rights as modern British values—ideology that would be incompatible with Manne's vision of patriarchy, particularly its heteronormativity. The EDL's website suggested that this agenda was necessary to combat concerns including the "denigration and oppression of women, organised sexual abuse of children, female genital mutilation, so-called honour killings, homophobia, racism, anti-Semitism."[36] However, the radical right has ridiculed trans rights. The radical right is also anti-feminist, and this is an important ideological strand of wider far-right ideology.[37] For some, therefore, radical-right narratives emphasising women's rights and protection represent little more than the instrumentalisation of a rights agenda. As Tania Modleski notes, if male subjectivities are in crisis due to threat from female power—as a result of feminism, or globalisation—one way to deal with this is to incorporate it.[38]

However, this incorporation is not meaningless. Ideology incorporating women's rights and agency, particularly in the face of male oppression, explicitly enables a different type of female gendered performance, including female masculinities. Lange and Mügge suggest that the way in which this manifests is related to populist ideology and varies, as different radical-right groups emphasise different ideas.[39] In work on the EDL, Hilary Pilkington has highlighted women's capacity to exercise active agency against structural patriarchy, even as a minority.[40] She concludes that women are keen and active participants, often transgressing 'traditional' notions of femininity and joining in with masculine aspects of protest such as crude chanting, casual sex and drinking culture, although this can exact a reputational cost.[41] Similarly, work on women in the Nordic Resistance Movement emphasises that there are penalties for participation, as well as benefits.[42] Women performing masculinities in far-right groups, taking on roles and behaviours typically associated with men, can see their agency set in tension with patriarchal structures seeking to exert power over them, as I now explore in the case of the British radical right.

Women in the radical right

As Pilkington notes, male dominance does not mean that the EDL does not appeal to women; nor does it necessarily equate to a lack of space in the movement for them.[43] Radical-right protests I attended evidenced a 7:3 ratio of men's to women's attendance. This was consistent with co-founder Tommy Robinson's suggestion that women constituted some 30 per cent of activists.[44] Both men and women engaged in all protest activities: chanting, filming, speaking, banner- and flag-waving, shouting propaganda slogans at passers-by and cheering, as well as some baiting of the public, Antifa and the police. Previous chapters explored how radical-right masculinities require men and male bodies, to support patriarchal ideologies and male bonding. Women's participation, and their bond with the group, is no less important. The EDL made claims of inclusivity and incorporated Jewish groups, LGB groups, Sikh groups and a separate section for women's groups, the EDL Angels, run by Hel Gower.[45] I encountered women in different roles, at the grassroots level but also, importantly, in authority and leadership roles—a traditionally masculine domain in the far right. The next section considers women as leaders, before turning to the challenges for grassroots members.

Female masculinities and fragmentation: women's leadership in the radical right

> My book is about the evils of feminism ... people find this really strange, coming from a woman ... because I get called ... it was Anne Marie Waters, actually—who is a socialist lesbian by the way ... it was her who called me a misogynist, which I always find quite ironic.
>
> Jayda Fransen[46]

Jayda Fransen was, during my research, the very visible female Deputy Leader of Britain First. In January 2019, following some months' imprisonment, Fransen announced that she was leaving Britain First to pursue her beliefs elsewhere.[47] She is now the leader of the British Freedom Party, which she created as an advocacy service during the COVID-19 pandemic.[48] She was one of two high-profile female radical-right leaders interviewed for this book, both of whom have since quit their groups—the other being Anne Marie Waters, then leader of For Britain, who has since rejoined UKIP. Each had a different strategic approach to leadership within the wider homosocial movement. Fransen embodied the hypermasculinity of the wider Britain First movement and an explicitly anti-feminist agenda, opposing gay rights and emphasising the 'need to breed'. Waters, meanwhile, as a gay woman, took an explicitly rights-based 'new right' approach centred on non-Muslim women. She aimed to fill a feminist gap in radical-right activism, whilst rejecting the term 'feminist'. Fransen's actions as Deputy Leader of Britain First were about portraying not just strong female leadership, but—consistent with the historic organisational involvement of women in nationalist groups—a symbolic presence, shaming men into action, mobilising mothers and acting on issues affecting women and children, all in support of a firmly masculinised space.

Jayda Fransen, Britain First

Field diary, Rochdale BF Protest, 22 July 2017:

> BF security is back, asking if I'm Antifa. I show my Twitter account. He scoffs. "Anyone can have a Twitter account." The rally eventually gets going—Golding gives a shout-out to the various nationalities from the UK represented, forgetting Northern Ireland, for which he has to apologise. The crowd is led in the Lord's Prayer, which feels odd, as even those who aren't Christian—surely the majority—join in, intoning the prayer in the familiar rhythms of children in a school assembly. There is a huge round of applause for Fransen as she takes to the stage, even as she struggles to get up onto the platform in her skirt—nobody brought a step. She says, "We are Christian, but people from all faiths or none are here. We know it is our Christian nation, so keep it that way." She then introduces fellow female activist Weronika Kania, from Poland, with, "I didn't realise there could be another female as crazy as me!" They both recently confronted a *Dawah* stall in Birmingham and the Polish press is apparently at the event, a number of supportive Poles in the crowd. Kania talks about grooming gangs, the threat of Muslims, media deception. Her speech is punctuated

by the crowd: "Disgraceful!" "BBC paedos!" "Down with the BBC scum!" As Kania finishes, Fransen thanks her: "It's totally inspiring to see a beautiful young lady say we need to be brave and 'no surrender'. Thrilled to have her here!" In the distance the counter-protest can be heard, above the crowd: "Nazi scum off our streets!" The next speaker, John 'Banksy' Banks, calls for unity across the far right, to "stop falling out". Then it is Fransen's turn. Golding introduces her: "She's been in more mosques than an imam, confronted more terrorists than the SAS." The crowd sings out, "We love you Jayda, we dooo!" and Fransen retakes the microphone.

In 2017, Jayda Fransen was the Deputy Leader of Britain First, apparently respected by Leader Golding, and loved by rank-and-file supporters. Since 2019, when she left BF, Fransen has sought to distance herself from the group. Her departure has been acrimonious. There are ongoing legal disputes, and she has talked publicly about being physically attacked by Golding.[49] Yet at Rochdale in July 2017, there was little sign of the falling-out to come. The key ideology mobilising Fransen and BF was evident that day. Fransen's active Christianity is important in her ideological approach to Islam, a faith which she told me she understands as "Satanic". She does not believe in free speech for trans people, gay people or Muslims, and has called to ban Islam in the UK; she opposes interracial marriage and LGBTQ+ rights;[50] and she adheres to Orientalist narratives of the Great Replacement Theory, framing British Muslims as hypersexual and committed to a programme in which they 'breed breed breed' to ultimately replace white populations.[51] As of Summer 2023, she is writing a book about the "evils of feminism", she told me. She has always been anti-feminist. At the December 2016 BF Annual General Meeting, which I attended, Fransen vocally opposed legal abortion—an argument across the far right which seeks to bolster white birth rates and challenge the Great Replacement—debating the few other women attending, most of whom did not agree. Indeed, Fransen also told me she was fully behind a speech at the December 2017 BF conference I attended during field research, in which activist Banksy suggested that women were less intelligent than men "in general". She told me she had discussed the content of his speech with him beforehand, as she had been uncertain it would be well received by other women.[52] In fact, unlike the discussion of abortion at the AGM in 2016, nobody protested.

The previous chapter explored BF's use of military cultures to foster support and communicate discipline, contrasted with the EDL. It also connected the group, which has explicitly racist ideology, with past fascist groups embodying a military culture. BF is a masculinist group, with confrontational tactics. Fransen and Golding have taken the cross into mosques in a series of so-called 'Mosque Invasions', and physically confronted Muslim men they believed were sex offenders at their homes. Golding's introduction to Fransen's speech at the Rochdale demonstration emphasised her female masculinity and capacity for disciplined confrontation. While supporting patriarchy, Fransen is not the typical nationalist woman: she has disrupted the gender binary in that she does not need protection, but instead offers it. This is something she prides herself on. In my interview with her, she contrasted her participation in BF 'direct action' with EDL protest, issuing a masculinity challenge concerning confrontation to radical-right men:

> The EDL are not confrontational. They gather, and people come to counter protest. … Standing in a crowd, miles from an Islamic extremist, that's not extreme or dangerous. Leave off! I've been in situations where I've confronted—now convicted—terrorists; they have roughed me up, grabbed me, they hold you, pull you about, drag you on the floor. … [Like] Tommy Robinson, he was just videoing Muslim groomers on trial. He had his phone in his hand, he said, "Come on then"—that takes more courage than standing with 100 other people shouting "EDL" and "Muslim bombers".[53]

Here Fransen highlights the group competition fragmenting the radical right; her remarks represent a means of shaming all men into action, while emphasising her ability as a woman to outperform men in masculinity challenges.

BF protest crowds appeared to admire her leadership as a woman, precisely because her actions did not disrupt the established patriarchal order, even while her identity as a female leader did: Britain First remained male-dominated, and Fransen supported patriarchy within it. This is not, however, the emphasised femininity of kitchen table activism. Fransen's was a robust female masculinity, yet advocating a kitchen table agenda. She both took for granted the masculinity of the movement and adopted its apparent ambition. She told me:

> I'm no stranger to male company. Most people who are outspoken on the right are male. Even further back in my life, I guess before Britain First, I had a business in recruitment, and I worked in law for 7 or 8 years. I'm not a feminist and there were always lots of men around. As I went higher up there were more. … I had no issues about it being a male environment. But it's changing, which is great.[54]

Fransen always emphasised her exceptionalism: the successful woman, thriving in the company of men. Yet she was keen to improve women's visibility in Britain First, and exploited her own visibility for publicity.[55] She acted as a figurehead, leading marches alongside other women she had invited and activists (see fig. 6).

Contacts were transnational, and Jayda's invitation to Weronika Kania came at a time of recruitment of British Poles.[56] However, this disrupted neither the militaristic culture nor the strong gender binary of the group. Fransen was careful to qualify the masculine qualities of Kania's actions—bravery, her call of "no surrender"—with a contrasting feminine essence—the "beautiful young lady".

This appeared successful, in that Britain First supporters apparently read Fransen as a feminine symbol of masculine nationalism. While I personally did not hear it articulated, Fransen was frequently depicted online as Boadicea, the historic female leader of the native Britons against the Romans.[57] Fransen has adopted an image of the Westminster statue of Boadicea and Her Daughters on her website, with a message to "support the resistance".[58] This semi-mythic female archetype importantly situates Fransen's activism within a specific cultural narrative: native British rebellion against foreign invaders.[59] This is also gendered. Boadicea is an important symbol of Roman sexual brutality, given that she was mutilated after she was captured.

Roman accounts of Boadicea's rebellion meanwhile monstered her, exceptionalising her as savage, unwomanly and evil.[60] As such, the symbol bridges tensions between Fransen's anomalous role as a woman leader—in this crisis situation of invasion—the patriarchal stance of the group, according to which her role is in the home,[61] and her perceived misrepresentation by mainstream society.

In a 2023 podcast, cited at the top of this chapter, Fransen acknowledged that she is a "hypocrite"—unmarried, not a mother, a public figure, a leader—given that she advocates heteronormativity, marriage and children for other women, in order to 'outbreed' Muslims.[62] However, she does not let this limit her own actions or ambition. Her disruption of the gender binary is framed as exceptional, as implied, for instance, by her reference to herself and Kania as "crazy". Here, Fransen explicitly referenced the transgressive nature of women's roles as leaders, and particularly as leaders engaged in masculinity challenges and confrontation. As in the case of Boadicea, women's violence has long been exceptionalised as the result of madness, or badness.[63] At Rochdale, Fransen reclaimed a label indicating women's instability to imply their ability to transgress in other ways, including the performance of violent female masculinities.

She also emphasised in a 2023 interview with me that the exceptionalism was necessitated by male weakness and 'incel'-like male leaders 'bastardising' the radical right through immoral and inauthentic practices, drugs, drink and using prostitutes:

> I am in this position because, yes, of feminism—but I resent that. If society wasn't as fucked as it is, men would be decent and strong. ... if it wasn't the case that men were weak and women were assuming this masculine role ... this isn't a position I like. It's a difficult life: no security, no husband, no kids. ... This isn't an easy gig. It's not. ... I am in exceptional circumstances, and throughout history there have been women that have found themselves in exceptional circumstances, in positions of leadership.[64]

Although women were in the minority at BF demonstrations, several I spoke to said that Fransen's leadership had inspired their attendance. Despite her denials, cited at the start of this chapter, Fransen's stance is consistent with both misogyny and patriarchy: her celebration of particular in-group women, active in the movement, does not undermine her contempt for out-group others—Muslims, feminists, liberals and other women leaders in the radical right, such as Waters.

Anne Marie Waters, For Britain

As women, Fransen and Waters did not fit the mould as far-right nationalist leaders. However, they did not share gender values and navigated this tension in different ways, each making their own bargain with patriarchy. Waters, as a gay woman, supported a 'progressive' secular approach mobilising first and foremost around non-Muslim women's rights, which she believed were threatened by Islam. She supported neither the heteronormativity nor the gender binary that constitute the logics of patriarchy and misogyny, as evident in Britain First. Her attempts at navigating a women-centred approach through radical-right activism appeared less successful than Fransen's, given that she faced constant misogynistic policing from within the radical right for her transgressive stance—an attempt to rewrite what constitutes hegemonic femininity in the wider movement.

This distinguishes Waters' activism from that of BF or the EDL, although she was involved with Robinson in the early days of *Pegida* in the UK, as noted in Chapter Three. Waters, born in Ireland but now a British citizen, told me she first engaged in LGB advocacy and politics as a student, and later became a Labour Party activist in South London. Women's rights were her primary motivation, she told me, as she felt that these were always subordinated to other agendas. She ran for selection as a Labour member of parliament as late as 2013, but told me she became disillusioned with Labour's stance on several issues. In 2014, she set up the Sharia Watch website "to monitor sharia law and how it affects the UK and might affect the UK in the future as the number of Muslims grows".[65] One of her highest-profile commitments during my research period was a series of events titled "Islam Kills Women" (see fig. 7). These focused on women's participation, with Waters telling me that only women would or could adequately represent their own interests.

In London in August 2016, I attended an "Islam Kills Women" event organised by Waters. This protest lacked any of the symbolic markers of hypermasculinity I witnessed at other protests, and constituted more of a conventional political protest. It took place outside Parliament and involved a majority of seasoned female speakers. Several came from the Flemish nationalist group *Vlaams Belang*, which opposes immigration and Islamist radicalisation and has links to both far-right and populist parties across Europe.[66] This protest specifically sought to engender connections between women. It excluded not women but Muslims, and, to a degree, men. Men I spoke to who did attend, however, appeared to endorse Waters as an anti-feminist due to her opposition to 'the left' and Islam.

Although she opposes liberal feminism, Waters is not, however, an anti-feminist, and this cast her in an aberrant role. Waters told me that her politics is underpinned by a "patriotic feminism" aimed at protecting in-group (non-Muslim) women and LGB communities from Islam and damaging cultural practices such as female genital mutilation (FGM). In 2017 she led an unsuccessful UKIP leadership bid and founded the radical-right political party For Britain. Waters' political experience and university education means she entered the radical right from a more politically conscious position than either Robinson or Fransen. She framed her ideology as both common-sense and necessary in order to fill a feminist gap in radical-right debate by opposing misogyny, first and foremost in Islam. However, her (non-Muslim) women's rights stance is quite different to an agenda based on protecting women. She told me:

> There are very few people speaking up for women. And a lot of opponents of Islam have views that I don't like. Anne Coulter thinks that women should not be allowed to vote![67] And she's got company. ... People say on Breitbart that feminism is unforgivable because working women means birth rates dropped. Causing the birth rates to drop and Muslims to come in! There's that end of it—and I don't want those ones to be the ones speaking out against Islam. I cannot bear lefty feminists—or women-hating.[68]

Waters "cannot bear" out-group feminists, but also the internally directed hatred of in-group women from factions of the far right.

Her anti-Islam politics put her in the company of those on the far right who would restrict all women's rights to the home, something she believes to be deeply regressive. The tensions are difficult to manage. She attempts to shore up her position by aligning herself with anti-feminists, against "lefty feminists".

Aspects of Waters' ideology, alongside her political identity as a gay woman, challenged heteronormative far-right misogyny and its complementary emphasised femininity in that she sought to represent (some) women, in terms of rights and the public space. Waters did not 'do hypermasculinities': she was not aggressive, although she was forthright; she sought representation through political process, standing in council elections, although she was not successful in this. However, her identity as a lesbian woman in a leadership position, advocating for women within the radical right, meant that Waters did not represent the normative femininity of the wider movement. The radical right is a movement that fights to protect the necessity of understanding masculinities through maleness, within which female masculinities accord women few privileges. Writing on female masculinity as threat, Halberstam judges that "where female masculinity conjoins with possibly queer identities, it is far less likely to meet with approval".[69] It becomes a pariah femininity. Many people I spoke to had experienced pushback from parts of the radical right at times: it is a fractious and fractured movement. However, Waters received much alt-right backlash through internally directed misogyny. She did not say that this was due to her sexuality, but felt that it resulted from her 'patriot feminism'. This was read as a pariah femininity challenging the far right's historic masculinity system and normative values. This both annoyed and frustrated her. She told me:

> This guy made this video, "women destroy societies" … men who think women should not vote. There's a few of them … people who thought they could write to me and say misogynist things. … They want us back in the kitchen, domestic servants, sex on demand … I block them. [I mean], have I been unclear in some way?[70]

Waters disbanded For Britain in 2022, and it is not clear if this decision was related to the stresses of her position as a gay woman advocating for gay and women's rights, an agenda that more masculinist strains of the wider far right read as a threat to patriarchal order. Gender and the issue of women's rights represent another fracture in the radical right. Waters' politics did not change the movement; given her current retreat from leadership of her own group into UKIP activism, it is more likely that its relentless masculinism changed her.

Grassroots activists: maintaining the binary

Consistent with the literature on nationalist and traditional far-right division of gender norms, several interviewees referenced a nostalgic vision of both sexual morality and the gendered division of labour they understood as part of pre-multicultural Britain. In fact, working-class women have rarely been stay-at-home mothers, as they have needed paid employment.[71] Despite assertions by radical-right groups that they represent modern British norms, in contrast to Islam, the picture was less progressive. Participants supported stereotypical, binary gender roles which were considered normative. Protective, bread-winner masculinities were hegemonic for men, and domestic, chaste femininities for women:

> I know people with kids from different fathers and you know, it doesn't matter to me. I just wouldn't ... do it ... I had three children by the same father, and I didn't want any more, and not from all different fathers. Call me old-fashioned [Jane, fifties].[72]

> A woman should stay at home and cook and clean, that's the way I've been brought up. The man should work. [Q: Are they equal?] Everyone is equal. I think everyone should be equal—I think that's a woman's role though. [Q: Isn't what you're saying a bit like how you see what Islam says about men and women?] [But] I would not make a woman stand in the kitchen and cook. You wouldn't make them. A Muslim would make them [Iain, nineteen].[73]

> Biologically, with regards to gender, I think that, from observation ... I'm convinced that most men are analytical, and most women are focused on, say ... represented by a diamond and a lotus. The

diamond shines and shows off, and the lotus is nourishing. It's the perfect metaphor [Jacek, thirties].[74]

What I find very unattractive is the defeminising, that there is 'no difference between the sexes'—it's just not true. Just physically, a fireman or builders, or the army. ... Men have got a third more muscle mass than women. ... You won't get rid of chauvinism ever, no matter how much you demand it; it's a natural phenomena [Lydia, fifties].[75]

By nature, men follow logic and principles, and women make their decisions based on emotion [Jason, thirties].[76]

The above accounts express interviewees' essentialist belief in the innate nature of binary gender norms, either through biology, or through socialisation and cultural practice—for example, "the way I've been brought up" (Iain). They regard these opposing binary gender qualities as "essential", "traditional" and so well-established as to be part of a "natural" order, which they do not like to see challenged. Bourdieu understands the naturalisation of sexed division as the basis of masculine order, its strength being "the fact that it dispenses with justification".[77] Instead of justification, sexed division "appears to be 'in the order of things' ... normal, natural, to the point of being inevitable".[78] This inevitability extended to nation. Interviewees frequently demonstrated slippage between concepts of 'natural', 'biological', 'British', 'traditional' and 'Christian' roles. Only one interviewee (Jayda Fransen) described herself as actively Christian. For others, Christian values were symbolically important in determining both gender norms and hegemonic (and subordinate) masculinities. As Jason, one of two openly white-supremacist participants, suggested of British people, "We [white Britons] are derived from Christianity. I'm not religious, but I do appreciate the values that we once had. The stability of the family, the role of women—working women has damaged the traditional family and Britain."[79] Indeed, this theme is central to radical-right rhetoric. Christianity is the implied provider of strength and morality; Islam its implied opposite.

For each interviewee, understandings of gender roles and associated practices appeared deeply ingrained and foundational to other beliefs about state, nation and politics. Indeed, interviewees regarded binary gender relations as foundational, even when their own lives challenged this. For instance, the above-cited interviewees lived in circumstances that included divorce, single parenthood as an unmarried father and having a wife who worked.

Patriarchal bargains: 'feminazis' and patriot women

Kandiyoti's concept of 'patriarchal bargains' suggests that patriarchy does not uniformly oppress women and reward men. Instead, both genders "resist, accommodate, adapt, and conflict with each other over resources, rights, and responsibilities".[80] This means that aspects of patriarchy can prove rewarding for women. All radical-right groups have mobilised around the narrative of protecting women from grooming gangs, while contesting (aspects of liberal) feminism. They believe that this has not protected women from, in their view, a dangerous Islam because white liberal feminism prioritises Muslim Others over its 'own' women. Liberal feminism clearly also disrupts the traditional gender roles outlined in the previous section, and is perceived to undermine men. Patriarchal gender values across the movement meant that some participants opposed feminism. Women participants broadly echoed Anne Marie Waters, who felt betrayed by "lefty feminists". For Waters this feminism, "is not about women, that's for sure. The types who applaud men, praise the Taliban … invite Moazzam Begg to speak. [This type of feminist] maybe thinks she cares about women, in some shallow place. But racism will always be seen as the ultimate crime."[81]

Feminism has, in the past, divided itself along race, faith and class lines. Todd notes that working-class women in the 1970s resisted the label 'feminist', perhaps recognising that middle-class women's liberation had depended on their labour.[82] Georgey, in her thirties and working in childcare, perceived two tiers of feminists: self-identifying (liberal) feminists who she believed appropriate the label to virtue-signal; and those like herself, who reject the title entirely yet actively mobilise to protect women, particularly those understood as socio-economically disadvantaged and white working-class, from the abuses of Islam. I asked if she considered herself a feminist:

> No, I bloody don't. I would say I'm more of a feminist though than those stupid cows out there. More worried about tits in a tabloid than girls getting their clits cut off. If you are a feminist you should be concerned by that issue … [FGM is] all about male dominance and pleasure, and I think if you're a proper feminist you should be concerned about Islam and the oppression of women.[83]

Radical-right patriarchy represents an inconsistency it cannot right. It seeks to represent women, and 'proper feminism'. Yet in a masculinist movement, women's rights are a threat to men's power and remain contested when embodied by particular women—those of another (middle-) class; the feminism of Muslim women or women of colour is not recognised at all. Despite the allegedly progressive gender agenda of the radical right, misogyny is very much present, and not just against Muslim women. Some radical-right women are included in activism, but some are still reviled. Abuses of women are positioned hierarchically, with race-based abuses foremost. While aspects of Georgey's concerns were consistent with various feminist agendas, she explicitly rejected the label 'feminist' and expressed misogynist abuse towards feminists. Female power is incorporated into the radical right, only to be turned back onto othered women.[84]

I met Jacek, the regular *Daily Stormer* reader who identified as racist, at one of Waters' demonstrations. He also suggested a two-tiered feminism, distinguishing between women like Waters and those who opposed her. "I'm happy that there are [new] feminists who are risking ostracism from the third-wave feminists, the 'feminazis'. The [new] feminists are being dismissed for stating that Muslim countries are terminating women! If you don't hide in a bubble, you are an enemy. It's quite ironic."[85] Jacek held misogynist views; he did not believe that women were men's equals. Yet he accepted Waters' explicitly women's rights-based agenda, because of her hostility to liberal feminists. However, for National Action sympathiser Jason, a more general contempt for liberal values encompassed women's rights itself. It did not matter to participants that both women and immigrants have always contributed to the economy.[86] Radical-right participants opposed liberal feminism as a deviation from a natural gender order: the gender binary. The status of women's rights represents a point of tension within the movement as a whole.

This is not to say that women did not genuinely believe in the worth of their participation in the radical right and their agency within it. Aspects of patriarchy clearly proved rewarding for some women. Jane's story is illustrative. Jane, whom I introduced at the start of this chapter, had been unhappy long before becoming involved in radical-right activism: with immigration levels, Islam, fears for her grandchildren and domestic violence from her partner. The internet was the key arena of her politicisation, but also a site of refuge from this abusive male partner of 22 years. He did not allow her out on her own, or to see friends. He abused her daughter. "Maybe I was a slave", she told me.[87] Jane began to engage in Facebook chat about the EDL from her living room. "[My husband] didn't read and write, so he didn't know what I was up to online. It was an escape; I felt like it was helping a cause."[88] She told me that the friends she made on social media were key in empowering her to leave the situation and find a refuge. Now, she says, she is "strong enough to stand up to do what other women can't do".[89] For Jane, the radical right represented the only possibility for exercising personal agency against a man who was abusive towards both her and her child. This empowered and politicised her. Radicalisation was not an entry to patriarchy for Jane, but a means to resist it as manifest in domestic abuse. Radical-right participation meant Jane finally felt she had a voice, speaking out against men's exploitation of women and exercising, for the first time, personal and political agency. However, this voice was one centred on race, faith and the exclusion of Muslim women.

Masculine protest, feminine exclusion

It is by now likely no surprise that while masculine group structures in the radical right enable both homosocial participation and men's agency, expressed in particular ways, they can challenge women's participation. All the participants noted that men were in the majority at events, and this produced an atmosphere laden with potential for violence. In the early days of EDL protest, male leaders anticipated violence and therefore wanted to exclude women, in order to protect them. Robinson said, "When we were first going to Bradford ... for us, the men, we were thinking—this is the battleground, like. We're going to come under huge attack. So, we tried saying women weren't allowed to go [laughs]—fucking hell, they went nuts, man!"[90] Women did indeed succeed in attending EDL demonstrations, despite men's opposition. In 2011, they organised a protest to challenge David Cameron's labelling of the EDL as "sick".[91] Although EDL men were not wanted at this event, they did eventually march behind the women, apparently to protect them.

Hel Gower, now in her sixties, is a divisive figure who remains close to Robinson and had a leadership role in the EDL. Discussing this episode, she suggested that the men's march was not protective, but rather representative of a misogyny within the movement as a whole. For Gower, the masculine norms and gendered ideology of the group, while claiming to protect and serve women, in fact relegated female agency—a form of misogyny Francesca Scrinzi labels "gender antagonism".[92] This describes how the broad domination of masculine cultures necessitates the marginalisation of women, who must struggle to find their place within systems that do not favour their participation except in symbolic ways. One consequence is the division of a movement along gender lines.

Some female grassroots participants related the male domination of the radical-right protest scene to its potential for violence. Only one of the women who contributed to this research told me that this had deterred her from involvement. Hel Gower remembered, "A lot of our people were fighting. I don't approve of it. I never approved. ... I felt, isn't this embarrassing? They were pissed, and I didn't respect the people on the demos, they were thugs."[93] Other participants also expressed disgust at some of those involved in protest and used this to distance themselves from a perceived radical-right 'underclass'. After a Britain First demonstration held at the same time as an EDL event in London, BF activist Lydia noted of EDL activists as they dispersed: "If you were choosing people to be representative of England, you wouldn't exactly choose them."[94] Radical-right fractures engaged class-based bias.

Other women were happy to attend demonstrations, although they sought to avoid violence, which they felt was inevitable, and which they blamed on far-left Antifa protestors. Jane was unusual among participants in attending a range of radical-right events, including some associated with explicitly racist organisations. She told me:

> I've had women inbox me and say, aren't you scared at demos? No, to be honest. Personally, I don't get scared. No, not anymore. I've come out of all these experiences much stronger than I ever was. But yeah, a lot of women won't go because they are scared of it kicking off and if the left are there, the Antifa are there, it does kick off.[95]

At a protest in Dover 2016, which included National Front groups,[96] she said she had witnessed aggression which she blamed on Antifa: "The police let the left throw bottles. They didn't stop them. But I personally didn't show violence. I'll stick up for myself, but I'm not going to pick up rocks and bottles and start throwing them back."[97] She believed that the fear of such violence might, however, deter other, less confident women. Iain, a veteran demonstrator agreed. Although he had actively participated in crude chanting at EDL events, he felt that such an activity would not appeal to women. He believed that Robinson's attempts, with Anne Marie Waters, to institute *Pegida* in the UK as an explicitly more middle-class and family-oriented movement could have enabled more female involvement: "It was a platform for women and kids to demonstrate and take the fear out of the football hooligans of the EDL. It was ... for families. Who's going to listen to 300 football hooligans? ... I would not want kids to see that. That ain't a demonstration."[98] His comments evidence a tension between different masculinity performances at demonstrations, and wider gender norms.

The prospect of protest violence deterred some women, but for others it offered an opportunity to engage in masculinity challenges involving confrontation with counter-protestors. I witnessed one woman participant being hit by a missile thrown by an Antifa demonstrator at a Britain First demonstration. Police quickly arrested a man at the scene and officers were supportive. However, to the participant's dismay, the Crown Prosecution Service (CPS) did not bring the case to court. She saw this as evidence of a two-tier legal system geared against 'the right'. Her anger and sense of betrayal grew and fuelled increasingly more provocative attendance at events. She began aggressively to confront large groups of Muslim men, on her own, at demonstrations and in other contexts. In this case, the act of protest violence against her did not deter her; it motivated her to take ever greater risks, to gain influence in the movement and to gain an online following as a result. This seemed to give her a new sense of status within the movement, and of self-esteem and pride. Like Jayda or Georgey, she felt stronger for facing down opposition through masculine confrontation, and feminising Muslim men. Masculinity challenges by women against men have power, as they transgress the gender binary of patriarchy and inevitably risk potentially greater emasculation for the objects of this challenge. The higher stakes increase the risk to women, but also any resultant status.

Masculinity challenges in digital space

The online domain is also a radical-right space where paranoia, accusation and conspiracy theory are the norm; participants Jane and Hel Gower told me that they were reluctant to engage online, due to in-fighting.[99] However, it was also therefore a space where the most confrontational would thrive. For some participants, the online was a substitute for the offline protest space. Georgey and Iain were highly invested in social media, particularly Twitter, where Georgey regularly engaged in spats with 'liberal' commentators and Muslims. She told me she enjoyed abusing both, using offensive language. She was frequently blocked and threatened but dismissed as laughable my suggestion that she could report threats rather than retaliate. Her approach to social media was combative, and she used the space to prove herself according to hypermasculine norms, forcing aggressive men to back down and confronting both liberal and Islamic values. For Georgey, the opportunity not just to participate but to win in masculinity challenges was central to engagement:

I used to at the beginning, get abuse, but because I wiped the floor with them, usually, not anymore. To be honest with you, it's Muslims. I've been threatened with rape. A guy on Facebook the other day said I should be beaten up. And that was just because I commented on a video that said 30,000 Muslims gathered [to condemn war]. ... [Another] guy said I should get a beating, that I was a redneck racist bitch [she shows me the comments: "you pale dirty ho", "you dirty fucking pig", and so on]. I have got them here. I tell them, come round then! You can't be scared of these people ... I'm going down fighting, whatever happens. These people, if you go "he said he's going to rape you"—I say, well, come round then and do it! We'll go toe to toe, I said. They soon shut up.[100]

At the time of our interview, Georgey no longer attended street demonstrations, instead using social media as her main space of protest. Offline, she worked in childcare, but online she was something of an influencer, with her tweets often retweeted thousands of times. When Twitter suspended her account of more than 10,000 followers, she reinstated it under a new name. She was suspended again. Georgey used Twitter to engage in a series of masculinity challenges, abusing those who did not agree with her, with like-minded followers as the peer group to whom she performed.

Georgey's online behaviour was mirrored offline, where she also 'did' masculinities, emulating combative masculine behaviours. In one example, she proudly told me of an incident in which she confronted Anjem Choudary and his followers when she found them giving Dawah in her hometown. The most important aspect of this was her ability to surprise the men, adopting a provocatively unfeminine and aggressive response: "They didn't know what to do. They're not used to women being so volatile. Speaking back to them."[101] EDL involvement was a way of proving herself as 'one of the boys' and provided a contrast to her maternal offline job, where she cared for small children. It was not a threat to the patriarchal structures of the radical right, however, and was therefore not considered transgressive within the wider movement.

Patriarchal pushback, misogyny and policing pariah femininities

Women's participation in any dominantly masculine power structure represents a form of gendered transgression.[102] The gender divide within the radical right, and particularly the EDL, was not simply about men and women. Consistent with the logic of patriarchy, which is policed through misogyny, women are categorised along multiple axes. We have already explored some binary categorisations of women in the radical-right movement: Muslim or non-Muslim, proper feminist or so-called 'feminazi', liberal or patriot. However, participants attending EDL demonstrations for some years also distinguished between patriot women, in particular between hegemonic femininities and pariah femininities (not their terms). Central to this were sexual slurs, which intersected with race- and class-based tropes about women from the EDL's own social demographic.

Sex and 'coupling up' were features of protest away-days, and women's perceived behaviours within this protest subculture became an active element of how they were labelled. Gower suggested that sexual encounters were common between EDL activists and a fundamental aspect of the scene: "I think it's fair to say that most EDL women used [the EDL] as a dating agency. [Pause.] Or shagging."[103] She also felt that some women sought status in the EDL through sexual association with high-status male leaders known to be widely revered. It was true that among participants in this research, admiration for Robinson as a charismatic leader was strong across genders. Britain First supporter Lydia had, for example, seen Robinson in the street in London and posed for a selfie that she proudly messaged to me. Georgey, a friend of Robinson, set her profile picture to an image of the two of them for a brief time. Gower said that there was a sexual element to Robinson's appeal to women and that he and other leading figures attracted 'groupies'. She explained:

> They would see it as an opportunity to say they'd had sex with Tommy or Kev ... it was a status thing ... and maybe also some infiltration ... throwing themselves at [Tommy]. It was my job to protect him. When I was going to the demos, I was right there

behind him, and I would move in if I saw them trying to latch onto him. ... It became a joke—"Tommy's rottweiler will deal with them", i.e. me.[104]

To some women, the male leader featured as an object of desire; to men, he was a role model. Additionally, some leaders, such as Robinson, had additional status due to their infamy nationwide and their image as a persecuted everyman figure, symbolising the wider perceived victimisation of the group. Gower suggested that such men presented an opportunity for status by association.

However, participation in masculine behaviours, such as casual sex, as part of the protest scene was far riskier for women than for men, for whom such behaviour would not provoke censure. Both men and women participants framed the sexual activity of the women in the movement through highly masculinised group norms, and patriarchal "ideals of love which make monogamy compulsory".[105] Many understood female bodies at events in binary terms: those who were sexually honourable and those who were not. The EDL Angels were a sub-group which Gower was initially involved in organising, in order to give women a voice. Many women wanted to campaign on issues particularly important to them, such as CSE and grooming. Gower was, however, clear about her views on the EDL Angels:

> I saw them at demos. And [others among your research participants] were quite correct about them being slappers ... it worried me how the whole of the EDL was turning out. But ... the Angels became a joke in the whole movement because of the shagging. ... They didn't have any interest in what the EDL stood for—it was more "the call of the cock". Rough as fucking shit, is what most people described them as.[106]

Similar judgments were expressed by both men and women participants who had regularly attended EDL demonstrations. Manliness entails the capacity to exercise violence, but it is also about sexual capacity, while femininity is the perceived absence of this.[107] Within patriarchy, women's chastity, appearance and vulnerability to out-group men are indicators of in-group dominance and status.[108] Interviewees described Angels in ways that questioned their femininity, positioning it as pariah, and emphasised the masculine aspects of their behaviour as denigrating:

> With me it was never an Angels thing; I was just going as me. They had their own in-group of people. A lot of them are bigger fighters than the men. Some of those northern birds, I wouldn't want to fight with them [Georgey, thirties].[109]

> Female by birth, but you wouldn't say they were ladies, put it that way. ... They call themselves EDL Angels. ... They're like Anchor butter; they spread their legs like slappers. The men go through them. I wouldn't. I despise them all, they are filth-bags [Darren, forties].[110]

> I would never join an Angels group. I don't know a lot of them, but to me the Angels seem to be there just to find a man. ... I don't know why they think they have to do it, I really don't ... it's—going through them, it is literally going through them. It's awful [we laugh] but they probably have their reasons [Jane, fifties].[111]

> People was there just to sleep with anyone. I don't know—it was their way of finding company for the weekend. ... some of them [Angels] had a bad reputation. [Q: What sort of guys would go with them?] I don't know—the football lads—those who don't have nothing to live for ... some of the broads were just out for the dick. Some was old. You wouldn't actually believe it. There was one woman, she was 50 years old and she ... done a good 70 per cent. Easy! She was disgusting. [Q: Do you think the guys were equally disgusting?] They was disgusting. Just for the demos. Just for sex in hotels, things like that [Iain, nineteen].[112]

In fact, Iain subsequently told me that some of the Angels who had formerly engaged in casual sex were now in leadership roles, "so fair play to them".[113] While Iain suggested some censure of promiscuous "football lads", participants did not similarly judge men unless prompted by interview questions. The tone of critique was also different, with disgust reserved for women and something closer to bewilderment for men. When I suggested the existence of a double standard to Jane, she said, "Yes, definitely. I can't count the number of times I had to block [men] on Facebook when they have sent disgusting pictures. A photo just popped up. But the EDL Angels—the men know it, so they do, they just use them."[114]

'Doing masculinity', being sexually active, is positioned against femininity; rewarded in men, for women it simply entails abuse and misogyny.[115] Participants regarded women's sexual activity at protests as transgressive of wider norms, and evidence of an inappropriate masculinisation; or as exploitation and lack of agency, deserving pity. Indeed, the term 'Angel' was applied in derogatory ways to women who had never belonged to Angels groups. Negative attitudes towards Angels possibly contributed to my inability to find any woman to interview who identified as an Angel. Men I spoke to as 'gatekeepers' of current or former Angels groups ultimately did not provide access for the research, for a variety of stated reasons.

As explored in the last chapter, demonstration is a highly affective event, drawing from masculine subcultures to better enable group bonding. The affective bonds of demonstration were also clearly evident in accounts of a subculture of sexual relationships, both serious and casual. Such behaviour need not necessarily disrupt group cohesion or gender norms, given that it is consistent with heteronormativity and the high status of men regarded as embodying an authentic masculinity within the movement. However, Pilkington notes that relationships between EDL members could at times prove disruptive to group dynamics. As partnerships broke up and rifts were made public, community fragmentations occurred.[116] Participants also referenced these dynamics. Jane told me, "[I]f they have a falling out they all accuse people of this, [that] and the other, and they are slagging them off on Facebook for all of us to see. ... Private messages get screenshotted ... these poor girls trying to defend themselves, and in many cases they've been used by the lads."[117] To Jane, the women had little agency: they were in effect victims of EDL men. Despite her own Twitter influence, Georgey described EDL culture online as "people who have nothing better to do with their time ... people who like to bitch on Facebook and have arguments".[118] She distanced herself from other women in the group, but such distancing can also serve to protect oneself from similar censure.

These attitudes to women's sexual behaviour are perhaps not surprising. Discussion of sexual and gender norms with interviewees evidenced a wider misogyny that was inconsistent with the compromises and practicalities of their own lives. Participants appeared to reframe women exhibiting particular masculine behaviours (fighting, casual sex) as a sub-category who should not be respected, honoured or protected. This designation is enabled through expressions of shared disgust, which are raced and classed. As Ahmed suggests, the physicality of affect can reveal socially internalised hierarchies and reinstitute them. This has implications for how affect is evident within 'extreme' public events. Affect is central to body-reflexive practice and emphasises how sexed and gendered bodies interact. Gender orders subjects according to the affect produced.[119] Ahmed argues that our affective responses to labels, through pain, grief, love or anger, serve to create political actors and mobilise them into resistance, in what constitute entirely rational means.[120]

Outrage and disgust are affects that institute boundaries between bodies and create gendered hierarchies between them.[121] Affect is, however, not uniformly distributed, and particular affects might 'stick' more to one class, gender or race than another—for example, the trope of the 'angry black woman'.[122] In his work on class, William Ian Miller notes that misogyny and disgust for women can emotionally mediate social class.[123] Disgust towards working-class women, for instance, can be particularly pronounced.[124] Feminist scholar Bev Skeggs suggests that this can also be raced, and that "the excessive, unhealthy, publicly immoral white working-class woman … epitomizes the zeitgeist of the moment", a zeitgeist that denigrates the working class.[125] Mainstream depictions of 'chav' women have cast them as over-sexed and overly fertile,[126] juxtaposing 'underclass' women with middle-class sexual norms.[127] Misogynist slurs are in fact commonplace and are also used against far-right women online, turning their class against them.[128]

In his discussion of social movements, Philip Slater suggests that "dyadic" (couple) relationships can fragment such movements, through the transference of loyalty from group to partner.[129] In this research, however, it was not the 'casual dyadic relationships'

or couplings that caused fragmentations, but the negative affect—
particularly disgust—generated when participants applied
masculinised gender norms to women in the group. Participant
perspectives on 'unworthy' women also revealed socially internalised
attitudes towards women evident in broader society.[130] This was
particularly true for working-class white women. In fact, attitudes
of disgust for those women within the EDL denigrated using sexual
slurs mirror the disrespect that EDL participants say Muslim men
have for white, non-Muslim women. I raised this contradiction
with Tommy Robinson. He reflected on a girl from his childhood
regarded at the time as a "slag" because "she used to give all the taxi
drivers blow-jobs to get free lifts. … She was 13 years old. That was
it—she's a slag. Straight away. … You look at it now, as an adult—
she's a victim."[131] Robinson did not, however, disagree with the
derogatory assessment of the Angels shared by other participants. He
told me that the Angels were an unnecessary EDL sub-group, who
had caused friction from the start.[132] While women's victimisation
by Muslim men resulted in censure of those men, and fuelled the
radical-right movement, the same victimisation by non-Muslim men
resulted only in disgust for the women in question.

Summary

In this chapter, the radical right emerges as distinct from the traditional
far right. However, it has not entirely transformed traditional far-
right gender politics. Women demonstrating hegemonic femininity
can find space as effective and motivational leaders, supported by
men and women alike, as long as they do not challenge dominant
patriarchal narratives. I met women for whom women's rights
appeared to be a genuine priority and who mobilised around them,
believing themselves committed to ending misogyny. Jane's life
had transformed since becoming part of the EDL, and, through
activism, she had escaped a personal situation of domestic violence.
Anne Marie Waters' political mobilisation was also rooted in her
own identity, as a lesbian woman. An assertion of the protection
of women's rights—narrowly defined as the rights of non-Muslim
women—was central to the activism of influencers, as well as

grassroots participants. However, this was not feminist activism. All regarded liberal feminists as traitors. The wider movement is avowedly anti-feminist, and, indeed, prominent women leaders who centre women's agency will always face censure, abuse and pushback—including, as Waters attested, from other women. This internally directed misogyny is consistent with nationalist ideology and is aimed at controlling women, through narratives of 'care', to protect patriarchy.

Women's presence at protest alters and disrupts its gendered and masculinist dynamics. Men's successful feminisation of the (male) enemy relies on women being absent from the fight;[133] women's presence in the movement therefore still represents a transgression. In their work on the far right, Blee and Annette Linden found that, "In the end, the needs and ambitions of women activists never fit into right-wing extremist parties and organizations dominated by men."[134] The same might be said here. The radical-right groups explored in this book are also dominated by men—men who rhetorically assert the importance of women's rights, and gay rights, as a means of reviling Islam as oppressive, yet maintain both patriarchal and masculinist values.

The picture is, however, complex. The three radical-right leaders interviewed represent different responses to Islam, and to gender. Discourses meet at points and then separate. Women make bargains with the radical-right patriarchy to gain from it what they believe in, but also what they want and need. Fransen's leadership of BF conformed to hegemonic femininity until she challenged Golding as a misogynist engaged in domestic violence against her; her status has therefore shifted from hegemonic to pariah femininity. Waters, as a gay woman, represents a fundamental challenge to the heteronormative masculinity system of the far right, and the assertion of a new hegemonic femininity. She was unable to stop her politics being understood as a product of pariah femininity by the wider movement.

Sjoberg suggests that masculinist organisations into which women intrude must shore up their masculinities or seek alternative strategies to maintain power.[135] At EDL protests, that shoring up came at the expense of particular EDL women demonstrating pariah femininities, dismissed by men and women alike through class-based misogyny, and from whom other women distanced themselves lest they, too, be stigmatised. The EDL reflected the culture identifiable with Robinson. Responses to EDL women who adopted masculinities through engagement in behaviours men believed themselves entitled to—sexual choice and promiscuity—saw them subject to censure and disgust. When (white, working-class) women were allegedly victimised by Muslim men, the radical right mobilised around them; when they were victimised by EDL men, or engaged in behaviours understood as sexually immoral, they were stigmatised and viewed as pariahs, through an internally-directed misogyny shared with mainstream norms. This was not aimed at care for in-group women, but their class-based control and stigmatisation. The ultimately patriarchal nature of the movement requires misogyny to keep women in check.

6

ALM

SITUATING MASCULINITIES

[My brother] asked me if I would keep someone from being gay. I asked,
"Which cap am I wearing? My 'Muslim' cap or my 'British Muslim' cap?
If my Muslim cap, completely; then it's not allowed."[1]

Aisha

Introduction

The book now turns to al-Muhajiroun, the most infamous banned branch of British Islamism, and a network of Islamists loosely associated with it. My first interviewee was Anjem Choudary, the controversial group leader, whom I met near his East London home. He was ebullient as he regaled myself and my *mahram* with tales of his Twitter popularity. There was no sense of his ongoing trial at the Old Bailey, and when I thanked him for his time—some hours—and noted that he might soon have little of it, he seemed unsure of my meaning. Choudary was on form: confident and friendly, pristinely turned out and assured. Choudary has openly supported Islamic State and endorsed the Salafi jihad; he has also been associated with several individuals who have committed terror offences.[2] Police and analysts have linked Choudary with almost half of British terror plots from 2000 to 2015 (twenty-three of fifty-one),[3] and several of his followers and associates have travelled to Syria and Iraq since 2013 to join Islamic State. In July 2023 Choudary was arrested once again in connection with suspected terrorism offences.[4]

The aim of this chapter is to situate and identify masculinities within narratives participants told about pivotal moments in their lives before their association with ALM. Masculinities emerge as constructed in three ways: in geographic space, in particular a hypermasculine street culture echoing that discussed in Chapter Three; through a process of gendered meta-reflexivity that constitutes the 'identity crisis' of radicalisation literature; and in the discursive space constructed post-9/11 through the gendered securitisation of Muslims and Islam. The chapter therefore expands the understanding of identity crisis as less 'crisis', more cumulative process. Reflexivity is constant, and while there appears to be a pivotal moment for each participant, this cannot be predicted. It follows years of reflexive thinking about identity and their own assimilation. What is clear is that gender is fundamental in that process, given that participants internalise conflicting masculinity systems and conflicting normative gender frameworks. Participants judge behaviour against a masculinity system's moral and sexual norms, producing affective responses. As in Chapter Three, this means that gender and sexual norms are important in distinguishing in- from out-group. The construction of and preference for particular masculinities is also important in mobilisation to the group, where these produce an affect of 'fit'.

The next section contextualises the findings with a discussion of identity and Islam in Britain today, before introducing the reader to the participants.

Extreme Britain and Muslim masculinities

Gendered and sexed identities emerge as central to participant narratives of the path to ALM. It is useful, therefore, to reflect on the degree to which participant accounts cohere with the existing literature on Muslim identity, which is extensive and growing, and tackles themes of family, security, faith and Britishness. As Shahin

Gerami notes, Islamist—and jihadist—identities entail labelling by others; Muslim identities are produced through individual or group agency, and they are multiple, across region, time and culture.[5] Marcia Inhorn observes that Western authors have created a "toxic list" of Muslim Middle Eastern hegemonic masculinity attributes, incorporating male oppressors, marriages without love, aggression and honour. She demonstrates that the reality is diverse, despite these stereotypes.[6] One difficulty for this chapter and Chapter Seven is that my discussion of Muslim identities, as a security-oriented non-Muslim, necessarily risks contributing to stigmatising discourse in which Muslim identity is securitised.

A key concern for me in writing this book, which belongs to the security literature, has therefore been to take a nuanced and empathetic approach. I hope to avoid the pitfalls of Western Muslim masculinity studies as well as security studies, which can see Muslim men demonised,[7] with their identities only of interest because 'identity crisis' has been identified as key to radicalisation processes.[8] Muslim men, Muslim women and Muslim families have been subject in past years to policy and discourse generated in the aftermath of the War on Terror. The pernicious effects of Western government policy assumptions about Muslim masculinities during that time cast a long shadow across any scholarly attempts to engage masculinities in order to understand jihadist extremism. Muslim masculinities' construction is complex;[9] young men construct, negotiate and perform different masculinities in different contexts.[10] Yet securitisation discourses have occluded this.

Indeed, the so-called identity crisis has, since Wiktorowicz, been a fundamental explanatory factor in understanding radicalisation to jihadism. It is apparently caused by either economic, social, political or personal difficulties.[11] In his study of Muslim masculinities and radicalisation, Tufyal Choudhury suggests that this crisis occurs when previous belief systems are shown as inadequate; when Muslims are not accepted, and are forced to construct a new Muslim identity.[12] Choudhury, and other Muslim authors who conclude similarly, therefore situate 'riskiness' and insecurity not in the bodies of young Muslim men, but in British society's response to them and the insecurity that this produces.[13] British Muslim identity is widely recognised as hybrid, but Yasmin Hussain and Paul Bagguley show that little work has been done to explore what hybridity really entails. In particular, they suggest that the hybrid experience is centred on "meta-reflexivity", a term produced by Archer and related to sociological analysis of the decades that Ulrich Beck, Anthony Giddens, Scott Lash and John Urry identify as late modernity.[14] Drawing on Margaret S. Archer's interpretation of it as emergent "in situations of 'contextual discontinuity' and 'contextual incongruity' relating to the experience of migration",[15] Hussain and Bagguley argue that meta-reflexivity, for some British Muslims, can be especially heightened by "political crises" related to the War on Terror;[16] this can destabilise identities.[17]

In the UK context particularly, decades of debate around the role of religion have contributed to any instability British Muslims might perceive in Muslim identity. The Rushdie affair in the 1990s was pivotal in forcing many British Muslims into engaging with the hybridity of their identities.[18] British Muslims protested en masse in favour of banning Salman Rushdie's book *The Satanic Verses,* a politicising moment;[19] author Tariq Modood has linked this to Muslim "working-class anger and hurt pride".[20] Such events result from polarisation but can also increase it. For instance, some multiculturalism scholars have taken the contentious view that, across Western national contexts, Islam as a religion has become problematic through demands for greater public accommodation.[21] Such assertions can clearly stoke Islamophobia. However, many other authors have asserted the importance of deprivation, discrimination and rejection by white non-Muslim majorities in the foregrounding of religious identities leading to radicalisation. Additionally, Hopkins, in work on the UK, notes that mainstream discourses can racialise Muslim masculinities, framing them as failing, as nerdy or passive and, contrasted with black masculinities, as physically weak. Such discourses can therefore position Muslim masculinities as subordinate to non-Muslim black and white masculinities, and therefore in particular need of state attention.[22]

Both scholars and community activists have pointed to the Prevent counter-radicalisation strategy as unpopular, discriminatory and even racist.[23] As such, it has been important in producing discourses damaging to Muslim men and masculinities.[24] The strategy's maternalist and paternalist logics and gendered assumptions of Muslim men and masculinities as 'risky' and 'suspect' have appeared in many studies as damagingly influential in the construction of British Muslim masculinities, and British life.[25] This framing of young Muslim men ignores other ways in which masculine agency is expressed. As for other young British men, aggression is only one masculinity performance; Hopkins has noted, for instance, the importance of scholarly masculinities and academic success in achieving status for young British Muslims.[26] Yet assumptions of young men as hypermasculine factored into the broad securitisation of Muslim youth in Western countries,[27] and a punitive interest in their integration as proof of invulnerability to radicalisation.[28] Additionally, research has evidenced a globally shared perception in Muslim communities that diverse Western governments allied to the War on Terror sought to alienate Muslims from their culture, in part through projects to empower women and monitor men.[29]

Jihadist propaganda explicitly exploited alienation caused by counter-terrorism strategies and mobilised around masculinities post-9/11, on a global and a national scale. That alienation, as will be explored in this chapter, is centred on gender. In the United Kingdom, Brown has argued that Prevent reified the paternalist state as the site of hegemonic and chivalric masculinity.[30] This both feminised Muslim men, by suggesting that they required protection from jihadism, and simultaneously hypermasculinised them through emphasising their potential for radicalisation and violence.[31] This tension inevitably impacts young British Muslims, who experience a resultant instability in the term 'Muslim' itself.[32] Mairtin Mac an Ghaill and Chris Haywood argue that this instability contributes to young men's search for more stable masculine subjectivities.[33] The radicalisation literature has paid less attention to the question of young Muslim women's identity; yet young women, too, are engaged in an ongoing negotiation of identities constructed both within and outside their own community.[34] Dominant discourses dichotomise Muslim women into essentialised roles: they are victims of Muslim men; or they are the 'heart of the community', feminine pacifying influences.[35] How both to navigate and to stabilise identity is indeed a theme for both the men and the women whose narratives I explore in the findings sections of this chapter, following an introduction to the participants.

Introducing the participants: ALM network

Following the arrests of key figures in September 2014, ALM became less centralised, using a diffuse network organisation to ensure greater resilience.[36] In 2003, Bakri Mohammed suggested that the British al-Muhajiroun numbered 700.[37] Today, the group is much smaller. It is still active, but not openly so. The twelve Islamists interviewed for this book include the leader Anjem Choudary himself and eight men connected either offline or online to his network (Akash, Rifat, Adam, Zakir, Abu M., Ahmed, Anhar and Mo). It also includes three women (Saleha, Aisha and Umm M.), two of whom were linked online to Choudary (Saleha and Umm M.). Aisha was linked to ALM through offline connections. For context, I conducted another interview with Farhan, who is not an Islamist but a friend of two teenaged women who travelled to join Islamic State in Syria, and who do not appear to be directly linked to Choudary.[38] And I also spoke to Kate, the mother of another man currently in prison for terrorism offences. Neither Kate nor her son had affiliations to Choudary. Network links to Choudary for the others were evident in three ways: first, as part of his inner circle; second, as offline associates—people who 'tag along';[39] third, within an online network, which included members of Choudary's inner 'offline' circle.

Both Bakri Mohammed and Choudary have, over the past 20 years, been regarded as engines of the British Islamist scene, and within the network they have been influential leaders.[40] While some participants in this research were relative newcomers to the scene, others had been active within it since the late 1980s and early 1990s. Bakri Mohammed, along with other radical preachers Abu Qatada and Abu Hamza, was influential in consolidating a network of radical Islamism, preaching violent jihadi doctrine in a number of British mosques during this period and fomenting a followership among student groups.

The participants cannot be easily categorised into roles. Choudary, known as 'the Sheikh', is a clear leader. He is a well-known speaker, teacher, authority, scholar and one-time media spokesman. Anhar, Akash, Zakir and Mo are among his offline circle. They attended classes, recruited, set up street *Dawah* stalls to carry out 'jihad of the tongue',[41] attended trials, mobilised in support of Muslim prisoners and filled their time by studying Choudary's teachings. Mo and Zakir also produced online video materials. Ahmed was convicted in 2017 for a serious terrorist plot. His connection to ALM was via the online social media network, and additionally through a contact offline. Abu M. was linked to the network online and Adam was peripheral to the circle but also active in the online social media network. Rifat's connection was through Akash, a British Muslim in his forties whose parents are from Bangladesh; Rifat does not appear to have attended any of Choudary's meetings. Of the women, Saleha was part of Choudary's social media network and was active in 2015–16 in disseminating propaganda for Islamic State; however, she no longer supported them at the time of interview. Aisha was committed to Islamist teachings and close to one of Choudary's study circle but has not herself attended. Umm M. was the wife of a prominent Islamist scholar and therefore had high status within the online network. Farhan was not connected to Choudary.

Choudary and two other male participants began to actively engage with ALM in their twenties, one in his thirties and five became involved with the ALM network in their teens. Their ages at time of interview ranged from twenty-one to forty-three (excluding Choudary himself, who was forty-nine). Of the women, two had become active in Islamic State-supporting networks in their teens. Aisha, in her thirties, became involved in Islamism via Hizb ut-Tahrir as a university student in her late teens. Umm M., the high-status female participant, became involved in Islamism after conversion from another religion in her twenties. Initial interest and engagement was therefore mostly limited to the period of the late teens and twenties. However, the 'scene' surrounding Choudary was not uniformly young. There were several followers in their thirties, some of whom had been with Choudary for years. In terms of education, the sample was more mixed than it was for those in the radical right. Of the men, three were university-educated. Zakir, who was imprisoned for funding terrorism in 2016, had two master's degrees in natural sciences; Akash had a master's in politics. Choudary studied law to a professional level. Of the others, Adam, who was a white revert, had been excluded from school in his teens.[42] The other participants did not attend university, but did finish school, staying on to the age of eighteen.

The next sections explore masculinities and radicalisation in participant narratives. They demonstrate how masculinities are produced in the intersections of race, sex, class and faith in three spaces: geographic; cognitive and affective, through meta-reflexivity; and discursive. Participants police their own gendered identities through self-reflexion; their own communities police these identities; and hostile non-Muslim Others also police Muslim identities in shared public spaces.

Gender, masculinities and place

In the previous chapters on the radical right, exploration of pre-group masculinities revealed how masculine identity and notions of community were situated and constructed through interactions in local geographic space. ALM interviewees, by contrast, understood community as something constructed and maintained in spite of space. Neither movement supported multiculturalism as assimilation; both regarded multiculturalism with suspicion, from what Modood has characterised as a position of "cultural separatism and self-imposed segregation".[43] ALM-linked participants suggested they believed community divisions along ethnoreligious lines constituted a 'natural' human response to perceptions of difference: that shared race or faith defined community and represented a distinct habitus, with separatism therefore inevitable. However, they did not regard separatism as racism. Adam was in his twenties, white and English, with an Irish father. He is a revert to Islam and a *Wahhabi* and was, during the research, found not guilty of terrorism charges. He suggested, "it's like in Brixton you have blacks, in Southall you have Sikhs, you've got things, cultural groups, like, if you have the same language. If I see a white revert, we have a lot in common."[44]

Echoing this was Farhan, part of the same friendship group as two teenaged Muslim women who had travelled to join Islamic State in Syria. She said of their majority Asian school, "If there was a white girl ... they would get the attention and be teacher's favourite. ... most of the teachers are white, but most students are of a different race. [Q: Is that racist bias?] ... they're not racist, I just think it's human nature."[45] Saleha, a 19-year-old British Muslim of Bangladeshi heritage who had supported Islamic State and was linked to al-Muhajiroun on social media, defined her community as "my Muslim Asian community, and the wider family as well. [Q: Do you include non-Muslim friends in that?] [Laughs.] Maybe I'm the only one that does have non-Muslim friends."[46] Like the radical-right participants, Islamists, but also the wider milieu including Farhan, reflected a view of society as naturally segregating into racial or religious groups, yet not necessarily with hostility; there is a perceived essentialism to ethnic identities.

The formative masculine identities enabling entry to radical-right activism were constructed on the streets, in the intersections of race, sex and class, and through masculinity challenges with Muslim and non-Muslim men alike. To some degree ALM masculinities were produced in similar ways. Muslim masculinities scholar Hopkins has written about the importance to young Muslim men of the local environment—home, mosque, friends and leisure spaces. Echoing narratives in the radical right, area provokes loyalty. However, there is also exclusion, from *haram* culture, such as drinking, and in some degree of discrimination.[47] The local space is one in which aggression functions as one dominant masculinities discourse, but unlike in the radical right, it competes with a second—what Hopkins terms "academic nerd" masculinities.[48] Numerous authors suggest that aggression and violence, as well as participation in street culture hypermasculinities, can function as a means of projecting 'potent' masculinity; this would resemble radical-right narratives, but in this case the masculinity is directed against racist attack.[49]

Several participants nonetheless described how street culture had shaped their early identity towards aggression. The public space was a site of insecurity and of vulnerability, a place where the projection of a hypermasculine physicality was important in defending oneself

189

and projecting status. Kate has a revert son in prison for terrorism offences. Before his reversion to Islam, she remembers his failed struggle to assert a strong masculine body-image: "I feel that he felt insecure. ... The gym, the piercings, the tattoos, trying to make himself feel better. To impress."[50] The family was middle-class. Her son's expressions of masculinity, along with his adoption of Islam, were unfamiliar to his mother—an attempt to gain status, to 'impress' other men. Other participants, however, described little agency around the masculinity performances of their teenage years. Adam is a revert who adopted Islam in prison. He described the working-class area he grew up in as formative in youthful crime, but also his reversion:

> Like you look at Lee Rigby [his killers].[51] ... The media said that they used to sell drugs—why were they doing that? I used to do all that stuff too. They grew up among all that street culture—and so did I. But I chose to use Islam to leave that. And they didn't. ... All the people I used to know, I do see them, and I say hello. But I don't hang out with them. Because you are who you hang out with.[52]

A key difference here is that, unlike participants cited in Chapter Three, Adam does not understand street masculinity as a source of pride or positivity; involvement in crime and drugs was a uniform bad, which he said he engaged in out of economic necessity. While radical-right participants who had been involved in crime associated with street culture framed their later activism as a form of desistance from that crime, they still engaged in many of the same behaviours, with the same people. Echoing other findings,[53] Adam also regarded his reversion and activism as desistance. In his case, however, it enabled distance not from the place he grew up, but from his former peer group—bar one who also reverted—for whom street culture, 'postcode pride' and crime meant un-Islamic values centred on money and drugs-centred esteem.

As noted, Islamist participants—unlike radical-right interviewees —defined community not through space, but in spite of space. Akash is one of the older Islamist participants, and his interviews revealed a gradual route to Choudary's study circle. He was born in

Bangladesh, moved to the UK as a small child and has several siblings, both older and younger. He found Choudary in his late thirties, and by the time of interview had followed him for some years. Akash no longer celebrated birthdays, or watched films, as this was un-Islamic. He did, however, smoke and allowed himself (his framing) to check football scores. Sport was one of only two activities that Akash described as unifying working-class Muslim and non-Muslim young men and boys within their shared geographic space; the other was fighting. The 'warrior' and the 'sportsman' were masculine archetypes that proved hegemonic across divides of race and faith.

For a while, shared public space was important to Akash in defining himself. Before he found al-Muhajiroun, he said, he'd led a secular life, but he later felt abstracted from place as a marker of identity. He had, for example, rejected masculinities linking him to place, such as supporting a football team. Yet he told me, "I still get upset when [my old team] lose—why on earth, I don't know. ... I see the FA cup now and it's as if [it is] the reason to live and the proudest moments of some people's lives ... that is success. Success for a Muslim is only determined by your place in Heaven."[54] Football and place were literal signifiers of distinctly earthly values, which he had rejected since finding ALM.

Likewise, white revert Adam adopted a concept of community based solely around Islam after his prison reversion several years ago. He explicitly contrasted this identity with those rooted in neighbourhood and space: "For me, if someone is Muslim, whatever colour they are, I'll have more love for them—even if they are my own brother, or from my hometown in Ireland. That's how it is."[55] His definition of Muslim however, is—like that of radical-right participants Daniel and Iain—narrow, and excludes Muslims who do not conform to the most fundamentalist of creeds. It does not, therefore, include most British Muslims, but only those who adhere to Wahhabism,[56] support Shariah and oppose practices of democracy, including voting. The 'hometown' he refers to is his father's hometown in Ireland; in fact, Adam has never lived outside his inner-city area, although he told me that he spent childhood holidays in Ireland. Both Adam and Akash also used interviews to stress Islamism as an escape from immoral secularity and an immersion in a new spiritual

191

community, which freed them from the masculinity demands of their geographic community.

Previous research has found spatial location to be of minor importance in people's narratives of jihadist radicalisation.[57] This was borne out here in the sense that while participant stories suggested ALM masculinities were produced in physical space, their emphasis was on communities of faith: Islam was a choice, one they had asserted agency to pursue. This choice was rooted in affect, and feelings of inauthenticity. In contrast, radical-right participants emphasised the authenticities of their lives, both before and during activism in the group. Adam and Akash both described Islamist activism as a refuge from inauthentic masculine behaviours that had brought them into conflict with the law. Akash was an active member of Anjem Choudary's study circle and came to this more radical Islam (in his eyes, the only Islam) some 5 years before we met. Akash described a brush with the law before he followed Choudary. It was typical of the life he led in what he termed his "model British" existence: "Fisticuffs after work out on a Friday night. The magistrates said it needs to go to court ... [but] it's only what happens every Friday night."[58] Like Tommy Robinson and others in earlier chapters, Akash regarded casual violence between men as part of a particular habitus associated with other practices (Friday night drinking, for instance), and within a particular non-Muslim culture. He understood the punishment he received for this infraction as evidence that the rules, nonetheless, would not be the same for him, as a Muslim, as for other men who were not. The street in these accounts was an important site of identity formation, but one that participants resented and resisted.

Gendered difference and identity boundaries

Zakir, who went to prison for funding weapons for a relative in Syria during the period of my research, was somewhat typical. He had not always lived a devout life. In fact, he told me, he led a "fully secular" existence before he found Islam. I asked him what that meant. It meant that he "did everything", he said, with a shy smile.[59] Other interviewees also told me that they had once been entirely assimilated, with non-Muslim friends, relationships and jobs. Yet throughout, participants also described how everyday gendered encounters with secular Others as well as members of their Muslim communities, and in particular their reflections on these, served to produce specific masculinities and femininities, through which they constructed difference. These were the boundaries of in-group and out-group that Berger discusses in his definition of extremism. Participants credited such reflections as a vital step in their journeys to Islamism and ALM, or its network.

Both male and female participants linked to ALM who had hybrid identities (for instance, British–Asian) suggested that their upbringing was marked by a growing reflexivity around two separate sets of rules and practices, two separate habitus, each of which represented different gender and sexual norms, and different hegemonic masculinities. As in Chapter Three, gendered and sexual practices were an important marker of difference between in- and out-group; yet reflexivity around these differences also manifested internal tensions between simultaneously held, but conflicting, hegemonic masculinities and femininities within participants' own identities. This tension created a feeling of dis-ease, manifested through a series of participant-identified events that could be read as "microradicalisations", a term coined by Bailey to describe how an accumulation of small changes in perception influences progress towards a 'radical' identity.[60] This differs in quality and duration from the concept of 'identity crisis' in radicalisation theories.

Class is an important aspect of British immigrant discrimination and was the subject of much participant reflexion. The issue of class-based exclusion affecting British Muslims can be lost, however, in discourses centred on Islamophobia as the sole axis of discrimination.[61] Recalling accounts from radical-right participants, Akash described how, while growing up, his gendered understanding of normative values experienced in public space was fundamental in constructing a boundary between in-group and out-group, Muslims and non-Muslims. Despite sharing a 'working-class' socio-economic background, and local spaces, with non-Muslims living nearby, their gendered habitus (routines, rules and practices) was not one he recognised. His account demonstrates slippage between 'white' and non-Muslim:

As disparaging as it may sound, the uneducated working class has a different outlook to the working-class Muslim ... there was a dim view of each other's cultures. We think white men get paid Friday and are pissed up all weekend. Monday comes, he's up and at the factory and he'll slog all week and then get pissed up again. The women are the same. They drop their children off and then smoke and drink coffee all day. Go out wearing nothing at weekends. I think, "Really? What a life." I thought all this even as a kid. Having worked in restaurants you see it. ... They would come out with their girlfriends and wives, the complaining type, the babysitter looking after the children. The idea of women arguing in public, if you're having a pint. ... [Q: Was someone at home telling you this was wrong?] Nobody is telling me this. It must just be that I'm just not seeing this at home. But I'm seeing it every week [when I'm out].[62]

Akash suggests a gendered superiority to others around him, and indeed a class-based misogyny towards the non-Muslim women he sees that is later mirrored in the superiority and beliefs projected by ALM.[63] Here, Akash constructs and reifies a particular gender binary. In what Hussain and Bagguley might identify as an incongruence of the migration experience,[64] Akash contrasts working-class Muslims with "uneducated" white men and women. The important point about this incongruence is that it is gendered. Women's dress, again, as in discussion of radical-right activism, becomes a point of perceived difference, along with the use of drugs such as alcohol and nicotine, and women arguing with one another and with men in public spaces: all are conflated into a picture of a set of practices that is devoid of faith and its strictures, and therefore meaningless. Akash was alienated from this picture of assimilated behaviour, which formed a barrier between him and a perceived full integration. In this account it is not simply hegemonic masculinities that matter in establishing difference, but femininities. The behaviour of women reflects on the status of men. When women are opinionated and sexual, not chaste, respectful, modest—stereotypical passive behaviours for women—men's patriarchal power as imagined for Akash through a gender binary is reduced.

Meta-reflexivity, masculinity systems and lack of fit

As in the wider radicalisation literature, a feeling of 'not fitting' or life not feeling 'right' or 'truthful' before finding spirituality through Islamism was a common theme, and not always linked to dissonance in gendered habitus and hybrid identities. Ahmed is a British–Pakistani Muslim in his twenties who, after our final contact, was sentenced to life for his part in a bomb plot. He had already spent his early twenties in jail after attending an al-Qaeda training camp in Pakistan. In the summer of 2016, he was frequently online, where we met. In discussion of his beliefs, he suggested that his "meaningless life" had something "lacking", an "emptiness" and a "dead heart", before finding Islam. He messaged me, "life is serious we are not here to fulfil our desires. Work eat sleep mate... theres more to it."[65] It is important to jihadists to proselytise, and much of my initial interaction with participants involved their attempts to convert me. Ahmed suggested that, like him, I was a "seeker", for instance. Spiritual identities, both masculinities and femininities, and selling those identities to others mattered to participants.

Questions about my life and faith were common among participants, for whom they constituted the beginnings of *Dawah*,[66] and an attempt to convert me. However, they were also expressions of spiritual dis-ease and existential 'emptiness' before the group, a repeated theme. As Catherine Zara Raymond notes of her al-Muhajiroun research, an important motif was evident when a participant told her, "I always had this feeling that there was something wrong."[67] Mo, a black revert to Islam in his twenties, had similarly asked me, "Do you ever feel like your life is not right?" I responded, "Doesn't everybody?"[68] No, he said. Since finding Islamism, Mo had felt he was on the right path. A friend's suicide bolstered his belief: "He had everything; he even had a [trade]. But he had no connection with Allah ... Our life is a cursed life ... unless you are connected with Allah ... life will be a lie."[69] For the Islamists, spirituality was key to 'fit'; this spirituality embodied a particular masculinity system, with a repertoire of gendered practice. There will be more on this in the next chapter.

Aisha was another participant who described a particularly gendered incongruence in her life before the group. She presented a complex narrative of perceived conflict between the secular gendered habitus of her 'assimilated' life, and an imagined habitus she always felt she should inhabit. Aisha was in her thirties, and had four children she cared for alone, as her husband was in prison for terrorism offences—a charge she rejected as another example of state bias against Muslims. My question to Aisha was about the formative events and milestones she felt mattered in her path to Islamism. Her answers suggested that these events were ones in which the dissonance between her life as a young, assimilated British Muslim Bangladeshi woman and an idealised habitus based on her understanding of what constitutes a good British–Bangladeshi daughter was most pronounced.

Participant narratives resonated with other research in the field that notes a generation gap between young Islamists and their parents, against whose secularism youth push back.[70] Aisha suggested an idealised habitus dominated by Islamic gender norms. This was despite the fact that her parents did not enforce religion at home and were, in her words, "Friday and Ramadan Muslims". Her Bengali father presented a contradictory experience of assimilation; "he hated religion" and would turn off the television if it was mentioned. He owned a restaurant which sold alcohol and sent his children to a Catholic school. Yet he had also been on the *Hajj*, the pilgrimage to Mecca all Muslims should undertake in their lifetime, and by an apparently unspoken rule—the essence of habitus the eight children were, when older, not allowed to do the things non-Bengalis did, such as socialising in clubs or pubs. Aisha did this anyway, she told me, in order to gain influence with non-Muslim peers: "I had to do those things to get on. Go to clubs, have boyfriends, drink, smoke."[71] However, for her, such activities were accompanied by permanent reflexive judgment. Secular norms felt wrong; idealised Islamic norms were ever-present, exercised through constant reflexivity.

As a teenager, Aisha's father enlisted her help working behind the bar of his restaurant, where she felt conflicted about her role, as expressed in a series of 'buts':

I thought, I can't work there—because I'm wearing a scarf [*hijab*]. But when I worked, I had to take my scarf off. But then, I felt like a hypocrite—so, I couldn't say no … but then the Bengalis that work in the back think like—mixed messages. Then I felt there was a day where—I can't [work there] anymore. [Q: Did you miss it?] … a bit of me did miss it there, it was a buzz about working there—it was a laugh.[72]

For Aisha, the tension between the identity she was forging as a *hijab*-wearing young Muslim woman and her role working behind the bar presented a conflict of norms. Bar work saw her handling alcohol and not wearing a *hijab*, at the request of her father, who owned the restaurant. Other British–Bengalis also worked in the restaurant, and she felt judged by them. By her own account, Aisha lived a relatively strict but well-integrated childhood and youth. It was a rejection of the gendered norms of that assimilation, and her own uneasy feelings about this, that she identified as an important part of her later radicalisation, although 'radicalisation' is a word she rejects as politicised. In her narrative, the tension between the two sets of gendered norms focused, as it did in various participant interviews—whether with the jihadists or the radical right—on an item of women's clothing, the *hijab*, a symbol of Islamic modesty.

When the tensions inherent in her situation were too much, Aisha discontinued the bar work. This did not put a stop to her lack of clarity about which habitus she could most authentically inhabit; to which group she belonged. Aisha continued to university in the 2000s with these difficulties unresolved. She said, "I was a typical student, I would be out drinking … I would feel guilty—I knew that it was not something that I should be doing."[73] For Aisha, secular behaviour was a source of guilt, because it was not the behaviour of a proper young Muslim woman, she told me. Gendered norms were fundamental to her construction of a boundary not just between Muslim and non-Muslim (secular) communities, but between two aspects of herself: secular and assimilated, and 'Islamic'. Nobody told Aisha she should not adhere to secular norms; it was a seemingly internalised habitus (rules), which elicited an almost constant reflexivity about her actions.

Participant narratives about such tensions did not focus on exclusion, but on a 'self-exclusion' which Roy identifies with group activism.[74] In common with other radicals interviewed, Aisha was not the least integrated or poorest of British Muslims;[75] she did not feel herself to be humiliated by her daily life. She was popular, well-integrated and successful, she told me. She had, however, always believed that life should have meaning beyond secular values. Her later fundamentalism was apparently derived in part from a rejection of her self-perceived transgression of what she believed were the correct gender norms.

Bolstering the binary: feminism, patriarchy and heteronormativity

For all the Islamists interviewed, Shariah as a patriarchal institution was important. They believed that "Western feminism" was not consistent with Quranic scriptures and therefore should be rejected. Feminism as part of a repertoire of non-Muslim female behaviour produced affects of disgust and dishonour. Women's behaviour and bodies have been the focus of fundamentalist actors within Muslim communities for some years.[76] Muslim women's bodies in particular, and how Muslim men should behave towards them, have become a 'discursive arena' for boundary maintenance between Islamic and secular norms.[77] The question of feminism was therefore perhaps contentious, although some of the women participants previously wanted to be feminists. Saleha, the 19-year-old former Islamic State supporter, described how she had briefly identified as a feminist, but rejected this when the consequences meant stigma and risk:

> I was one at first [a feminist]. Then I realised it was wrong. If you want respect you have to respect yourself. Not going out on the street naked—that will not get respect and so I rejected it.[78] [Q: Did you have feminist friends?] No—if you were, you didn't say it. Like if you're a homosexual you'd just keep it to yourself. ... [Q: Why? Is being gay and feminist the same?] In school if you give any hint that you are gay, then you were bullied so badly. ... If I as a Muslim said I was into feminism, then I would have got so much hate. I would have seen my scarf pulled off my head. I'd

be called horrible names. So, I thought, I will keep it to myself.
[Q: Who would the hate come from?] Girls in my year, families,
my community, my culture. Asians. I'm not saying they're all
like this, but the majority, their mindset, their mentality, is old-
fashioned. There are also some extreme Muslims out there who
will say, "You're a slag, you're this, you're supporting British
ideology. Look at what the British have done to Muslims in the
past." ... In my community I'm seen as a respectful young lady,
and if I did that, that reputation would be diminished.[79]

Feminism and homosexuality, in this account, are both deviant:
they both jeopardise community respect, apparently built around a
heterosexual normativity. In contrast to government securitisation
discourses and far-right rhetoric, which both produce Muslim men
as hypersexualised and a threat, Saleha suggests that it is feminism and
non-Muslim women who represent the hypersexual threat. Echoing
the abuse of radical-right and underclass white women discussed
in the previous chapter, Saleha's eventual rejection of Western
feminism as a perceived form of wanton sexuality was a product of
social stigma and misogyny. Saleha indicates that anti-feminist norms
within her own (Asian Muslim) community produced two choices:
conformity or punishment, with misogynist punishments of name-
calling and scarf-pulling echoing Islamophobic hate crimes by non-
Muslims against Muslim women.[80] The result was her adoption of an
explicitly anti-feminist stance, one that later led to her support of
Islamic State.

Peers were clearly important here. Saleha's description of feminine
identity reveals that it is understood as subordinate to masculine
identity. Yet its formation has some similarity with that of masculine
identity: it is shaped through performance to peers, and liable to
challenge. The first group that she mentions in that challenge are her
immediate peers, "girls in my year". Gender norms that deviated from
binary norms compatible with understandings of Islamic scripture—
which like Christian scripture sees homosexuality as unnatural and
understands men as being created to be responsible for women and
family—were liable to be punished by men and women alike. Within
this narrative, feminism becomes an irreconcilable and fundamental

aspect of British culture, harmful to Muslims and resonating with the past and present injustices of colonialism implied by the term "British ideology". Saleha was unable to forge her own relationship with feminism, as it is mired in wider discourses positioning it as 'Other'. It was unclear whether the British ideology referred to signified Prevent, which has instrumentalised feminism to 'empower' Muslim women in ways that Muslim women have contested;[81] or if it was understood as part of a legacy of past colonialism, which broadly pre-dates feminism.

The issue of secular rights for homosexual men and women was a wider theme in participant narratives. To Saleha, both homosexuality and feminism are wrong; both challenge men's power as exercised through heterosexual, protector masculinities within patriarchal structures. Men who have sex with other men appear as feminised in interviews with participants—a disruption to traditional gender norms. Aisha also expressed concern about homosexuality in British society. She remembered discussing this with one of her brothers:

> It's because we're here, that we're in this country, in this environment, that our moral compass gets [pause]—we were having arguments about homosexuals. I said, just because [non-Muslims] allow it, it doesn't mean we have to. I said, we don't go by what they want us to think and feel ... sometimes you need to take a step out of where they are, to realise how far they are from the truth. ... [My brother] asked me if I would keep someone from being gay. I asked, "Which cap am I wearing? My 'Muslim' cap or my 'British Muslim' cap? If my Muslim cap, completely; then it's not allowed."[82]

The account was dominated by the Muslim 'we' versus the non-Muslim 'they', a constant back-and-forth referencing of in-group and out-group. While Aisha's narratives show her constantly engaged in policing of her own gendered identity, Saleha suggested that her community openly policed her, and in abusive terms. Ultimately, Saleha indicated that she conformed to this policing; it was a necessary part of belonging to a collective.

Enforcing patriarchy: policing masculinities

Previous chapters on the radical right have shown their policing of women and gender relations; this is not the sole preserve of Muslim men. Nonetheless, both scholars of masculinities and Muslim women's rights campaigners have noted policing tendencies in young Muslim men centred on the control of women, and projecting strength.[83] In my research, men discussed policing behaviours to 'help' women, enforcing norms of chastity and abstinence. These behaviours represented an internal misogyny, directed at in-group women, through claims for care and in order to exert control, echoing similar behaviour in radical-right milieus. I spoke to few Islamist women for this book, and only one in person; however, Aisha's attitude to control was interesting. She actively sought male policing, as a performance of a particular set of gendered values, contrasting with secular norms. She wanted men in her family to assert power through policing masculinities, in order to reinstate norms she feared were lost. For instance, she described a public encounter with one of her brothers at a nightclub which left her feeling ashamed. Patriarchal community norms she felt other families were abiding by, in which young women were shielded from alcohol and sexuality, but which she did not herself adhere to were not being enforced. This indicated how far her family had drifted from her internalised and idealised gender values:

> I remember being outside a club one night and seeing one of my brothers there. ... we both shouldn't really have been there. We should have said it wasn't good. Any other family, they would have said, get home! ... It's not good that we were so laidback and casual about it. He [dad] wouldn't want his daughter to be in this sort of place. The fact that we were so Western...[84]

In his work on Muslim identity, Hopkins suggests that young Muslims experience local spaces dichotomously,[85] and this is evidenced here. Aisha judged her older brother's behaviour in the public arena against what she understood as the gender norms of Bengali culture, according to which male family members should discipline female members who transgress moral strictures—for example, by going to a nightclub. This disciplinary masculinity, which is understood by Aisha as incompatible with secular norms, is presented as ultimately hegemonic. Aisha, however, demonstrated an ambivalent attitude to other aspects of patriarchy. She remembered that at home, "My mum just cooked and cleaned. … She was cooking, cleaning and [it] was just for the brothers and for dad. … I never saw mum and dad really speak to each other even. She just served him. I didn't like that."[86] Aisha judged the absence of a public patriarchal order as "not good" even as she felt ambivalence to this order at home. At home, only family can see; in public, Aisha's behaviour becomes part of a much wider gendered discourse and all that that entails, given that it is associated with being "Western". It seems impossible for personal behaviour to remain personal; it is either Bengali or Western, with all the attendant complexities and discursive baggage of colonialism.

Male participants described how they judged those around them, particularly women. In his study of Muslim masculinities, Hopkins describes such behaviours as falling within a "policing masculinity";[87] it is precisely this form of policing that Manne identifies with misogyny, given that it enforces patriarchal order.[88] Eventually this led the participants to reject secular gender values, believed to challenge both the gendered morality of an internalised and as yet dormant Islamic habitus and men's power within it. There were other ways of exercising that power against secular norms. Anhar, a young man in his twenties and an associate of Choudary, told me he gave up his job in retail due to his gradual inability to tolerate the revealing clothes of his female colleagues. Similarly, Rifat, in his thirties and part of Choudary's study and protest circle for many years, told me he was previously "well-assimilated", also with a job in retail. He was popular and a joker, he said, with "good banter" with non-Muslim colleagues. Even before he found both his faith and ALM, he was nonetheless uncomfortable with some of the firm's institutional norms, particularly regarding female dress. He described an attempt to change the behaviour of a non-Muslim female friend and colleague:

> I said, "Don't be offended, but why do you wear so much make-up?" … she said, "I want to look pretty." I said, "You could be

pretty with less make-up on." She was very [pause]—[Q: Low self-esteem?] Yeah, she had low self-esteem. As a friend, I cared about her. I said, "Take away the make-up, you are very beautiful." ... I said, "Can you just, one day, come in with no make-up to work?" She said, "No, I can't do that." I said, "At the most, wear a light lipstick and eyeliner." ... [Then] she did it! And I was like, "Oh my God, but how do you feel?" She said, "I feel all right." No—she said, "Why was I burdening myself with so much make-up??"This was actually the period where I wasn't practising. [Pause.] I believed everything from day one really.[89]

Here, Rifat effectively polices secular norms through women's bodies: in particular, through his apparent attempts to desexualise his colleague. Heavy make-up becomes synonymous with an open display of sexuality and an apparent lack of modesty that challenged him.

Expressions of misogyny have been a concern in British society for some time. In March 2022 the government spearheaded the Enough campaign in television adverts and on billboards to change some (young) men's harmful attitudes towards women.[90] In 2023, the Welsh government launched the anti-misogyny 'Sound' campaign, and in London Mayor Sadiq Khan produced the new 'Maaate' campaign with the same aim.[91] Women campaigners in Muslim communities have also discussed and worked on these issues for years, and British Muslim women's rights activist and former Commissioner for Countering Extremism Sara Khan has highlighted the links between misogyny and extremism.[92] In specific research on British Muslim identity construction, Claire Dwyer has documented the experiences of some Muslim women, and the ways in which young Muslim men have attempted to reinforce gender relations through policing women in order to maintain their own identities.[93] In other research, Hopkins has found that British Muslim men map the lived experiences of their dichotomous hybrid masculine identities onto local space, and onto women within that space.[94]

It is hard, though, to know Rifat's motives, beyond his own narrative in which care and friendship were central. I do not want to disregard the scholarship on the production of British Muslim men's masculinities; however, nor do I want to assume that Rifat's masculinity journey is primarily to do with his Muslim identity, rather than his journey as a British man. He told the story in response to my question about why he became involved with ALM, and how he came to the group. He emphasised the high level of continuity between the gendered beliefs he said he had held before the group and those he held once in the group, where these beliefs were mobilised towards the collective identity of ALM. Rifat used this incident to emphasise to me that from "day one" the norms of ALM, within which women wear the *niqab* and a particular form of female modesty is valued, were instinctive to him. He also saw it as his role—in fulfilment of what it means to be a man—to impose his sexual norms on others through effectively policing their behaviour. He did this because he cared, he said, but also because he believed that moral ethics were absent from secular life, yet needed. He reflected, "I understand why [non-Muslims in his home-town] don't like us because of the rhetoric we've pushed. ... they can't stand women covering their faces. Many people say it to me."[95] Still, he continued to police women's behaviour, particularly their dress, in an attempt to alter local norms, he told me.

Similarly, white revert Adam suggested that Islamism made sense to him as it was representative of a 'natural' set of gender norms he already believed in:

> [Islam teaches that] if you are a woman alone with a man in a room ... that's not right. ... If a man and woman are alone in a room that woman has to be his wife! It shouldn't be allowed. That's what is taught, even in Christianity. ... I don't know really—I just thought, it makes sense.[96]

All of the participants agreed with this. Yet none of the male participants, except Choudary, insisted that I meet them with a *mahram*. Mo, Adam, Rifat, Zakir, Akash and Anhar were all apparently happy to speak to me unaccompanied, in public spaces.

Islamophobia, masculinity challenges and post-colonial discourse

So far, the chapter has considered how participants experienced their own (Muslim) communities, and how their own reflexivity was instrumental in producing particular gendered behaviours as a mark of group membership. These included policing masculinities and femininities, protector and disciplinary masculinities and an understanding of any behaviours that threaten male power as immoral: expressions of female sexuality such as clothing described as revealing, make-up viewed as excessive or the support of feminism, for example. Few participants explicitly referenced Islamophobia, racism or global events, and yet they were ever-present in their narratives. In his discussion of Muslim masculinities, Gerami notes that the hegemony of white heterosexual masculinity forces global masculinities into a secondary and subordinate position. This is a familiar pattern: colonial powers have always threatened local masculinities.[97] Echoing this in their account of reflexive ethnicities, Hussain and Bagguley link meta-reflexivity to:

> [global political crisis events] promoting or requiring reflexivity about ethnicity, nationhood and citizenship. Moments of 'identity crisis' are when people are forced to think about who they are, and where they belong. Processes or events experienced 'objectively' generate crisis effects if they cannot be handled without 'changing the rules of the game'.[98]

Post-9/11, such crisis events frequently involve displays of Western colonial power and hegemonic masculinity. Singular events become understood within a particular—gendered—political context and wider discourse. For instance, Saleha understands her feminism within a narrative of "British ideology". As such, the power of singular events is amplified within a transnational discourse of contestation and challenge. However, instead of an 'identity crisis', singular, participants describe a series of microradicalisations, plural, centred on tension around gender and sexual identity and gendered norms. The 'rules of the game' are represented by Bourdieu's habitus, and the switch to support one favoured habitus over another.

Participants also described how public interactions with Islamophobic non-Muslim Others impacted the dynamic of radicalisation. Some described situations of reciprocal tension, hostility and fear, and encounters that enabled the reproduction and reification of norms reducing Muslim women's agency and promoting Muslim men's power through their apparent protection of women and children from non-Muslim men. For Saleha, experiences with non-Muslim men in her local area, which has a large Muslim demographic, were marked by fear. This was heightened for her by her decision to become a '*niqabi*'—that is, to wear the *niqab* (face veil):

> There's a lot of repeated attacks on *niqabis* ... I'm sometimes very scared, even if it's like verbal abuse. I've had that, [I've] never [actually] been attacked. But I'm still affected by it. Even my sister with her baby, she has been abused, like verbal abuse, like "Oh, you're a terrorist", and like, kicking the pushchair.[99]

Such experiences led her older brothers to restrict her movements, justifying this as being for her own good. The gendered norms of public space and encounters with hostile men and masculinities within it constructed that space for Saleha as a threat, and her place within it as both subordinate and a disruption to its norms. This in turn enabled further subordination within her own home, as male family members imposed their authority to keep her 'safe' by restricting her access to public spaces. Saleha cited these dual subordinations within the family (private) and shared (public) sphere as reasons she felt initially empowered by association with Islamic State, who she believed promised the fulfilment of agency as a Muslim woman. Here one instance of misogyny provokes a series of misogynist subordinations.

In what could be read as an assertion of agency, participants themselves did not explicitly suggest that radicalisation was a response to racism preventing them from adequately assimilating, but a rejection of their actual assimilation and the unacceptable moral compromise they believed that entailed, particularly concerning gender and sexual norms. The greatest challenge participants described was not abuse or Islamophobia, although these were hard; it was the choice between the secular doxa—beliefs—and Islamic habitus, which suggest completely different gender norms. Ideally, Aisha told me, she would like to avoid this tension by living abroad, in a Muslim country.

Perhaps Aisha and others did not want to detail to me, a white non-Muslim, the impact that racism and discrimination had had on them and their beliefs. Yet in both of my meetings with Aisha, which lasted some hours, she did not herself explicitly cite racist experiences as factors in her Islamism, except as the unfortunate background noise of British Muslim life. For example, Aisha also told me she found it hard to wear her *niqab* in public anywhere but London, because she fears Islamophobia in her less diverse hometown. However, Islamophobia was so commonplace that Aisha and other participants narrated it almost as an aside. Racism was not what Aisha said she rebelled against; her Islamism challenged assimilation into an immoral society, and the values which that society represented. Others echoed her. All except white revert Adam had experienced racism or Islamophobia, although "not to the level our parents did",[100] as Rifat told me. All saw this as an unpleasant and inevitable, yet ultimately manageable, aspect of British life for British–Asian Muslims.

This surprised me. Grievances and discrimination are an important part of the radicalisation literature.[101] Participants regarded racism as intrinsic to British public and institutional life and, in particular, state responses to Islam and Muslims. Ahmed, who I noted had already spent time in prison after training with al-Qaeda, messaged me about "the racism from prison officers".[102] Yet while racism mattered in their lives, participants did not explicitly implicate it in the microradicalisations that form this chapter. What Rifat, Mo, Akash, Zakir, Saleha and Aisha described was not how racism prevented them from adequately assimilating, but how a constant reflexivity saw them reject their actual assimilation because of the moral and gendered compromises that they believed came with it.

Race cannot be ignored in the processes and experiences that shaped later participant activism, given that scholarship suggests masculine subjectivities post-9/11 are both highly securitised and rendered unstable via contradictory discourses.[103] ALM participants were mostly people of colour. Mo, a black revert, born in the UK, had Jamaican grandparents; and Kate's son, in prison for terrorism, is a mixed-race man, half white British and half North African. Seven of the male participants were of South Asian heritage, and all of the women. Anjem Choudary, Ahmed and Abu M. were born in the UK to parents of South Asian origin. Anhar did not reveal his heritage in the one interview he gave. Akash, Zakir and Rifat were all born in Bangladesh, moving to the UK as small children and with little or no memory of the early years abroad. However, their Bengali identity had deep roots, they suggested, and was important in recognising subaltern masculinities, successfully engaged in post-colonial resistance. Akash, in his forties, remembered his father's stories of political activism in fighting for the liberation of Bangladesh from Pakistan in 1971. He suggested:

> I would describe myself now as a 'third-world boy'. That means that it's very important that my children see how the other half lives. The example I give is, if there's a football match between an African country or Latin American country or Jamaican, and a European country, then I always support the third-world country. [Q: You didn't feel British?] Before I did, yeah–but now I don't.[104]

The 'before' period ended when Akash joined Choudary's study group aged thirty-nine and became ideologically committed to the cause of Shariah for the UK. It was at this point that he adopted a masculinity he suggested was subordinated—"third-world". However, Akash also referenced the far earlier Rushdie affair, which was a turning point for British Muslim identity.[105] Anthias and Yuval-Davis describe its effects as "a process of racialization that especially relates to Muslims".[106] With their experience formerly defined as a dichotomy between British or Asian identities, after Rushdie the question for young British Asians was whether they were Muslim or not. Akash attended rallies aged fourteen or fifteen, with friends from school. He remembered, "Definitely after the Salman Rushdie incident, people were unified around that. … it was something that brought Muslims together on platforms—this kind of slur." For other participants, the relationship with a second Asian country was strong; however, it was unclear to what degree this impacted feelings of Britishness. Few participants chose to discuss this and although I pursued the theme, I did not press. In some instances, participants described what I framed as racism in other terms. In one account, Akash, for example, emphasised the casual violence in what he regarded as a milestone incident on his path to ALM; I, meanwhile, understood the incident he narrated as a racist attack and a masculinity challenge. He described being attacked by a work colleague during the period of the war in Iraq:

> I got assaulted by a [colleague] on a drinks night out. . . . And after this happened, he still worked with me. I said, "Suspend him, it's not right." But they didn't. Mentally I must have thought—it wasn't the real me. Then I made the decision to get a girl from back home. I got married then in 2003, when I was twenty-nine, thirty. Which is quite old for a Bangladeshi.[107]

Feelings of injustice at the outcome of this incident mirror some of Daniel's feelings about being attacked in Chapter Three. Akash had an expectation of protection at work, and for his employers to condemn racist abuse from a colleague, whether in the office or in a social situation associated with work. However, they did not support him. In effect, his social mobility was challenged, a factor that Tufyal Choudhury considers vital in progression to groups including ALM.[108] Considering hybrid identity, Christian Karner has observed that "culture becomes ethnicity when – in the context of rapid and drastic changes and their far-reaching effects – social actors begin to reflect on what they used to think and do".[109] This observation perhaps has relevance to the factors influencing the marriage decision Akash made. This was an identity choice based on an episode of cultural dis-ease, linked to an international event perceived as colonialist intervention and contextualised by racism— and a history of similar episodes. Akash apparently ceded to both a situation and a particular masculine subjectivity he had previously resisted: traditional Bengali husband, in an arranged marriage with an educated woman from Bangladesh. This represented a pivot in his own identity, and his sexual and gendered behaviour. However, it was not a 'new identity'; he had lived in its shadow all his life. Nor was his reflexivity related to crisis. It was one in an ongoing series of microradicalisations. He could offer no explanation, nor could I see one, for why particular moments mattered more than others in leading him to ALM.

Here the concept of scale is important. Sallie A. Marston suggests that scale, whether local, global or national, is constructed and produced in the tensions between structural forces and the practices of people. It is therefore always open to negotiation and transformation.[110] The account above shows Akash reframing the assault by a colleague according to a new scale. Rifat described a similarly transformative experience. He told me that his further exploration of Islam evolved after 9/11 and questions about the attack from non-Muslim colleagues. He suggested that these conversations arose in part because he was assimilated. However, there is clearly a fine line in his story between questions derived from curiosity and racism:

> A lot of my colleagues—non-Muslim colleagues—asked questions I didn't have the answers to. [Q: Did you feel they were blaming you?] Some blaming, and some blaming the faith, and some had been working with me for 2 years plus, and they knew the person I was, or am—I'm a joker, I don't take things too seriously. They're like, "We're not pointing fingers at you, but what about your faith? Is it ok for your faith to say things like 9/11 is legitimate?" ... so, I said, "Look, don't think that the issue of retaliation and insurgency and jihad—yes, that—is not mentioned in the Quran. Islam covers everything."[111]

Non-Muslims holding one Muslim colleague accountable for the events of 9/11, or expecting them to provide an explanation for it, does constitute Islamophobia. In this account, colleagues effectively use the device of 'not blaming' to blame. Rifat is forced into a position where he is Othered and must defend or justify the most extreme acts of an Islamist group, which he apparently does.

As discussed in Chapter One, the global conflict of the post-9/11 landscape represented for feminist scholars 'a manly moment' in international relations:[112] a time in which masculinity challenges took place on the global stage and between states and male leaders. Western media was infused with Orientalist discourse, and military intervention in Afghanistan was justified through reference to women's rights and the paternalist oppression of Islam.[113] Global masculinity challenges were also scaled down, as evident in interpersonal relationships. On a personal level, participants contextualised both altercations and robust discussion with colleagues within the context of global politics. They later became active in local manifestations of that politics. The international political space is a site for the production of masculinities.[114] The global hypermasculinity of the international arena is produced here in men's interactions, one on one.

Participants could have framed these challenges as Islamophobic, given that they apparently held individual Muslims accountable for a whole faith. However, they chose not to. Rifat recalled his defence of jihad as formative in his own journey to ALM. It was an 'identity crisis', perhaps, but one of many along his path. While a person of any ethnicity and background can support Islamist ideology, the experiences of this very small sample support the suggestion from authors such as Farhad Khosrokhavar or Wiktorowicz that racism and discrimination do factor into radicalisation.[115] ALM leaders, too, have emphasised the importance of racism and discrimination in recruitment.[116] However, it is important to note that, as in interviews with Kenney and others,[117] participants did not emphasise this themselves, and indeed appeared to regard my questions about the role of racism as a failure to listen; another attempt by a non-Muslim white person to position white people, once again, at the centre of their stories.

Summary

This chapter has explored how masculinities and femininities later mobilised towards ALM activism are produced in three sites: public space (external); a meta-reflexivity that is both cognitive and affective, in which participants subject their assimilation to a gendered critique (internal); and a third space necessitated by both of these, a discursive gendered space in which global understandings of gender, Britishness and Islam are reconstituted in everyday interactions. As with the radical-right participants in Chapter Three, gender and sexual norms were important in determining in- and out-groups, Muslim and non-Muslim, the first part of Berger's extremism definition. Two gendered masculinity systems—idealised Islamic, and British secular—were incorporated into identity, and appeared to compete for dominance. What is important here is that diverse masculinities, and masculinity systems, were simultaneously experienced. Writing on inner-city masculinities construction, Louise Archer and Hiromi Yamashita note that young men "did not construct 'fixed' or consistent masculinities; they shifted between alternative identity positions. In particular, the young men talked about trying to 'leave' some identities."[118] This finding is repeated here. The simultaneous experience of two habitus, two contradictory masculinity systems, produced an ongoing reflexivity through which participants policed their own behaviours, but also the behaviours of those around them.

Some of the policing of women by men was framed as care, yet is consistent with Manne's definition of misogyny. Misogyny in this chapter has had different expressions, as in the radical right. Care and control are exerted towards in-group women, who suggest that this is both resisted and wanted. What is more, this gender binary of protector/protected feels like a 'fit'. Internal misogyny is enabled by external misogynies, from out-group men; a kicked pushchair or racial slur are examples of wider misogyny situated in transnational discourses of Islamophobia. Gendered discourse around women's rights is viewed as problematic, and participants oppose gender equality and feminism, showing misogyny in their narratives towards out-group non-Muslim women. None of the expressions of misogyny is isolated; each is evident in wider communities, groups and discourses.

Gender and sexual norms are central here. Prior to finding ALM or its network, participants described struggling to resolve tensions between the routines and practices of two simultaneously internalised gendered habitus—Islamo-cultural and 'British'—with each masculinity system a particular rendering of patriarchy, yet each endowing different masculinities with different powers. Participants suggested that conflicting sexual and gender norms, over, for instance, feminism or homosexuality, were often at the root of the tension. Islamo-cultural masculinity systems took precedence.

Here not one but numerous masculinities in combination are hegemonic: heterosexual, hypermasculine, spiritual, abstemious, resistive, paternalist, protective/chivalric, policing in order to maintain patriarchy. Within this system, there are complementary femininities: chaste, modest, protected, covered, anti-feminist. The gendered ways participants continually engaged with their communities of origin (both of space and of faith), and associated masculinity systems, are key to understanding their later adherence to extreme collectives. This chapter therefore diverges from the current understanding of radicalisation processes in one significant way: while much of the literature emphasises the inability of Islamists to integrate due to external factors, participant narratives focus on their own internal rejection of assimilation, because of the inauthenticity of the manhood or womanhood acts that it produces.[119] This echoes Roy, who has noted that young radicals have no wish to integrate;[120] however, this assertation fails to encapsulate the complex gendered experience behind that wish.

This chapter therefore builds on the radicalisation literature and Wiktorowicz's so-called 'identity crisis'. Although Kenney notes the importance of identity crisis to ALM, he offers no account of its mechanisms.[121] By contrast, this chapter enhances accounts of pathways to ALM by other authors, through inclusion of gender. There is no transformational moment, no sudden embrace of religion, as Roy asserts.[122] The chapter clearly resonates with the established concept of the 'identity crisis'; yet here, gender is the salient aspect of identity. However, this is not a 'masculinity crisis' as such, because it is both men and women who are engaged in reconciling competing sets of norms—moral, sexual—in a constantly reflexive process, also engaging feminities.

Race and gender are intertwined in these narratives,[123] as lived in local spaces. Gendered identities are, as with the radical right, created in the intersections of race and sex in public space. Participants link personal choices to wider political and racialised discourses in which gendered decision-making is understood as aligning either with Islam or against it. The stakes of personal decisions—going out to a nightclub, becoming a feminist—are collectivised and read according to global scripts produced both before and after 9/11 in which gendered practices become symbolic of colonial projects, or post-colonial practices. Throughout, participants emphasise their agency, and frame their activism accordingly. While racism and Islamophobia are factors in the journeys taken, participants minimise these. Participants minimise the importance of non-Muslim Others in their narratives. To some degree, local space appears as a site for the constitution of masculine 'street' identities, with the performance of aggressive hypermasculinities necessitated to acquire status in working-class areas for both radical-right and Islamist participants. Success in fighting is one of the few gendered practices that is a hegemonic masculinity across the two movements.

From this chapter, situating masculinities, Chapter Seven moves on to consider how these masculinities are mobilised within ALM and its network.

7

ALM
MOBILISING MASCULINITIES

Introduction

It is May 2017. I meet Rifat, a long-term member of ALM, and we spend some time discussing how he joined the group, and why he would never leave it. In the car back to Rifat's house we discuss Anjem Choudary. Rifat wants to know what I made of our meeting, some months earlier. I can see why people like him, I say. He's funny, charismatic. Generous with his time. But—he has something of the Citizen Khans about him? Rifat asks what I mean. He's never watched *Citizen Khan*, the television comedy about the hapless Muslim community leader. You know, I say, like, he was telling my *mahram*, a female friend who had never even heard of him, how many Twitter followers he has, how 'they all know him' in East London where he lives. They all like him; they all shake his hand. He just has—I risk it—quite a big ego? Rifat protests. Not at all—Choudary has no ego, he says, and that is why he has stuck with him, despite all the hardships. What is so appealing about Anjem is that he is "totally uncompromising", adhering steadfastly to his principles. Now that he is in prison for his beliefs, there is nobody like him left, Rifat tells me.

215

This chapter explores the mobilisation of the masculinities emergent in the last chapter in the ideology and activism of the Islamist participants. It sets out what the ALM participants believe, with a focus on their understanding of doctrine, and how this positions them in relation to women, to gender and to jihad. While radical-right participants deemphasised adherence to any explicit 'ideology', ideology has an important status within ALM and the network. There is far more coherence around a particular gendered ideological position among both ALM and its network than there is for the radical-right participants, and ideological knowledge endows status. It is not just reading that endows learning, however; as Kenney notes, "'companionship' with more experienced activists" is a "'learning process' that never ends".[1] This learning process is an induction into a particular gendered outlook, entailing the acceptance and propagation of explicitly gendered norms, and, as will be examined, it constitutes a particular kind of masculinity project.

This chapter considers the three different sites of the production of masculinities explored in Chapter Six: the street, the cognitive and affective space of the meta-reflexive process, and the discursive space emerging from the problematisation and securitisation of Islam following 9/11. In this chapter, I do not discuss protest, as the protest scene was curtailed. However, I did attend *Dawah* stalls manned by activists, although I saw no women on stalls. It should also be noted that, as outlined in Chapter Two, due to the criminalisation of support for Islamic State (IS), conversations about ideology were limited, in terms of both the questions I was able to ask while maintaining trust and the answers activists gave. It was difficult to discuss participant belief, because of the threat of prosecution for support of Islamic State. However, four of the men I talked to were jailed during the research period, for a plot in support of Islamic State (Ahmed), activities to support Islamic State (Choudary), breach of an ASBO (Mo) and funding terrorism (Zakir). Adam was charged with downloading Islamic State and bomb-making materials and found not guilty. Rifat, Mo, Anhar and Akash belonged to Choudary's inner circle and could therefore reasonably be assumed to share his philosophy. Meanwhile, Abu M.

and Saleha were once active Islamic State supporters online. Islamic State was supported by many in the wider transnational online network to which participants belonged, and many also engaged in (legal) online discussion of issues surrounding aspects of Islamic State ideology. The participants were all interested in Syria, Islamic State and Western engagement in the situation, whether they expressed support for any specific group or not.

Jihadist masculinities

Before moving to the findings, this chapter considers some of the background literature on jihadist masculinities. In past years, and in particular since the rise of so-called Islamic State, there has been greater public and academic interest in this topic. The timeliness of questions about jihadist masculinities was self-evident. IS propaganda exhorted 'real men' to fight, accompanied by images of what these real men should look like: fighters clad in combat fatigues and *keffiyeh* scarves which cover the face, on horseback or in jeeps, carrying weapons and IS flags. Such hypermasculine imagery is important in establishing an ideal and a norm of violence and warriors as hegemonic.[2] There is nothing new in this. Militaries of diverse ideologies have long relied on projecting themselves as "bastions" for 'real men',[3] and the "soldier hero" is perhaps the most "durable form of idealised masculinity".[4] Writer on masculinities John Stoltenberg explains that the "delusion of 'real manhood'" is far-reaching, and has long compelled men to "acts that violate and subjugate others".[5]

How is such masculinity constructed? Connell amended her original conceptualisation of masculinities as framed within national boundaries; Connell and Messerschmidt later note "... the geography of masculinities, emphasizing the interplay among local, regional, and global levels."[6] Jihadist masculinities have indeed been forged across decades, continents and conflicts, with different cultural influences.[7] Specific studies, such as Hegghammer's, identify multiple masculinities in jihadi culture: scholarly, emotional and weeping, and the warrior.[8] In her book *Gender-Based Explosions*, Maleeha Aslam explores how different layers of local and regional masculinities, rooted in patriarchal values, are expressed in jihadism.[9]

A significant body of research follows Aslam in suggesting that jihadist masculinity is composite. It is constructed from the post-colonial, and is often situated in place, the regional and the tribal. For instance, Duriesmith and Ismail's work on Indonesian jihadist fighters reveals the complex identities at play: ethnicity, nationality and faith are amongst the many masculine identities mobilised into violence, and employed in justification thereof.[10] This was the goal of al-Qaeda and, Messerschmidt and Rohde suggest, Osama bin Laden's key aim: to unite diverse masculinities in Muslim men worldwide in service of jihad. Bin Laden's propaganda constructed the jihadist as a global and hegemonic masculinity.[11] The central idea of jihadism is almost the opposite of nationalism; jihadism ultimately transcends space and borders. Jihadist masculinities are situated in a collective spiritual community, not a spatial one.

There has been much scholarly debate about the role of ideology and religion in radicalisation processes, as discussed in Chapter One. In his work on radicalisation, Tufyal Choudhury suggests that men use Islam to rebuild an identity towards jihad.[12] However much Islam might mask other issues, jihadists repeatedly justify their fight through reference to Islam, jihad and the Quran. Quranic literalism can be traced back to early Islam.[13] Historic leaders such as Muhammad Ibn Abd al-Wahhab, influenced by the mediaeval Islamic scholar Ibn Taymiyyah, encouraged a literalist interpretation of the Quran and a return to the values and practices of the time of the Prophet, without innovation (*bidah*).[14] These ideas were later reproduced in the post-colonial movements of the twentieth-century Middle East. In the 1970s, the Iranian revolution contributed to the dominance of Islamist masculinities as hegemonic within certain militant groups and cultures across the region. It was informed by two narratives: jihad and martyrdom (*shahada*).[15] These relied on the earlier work of twentieth-century Islamists, including Hassan al-Banna, Sayyid Abul A'la al-Maududi and Sayyid Qutb, author of the core Islamist text *Milestones*. Qutb constructed his philosophy from the content of the Quran, but drew his ideology from two other sources: Islamic societies, which he regarded as facing decline; and secular society, towards which the new proactive jihad was directed as moral antidote.[16] The jihadist, therefore, might draw on the "Islamic imaginary", but also cultivates a "modern aesthetic", given that they remain of their time.[17]

Qutb's Islamism represents one masculinity system, one set of gendered and sexual norms, pitted against another. Qutb emphasises concepts in the Quran and Islamic society he fears are being lost, noting widespread *jahiliyyah*—the ignorance of God's supremacy and the dominance of man-made laws. In response, he constructs a muscular ideology around Islamic opposition to the 'backward' secular sphere and its nationalism. His revolutionary movement envisages the creation of Islamic states embodying Islamic values constructed around proscriptive ideas about gender, sex and morality. Qutb emphasises the contrasting roles of men and women—a gender binary—as central to Quranic teaching, and therefore his new political philosophy. A binary differentiation between sexes and an adherence to Islamic social norms concerning conduct and appearance are for him the basis of Islamic morality and what distinguishes Islamic civilisation from the 'backward' *jahiliyyah* of secular society. For Qutb, the pursuit of a pure Islam is centred on naturalising male and female roles as God-given. Qutb writes of "degenerate", "man-made" (secular) society, and of his brand of Islam as "harmonious with human nature".[18]

To be a warrior—and there is much emphasis on 'warriors', not soldiers, in jihadist propaganda, with all the symbolic weight of just masculinity that this entails—knowledge and the right intent are vitally important in legitimising violence.[19] War without faith is not jihad, it is brutality. Religiosity is a means to righteousness, and therefore to respect.[20] The only law to be followed is Shariah; "anything else is mere emotionalism and impulsiveness", characteristics Qutb notes are central to the sexual immorality of the West.[21] His depiction of secularism is one of moral decline,[22] threatening not only the West but the Islamic practices of the Middle East and Islamic societies.[23] For Qutb, the goal is simple and corrective—namely, "Jihaad in Islam … simply a name for striving to make this system of life dominant in the world."[24] This new movement was not just about belief, but about belief supporting action in furtherance of a particular masculinity system. Indeed, from Sheikh Abdullah Yusuf Azzam's call for fighters to unite in Afghanistan to wage jihad as an individual obligation to

Osama bin Laden's veneration of martyrdom, Abu Muhammad al-Maqdisi's influence on al-Qaeda in Iraq and Abu Bakr al-Baghdadi's focus on the growth of a functioning Islamic State,[25] Islamism, and the Salafi jihadism which fights for it, has evolved around a highly militarised, codified and explicitly gendered vision of Islam as a masculinity system.[26] Hegemonic masculinity, centred on the necessity of fighting, is complemented by emphasised femininities, with women in domestic roles supporting and enabling this.

Women and jihad

The jihadist is positioned as the male warrior–protector, in service of a feminised *Ummah*, the global Islamic community. Jihadists both protect their community from the secularism and militarism of the West and, in the right circumstances, take Islam to it. Women constitute part of the collective jihad but may not fight, except in exceptional circumstances of defensive jihad.[27] Jihadist masculinity centres on the collective, with martyrdom for the cause rooted in understandings of altruism.[28] Self-sacrifice is framed as the ultimate hegemonic masculinity: the erasure of the male body—women are not permitted to fight or carry out suicide attacks, although some have, even with the blessing of male leaders—in order to protect an imagined global populace, as well as a material local one.[29] The role of women is to support men through an emphasised femininity that is anything but inactive, given that it encompasses financing, spying, recruiting and propagandising; absent, however, is the role of fighter–warrior.[30] The binary separation of men and women was intrinsic to the jihadist masculine standard set through bin Laden and, later, IS to unite Muslim men around a jihad, legitimised across the artificial borders of nation states.[31]

Women are vitally important to jihad, and the appeal to women to join Islamic State was central to the IS project: without the family, there could be no state.[32] The jihadist lifestyle is, as Brown has noted, often one in which family life is ignored.[33] Yet family is central to Islamic values and forms a contrast with non-Muslim practice, duties and responsibilities.[34] It was, therefore, a useful recruitment point for jihadist groups such as IS. Aslam notes that women are neither passive nor without power in Islam; mothers have a central social status, and Heaven is said to "lie beneath a mother's feet".[35] Jihadist groups have exploited family roles accordingly. As much as it mobilised propaganda focused on war, Islamic State built its identity on a principle of family and fatherhood—as much as motherhood— as central to the state project. However, Aslam notes that jihadists must twist the meanings of texts to reach their violent position. What is more, the gender binary that legitimises this violence through the relative position and status of the masculine and feminine in the Quran is far more complex, she asserts.[36]

Jihadist ideological inconsistencies around gender do not mean that women cannot exercise agency through hegemonic femininities in jihadist groups. Islamic State women, for instance, both enabled and policed strict gendered norms prohibiting particular forms of female behaviour.[37] Online, women have collectively censured other women for transgressions including use of photographs showing their hair in social media profiles, or men for failing to travel to Islamic State territory to fight jihad. There is also evidence of women's enthusiastic participation in the all-female Islamic State *al-Khansaa* Brigade, a women's police force which became notorious for brutality against women infringing jihadi norms.[38] A gendered approach to radicalisation considering individual responses to structural inequalities, and their effects in further constituting these, is important. It enables scholars to outline the mechanisms by which women, particularly young women experiencing Islamophobia and marginalisation in the West, can be drawn towards ideologies in which hypermasculinities of warriordom and violence have high status and women's support of these are read as empowerment.

The chapter now moves to the findings. Here it is clear that the masculinities and femininities explored evidence the importance of faith, but also the inescapability of modern norms; this is seen in the mobilisation of street masculinities, and both feminist and anti-feminist arguments in furtherance of ideology. What is also clear is the importance of mutually supportive and coexistent masculinities: the violent masculinity of the jihadist fighter, for instance, is reliant for its validity on the learning masculinity of the Islamic scholar. The findings section begins with consideration of the role of street masculinities, including policing masculinities, in recruitment to and activism for the group.

Street masculinities, redemption and recruitment

Street outreach is an important part of recruitment to al-Muhajiroun and one in which Choudary, Akash, Mo, Anhar and Rifat have all been actively engaged. *Dawah* activities are generally gender-segregated, with separate men's and women's groups. *Dawah* continued during my research, despite some legal restrictions on activity and loss of ALM members to prison or to ASBOs. I witnessed followers assemble stall materials, leaflets and speaker and PA equipment, in order to engage with passers-by. They answered questions, asked questions, discussed Islam and preached. The street was an important outreach space. Although *Dawah* was segregated, I witnessed men engaging women passers-by, with leaflets specifically targeting them. Participants followed a particular—learned—recruitment strategy. Akash told me that ALM classes offered specific instruction on how to engage young people in conversation and educate them on the ALM brand. He showed me a folder with notes and materials from a recruitment class he attended. The strategy was to become a figure of absolute male authority to Muslim-heritage men by demonstrating mastery of Islam, learning being an important aspect of jihadist hegemonic masculinity:

> I went last week to a class, and they said... [He gets out an A4 booklet and reads.] It was on the importance of *Dawah* ... the different types of people there are and how to give *Dawah* to them. There is, for example, such a thing as a 'non-practising Muslim'. Someone with a Muslim name who doesn't worship. They're the best to convert. Also, [topics are] current affairs, the government mood, to capitalise on that. Or if someone has just passed away... [Q: Well, that sounds like you're taking advantage of someone very vulnerable.] Because someone is vulnerable then? Well, yes, they are. ... They will be questioning, "What will happen to me after I die?" ... The most difficult ones [to recruit] are the ones who are already practising Muslims, who

belong to a sect already ... because he has a Sheikh that he refers back to.[39]

Through engagement with topical issues and current affairs ALM sought explicitly to situate their ideology within the discursive space generated post-9/11, in which masculine identity was destabilised through decades of Orientalist discourse and gendered securitisation practices.

From street *Dawah*, Akash told me, the next stage was to relocate conversation from the public space to the more private space of the mosque. This strategy worked successfully some years ago on Rifat. Although already interested in Palestine, Rifat was not mobilised to join ALM until he encountered street *Dawah* that reframed conflict between Israelis and Palestinians as something he could personally counter. The gender-segregated nature of *Dawah* was successful in presenting a strong male front; he was sold the group as a "brotherhood", he said, which both motivated and empowered him. Rifat's dis-ease, outlined in the previous chapter, was resolved through the stable masculine subjectivity he found in the group. He soon began to attend a mosque frequented by Omar Bakri Mohammed, and has been part of Choudary's circle ever since. Rifat described his encounter with street *Dawah* as a milestone on his journey.

The new ALM brotherhood also enabled better relations for Rifat with his actual older brother, an important role model. Rifat said that his brother was pleased when he first found a more pious Islam:

He supported it because he didn't want me to be—there were a lot of bad influences around us—like drug dealing and gangs. Family friends—like, you know, a lot of people that were addicted to gambling and petty crime. ... My brother was worried that I may get involved in that. ... So, when I started to practice and go to prayers, he was relieved. ... he was proud of me.[40]

The redemption narrative common to radical-right radicalisation noted in Chapter Three, and highlighted by Basra, Neumann and Brunner in their work on criminality and Islamism, is evident here.[41] Rifat had, in fact, rejected one set of criminal street masculinities for another; where before the threat was drugs and gangs, his association with ALM had consequences. Despite his trust that he was on the right path with ALM, Rifat was still concerned about his older brother's views about the government's removal of his passport in order to prevent travel to IS, and an anti-social behaviour order against him.

The sense of brotherhood derived from joining the network was also crucial to Adam. The revert, in his twenties, told me that he had been a *Wahhab* and part of the 'brotherhood' for 2 years. He believed in the principle of *takfir*—the validity of declaring another Muslim a non-believer—and followed the teachings of Ibn Taymiyyah. One of Adam's most important 'neighbourhood' friends was Mo, another revert in his twenties who belonged to Choudary's study circle. Adam's transition to the *Wahhabi* creed of Islam was locally, "through friends" on the street, whom he described as "knowledgeable people"—an indication of masculine status.[42] Although Adam did not name the friends, he told me that they had introduced him to people with influence in British *takfiri* Islamist circles, including Abu Haleema. Abu Haleema, also called Shakil Chapra, is another associate of Choudary. Chapra is an outspoken preacher who joined ALM in 2013 and had his passport removed in 2014—again to prevent travel to Islamic State.[43] In 2021 he was jailed for distributing a terrorist publication.[44]

Prison masculinities and street policing

Prison represented an important location for *Dawah* and recruitment, and participant narratives cited it as a significant site of conversion. Several participants said that prison was important in their mobilisation to al-Muhajiroun, and it is perhaps here that the redemption narrative is strongest. Ahmed, whom I met online in the Islamic State/ALM support network, was British of Pakistani heritage and in his twenties. As previously noted, he is now serving a second term in prison for a terror plot with others he met during a previous prison sentence. Other participants had also been in prison. Mo, the revert in his twenties, did not disclose how he first encountered Choudary's group, but it was not prison. However, he had twice been imprisoned and was positive about the opportunity it gave him to mobilise others through *Dawah*. He found the experience liberating:

> To be honest, [prison] was one of the best things that ever happened to me as a Muslim. I could really think and contemplate—and I met a lot of Muslims in prison. I met a lot of people who helped me to understand in a better context. A lot of Muslims don't speak the truth when they are afraid of it [prison]. People outside don't speak the truth, like the imams, and that. ... It was so easy—prison. You have ... a TV, PlayStation. ... There are many books to read. I did a lot of exercise. I gained a lot of knowledge in prison. I could reflect and contemplate a lot. You don't have time otherwise, but in prison you had all the time in the world—even to talk to non-Muslims. They are very receptive to Islam. One of the guys even wanted to iron my clothes for me![45]

In prison, Mo met other men who shared his values. In this all-male environment, masculine norms circulate and are constantly reproduced. Mo noted that this sex-segregated environment was also conducive to Islamic learning. In prison, Mo become one of an instant community of young Muslim men, who can support and protect one another.[46] The norms and status of street masculinity still applied, physicality still mattered, and Mo worked out. However, hypermasculinity based on physicality was not the primary frame used by Mo here, contrary to Bengtsson's work on prison masculinities, referenced in Chapter One.[47] This physicality now had a spiritual dimension, and Mo emphasised the presence of books and the time for reflection and contemplation. As his first offence was classified as terrorism, Mo perhaps enjoyed a high masculine status in jail, as suggested by the offer to perform chores for him by other inmates. He did not have to use violence, or his physicality, to gain status; his reputation positioned him towards the top of the prisoner hierarchy.

Without the possibility of further sanction (he was already in prison), Mo told me he was free to convert others to ALM ideology. This ability to mobilise others was predicated on the way that gender constitutes the power dynamics and social relations of prison culture. Prison afforded status. Its dynamics mirrored the street culture from which Mo told me he emerged, and in which he knew how to gain

225

status. Prison both consolidated and amplified his status. In prison, Mo performed masculinities according to familiar masculinity systems; however, he was also able to adopt roles he did not possess before his involvement with Choudary: scholar, role model, preacher and, like Choudary, a martyr to the cause.

Street masculinities, misogyny and masculinity challenges

In the past, core ALM activities centred on generating publicity through deliberately provocative events and demonstrations organised to gain media coverage.[48] For example, al-Muhajiroun arranged a press briefing where it lauded the 9/11 attackers as the "magnificent nineteen". In central London, other activities grabbing the headlines included a poppy-burning incident on Armistice Day under the banner of Muslims Against Crusades (MAC), which led to clashes with the police.[49] Additionally, they have organised demonstrations outside mainstream mosques aimed at persuading Muslims not to vote—for example, a rally at the Regent's Park Mosque shortly ahead of the 2015 elections. This led to clashes with the EDL, which also meant publicity.[50]

As explored in Chapter Five, patriarchal—and nationalist— movements fear the targeting, particularly the sexual targeting, of 'their' women. When hegemonic masculinity positions men as protectors, failure to protect is emasculating and potentially feminising. ALM members suggested that they had at times instrumentalised women as a tool to provoke non-Muslim men. Rifat referenced an episode in which some white non-Muslim women had reverted to Islam and joined ALM following domestic violence. This had antagonised the local white non-Muslim men they sought to escape. The protection of non-Muslim women by Muslims constituted a masculinity challenge to non-Muslim men, given that it implied the superiority of Muslim men and Islamic culture and masculinity. The women had effectively, Rifat said, switched sides. Women (particularly white) reverts were symbolically useful to emasculate non-Muslim men, who regarded such women as 'stolen' by Muslim men. Rifat accepted that issues of gender and the treatment of women were a point of high tension between Muslims and non-Muslims in his area. Rifat said, "We met an EDL guy, he was sociable, more civilised—he said, you guys love wearing dresses. We said, your wife prefers a Muslim guy rather than one of you guys. There was this joke of English women preferring [Muslims]."[51] Each group used women to feminise the other, as evidenced in local banter and insults between Islamists and the EDL. Here the "EDL guy" challenges ALM sexuality, with reference to their *kamees*— tunics—and Rifat challenges his virility and ability to hold onto women in turn. This 'banter' recalls the far-right insult 'cuck', short for 'cuckold': a man whose wife is unfaithful to him and leaves him. Such words are only offensive if heterosexuality and virility are understood as hegemonic.

Not all masculinity challenges were light-hearted. Participants also described more serious masculinity challenges involving gender-based violence and sexuality-based violence. Between 2013 and 2014, some male ALM activists participated in so-called 'Muslim Patrol': the vigilante enforcement, sometimes through violence, of Islamist norms in shared public space. Al-Muhajiroun members attempted to prohibit the consumption of alcohol, and to intimidate non-Muslim women wearing short skirts or openly gay couples.[52] The action was an echo of Qutb's ideology. As John Calvert notes, "Qutb's American writings are laced with anecdotes ... which reveal an almost obsessive concern with moral issues, especially concerning matters of sexuality";[53] this includes depictions of a would-be seductress on the boat to the United States ("drunken", "semi-naked") and a suburban church dance ("Arms circled arms, lips met lips, chests met chests, and the atmosphere was full of love").[54] The misogynist actions of ALM's Muslim Patrol, mirroring those of IS, were perhaps predicated on fear, hatred and desire too.

Sara Khan suggests that Qutb's ideology of Islamism constitutes a "sex-segregated dream",[55] and ALM participants were active in attempts to enforce such ideology in public spaces. A similar focus on matters of public sex and sexuality was evident in the accounts of some participants in this research, men and women alike. Mo distinguished between the passivity of women in Islam, which treats them as a "diamond", and their immoral behaviour in secular society, which does not offer them respect or protection: "Many people are getting drunk. There was a woman I saw, just drunk out of her face in the street."[56] Mo noted the absence of a gender order in secular society and the resulting dangers for women; he responded by attempting to regulate their behaviour using his physicality. This intimidation had the effect of attempting to limit women's access to the public space, unless they conformed to specific ALM norms around behaviour. This was an attempt to impose the masculinity system represented by ALM onto public space. Mo justified women's seclusion from public space as both a protection and a form of freedom. He did not want to discuss his violence, except obliquely, in discussion of prison. I noted in my October 2017 field diary:

> After meeting locally, Mo offers to walk me in the direction of my car, as the area can be unsafe, and I have been mugged before. … We chat as we walk, and he reassures me that it would be impossible for me to be mugged if we lived in an Islamic state. I ask why. He replies that in an Islamic state I would not be allowed outside on my own. So, I could never be attacked. I ask, would I be able to complete my [research] in an Islamic state? No, he admits, but I wouldn't need to because I'd be married. I couldn't just—be unmarried; they would find someone for me. I tell him with a laugh that I'd probably rather be mugged, and he looks momentarily bewildered. He asks me to text once I am safely home, which I do.[57]

Mo's interpretation of Islamic law is one which gives him an important role in ensuring the safety of others, and a protectionist justification for the misogynist violence of Muslim Patrol.

Muslim Patrol activism was endorsed by Choudary, whose understanding of gender roles closely follows Qutb in its fundamental rejection of the secular and is also focused on public space. He told me, "I mean if you walk down the street in London … you see naked women on billboards, there's the sale of pornography in shops. … All of this exploitation of both the man and the woman in the West—it would be eradicated in Islam." Choudary believes this is a factor motivating women to join Islamic State, "because they know from our own beautiful history that women are elevated— they're mothers, they're sisters, they're aunts, they're nieces, they're daughters. They're not sex objects as in the West."[58] Choudary contrasted the sexual and gender values of ALM's masculinity system with those of secular society and noted that it was ALM's ultimate intention to impose their norms on public spaces. What constitutes the removal of agency for women is framed as their protection; however, unlike the case of the EDL and men's attempts to control women's marches discussed in Chapter Five, ALM men appear more successful in controlling, if not women in public space, women in their own group.

Jihadist violence and the ALM activist

As noted in Chapter One, one dimension of jihadist violence is gender-based violence. IS has targeted and killed gay men, and enslaved Yezidi women. ALM supporters share a gendered belief system with IS, and ALM has always had links to global jihad. As Lorenzo Vidino notes, the ALM "worldview ... is virtually identical to that of groups like al-Qaeda or the Islamic State."[59] For Maéva Clément, this ideology is "hubristic" in that it is based on prestige, and non-recognition equates to disrespect.[60] ALM shares ideological roots with groups including al-Qaeda and Islamic State, and the many other violent offshoots of Islamism.[61] The historic leaders previously mentioned—Muhammad Ibn Abd al-Wahhab and Ibn Taymiyyah— are among those ideologues cited as influencers to the participants in the research, and within IS.

Islamist Omar Bakri Mohammed founded two global Islamist groups in the UK: Hizb ut-Tahrir (HT) in 1986, and, in 1996, the UK branch of al-Muhajiroun.[62] Both ALM and HT support the creation of a Caliphate ruled with Shariah law and adhering to a Salafi Islam; however, they have different stances on violence.[63] HT, although rejectionist, in that it rejects the legitimacy of the nation state, does not officially advocate violence. ALM supporters, however, are ready to use violence if necessary and understand *Dawah* (evangelism) and jihad (to them, the Islamic 'lesser' or violent jihad) as twin aspects of a single individual Islamic duty. Al-Muhajiroun in the UK has nevertheless preached a doctrine of active involvement in violence overseas only. Within the UK it has called for peaceful but provocative protest for Shariah.[64] Indeed, a focus on Shariah and a Caliphate for the West is one of the features of al-Muhajiroun that distinguishes it from other groups with a jihadist ideology.

Numerous authors have linked ALM to transnational terror plots, although Choudary told me that violent actors simply "passed through" his circles.[65] Bakri Mohammed was born in Syria and schooled in the Middle East, and in 2003 told an interviewer that he was proud to be known as a follower of bin Laden, "the lion of the Muslim nation".[66] Choudary has been active in setting up splinter networks in Belgium and Norway and across Europe, including Sharia4Belgium, Shariah4Holland, Forsane Alizza in France and the Prophet's Ummah in Norway. Petter Nesser notes the role of activists from these groups in increased jihadi activism over the years, including protest and terror plots.[67] In recent years al-Muhajiroun has been linked with support of Islamic State in the UK and abroad. While careful not to profess support of IS, Choudary told me, "The declaration of the *Khilafah* [IS Caliphate] in June 2014 is something that Muslims around the world have been waiting 90 years for. ... this is a momentous occasion."[68] Several ALM members did travel to the Caliphate,[69] and in 2018 the UK's CONTEST strategy noted the alignment of al-Muhajiroun and Islamic State ideology.[70] ALM is absent from the 2023 CONTEST strategy, although the new strategy emphasises the broad threat from groups with a jihadist ideology.[71]

Both Bakri Mohammed and Choudary had in the past led regular classroom sessions attended by a variety of people, including some later convicted of terrorism. With Bakri Mohammed gone, much of participants' understanding of ideology and the requirement for violence was derived from one man with unique importance to the network: Anjem Choudary. He was the only ALM leadership figure I interviewed and, while he did not discuss violence, he emphasised several gendered ideological points which closely resembled the position of Islamic State. Two other supporters of Choudary (Mo and Akash) suggested that they were in principle behind a functional Islamic state, without explicitly referring to IS. Choudary advocated Islam as a solution to the inequalities for women in Western society, and as a comprehensive system of human rights. He had a clear-cut attitude towards the status of warrior masculinity as hegemonic for ALM women and men:

The *Mujahid* [warrior] is a very honourable person, one who sacrifices his life for the sake of Allah; he's going to the battlefield, you know, defending others. So why isn't that something that— er—should be promoted! Why should not people want to get married to people like that? ... But definitely like you would say—hey, I guess you'd say—a fireman or a member of the armed forces is someone who's respected. So, it's the same thing in Islam. They are respected people ... who sacrifice their lives for what they believe in.[72]

According to this view, women's key duties are those of a wife, in the home, and men's are in violent struggle to establish a Caliphate. Choudary told me, "It's not obliged for the woman to fight. ... even the offensive campaigns that the Prophet launched, women would go with the men, but they would have a different role ... a kind of medical role."[73] This essentialist demarcation of roles ensures that it is men alone who have access to the highest-status role (warrior) in times of conflict, and that this is secured through the delegitimisation of women's violence and the claim that they need to be protected. Choudary asserts the Caliphate as an essentially ideological space in which women are protected first and foremost for Islamic reasons. He dismisses as un-Islamic emotionally motivated actions, including the abuse of women—he told me that "there is nothing called rape in Islam"—because they are not consistent with ideology. Indeed, Choudary himself acted to protect his female associates by telling me that there had been no women activists in his circles since al-Muhajiroun disbanded, a claim that contradicts numerous documentaries and much research.[74] Choudary also suggested that women frequently asked for his advice, particularly around issues of marriage, and that his lectures remained well-attended by them.

Choudary emphasised the status of the warrior as a marker of difference between secular non-Muslim community, and its masculinity system, and his community. Additionally, he suggested that ALM occupied not a different but a parallel gendered space, in which societal gender structures were mirrored (high status for men in dangerous 'rescue' roles), but the ideological content was different (warriors revered instead of firemen). ALM therefore represented a space in which Muslims who do not believe in the state had a home. The group's gendered ideology also resolved the dis-ease, explored in the previous chapter, created through reflexion on the tension between an Islamo-cultural masculinity system and the secular Other.

Violence, jihad and hypermasculinities as moral purpose

Despite the above, Choudary and all male participants emphasised that they were bound by the 'Covenant of Security', according to which UK civilians are safe from attack from al-Muhajiroun members living within the UK's borders.[75] Mo texted me about this after the London Bridge attacks of June 2017. Choudary was being linked in the press with one of the attackers. Mo felt that this was unfair, because of Choudary's belief in the Covenant: "[Choudary] emphasised that a lot so the connection is simply a sensational one", he texted.[76] Participants and their wider network online liked to debate what should or should not be counted as a valid attack. Adam understood jihadi violence as adhering to strict moral rules underpinned by Islamist theology. He believed some attacks did not conform to correct values: "Like Lee Rigby—it's the way they did it, that wasn't on the battlefield, so that wasn't right."[77] Choudary was adamant about the importance of the Covenant in his interview with me. However, he has shown willingness to support violence overseas. The participants, too, seemed to regard the Covenant as malleable. Akash suggested that the pressure of increased arrests and surveillance at the time I was interviewing might have unwanted side effects, and said, "My fear is that if this continues then the Covenant of Security will no longer be respected."[78] There has been no public evidence to support this fear; however, the 2023 CONTEST strategy prioritisation of jihadist threat suggests there is no room for complacency.

While participants were careful not to express open support for Islamic State, some appeared to be active supporters of transnational Salafi–jihadi groups endorsing violence, without necessarily having contact with them. Abu M., for example, is a British Pakistani in his early twenties whom I met online. He at times expressed support for Islamic State online, although he told me that this was just "for show", to maintain status within the online network. For him, the strength of Islamic State and Islamism was in the ideology; "an ideology cannot be defeated", he messaged.[79] Participants looked to Islamic doctrine, scholars and the Quran for guidance on when and how to use violence. They linked violence to self-defence, and the notion of honour, status and respect.

Jihadist hypermasculinity and violence are therefore not on their own hegemonic for participants. They function within a system of masculinities. It is ideology and scholarship, the 'learning masculinity', that legitimises hypermasculine violence. The two operate dyadically, within the system of masculinities that constitutes ALM's patriarchal ideology. Zakir was accused, and found guilty, of funding terrorism during my research, and he provided perhaps the most honest discussion of the ALM understanding of rules for jihad in his court appearance. What is clear from Zakir's reading of violence in war, as recorded in my notes from his trial, is that only adherence to strict Islamic rules gives hypermasculine violence the authority of Islam, and the fighter the honour of being a warrior rather than a killer. The court discussed messaging between Zakir and a male relative he sent money to in Syria:

> Zakir says there should be "no mutilating, just beheading". The barrister says, you advise him that beheading is acceptable, but that mutilation by being dragged behind a car is not. Zakir says, "No, I was saying—don't go out of the bounds of Islam. Only if you need to are you allowed to execute. If you hate, it must be for the right reasons. I'm taken aback by what he is saying ... I told him back, remember what you are doing." The barrister asks: So, help us with the legal jurisprudence in Islam on this, help us to understand the beheading.

> Zakir: You can execute an enemy combatant in war. You could execute people with swords 1,400 years ago.

> Judge: Has it not moved on since the fourteenth century?

> Zakir: You should not behead people—there are principles. I tell my [relative] this. The [relative] replies: You can kill whether

[fighters] are male or female and asks me to read *The Management of Savagery*.

Barrister: So, you don't tell him, "I'm shocked, you need to step back"?

Zakir: I tell him not to act from emotions. I don't withdraw my support.

Barrister: did you not have a concern that radicalised trained people would return to the UK? You know that your [relative] had been 'radicalised', he was dragging heads behind trucks. Zakir ends this exchange by telling the Barrister, "My [relative] was not 'radicalised' at any time."[80]

Zakir did not believe that his relative was radicalised; he perceived his actions as morally correct and entirely consistent with the tenets of Islam. This behaviour is also consistent with Choudary's description of the 'honourable fighter'. There is no sense in which the actions of Zakir's relative would appear 'radical' to any of the participants, whose faith in Islam prescribes this as correct behaviour for jihad. Aisha expressed a similar belief. Her cousin travelled to join Islamic State, but Aisha believes this was linked to problems at home, as he was abusive to his mother and not settled. Although she did not support his jihad, she said, "I would encourage it. The principle I would support, I mean. Not going off to be bogus in Syria. It has to be in the right context; it has to be actual jihad, which this wasn't."[81] What made her cousin's jihad "bogus" was her belief that emotional issues, rather than purely ideological ones, drove him. What these narratives demonstrate is that hypermasculinity—the archetype of the jihadist warrior—is not hegemonic unless accompanied by scholarship and learning masculinity. Hegemony is produced from their conjunction.

Dyadic masculinity and the learning masculinity

Participants rarely used the terms *Wahhabi* or Salafi. However, they regarded their creed as a whole political system. This was hegemonic and inherently anti-secular. All regarded this Islam, and those ideologues who adhered to it, as possessing a unique truth. Faith dictates all action, is fundamentally ideological and is about enacting system change. Developing the findings of the last chapter's section on meta-reflexivity and tensions between masculinity systems, participants here suggested they regarded ALM ideology as a choice between systems:

> When I see people rejecting Islam, people not caring about life—aimlessly going through life, I realised that I needed to, as a Muslim, I wanted to change society, you know. … [the prophet] Jesus. He was persecuted because he didn't respect the rules of government [Mo, twenties].[82]

> It's about religion; teaching Islam and giving *Dawah*, the invitation to Islam, is the essence of a Muslim—the very reason for being and us existing is to give *Dawah*. Every nation, every regime, every agency that is built on this liberal democratic ideal is not consistent with everything that I base my thoughts and actions on, the Quran and the Sunnah [Akash, forties].[83]

> Islam is a beautiful way of life despite the propaganda on the news it's liberating man from the shackles of manmade systems and returning you to worship God as one [Ahmed, twenties].[84]

> [Q: Do you think it's possible to be Muslim and not political?] It's not remotely possible. One thing people think—it's about fasting, praying, going to the *Hajj*. It's not just that—but those are part and parcel of the faith, yes. … It [Islam] is both public and private. The issue of evil. Rape, drugs, prostitution. Or domestic violence [Rifat, thirties].[85]

The ideology which participants followed echoes that of Qutb, with Islam regarded as a 'whole system' that is completely inconsistent with democracy and represents, as Rifat noted, a set of gender and sexual norms that differ from those of secular society. A key difference between the radical-right participants and ALM, therefore, is the attitude towards ideology and learning. While radical-right actors tend to reject the assertion that they hold an ideological position, due to the negative associations it holds for them with the 'extreme' right, fascism and weak liberal masculinities, the acquisition of Islamic knowledge in and of itself gave Islamist participants masculine status. Knowledge of the Arabic language, alongside key Quranic concepts and the teachings of scholars, and strict observation of rules surrounding prayer contribute to the creation of a particular identity and an accordingly high status. Participants used smatterings of Arabic in online discussions, and could speak Arabic or were learning it. The sample frequently showed their knowledge through the use of Arabic terminology in our interviews. They referred to concepts such as *Tawheed*, the oneness of God (as opposed to the Trinity of Christianity); the *kufar,* a person who prefers democracy and man-made systems over and above Islam and who will finally go to the hell-fire; and jihad as a necessary defence when attacked. Mo even offered to help teach me Arabic so that I would be able to understand Islam better.

Kenney notes the importance of scholarship to ALM activists, who identify as both "students" of Islam and "intellectual affiliates".[86] Scholarship was similarly important to participants, and they were keen to demonstrate their Islamic knowledge to me and emphasise that they followed renowned scholars and took knowledge seriously. To some (Akash, Anhar, Mo and Rifat), Choudary and the younger Mizanur Rahman, also known as 'Abu Baraa', with whom he was tried and sentenced for support of Islamic State, have been role models and father figures. To others, Choudary was not the key ideologue; they looked to the scholars of the past, men like Ibn Taymiyyah (Adam), also revered by Islamic State; or to internet preachers affiliated to al-Qaeda, such as Anwar al-Awlaki (Rifat); or to Islamic State itself (Saleha, Ahmed, and Abu M.); or to preachers with no group connections at all, such as the Trinidadian preacher Imran Nazar Hosein (Aisha and Zakir), a man who believes, in keeping with apocalyptic Quranic tradition, that the signs of the last day are already here.[87]

As Robinson was revered in the radical right, Choudary also embodied an aspirational masculinity within the ALM research sample, and participants sought to emulate his devotion and knowledge. Choudary and his junior colleague Abu Baraa had the highest masculine status within the group, partly because they embodied a scholarly masculinity. Akash suggested that their imprisonment impacted everyone: "Once that knowledgeable person has been locked up, there's no point of reference, you can't ask anyone anything." He despaired; the knowledge base was being depleted, and there were few left with the authority to advise. "These are the real effects. ... Abdul M----, he's on a TPIM, also Abdul S----. Abu H-----, he's on a TPIM ..."[88] ALM is a community of practice, in which members learn by doing; the more they engage with the culture, the more they are considered a part of the group.[89] At the time of research, ALM members had few to learn from.

Participants attained knowledge, but also 'wore' their ideology and knowledge, in a demonstration of masculine status, and to communicate this to like-minds. This resonates with the use of clothing by radical-right participants involved in the football hooliganism scene, who chose fashion brands to communicate a desire to fight. All male ALM research participants grew a beard as a sign of devotion, although this proved problematic for Adam, the white revert in his twenties. He told me, "Yeah, this beard, people mock me. I hear them when I'm working. Not that they bully me, because I'm quite big, you know. ... But they mock it. ... [Because] I look Muslim."[90] They all at times chose to wear the dress associated with the Prophet in his era and saw this as a way of distinguishing their Islam from 'incorrect' versions, as Adam again explained: "Saudis. They're not really—look at their clothes, the *thaub*, that is not from Islam. The Prophet didn't wear that. He wore—like what I'm wearing, like trousers and a *kamees* [loose long shirt]."[91]

Ideology matters, but it is the display of knowledge through both language and apparel which communicates members of the group to one another as part of the same "epistemic community",[92] united through a new shared habitus.

Within the ALM masculinity system, learning is hegemonic; in the old pre-ALM system, school learning was not. For Adam, Islamic knowledge, unlike academic knowledge, was attainable. He said, "I was expelled from college and school—and then I studied '*Aqeedah* [Islamic knowledge]. [Q: When were you were expelled?] That was when I was fourteen, fifteen, I was expelled. They let me do three exams—English, maths, you know—but I didn't revise, so they didn't go too well."[93] Islamic learning was a way for Adam to redeem himself after being jailed for crimes involving drugs and violence, and it also identified him to a particular community.

Kenney has explored how ALM uses events to produce a strong brotherhood as an organisational strategy, strengthening action and making leaving the group difficult.[94] For Adam, the brotherhood of Muslim friends was one of the most important aspects of Islam, because it is a form of club. Furthermore, it is a club within which Adam believes members always recognise and reward one another as part of the path to *Jannah* (Heaven). Kenney cites one ALM activist who described Omar Bakri Mohammed as "big brother, our dad. He was everything".[95] Adam went further; not just the leader but the network itself represented a family of male role models. He said, "There's a group of people, growing up, that maybe didn't have a dad, and then when they came to Islam—it's like a brotherhood."[96] This suggests the impossibility of separating the ideological aspects of mobilisation to the movement from the affective advantages and unconditional acceptance enabled through masculine bonds, "brotherhood" or male mentorship, despite the participants' belief that emotion can serve to dilute the purity of the ideology.

This was a whole system for participants' lives, not just their faith. The feeling of brotherhood within the movement and the depth of relationships meant that participants rejected labels, including 'radicalisation', that removed their agency. Rifat and I discussed what I termed his 'recruitment' to Choudary's circles, and his frustration with the misrepresentation of Choudary and the terminology of 'radicalisation' and security studies. He cited an experience with a national newspaper journalist, after which he felt misrepresented and misled:

> He called me "an acolyte of Anjem Choudary". People spend time with you, and they say they understand you and they sympathise—"oh we agree with you, your cause"—then they describe you as an 'extremist', 'radical', 'crazy', 'fanatical.' I think, "You never said that when we were having a meal together." [Q: Well—how would you describe your relationship with Anjem Choudary?] I'm a friend of Anjem Choudary.[97]

Rifat reframes his relationship with Choudary in terms which endow it with the authenticity he experiences, and as a challenge to the dominant narrative of radicals as 'misguided', 'vulnerable', 'extreme' and inauthentic Muslims, who misinterpret the Quran. He dismisses this language, and asserts his agency in the face of discourses he feels seek to deny this. Every small event on the path to Choudary felt simple, real and authentic and none of the experiences were correctly encapsulated by the politicised language of terrorism studies, as far as Rifat is concerned. This means that participants do not feel 'radicalised', as the term in no way represents the authenticity of their experience, mirroring the narratives of those in the radical right.

Emotion, affect and racialising discourse

So far, this chapter has explored how both street masculinities and Islamic identities resulting from meta-reflexivity discussed in the last chapter are mobilised in ALM activism. A few participants also noted the online space as a factor in their mobilisation, and their narratives suggest that this was especially effective in mobilising those Muslim protector masculinities generated in the discursive space after 9/11. This is a space in which subjectivity is produced in reference to post-colonial and subaltern masculinities and resistance.

Participants, for instance, talked about the importance of video material viewed online in evoking the masculine protector response and mobilising them to the network and to action. Zakir's provision of money for weapons to a relative fighting in Syria, for example, was a result in part of emotions stirred not just by family duty, but by a desire to right an injustice he believed was not addressed by foreign policy. This was made more urgent by images viewed online of atrocities in Syria. At his trial, his legal team argued that their effect was so compelling that the jury needed to watch them to understand their role in his mobilisation. The judge dismissed the request, but Zakir described their impact, as I recorded in my field notes:

> The court discusses video of an Assad gas attack; the deaths of babies, foaming at the mouth; many children dying. They discuss

the fact that Zakir also has young children, and he is asked the impact of the videos on him as a father. He replies, "heart-wrenching". The judge asks, "Were you angry?" He says, "I don't know. I was emotional, upset—it was not rage that I felt." Later, in the café, we talk about the Syrian gas attack videos the court would not show, and his eyes fill with tears. He is clearly deeply emotionally affected by the conflict, by what he sees as a moral imperative to resist, alongside the plight of his relative, who has chosen—rightly, he believes—to fight Assad.[98]

Zakir's mobilisation took place at the intersection of diverse gendered discourses, triggering the necessity for particular masculinity performances, intrinsic to the normative gendered values of ALM. This mobilisation is familiar from radicalisation theory, yet without emphasis on the gendered component. State injustice situates Zakir as a Muslim man within discourses of global injustices to Muslims, which specifically centre on Muslim men as unstable subjects (foreign policy); a male family member already fighting in Syria and Iraq elicits a specific masculine response as a family member (kinship connections); the distressing images he has seen related to the conflict on the internet (online imagery) and the affect that this has produced ("upset") motivates him to action through a protector masculinity. Such images are commonly used by Islamist movements to highlight the inaction of non-Muslims to defend Muslims and to evoke an emotional response necessitating action; or, as expressed in language ALM has rejected, to 'recruit'.[99]

The online terrain was significant in mobilisation because participants perceived it as an important site of 'unbiased' information, unlike the mainstream media, which they situated as part of a colonialist anti-Muslim agenda. Within Saleha's online network there was widespread sharing of information about Iraq and Syria, Western persecution of Muslims and Palestine. Commenting on why social media mattered to him, a member of Saleha's network, Oliver, messaged me to say that it was important in its authenticity, as "without social media would we know what goes on in Palestine, Syria, the racist French banning and harassing our women on beaches. ... Today due to social media we know who our enemies are."[100] With the enemy clearly demarcated—Israel, Western values, feminism, democracy, Western states and those acting against the global *Ummah*—images lionising warlike male behaviour in defence of Islam have resonance. These normalise the idea of both violence and a warrior masculinity as necessary to jihad. While some images posted by the network are stylised so that the violence is obscured, others do not hold back from displaying the brutality of war. To fulfil the male Islamist duty, men must, after all, be warriors. Emasculating images of Muslims as defenceless victims require a hypermasculine mobilisation and response.

Rifat also described how his entry into the protest scene was catalysed by conflict images of injustice eliciting a protective Islamic masculinity. He said he was attracted to Choudary's group as it gave him a platform, as (primarily) an anti-war activist. The 'war' he first protested was Israel–Palestine. He remembers watching the television news as a teenager:

> The footage was heart-breaking. It was of an IDF [Israeli Defence Force] personnel dragging a child … off the street—I thought that was horrible—why would they do that to a child? … Then I saw a pamphlet in my area by some anti-war campaigners. … Don't know if they were Choudary's group or not; so, I went down [to a protest] because I felt guilty and didn't want to not do anything.[101]

Other participants described how the internet mobilised them to extreme movements in similar terms. Oliver, an Islamic State supporter in the ALM social media network but living outside of the UK, suggested, without shame or emasculation, a similar response to imagery as Zakir: "You know I am bursted in tears so much *wallah* [I swear to God]—I watched something, and I am draining with tears."[102] Akash told me he tried to join a convoy to Syria and was stopped and turned back at the port of Dover. He was similarly emotionally motivated. He saw a poem posted online about a young girl, Zainab, tortured and killed by the Syrian security services. For Akash, Oliver, Rifat and Zakir, the power of these images was not just in the humiliation of Muslims and the injustice they represented, but in their evocation of a hegemonic protective masculinity as a response, which endowed a sense of status. This Islamic status eventually compensated for a corresponding loss of status within secular society as they were drawn deeper into ALM; it involved a transgression of secular limits on what masculinity should resemble, who it should protect and how it should be expressed.

I discussed ALM recruitment, including the discredited term 'brainwashing', with Umm M., in her thirties and on the fringes of the online network supportive of Islamic State. She preferred a different term: "They have materials out there, with the help of the internet. It was easy for people to get carried away. I don't know if it's 'brainwashing'; they are not using their brains on this—they are using their hearts. It is heart-washing ... driven by emotions."[103] Heart-washing is the affective mobilisation of men and women. Images of Muslim emasculation invoke a feeling of (feminised) powerlessness. The response is hypermasculinity, but not as an "avenging hero",[104] as Roy suggests—rather, as a 'protective hero'. Indeed, Abu M. texted me that he began to support Islamic State online as he was looking for someone to defend Muslims: "I was upset at the oppression the Western governments did to the Muslim lands like Iraq and Afghanistan, I thought ISIS were the ones to bring about change at first."[105] It is action that participants all emphasise: Islamic State were actually doing something, and becoming involved resolved the unstable Muslim subjectivities produced between securitising and post-colonial discourses discussed in the previous chapter. Images prompting other participants to action, a common theme in 'radicalisation' models,[106] present the emasculation of Muslims as a form of impotence and a gendered disempowerment, with Muslim men unable to protect Muslim children and women.[107] This both necessitates and elicits a particular gendered—and masculinised—active response. The response is justified by ideology. However, it is also highly affective.

Online mobilisation, women and hegemonic femininities

The final sections of this chapter discuss women's participation and the complex femininity this entailed. The research for this book was aimed at offline, not online, domains, given that the online realm constitutes its own topic of analysis. However, it is worth noting that Choudary mobilised many into online followership. Before his arrest, he had as many as sixteen Twitter accounts encouraging support for Islamic State.[108] His colleague Abu Baraa ran Twitter accounts with followers in the hundreds of thousands. He was a regular user of Islamic State hashtags, and popular among Islamic State 'fanboys' and 'fangirls'.[109] ALM and Choudary prized their online popularity,[110] and many Islamic State supporters whose accounts I saw online expressed anger and regret when Choudary was jailed. Online gender norms in the network supporting Choudary appeared to mirror the offline norms that Adam and Mo described on the streets, or even in jail. Additionally, online status functioned 'by association', based on a hierarchy where not just the most pious, but also the most famous—or 'infamous'—gain social capital and are able to mobilise others into the movement.

Leaders were revered for many reasons. Umm M. pointed to important overlap between cultures of reverence for knowledge in the online Islamic State-supporting network and a—less pious—celebrity culture, which she suggested was highly sexualised. Mirroring radical-right subculture, she said that women sought status through association, particularly sexual association, with high-status men. Umm M. was previously married to an important ideologue. She told me that the fundamentalist gender norms which the Islamic State-supporting online network openly policed and promoted (no free mixing, no messaging the opposite sex, and so on) contrasted with other covert behaviours. She said:

> It's a celebrity thing. Well, you know [my ex-husband] has got a lot of fans. He has charm—all the girls, a lot of girls were after him. I'm not insecure but... [Q: He had *burqa*-wearing 'groupies'?] [Laughs.] Yes. 'Groupies'. They are watching him. I don't like that he's so conscious and—so much attention. ... Anyone tells him, "oh, I'm connected", he gets excited, talks to them. ... They want attention. "Oh, I'm talking to the famous [x]!" ... [Q: You make it sound like a celebrity culture as much as

on the outside.] It is a celebrity culture. Yeah, he was living that life and can't get out.[111]

The online Islamist network's ideological gender norms, which prohibited sex outside of marriage, operated alongside other sexualised behaviours. Men became attractive to women, as well as men, when they embodied Islamic knowledge and had status in the group.

Hypermasculinities mobilised women as well as men to ALM and support of jihad. I met Saleha, a 19-year-old British–Bangladeshi woman, through her online connections to a network of Islamic State supporters. She told me she no longer supported Islamic State but described how past support developed through online exploration. Like Rifat, this began with an initial interest in the Israel–Palestine conflict, sparked through a debate at school, and subsequent attendance at a demonstration. These events prompted her to conduct related research on Google, learning about Hamas, Hezbollah, then al-Qaeda and 'African groups'. She made friends online with similar interests. Eventually she began to read about Islamic State, and found their vision appealing:

When you heard of them, it was like everybody was looking for something like this. Muslims were being killed left, right and centre, and there it was, like this amazing group fighting back and taking back what's ours. You feel like you belong. This is what you've been waiting for… Islamic State was something really good. It's weird, it felt bad and good at that same time, I don't know how to explain it.[112]

The image of the "amazing" heroic fighter represents a figure who sits at the intersection of two masculinity systems, echoing the tensions evident through meta-reflexivity in the previous chapter; and Saleha could not decide whether this violence was positive, given his challenge to global discourse positioning Muslim men as victims, or negative, given his violence. Online encounters with such men were important within both Saleha's radicalisation story and Farhan's description of the journey pursued by her friends, who travelled to join Islamic State in Syria. The young women, all teenagers, were isolated from men in the offline space, were not allowed to date and were apparently coping with low self-esteem. For Saleha, an experience of sexual trauma meant that she suffered from agoraphobia and spent a lot of time online, where, consistent with other research on women's radicalisation stories,[113] she and her Muslim girlfriends used social media as a dating site. When Islamic State recruiters approached Saleha and other young women in her online circle, she felt both infantilised (lowered within the IS masculinity system) and deeply feminised (raised). The Islamic State approaches conformed to an idealised masculinity in which the ideal Muslim man is a protective warrior. She said:

> At first I think these guys were like properly what Muslims should be like. You build an image up and you feel flattered from that status when they contact you. … You're inside the ranks then, of these people who are so honoured. At first it was this, like, girly childish feeling. Like I was flattered. [Q: How long did this go on for?] That was like for maybe 3 months and 3 months to get over it. … We didn't tell anyone. They told us [not to].[114]

Farhan echoed this story in her explanation of the *hijrah* of her two friends to Islamic State. The young women, both still at school, had a brother already in Syria, and Farhan believed they were ultimately determined to meet a—high-status Islamic State fighter—husband. She suggested they were particularly 'vulnerable' to this and needed high-status men due to their intellectualised reputation at an all-girls' school, and their low sexual status. She said, "All the friendship group they all wore *hijab*, were religious … they found somebody who would look past all that. They were getting attention. You don't get much attention at all for 5 years, then—it's easy to get carried away … Boys don't go for girls in *hijab*."[115] Both Farhan and Saleha described the empowering effects for women of contact with male Islamic State supporters. These men had appeal because they presented female sexuality within the context of Islamic struggle and theology; they linked the approach to faith and marriage and did not discount women who wore *hijab* or *niqab*. This increased the young women's status and self-esteem. It is also possible that the contact with violence itself was empowering. In *Gender-Based*

Explosions, Aslam suggests that women supporters of jihad aspire to masculine practices, and, as a performative move, surrender their femininity when engaging in public spaces such as social media.[116] Saleha, who was an online Islamic State supporter, eventually found violence sickening, but at first she accepted it: "I thought about the violence—that to achieve peace sometimes you have to kill someone. You can't avoid it."[117] Men and women participants showed no difference in support for violent jihad when necessary, and this support was an important aspect of hegemonic femininity as well as masculinity in the ALM masculinity system.

Women's participation and feminism

While ALM, consistently with IS ideology, required a complementary emphasised femininity from women, this does not necessarily mean that women submitted. Earlier in this chapter, I referred to the Salafi jihad as a modern movement, mobilising an Islamic imaginary. The women I met were also modern British women, who mobilised modern arguments, such as a feminist agenda, to justify their support of ideology positioning them in the home and in subordinate positions within the group. This has some resonance with the so-called 'kitchen table activism' of far-right women, noted in Chapter Five. While ALM recognised the importance of female group membership and sought to recruit women, they had a specific role. During street *Dawah*, Mo distributed leaflets urging women specifically to take up their responsibilities and join him. "From the very beginning of Islam, women have played a vital role in the propagation of the *deen* [faith]", one read. It continued, "The question is will Muslim women be active participants or passive spectators in the Islamic revival?" The movement makes ideological space for agency, and active rather than passive female participation; however, it is clear from Choudary's vision that this can never be a public leadership role and must follow the demarcated roles of Shariah. ALM's hegemonic femininity is active, but must support men's authority and ultimately their violence.

Nonetheless, ALM ideology empowers women in different ways. Through clothing, they can signal a lack of conformity with secular society and with parental Islamic practices; Islamic authority can be used to challenge family prohibitions, and as a source of resistance.[118] Participants regarded secular feminism as unnecessary, given that they believed Islam as a practice and ideology enshrines women's and men's rights according to God's wishes. Yet some of the women framed their faith in feminist terms, borrowing from the rights discourse of secularism to do so. Saleha told me that Western feminism is unnecessary, not just because it is immoral, but also because Islam already contains all the rights women need:

> When Islam was first [invented] women didn't have any rights, then they were nothing, not even seen as human, that's how bad it was. Islam came into the world and gave us these rights. A woman was created, not to do what a man can do, but to do what a man cannot do. ... we have that balance, not to be like men.[119]

Saleha regarded relations between men and women as sacrosanct, with each having rights but not 'gender equality', as secular society posits it. It was preferable to marry, she said, but only to fulfil the *deen* or faith of Islam. Saleha dismissed feminism; Aisha, meanwhile, used it to justify her position. Chapter Six discussed Aisha's dis-ease with her assimilation, because it did not fit her interpretation of how a young Muslim woman should behave. She eventually became involved with an Islamist group who approached her through a University Women's Islamic Society, probably, she said, because she was seen as "susceptible". Years on and married to a man in prison for terrorism offences, she has ceded responsibility to her husband, in accordance with those norms:

> Now as a woman, happily, I say I do completely agree with my husband—I obey my husband. It doesn't sit well with feminists, but I like to think of myself as a feminist—but maybe not the same type as them. ... So, I do obey even where I have not wanted to. ... My husband is very, very clued up on affairs—I wonder, am I brainwashed? No, I'm not, I'm not that naïve.[120]

Aisha justified her reliance on her husband's thinking by framing this as a feminist choice. She embraced the empowerment message offered to Muslim women by the maternalist logic of counter-terrorism programming, and engaged this in an opposite direction.

Summary

This chapter has sought to demonstrate how the masculinities explored in the last chapter, situated in three sites, are mobilised into ALM and network activism. It has considered those masculinities in three sections. The importance of street masculinities as hegemonic was apparent in the accounts of several participants. Whilst they emphasised that ALM had enabled them to redeem themselves and leave street crime behind, they in effect mobilised the same masculinities for group activism, which led to censure within the criminal justice system. This is a finding consistent with radicalisation literature noting the prior involvement of a significant number of jihadist men in petty crime,[121] although most Muslim men involved in street culture do not go on to join extreme groups.

However, street masculinities without learning did not have status. Learning was hegemonic and necessary to endow not just street masculinities but the hypermasculinity of the jihadist warrior with status. Without learning, violence was not hegemonic. The finding suggests that learning and hypermasculinity function as a dyadic pair: hypermasculinity without learning is not hegemonic, as evidenced in narratives in which participants debated the legitimacy of certain acts. Learning masculinities also enabled participants to identify themselves within an epistemic community, as the body becomes a site for the display of knowledge. The importance of knowledge and learning contrasts with norms and masculinity systems within the radical right. The gendered content of learning is consistent with other jihadist and Islamist groups, in that it presents a rigid gender binary. Adherence to this resolves the existential tension of reflexivity concerning hybrid identities.

Misogyny is evident in the chapter in different ways. First there is the internal misogyny directed towards in-group women, and aimed at their control, and claims of care. This is also directed towards some out-group women: victims of domestic violence in non-Muslim communities, apparently, myself, walking home. Nonetheless, Rifat describes the instrumentalising of out-group women in masculinity challenges with EDL men. Care for in-group women does not preclude women's agency in the group, which is expected to be projected in support of men's violence. Then there is external misogyny directed towards out-group women, and evidenced in accounts of so-called 'Muslim Patrol'. This misogyny is reserved for non-Muslim women whose behaviour in public spaces is judged un-Islamic, and who are perhaps judged to be without the prospect of finding Islam. It involves a mobilisation of policing masculinities. As with women in the radical right, there is a complex relationship with misogyny for women. It can be internalised, and it can be mobilised using a rhetoric of feminism. Additionally, Umm M. described how some women seek to express sexuality unseen, online, knowing that to do so publicly would risk censure, from both men and women.

Finally, the chapter has considered online radicalisation, women and the affective nature of mobilisation to the group, termed "heart-washing" by one participant. Women and men support a strict gender ideology consistent with that of other Salafi–jihadi groups; however, some women justify this with appeals to feminism. Recruitment to both IS and ALM mobilised protector masculinities, protected femininities and securitised Muslim identities produced in the discursive space following 9/11, as discussed in the previous chapter. Hegemonic femininity demands the ceding of power to men, but also women's support of violence. It also emphasises sexuality, which is evident in online networks, whether accompanied by a legitimising ideology or not.

8

CONCLUSIONS

Introduction

Never has the subject of gender in terrorism and extremism been more pertinent. With the rise of the manosphere and the incel movement, questions of misogyny and masculinity, and the application of gender to understand extremism, have gained in popularity, even in mainstream security studies. The aim of this book has been to use gender to move beyond accounts of radicalisation that focus either on women or on men, and instead to engage in gendered analysis of relations of power within the movements. The research underpinning the book has undoubtedly taken me on a journey, and I am not unchanged by it. The day after the attacks by jihadists at London Bridge in June 2017, a participant I had come to know well texted to tell me that "two children are [now] without a father." This was a reference to the death of one of the attackers, someone he had apparently known. He seemed to praise the actions. I was angry. I replied, "I was out in South London that night. Would you care if it had been me?" He knew he should care about the death of any human being, he replied. But the truth was, he did not. Extremism exceeds the boundaries set not just by the state but by most people of what is acceptable and what is not. Poverty is never to blame. Yet this is

251

an age of austerity as well as extremism. It mattered to participants in both movements that we met in their hometowns, which, even before COVID-19, were often poor and neglected. It enabled me to get a sense of their lives, communities and experiences. Their situations do not justify their views, especially as most others living around them were not part of extremist groups. But they provide context.

To draw further conclusions from the research findings and process, this final chapter now proceeds in four sections. First, it summarises the findings of the book; second, it assesses the repercussions of understanding radicalisation as a masculinity project for terrorism studies and thinking on extremism; third, it engages with the possible consequences of this empirical research for future work on masculinities by gender scholars; finally, it briefly considers policy implications and the future of counter-extremism in the UK.

The findings

That gender matters in studying extremism is increasingly a given; this book answered calls within terrorism studies to outline the dynamics of precisely how it mattered. Based on the empirical data, I have argued throughout this book that both extremism and radicalisation should be understood as gendered processes. In particular, radicalisation to the two movements explored constitutes a 'masculinity project'. That is the first finding. Radicalisation is a process in which masculinities produced in different ways before group activism become mobilised in service of the group, where they are focused on policing others, fighting or justifying violence. Yet they can also be invested in protecting and in learning. Groups mobilise masculinity systems to facilitate exclusions: of the 'Other', external to the group; but also of some within their group—through pariah femininities, for instance.

This leads to the second finding. There is misogyny; that is clear. However, this is unevenly distributed, and it is rooted in the practices of communities wider than the extreme group or actors alone. Both movements exercise internal misogyny towards movement members, through the gender binary upholding patriarchy. This is framed as both care and control, and can be supported by in-group women. Both movements also exercise external misogyny towards out-group women, often focused on narratives around dress and sexual norms. Meanwhile, groups also mobilise internal misogyny towards particular in-group women who attempt to 'do' masculinities, or transgress binary norms. This was particularly evident in the radical-right narratives, and centred on women's presence at demonstrations. It was less evident in ALM, as women had less opportunity to be present in men's or public spaces. Both movements also at times expressed care towards out-group women, however. In the radical right, this was evident in some participants' seemingly genuinely-held desire to protect women from oppression, including Muslim women. In ALM Rifat described how out-group women married Muslim men to escape domestic violence. Some of the women participants (three from the radical right and one in the ALM network) additionally told me that domestic violence had been part of their path into the group. Misogyny therefore has different expressions. Gender is not the only basis for exclusion in the movements; sexuality, faith and race are evident as axes of exclusion and domination too. What is more, the radical right both presents opportunities for women's leadership, even as this produces fractures in the movement at large, and mobilises against misogyny, albeit the misogyny of the 'Other'. The third finding is therefore that women are enthusiastic participants in these masculinist movements, actively recruited within them and navigating the exclusions evident using diverse strategies.

The fourth finding concerns the nature of the masculinities explored in this book. These operate in systems: combinations of masculinities are hegemonic, which necessitate complementary hegemonic femininities (Connell's "emphasized femininities"). One masculinity performance might require another, complementary, masculinity to validate it. Validation has different primary audiences: women, for the warrior–protector, or other men, for the warrior–scholar. To be strong and chivalrous requires having a weak woman as the object of that chivalry.[1] What is more, Chapter Six demonstrated that individual people can internalise different masculinities, and different masculinity systems, simultaneously. Performing different masculinities simultaneously is more difficult. This existential tension was resolved via meta-reflexivity, and the ultimate prioritisation of one set of masculine values and behaviours.

The final finding relates to the masculinities evident in the radical right and ALM, which were not the same. In the radical right, gender was a point of fragmentation, and different masculinity systems across groups communicated different cultures and values as a means of group distinction. Women found the space for leadership and to shape the movement, as well as experiencing pushback. ALM and the radical right, importantly, perform masculinities according to different systems; what is hegemonic within one culture is not necessarily hegemonic in the other.

Chapter summaries and overall argument

In Chapter One I made an appeal to future terrorism studies scholars to incorporate gender as more than marginal, and concerning more than just women. I considered how radicalisation and extremism theory has frequently—and historically—failed to work with gender at all. Subsequently, in part because of Islamic State's call to recruit women, this was proven to be an incomplete approach. Counter-radicalisation programming and counter-terrorism work frequently include a gender component, in response to international United Nations Security Council Resolution mandates as much as anything else. Often this has done no more than consider gender as pertaining exclusively to women. Contemporary research is becoming interested in gender dynamics, masculinities and misogyny. I outlined some dangers: how narratives of toxic masculinity stigmatise and racialise men and render their actions "legible as masculinity where and when it leaves the white male middle-class body", as Halberstam puts it;[2] and how narratives of both toxic masculinity and misogyny fail to accommodate the actualities of women's extremist activism, outside of victimhood. I also explored how and why gender could provide a more detailed and nuanced picture of what radicalisation means, and what violence means. It is about masculinity and power, but women have a place within this too.[3] Much of this chapter will have felt familiar to gender scholars, who have been calling for a more nuanced approach for decades.

CONCLUSIONS

How to use gender and masculinities to analyse extremism is a
contentious question, and one on which scholars disagree. In Chapter
Two I explored the feminist empathetic methodology engaged for
the research underpinning this book. Here I argued that empathy
is an appropriate tool for engaging with extremists themselves, and
uncovering the gender dynamics of extremism and radicalisation. By
now the reader will have their own views on this. My hope is to have
fairly represented the narratives interviewees gave, while subjecting
them to critical analysis. These are narratives, not truth—something
researchers cannot aspire to. This chapter considered power and
positionality in the field, relating some of the realities of engaging in
this research, and some of its limitations. My whiteness, my class and
education, my non-Muslim-ness and, most of all, my being a woman;
these are all implicated in the analysis presented, and in the academic
and security discourses to which this book belongs. Nonetheless, I
believe we are not weighed down by our identity. It is possible to
carry out ethical research based on talking, with empathy, to people
we do not agree with, who exercise different power or no power, or
with whom we have nothing in common. I hope that Chapters Three
to Seven proved this to be the case.

Of the two movements, the radical right and al-Muhajiroun, the
first three findings chapters focused on the radical right. In Chapter
Three I sought better to understand extreme activism through
analysis of participant interviews, and the key events and background
participants identified as relevant to their later activism. If gender is
a constitutive element of social relationships, this chapter shows that
it is constitutive of these relationships as embodied within space.
Masculinities were situated in the intersections of race, gender, class
and faith, and in local spaces. Particular masculine subcultures and
identities were important, and firmly rooted in geographic space:
football masculinities, including football hooliganism; an idealised
'working-class' masculinity, strongly located in street culture and
produced through masculinity challenges with other white working-
class men; protector masculinities—fathers who take responsibility
for perceived harms to the community and to women within it;
patriot masculinities, substituting for a perceived failed state; and
white masculinities, whose frustrated entitlement is reproduced in

the street protests of the radical right, which lay claim to towns as theirs. The chapter also outlined which masculinities participants understood as weak and subordinate, and why.

In this chapter, women are also important—both Muslim women and in-group women. Radical-right women, like men, perform and valorise masculinities, adopting confrontational behaviours that they, too, associate with an idealised class and place. The chapter considered how both gendered and sexual norms function to create perceptions of difference and in- and out-groups, which are mobilised in action once participants become involved in the extreme group. This chapter introduced the term 'masculinity system', and the idea that participants understood their own system, familiar to their habitus, as incompatible and in confrontation with the masculinity system of the 'Other'. In particular, women's dress and behaviour as emblems of masculinity systems functioned as the boundary by which in- and out-groups were formed. The importance of this chapter was in establishing the later masculinities of activism as everyday, and continuous within and before the group itself.

Chapter Four explored how the masculinities introduced in Chapter Three were mobilised into group protest and activism perceived as moral good. This chapter considered the role of ideology and noted participants' association of formal learning with subordinated liberal masculinity. Ideology is nonetheless evident in participant activism, through shared symbolic practice. While participant behaviours vary little after group entry, some men understand group activism as redemptive, a form of desistance from prior criminality. Here particular subcultures demarcate the borders between group activism, enabling activists to identify which group is for them. Protest cultures separate into military and football, each representing a different set of values and activities. Britain First, with aspirations to more disciplined political activism, mobilised around military-style symbology; they also engaged a more explicitly Christian and confrontational agenda, 'invading' mosques and confronting Muslims they believed guilty of child sexual exploitation. The protest site emerges in this chapter as a gendered and affective space. The different masculinities represented in protest symbols elicit specific affective responses in the men and women activists attending.

I devoted Chapter Five to misogyny, masculinities and women's leadership in the radical right, in part because the two women leaders, Jayda Fransen, then the Deputy Leader of Britain First, and Anne Marie Waters, of For Britain and more recently UKIP, warranted detailed consideration. Hel Gower was an additional EDL leadership figure discussed in this chapter. Here, scholars' assertions of the radical right as 'new', due to its incorporation of narratives favouring women's equality and LGB rights, were considered. Women's leadership is significant. Waters represented, as a gay woman, a leader wholly inconsistent with traditional far-right norms. Women do have power within the radical right, and occupy public authority positions, something not seen in neo-Nazi and 'old' far-right groups in which men's and women's roles and spaces of activism were more strictly defined and separated. Women set agendas; they brought in other women speakers; they confronted Muslim men; they mobilised women recruits. However, the chapter also demonstrated that women's power had limits due to internally directed misogyny, and women had to negotiate this in different ways. Women leaders continue to represent a transgression and use anti-feminist narratives to manage this. Fransen, additionally, presented an emphasised/hegemonic femininity, supporting patriarchy: a conventional role for far-right women.

Sjoberg's suggestion that masculine spaces into which women intrude can work against them to maintain men's power was borne out here, to some degree.[4] Waters attempted change, but the movement pushed back, attempting to police her activism back into the kitchen. EDL Angels, meanwhile, experienced class-based misogyny from their fellow activists, with their participation in the masculine subculture—drinking, casual sex—regarded not as female masculinity but as pariah femininity by men and women alike. Both Fransen and Waters have now left the parties they led when I researched this book, Fransen alleging years of domestic abuse from Britain First leader Paul Golding. Misogyny is, without doubt, part of these women's stories within the radical right. Whether it is the defining one remains to be seen. However, misogyny is not evenly distributed across the radical right; nor is it evenly distributed between the radical right and al-Muhajiroun, given that it limits women's roles in these two movements in very different ways. It is also contiguous with mainstream misogyny and cannot easily be separated from this. Misogyny is not a distinguishing feature of the far right—as explored in these chapters.

Chapters Six and Seven explore masculinities in ALM. In common with other studies,[5] there are parallels with the radical right, in that working-class Muslim masculinity formation has something in common with that of non-Muslim working-class men. In both movements, male leadership figures have special power in representing idealised masculinities that mobilise men and women alike. Gender and sexual norms and the behaviour of women are again used to draw boundaries between in- and out-group. Success in violence is a masculinity that cuts across all others to prove dominance in both movements. There are also important differences. ALM masculinities and femininities are produced in three spaces: violent masculinities emerge in a physical space, similar to the street culture masculinities of the radical right; a meta-reflexive cognitive/affective space through which participants constantly police their assimilated gendered behaviour, and that of others, against an internalised masculinity system representing a different set of sexual and gender norms; and a discursive space produced by the War on Terror and the subsequent British counter-terrorism strategy. This is important in producing racism and discrimination on the one hand, and, on the other, activism as the only perceived means to resolve gendered feelings of dis-ease. While street culture is clearly a factor in ALM radicalisation, masculinities are primarily situated in faith, as opposition to local space, which is regarded as a negative environment.

The chapter shows how masculinities are not just multiple in the ALM network, but multiply experienced. The theme of 'identity crisis' has been integral to understanding radicalisation, and this chapter sheds light on how identity crisis is constituted and affectively experienced as 'dis-ease'. This is not 'crisis', not an event, but a constant raced and gendered process, over many years. The chapter uses the term 'masculinity system' to describe sets of gender values in which masculinities are dominant. Similarly, Hopkins employs the term "repertoire" to describe simultaneously held masculinities in his work on Muslim identities.[6] A masculinity system is a repertoire of masculine and feminine performances consistent with specific gendered values. It is masculinity systems, rather than individual masculinities, which function as hegemonic. Participants contrasted the masculinity system of a culture perceived as 'British' with an internalised Islamo-cultural system. In each, masculinities have complementary femininities; but masculinities, too, both complement and legitimise one another.

In Chapter Seven, it becomes clearer how masculinities are produced together. Unlike in the radical right, ideological adherence is extremely important to ALM activists. Warrior/violent masculinities are hegemonic, but only when legitimised through accompanying scholarly masculinities. These masculinities are dyadic; they have meaning when performed together. This chapter also noted the emphasised femininity of women activists. ALM is different from the radical right in that it does not allow space for women leaders on the same footing as men. Men's stated need to protect women meant that it was difficult for me to access them at all. Women nonetheless appeal to feminism, not just anti-feminism, to justify their acceptance of men's status. Some women are ascribed pariah femininity status, as they challenge the dominance of the fundamentalist and patriarchal model ALM embodies: moderate Muslim women and those whom participants understand as 'British' women, whom activists police as part of Muslim Patrol.

In a deviation from the structure of Chapters Three, Four and Five, which engage the radical-right material, there is no separate chapter devoted to ALM women. This asymmetry is important. Research with both movements was very different. I was lucky to secure multiple interviews with key women leaders in the radical right: Jayda Fransen, Anne Marie Waters and also Hel Gower, who organised the EDL Angels for some time. At the time of field research, no radical-right groups were banned, demonstrations were frequent and there was no shortage of people to talk to—men and women alike. It was not easy to interview women, as I reflect in Chapter Two, but I did, and on multiple occasions. I also talked to numerous men and women in conversations outside of the official interviews. This meant that I had a good sense of the radical right as a movement, and how women functioned within it. The existence of a stand-alone chapter for the radical-right women is an important feature of the book in and of itself, as it indicates my ability, as a white non-Muslim woman researcher, better to gain this access.

This also indicates the degree to which men controlled my access to ALM, and did not or could not in the radical right. This is, of itself, a finding. As noted, men in ALM were protective of women and did not facilitate my access to them as men in the radical right had. Choudary even told me that there were no women in ALM, which is not the case. I did interview women. However, these women were not in leadership positions, and they were not formally part of the ALM activist group; they therefore did not attend either seminars or meetings and other fundraising events. I only met one woman through other people; others I met online. As a result, I only met one woman participant in person, and we met several times. Others I talked to on the phone (or equivalent). It was therefore much harder to assess what these women told me through my own observations.

This means that there are three reasons why I did not write a separate chapter on women, female masculinities and misogyny in ALM. First, quantity: I did not speak to as many women in my research on jihadism as I did for the radical right. Second, quality: not only did I speak to fewer women, but I met them less, and spoke to them for fewer total hours. I also had less opportunity to observe their interactions with others in the movement, due to the nature of my meetings with them, which were mostly not in person. Third, to have included a chapter mirroring Chapter Five—and arguably I could have crafted one from the material gathered—would have implied that the depth of my research in this arena was equivalent to that of my research into the radical right, which was not the case. This would also have masked the various research barriers to discussion with ALM based on my positionality and identity, which I discussed in some detail in Chapter Two. Instead, I chose to integrate the interviews and reflect on both misogyny and women's activism in ALM in Chapters Six and Seven. The reader should not assume that this means there was less misogyny in ALM; this is not inferred by the lack of a corresponding chapter, which essentially relates to ALM men's control of my access to women participants, and perhaps women's mistrust of me online, which led to fewer interviews.

Masculinities in radicalisation and extremism

This book has argued not just that gender matters in radicalisation, but that radicalisation is a masculinity project. However, this is not simply a question of misogynist, toxic masculinity: neither toxicity nor misogyny are distinguishing features of extremism. Extremist ideologies, in common with Kimmel's findings, position enemies as having either too much or too little masculinity, often understood in sexual terms, prompting the use of the appropriate opposing masculinity against them. The masculinities they mobilise are produced in the intersections of class, sex, race and faith and through competing discourses: state, media and community. Gendered and raced discourses cannot be separated. In the radical right, masculinities situated in race and space are mobilised into the subcultural symbologies through which different strands of the movement can be identified. In ALM, masculinities situated in faith are mobilised alongside those situated in the discursive space produced by 9/11 in service of rejection of a masculinity system understood as secular and sexualised. Masculinity is mobilised at each stage of radicalisation. Chapters Three and Six demonstrated that it is sexual and gender norms and perceptions of contradictory masculinities and femininities that enable boundaries to be drawn between in- and out-group. Everyday masculinities—violent, policing, scholarly, protective—are fundamental to participant narratives of pathways into the extreme group, and it is these masculinities that continue into group activism and are mobilised when people, both men and women, engage in extreme activism. Understanding radicalisation as a masculinity project does not mean that it is only about men. Women, too, both support and 'do' masculinities, whether through confrontation and aggression or through leadership roles, and men's performances of particular masculinities appeal to men and women alike.

The gendered approach taken here has produced findings which challenge some conventional wisdoms of existing radicalisation theory and confirms the findings of other scholars in the field. For instance, Busher suggests of entry to the EDL that "by and large ... activism did not entail the degree of rupture in their lives ... as can sometimes be the case when joining a radical political or religious group."[7] He notes that the movement is about "bringing extant identities to the fore",[8] challenging the notion of radicalisation as transformational and emphasising continuity. Bailey, meanwhile, suggests that many social groups are capable of a series of shifts in thought that constitute "microradicalisations".[9] Confirming this, the gendered approach presented here demonstrates that radicalisation entails continuity as much as transformation. Masculine identities appear maintained through and beyond subcultures, and into extreme groups. So, too, are gendered belief systems, practices or ideologies. What participants do change is their level of commitment to a cause and to other activists. They take more risks, including arrest and imprisonment. The group becomes their life. I do not argue that radicalisation is not transformational in some ways; simply that it involves a higher degree of gendered continuity than is implied in existing models.

Berger's in-group/out-group characterisation of extremism incorporates radicalisation theories' emphasis on black-and-white thinking as a marker of radical groups. However, in the wake of emphasis on both gender and masculinities, such a theory is too simplistic. People have multiple identities. Patriarchy remains a compelling organisational structure, and this is particularly true of the extreme group. An amended gendered definition might now explain extremism as:

> The distinction of in-group and out-group through perceptions of conflicting gender and sexual norms. The belief that an in-group's success or survival can never be separated from the need for hostile exclusionary action against an out-group, and mobilising an in-group masculinity system of prescribed masculinities and femininities into action. Such action must be part of the in-group's definition of success. Hostile acts can range from verbal attacks and diminishment, policing of gender and sexual norms, violence and support of violence, including sexual violence, and even genocide and

other discriminatory behavior, *including to in-group members who deviate from gender norms.*[10]

This definition recognises gender as intrinsic to extremism, through a prescribed set of masculinities and femininities mobilised towards particular exclusionary actions. Here I include misogynistic acts in the range of extreme behaviours, which pivot on a gendered axis. However, I do not assert that misogyny is the distinguishing feature of the extreme movements in this book, given the prevalence of similar expressions of misogyny in wider society, and the movements' focus on wider ideological issues. Misogyny is a feature, not necessarily the focus.

Masculinity systems

This research was not simply about talking to women. Following Parpart and Zalewski, who have more than once in past decades posed 'the "Man" question' in IR, it problematises masculinities.[11] The book has attempted to interrogate and understand men's power and how it shapes men's and women's experiences, not within the institutions of international relations, but within those of extreme movements.[12] Scott writes of gender as "a way of referring to the social organization of the relationship between the sexes".[13] Masculinities are not simply multiple, or plural.[14] The book follows masculinities scholars who have found masculinities are multiply and sometimes contradictorily inhabited, as shown in the fourth finding above.

Masculinities are interconnected through systems of meaning, in which some masculinities validate others. In her book on Middle East masculinities, Inhorn notes that Connell's hierarchical masculinities of subordination or hegemony, despite amendments, remain too static; that masculinity concerns dynamic social practice.[15] Duriesmith and Ismail, in their study of Indonesian jihadist identity formation, consider "multiple, overlapping, and contradictory ways in which hierarchies of gender operate".[16] Their suggestion is that a new framework is needed; however, the key issue for them is one of scale, not the formulation of embodied masculinities as 'hierarchies'. In 1995, Sedgwick proposed another model, based on an empirical study by Sandra Bem, for the relationality of masculinities and femininities: that they are orthogonal to one another, which is to say, they are not at opposite ends of a scale. This necessitates "a leap from 2-dimensional into n-dimensional" thinking on this subject.[17] Yet the fundamental concept of masculinities as a linear, two-dimensional hierarchy has endured. This book, along with Sedgwick, Duriesmith, Archer, Inhorn and others, rethinks masculinities as n-dimensional, but also relational in systems. These are better described as heterarchies than hierarchies.

Masculinities and femininities, as mentioned earlier in the book, perform in chords, not notes. Some chords were melodious; they felt right to participants due to their consistency with a well-instituted habitus. Others were discordant and necessitated active prioritisation of some gender systems over others. Sometimes it seemed that this tension was the key reason people became active in their group: they prioritised those masculine performances that 'felt' right and which they believed only the extreme group to esteem. Outside of the group, they experienced censure.

What is more, the masculinities evident in the lives of participants in the research are only possible because of masculinity systems within which they are embedded. Radical-right masculinities and misogynies are not independent of multiple and simultaneously held articulations of masculinity: football masculinities, working-class masculinities—or idealised notions thereof—or nationalist masculinities. Radical-right masculinities are produced through masculinities that are part and parcel of British identity. It is fruitless to search for a single unit of masculinity, such as 'toxicity'; toxicity is not about masculinity, but its effects. Kupers' definition of toxic masculinity does not frame it as one thing; it is a "constellation", suggestive of a particular system.[18] Misogyny is a part of this system. Toxic masculinity, is a term that only hints at an understanding of how gender works, or how people obtain and wield power in extreme groups. Both misogyny and toxicity narratives have something to say about extremism; however, they once again reify assumptions that particular forms of masculinity are "a single monolithic category ... simply, unambiguously, essentially evil".[19] Indeed, for scholars such as Finn MacKay, who envisage a future without the constraints of gender roles, not just masculinities but all gender roles are toxic.

Discussing toxic masculinity, Syed Haider writes: "If violence is constitutive of masculinity, then violence becomes the mode by which one asserts one's masculinity."[20] In this book, the violence constituting extreme masculinities is produced in different places. It is in the local spaces where people live, at the coalface of multiculturalism. It is in decades of class exploitation and mobilisation to violence on behalf of hegemonic others. It is in the discourses engendered by the War on Terror. It is in the tensions between the conflicting gendered norms of masculinity systems, produced in reflexivity. For the men and women involved in this research, extreme activism meant time in prison, estrangement from family or simply reflecting on a life on the wrong path—having taken the wrong turn, as Darren suggested. Masculinities scholar Sally Robinson writes that "fictions of masculinity serve the interests of an abstract concept of male power ... but few individual men".[21] These fictions are ill-equipped to serve women too.

How gender matters for future research

A gendered approach has long suggested an empirical engagement with research. The new data and analysis of the empirical chapters in this book make an important contribution and will be of interest to other gender scholars seeking to understand contemporary political polarisation. Connell, the leading masculinities scholar, advocates life history interviews in particular as a means to knowing the masculine subject. As Nikki Wedgwood notes, "The life history case studies in [Connell's book] *Masculinities* explicitly link the minds and bodies of the men in the study to broad social structures like gender and class. In doing so, those being studied remain visible as real, living people with their own personalities and trajectories."[22] The findings speak for the importance of a gendered theoretical framework in terrorism studies that reads gender across multiple levels. The book has insisted on approaching gender as a way of engaging with structural norms, and how they interact in local space to impact agency and produce particular behaviours, group rules and identities. Analysis is focused on what people said, the words they used and how they chose to represent their stories, contextualised through the literature and participant observation. To return to Chapter Two, empathy as methodology was an important aspect of producing these interviews and disrupting narratives of the extreme actor as Other, whatever harm their ideology does.

This means that the work has in fact focused not just on women, nor just on masculinities, but on gender as a means of producing power in relations. As such, the project engaged a holistic approach to gender. The terms 'women', 'agency' and 'masculinity' are not separate. Masculinised ideologies and group norms produce communities of practice. They engender particular roles and channel the expression of agency in distinct ways. The resulting analysis is therefore at times conceptually 'messy'; however, it is important to see ideology and norms as expressions of the same gendered power dynamics and ideologies. The book therefore advocates empirical engagement with 'messy' subjects and concepts as a means of doing future gender work.

If this book yields anything, it is evidence of how gender concerns systems, relations, structures, spaces and power. To address one possible aspect of these systems of problematic power—'bad men'—is not, therefore, the solution. Nor is the solution to include men in existing theoretical structures as a new version of the gender variable—to 'add men and stir'. Gender as represented in this book is not a discrete entity,[23] available simply to be slotted into existing radicalisation theory. As V. Spike Peterson argues, gender is a perspective: "we do not experience or 'know' the world as abstract 'humans' but as embodied, gendered beings".[24] As long as that is the case, accurate understanding of actors—as knowable and as knowers—requires attention to the effects of our "gendered states".[25] This is as true for extreme actors as for any others.

While the book has sought to be comprehensive in its consideration of gender, there are limitations and omissions. One important omission is a detailed engagement with the queer theory literature on gender, sex and sexuality, and focus on sexuality in the chapters. There is potential within the interview transcripts to return to this question; however, the scope of this particular book is already broad. My hope is to return to the material and focus on sexuality in another publication. Sexualities work is specialist, and developing; Connell faced criticism in her comprehensive body of earlier work for neglecting sexuality as active in the construction of both femininities and masculinities.[26] I have tried hard to use this book to address a gap in mainstream terrorism literature; however, this one book is not able to do everything. It is my hope that its gender analysis, alongside an empathetic approach, presents a path forward for gender studies within the field of terrorism and extremism, and an inspiration to others to do more of this kind of work and address my gaps and inevitable errors.

Masculinities, misogyny and future policy

One of the key difficulties in utilising the research in this book is that of aim. As Stern and Zalewski write in their analysis of the future of feminism in IR, "we promise that if only we could do gender (read: produce masculinities) differently ... then real women and real men [would] live happily ever after".[27] The way forward is not engineering men to be otherwise or pathologising manhood—or even particular forms of it.

The new 2023 CONTEST strategy promises to transform Prevent; however, it is a missed opportunity in terms of gender. It refers to gender only in reference to overseas counter-terrorism. There is no mention of women, or of masculinities. This is despite years of calls from gender scholars better to integrate gender. It is not enough; misogyny is only mentioned in the context of conspiracy theories. As the national context evolves, and the role of gender in radicalisation is better understood, policy must move its language to meet it, recognising how policy itself has an impact on views. Those working to stop Britain's extremism, in counter-terrorism, the CCE, the police and Prevent, have known since at least 2015 and UNSCR 2242 that gender does matter. The question for Prevent teams, whatever the wording of CONTEST, is how they should engage it, and in recent years they, too, have discussed the role of misogyny. Misogyny and toxic masculinity are two sides of the same coin, in that both position women as victims, and both have become buzzwords in current academic and policy discourse on radicalisation, as discussed in Chapter One. Yet this book has shown that while misogyny is evident in the radical right and ALM—to the point of men blocking my access to women in ALM—it is not evenly distributed; it is also largely the same misogyny that is evident in wider British society, and in the lives of the participants before they found an extreme group. A focus on societal misogyny matters, including adequate funding for domestic violence prevention services which have for years suffered from cuts and underfunding, but misogyny should be dealt with in and of itself, not simply as a security issue. It would not be appropriate, as some have suggested, to refer DV cases to Prevent. It might, however, be appropriate to refer Prevent cases where misogyny is evident as domestic abuse to DV teams.

Prevent cases often present a range of complex social issues that require a multi-agency response, and DV resulting from misogyny is one of these. To securitise domestic violence means that women in already marginalised and suspect communities will have an additional layer of fear in reporting problems at home: that this will lead to their families coming under the radar of Prevent. This is unlikely to help anyone, least of all women. The book also shows that some women participants had faced domestic violence prior to joining the extreme movement; clearly this would not be an argument for profiling women survivors of DV.

Prevent referrals range from those who represent the genuine threat of attack to those who idolise school shooters, or Andrew Tate, or other social ills which are not extremism, and are included under the category MUU (the unhelpful *pot pourri* of 'mixed, unclear and unstable ideologies'). It is clear, looking at these referrals, that the programme risks becoming a repository for problems that cannot be solved elsewhere, and have come onto the radar of those mandated under the Prevent duty: teachers, doctors and lecturers. Misogyny and domestic violence resulting from this are prevalent in society, but if Prevent were to deal with all issues in the often complex lives of those referred—mental health, drug problems, family violence—it would not be able to focus on its actual task, which is combatting radicalisation.

While my focus in this book is on masculinities, and the movements concerned are studied as homosocial, it should also be clear that I am not advocating a policy return to the bad old days where women were invisible. The movements discussed in this book include men and women; gender dynamics affect everyone. Nor, despite the dominance of men and men's power, are the women in this book passive wallflowers. In the radical right they are leaders, in spite of any misogyny, and in both movements they were no less ideologically committed than men. Policymakers cannot ignore women, and they cannot assume that they are less ideologically driven, even if their actual roles differ from men's. This is worth repeating. It is also worth repeating that as part of gender mainstreaming in any approach, it is important to recognise intersectionality. Policymakers should consider impacts differentially—on men, on women, on boys, on girls, on Muslims, on non-Muslims, on the middle-aged (they are represented in this book) and on the young, as well as considering how sexuality, gender and disability impact identity. Gender is enacted differently at different ages, with different masculinities hegemonic at different times in life. Participants reference changes due to age and life situation, and this is important. There is no one gendered outcome, but there are ways of thinking about likely outcomes of policy for different demographic groups. This also applies to wider government policy. It is impossible to craft immigration policies that appease the far right, or education policies that focus not on education but on immigrant assimilation, without having tangible security outcomes. One of these is perceived hypocrisy when the same governments enforcing such policies then attempt to censure the radical right and label them as extreme. Ultimately this is likely to threaten not security, but the democratic function of the state.

Working with masculinities to understand crime more broadly has relied on a particular logic: if the two are connected, then changing one will produce a change in the other.[28] If only countering either crime or extremism were so simple. Amar has effectively critiqued how the "public-discourse versions of masculinity studies" employed within the academic and policy landscape of "terrorology" frame Islamist masculinities as "atavistic, misogynist and hypersexual".[29] Additionally, there is no such thing as 'a' working-class masculinity,[30] or, as this book has shown, one extreme masculinity. Given that the radical right is only one subset of the far-right family, and ALM one subset of Salafi jihadism, the possibility of identifying one type of masculinity to 'challenge' is small. Anyone seeking to engage masculinities in counter-terrorism should therefore proceed with care. Too frequently, gendered research has damaging effects when mobilised by governments with communities for whom radicalisation is only one of many more important issues.[31] Interesting work has been done by men who understand the norms and values of the masculinity systems of extremists; formers, for instance, who work with the transformation of masculinity in ways that feel authentic and that men understand. One example is the Unity Initiative's Usman Raja, who once held fundamentalist beliefs. His deradicalisation work engages mixed martial arts as "a battlefield for both the mind and the body" in mentoring, and recalls that he himself was "moulded by the streets with a ready fighting instinct and short fuse".[32] Such work still needs to be subject to adequate monitoring and evaluation.

This book is, of course, as much a part of 'terrorology' as any other on radicalisation. I hope not to have fallen into traps that either reduce activists to gendered stereotypes or elevate them to objects of sympathy, but I am aware that meeting them and writing about them risks this. Amar warns that tropes associated with "men in crisis" are implicated in "misrecognizing, racializing, moralistically-depoliticizing and class-displacing emergent social forces".[33] This cannot be conducive to ending extremism. Of course, extremism is read as morally offensive; however, easy characterisations of the men involved as uniformly deviant, distorted and dangerous do not help. Whether of 'angry young men' in the far right or vulnerable-turned-hypermasculine jihadists, such narratives are unrecognisable to the men and women involved in extreme movements. They also do little to enable us truly to work to prevent extremism.

Additionally, it is not just men who should do the work of transforming masculinities; masculinities and femininities are produced together, and within systems.[34] Changing them is the work of women too, but not their responsibility.[35] Gender norms can change. Increasingly, the situation on the far right is one of populism, not extremism. Discourse has shifted. In 2018, protests on behalf of Tommy Robinson brought thousands onto the streets. Now it is online influencer, and misogynist, Andrew Tate who appears to be a priority for the media, although he is not extreme by any standard definition of the extremism literature. It is not clear whether such figures are pushing views into the wider public or reflecting a public that feels unheard. As public thinking changes, policy must change too. Extremism, misogyny and populism, however ill-defined, are not the same thing. Policy designed to counter extremism cannot hope to counter populism. Ask any woman: misogyny is a societal issue, not just a security issue. Curiosity about the 'rank and file' should not distract us from asking questions about where the masculine power of patriarchy really lies.[36] States act to curtail masculinities that they themselves have had a role in producing, via the securitising practices of the policing of particular men.

Duriesmith has noted that the identity junctures that constitute radicalisation are structured through gender confrontations with different forms of masculinity.[37] He has emphasised the hybridity of masculinities often homogenised into one word: 'jihadist', or 'threat'. For ALM participants in this book, those confrontations were constant and often subconscious, engendered through feelings of the impossibility of living according to the gender practices of one's own habitus in a society in which these are not normative. Interviewees were all aware of how their local hegemonic masculinity was perceived outside of their activist circles. They had been aware of difference from the mainstream for most of their lives. Activism made sense to people. For those in the radical right, the sense was not rational, or ideological. It was affective and intuitive, based on interaction with the normative values that interviewees had grown up with, and the cultural practices they had absorbed. This means that dissuading people from activism is not simply a question of critical thinking, or telling them that they are wrong and need to change: you cannot argue people away from a position which they feel, and which they know that you do not. I tried, multiple times. It was an approach that could never work.

Summary

The 2023 CONTEST strategy noted the threat posed by both the far right and Islamist terrorists—threats linked to the subjects of this book.[38] In practice, particular terrorist and extreme groups come and go, and the influence of the key actors at the centre of this study has changed since 2016–18, when I carried out the research. Even as Anjem Choudary is again arrested, Jayda Fransen returns to Twitter and Tommy Robinson reportedly teams up with Paul Golding, who is 'liked' by Elon Musk, the EDL, Britain First and ALM will be understood by some as yesterday's extremism, problems of British society that have dissipated. The key groups that the Prevent strategy was structured to engage have changed over time. Is Britain therefore less extreme? No. Groups are banned; street movements fall from popularity. There are new extremisms, some based around the old ideologies, others with different causes. Group fragmentation is commonplace; a group can draw thousands to the streets and then dwindle. However, the ideas at an extreme movement's heart, and the framings of gender within them, have the power to endure. This book, importantly, provides a template for understanding future groups by using a gendered approach: how are masculinities situated, and how are they mobilised? How do they benefit and disadvantage the men and women who live by them?

A gendered approach presents the opportunity to work positively with communities in order to foster change by exploring gendered relations, clearly a source of tension. None of this is necessarily enabled by current discourses of 'extremism'. Extremism discourses have securitised groups of actors in particular ways. These actors are already marginalised by gender, race, class or power. Both Muslim and non-Muslim working-class masculinities are subordinated. Both groups engaged in this book are the subject of condescension, mistrust and surveillance.[39] All the participants reject discourses labelling them as extreme, and a number point to the hypocrisy of the state, which has acted on them in exclusionary ways: through arrest or through silencing. What is clear is that even if the political subjectivities of marginalised extreme actors are invalidated through securitising discourses, they do not disappear. They find alternative expression. The gender analysis of this book had the aim of recognising and understanding the constitution of these subjectivities; they clearly are not erased simply because they have been told they should not exist.

It is also clear that attempts by the state to treat the movements as manifestations of the same kind of thing ('extremism'), and therefore amenable to the same types of intervention, are flawed. Gender is frequently used as a way of drawing straightforward comparisons between movements. However, this book showed that comparisons are not straightforward; there are complex and diverse gender dynamics at play, particularly in the radical right. Additionally, comparisons need to be made not simply between movements, but with British society as a whole and 'mainstream' discourses. From an ideological perspective, the views of the Islamist participants are very far from the vision of Britishness communicated by the British government; the perspective of the radical right is less distinct.

In sum, this book suggests a rethinking of theory on extremism and radicalisation, and the policy aimed at tackling them. All the participants put themselves at considerable legal and social risk to adhere to their beliefs. If we are to understand how and why they seek power in society, we must also see how society seeks to withhold it from them. Intrinsic to this, as this book has sought to show, is a holistic study of gender and its complex manifestations. Both policy and mainstream security studies, from which it is often derived, have, until recently, neglected gender. Gender is perhaps the most fundamental of our identities as human beings. The fury of both sides of the 'gender wars' evidences the seriousness with which people engage with who they, and others, are: as gendered people and as sexed bodies.[40] Gender is also fundamental to understanding violence, and how it is structured and organised.[41] However, it is easy to get wrong, and the harms caused by poorly formulated gender policy can be devastating. Talk to any British Muslim community about Prevent and its policies, and there will be voices that attest to this. It is my hope, despite all the complexities of this space, that this book makes a contribution; that it is one step on the path to better understanding of gender in extremism, better ideas of how to research gender and terrorism and better security policy resulting from this. Extremism does not appear to be going anywhere and both gender and empathy are tools to understand it. I hope that these tools will help evolve our understanding of extremism, ultimately reducing the harms that radicalisation causes, for people in extreme movements, for their friends and families, for democracy and society, and us all.

APPENDIX

Interviews
Column D marks the key dates on which interviews took place that were later transcribed.

Additional conversations took place via social media, via phone, by text and at demonstrations, which also included participant observation. Additional meetings took place informally where notes were not taken. 'Age' in Column C indicates age at time of interviews, where known.

Radical right interviews

Name		Age	Dates	Primary Affiliations
Anne Marie Waters	F	40s	20/8/16 30/8/16 14/10/16	UKIP Pegida For Britain
Georgey	F	30s	28/9/16 17/10/16	EDL
Hel Gower	F	60s	2/11/16 16/12/16	EDL
Jane	F	50s	23/8/16 1/9/16 14/10/16 26/10/16	EDL WLM

Name		Age	Dates	Primary Affiliations
Jayda Fransen	F	30s	3/12/16 5/4/17 26/1/18 27/4/23	BF
Lydia	F	50s	27/2/17 28/2/17 1/4/17 25/5/17 15/7/17 19/8/17	BF
Alex	M	20s	25/8/16	EDL
Bonzer	M	40s	25/8/16	EDL +
Daniel	M	20s	25/8/16 5/11/16	EDL UP +
Darren	M	40s	4/8/16	EDL +
Glynn	M	?	23/8/16	EDL +
Henryk	M	60s	22/7/17	BF
Iain	M	19	25/8/16 5/11/16 10/12/16	EDL, UP +
Jacek	M	30s	7/9/16 22/10/16	FB BF WLM +
Jason	M	30s	9/8/16, 15/8/16 6/11/16	Independent
John Meighan	M	30s	5/7/17	FLA
Tommy Robinson aka Stephen Yaxley-Lennon	M	30s	26/9/16 10/3/17 11/4/17	EDL Pegida Independent

Islamist/al-Muhajiroun interviews

Name		Age	Dates	Primary Affiliations
Aisha	F	30s	10/4/17	Network

Name		Age	Dates	Primary Affiliations
Saleha	F	19	15/7/16 20/7/16 16/8/16	Online network
Umm M	F	30s	20/8/16	Online network
Farhan	M	20s	24/8/16	N/A (friend of women who had travelled to Islamic State)
Kate	F	60s	17/7/16	N/A (mother of convicted Islamist terrorist)
Abu M	M	20s	2016 (messaging only)	Online network
Adam	M	20s	16/6/16 12/7/16 28/3/17 4/4/17	Network
Ahmed	M	20s	May 2016 (messaging only)	Online network
Akash	M	30s	1/11/16 6/11/16 11/12/16 7/2/17 29/3/17 14/5/17	Network
Anhar	M	20s	29/9/16	Network
Anjem Choudary	M	40s	18/7/16	ALM Leader
Mo	M	20s	16/9/16 29/9/16 5/10/16 8/10/16	Network
Rifat	M	30s	21/5/17 16/7/17	Network
Zakir	M	30s	2/12/16	Network

Demonstrations and events: radical right

25 August 2016, undisclosable location, United Patriots
20 August 2016, London, Islam Kills Women
22 October 2016, Margate, White Lives Matter
5 November 2016, Telford, EDL
3 December 2016, undisclosable location, Britain First AGM
25 February 2017, Telford, Britain First
1 April 2017, Westminster, London, EDL
1 April 2017, Westminster, London, Britain First
22 July 2017, Rochdale, Britain First
4 November 2017, Bromley, Britain First
2 December 2017, undisclosable location, Britain First Conference

Al-Muhajiroun–linked events and trials attended are not listed for legal reasons and the preservation of participant anonymity.

GLOSSARY

Al-Muhajiroun The emigrants, a reference to the flight of the Prophet Mohammed from Mecca to Medina

Al-Qaeda In Arabic, the base, the jihadist group founded by Osama bin Laden

Antifa Left-wing anti-fascist and anti-racist political movement involved in protest against the far right

'Aqeedah Creed in Islam, the core set of beliefs followed

Bidah In Islam, any innovation to the practice established by the Prophet in the Sunnah

Burqa Islamic clothing covering a woman's body and hair.

Caliphate An Islamic state governing Muslims according to Shariah law and ruled by a Caliph, or spiritual leader

CONTEST The UK's counter-terrorism strategy

Dawah The propagation of the teachings of the Prophet

Gettr An alternative social media platform largely populated by those with radical-right views

Hajj One of the Five Pillars of Islam, this is the pilgrimage Muslims must make to Mecca at least once in their lifetime, if able

Haram Forbidden according to Islamic law

Hijab An Islamic hair covering or headscarf

Hijrah The migration of the Prophet Mohammed from Mecca to Medina, to escape persecution

Imam A Muslim religious prayer-leader, usually male

Incel Involuntary celibate; generally a young man who is part of an online community which believes that women are denying them sex

Jahiliyyah Ignorance in Islam, the period before the word of Allah was revealed to Mohammed in the Quran

Jamaat Ahlus Sunna Lidawati Wal Jihad Often known as Boko Haram, People Committed to the Prophet's Teachings for Propagation and Jihad

Jannah In Islam, Heaven, the reward for believers

Jihad The Islamic 'lesser jihad', specifically the violent struggle for Islam based on violent interpretations of fundamentalist Salafi beliefs

Kamees A long tunic worn by some Muslim men in emulation of the Prophet Mohammed

Keffiyeh A traditional headdress worn by men in desert regions of the Middle East, now also associated with the Palestinian cause

Khilafah See the entry for Caliphate

Kufar In Islam, a non-believer—derogatory

Mecca Islam's holiest city, and the birthplace of both the Prophet Mohammed and the Muslim faith

Mujahid In Islam, a warrior, one who undertakes jihad

Niqab A face covering worn by some Muslim women, leaving only the eyes uncovered

Pegida German acronym for *Patriotische Europäer gegen die Islamisierung des Abendlandes* or Patriotic Europeans Against the Islamification of the West

Prevent The UK's counter-radicalisation programme

Salafi In Arabic, 'predecessor'; Salafi Muslims follow a literalist interpretation of the Quran

Shahada The oath of faith to Islam

Shariah Islamic law; the regulations governing the practices of Muslims

Sheikh A respected male leader within a Muslim community

Sunnah In Islam, the sayings and practices of the Prophet Mohammed

Takfir The practice of one Muslim declaring another a non-believer

Tawheed The oneness of Allah

Thaub A traditional Arab garment for men

Ummah The global community of Muslims

Wahhab A follower of the teachings of Muhammad ibn Abd al-Wahhab, and the Islam practised in Saudi Arabia

Wallah(i) 'I swear to God', a phrase used in Arabic for emphasis

NOTES

INTRODUCTION

1. Jayda Fransen was then Deputy Leader of Britain First.
2. In a British context, 'Asian' most often refers to people whose heritage lies in the Indian subcontinent.
3. Hope Not Hate, "State of Hate Report 2023" (February 2023): https://hopenothate.org.uk/wp-content/uploads/2023/02/state-of-hate-2023-v7-1.pdf, last accessed 23 July 2023.
4. Lars Rensmann, "The New Politics of Prejudice: Comparative Perspectives on Extreme Right Parties in European Democracies", *German Politics & Society* vol. 21, no. 4 (2003): 93–123 (95), citing McGowan (2003) and also Simmons (1996).
5. Hope Not Hate tweeted, "Elon Musk says he wants Twitter to be a town square but it's clear his idea of a town square would be overrun by racists. Here he is liking tweets from Britain First's, Paul Golding." See https://twitter.com/hopenothate/status/1680507890702905346, last accessed 23 July 2023. Golding himself responded, "Got my first 'Likes' by Elon Musk. Far-left extremists 'Hope Not Hate' are absolutely furious. It's made my day 😂 #FreeSpeech": https://twitter.com/GoldingBF/status/1680558486273376262, last accessed 23 July 2023.
6. In January 2018, Twitter responded to criticism with a blog justifying the exemption of world leaders from blocks or bans: see https://blog.twitter.com/official/en_us/topics/company/2018/world-leaders-and-twitter.html, last accessed 23 July 2023.
7. Caron E. Gentry, "Misogynistic Terrorism: It Has Always Been Here", *Critical Studies on Terrorism* vol. 15, no. 1 (2022): 209–24 (216).
8. HM Government, "Counter-Extremism Strategy" (October 2015), 9: https://www.gov.uk/government/publications/counter-extremism-strategy, last accessed 26 July 2023.

283

9. HM Government, "CONTEST: The United Kingdom's Strategy for Countering Terrorism" (2009); HM Government, "CONTEST The United Kingdom's Strategy for Countering Terrorism Annual Report 2012" (March 2013): https://www.gov.uk/government/uploads/system/uploads/attachment_data/file/170644/28307_Cm_8583_v0_20.pdf, last accessed 26 July 2023; Home Office, "CONTEST: The United Kingdom's Strategy for Countering Terrorism" (June 2018): https://assets.publishing.service.gov.uk/government/uploads/system/uploads/attachment_data/file/716907/140618_CCS207_CCS0218929798-1_CONTEST_3.0_WEB.pdf, last accessed 26 July 2023; HM Government, "CONTEST 2023" (July 2023): https://assets.publishing.service.gov.uk/government/uploads/system/uploads/attachment_data/file/1171084/CONTEST_2023.pdf, last accessed 26 July 2023.
10. Home Office, "Prevent Strategy" (2011): https://www.gov.uk/government/uploads/system/uploads/attachment_data/file/97976/prevent-strategy-review.pdf, last accessed 26 July 2023.
11. David R. Mandel, "Radicalization: What Does It Mean?", in *Home-Grown Terrorism: Understanding and Addressing the Root Causes of Radicalisation Among Groups with an Immigrant Heritage in Europe*, eds Thomas M. Pick, Anne Speckhard and Beatrice Jacuch (2009), 101–13; Peter R. Neumann, "The Trouble with Radicalization", *International Affairs* vol. 89, no. 4 (2013): 873–93; Michael King and Donald M. Taylor, "The Radicalization of Homegrown Jihadists: A Review of Theoretical Models and Social Psychological Evidence", *Terrorism and Political Violence* vol. 23, no. 4 (2011): 602–22.
12. Anthony Richards, "Conceptualizing Terrorism", *Studies in Conflict & Terrorism* vol. 37, no. 3 (2014): 213–36.
13. Rachel Briggs, "Community Engagement for Counterterrorism: Lessons from the United Kingdom", *International Affairs* vol. 89, no. 4 (2010): 971–81 (975); HM Government, "CONTEST" (2009), 13 & 57.
14. Alex P. Schmid, "Radicalisation, De-Radicalisation, Counter-Radicalisation: A Conceptual Discussion and Literature Review", (International Centre for Counter-Terrorism, The Hague, 2013), 8: https://www.icct.nl/sites/default/files/import/publication/ICCT-Schmid-Radicalisation-De-Radicalisation-Counter-Radicalisation-March-2013_2.pdf, last accessed 26 July 2023.
15. J. M. Berger, *Extremism* (Cambridge, MA: MIT Press, 2018).
16. Henri Tajfel, ed., *Differentiation Between Social Groups: Studies in the Social Psychology of Intergroup Relations* (London; New York, NY: Academic Press, 1979).
17. Berger, *Extremism*, 44.
18. OSCE, "Women and Terrorist Radicalization" (2011): https://www.osce.org/files/f/documents/4/a/99919.pdf, last accessed 27 July 2023; Jane L. Parpart and Marysia Zalewski, "Introduction: Rethinking the Man Question", in *Rethinking the Man Question: Sex, Gender and Violence in International Relations*, eds Jane L. Parpart and Marysia Zalewski (London; New York, NY: Zed Books, 2008), 1–22 (1); Cynthia Enloe, *Bananas, Beaches and Bases: Making Feminist Sense of International Politics*, 2nd revised edition (Berkeley, CA: University of

284

California Press, 2001), 6; J. Ann Tickner, "You Just Don't Understand: Troubled Engagements between Feminists and IR Theorists", *International Studies Quarterly* vol. 41, no. 4 (1997): 611–32.

19. Michael Kimmel, *Healing from Hate: How Young Men Get Into—and Out of—Violent Extremism* (Oakland, CA: University of California Press, 2018), 5.

20. Jacob Zenn and Elizabeth Pearson, "Women, Gender and the Evolving Tactics of Boko Haram", *Journal of Terrorism Research* vol. 5, no. 1 (2014): 46–57; Atta Barkindo, Caroline K. Wesley and Benjamin Tyavkase Gudaku, "Our Bodies, Their Battleground: Boko Haram and Gender-Based Violence Against Christian Women and Children in North-Eastern Nigeria Since 1999" (World Watch Research Unit of Open Doors International, the Netherlands, November 2013): https://www.worldwatchmonitor.org/research/3117403, last accessed 27 July 2023; Mausi Segun and Samer Muscati, "'Those Terrible Weeks in Their Camp': Boko Haram Violence Against Women and Girls in Northeast Nigeria" (Human Rights Watch, 2014): http://www.hrw.org/sites/default/files/reports/nigeria1014web.pdf, last accessed 27 July 2023.

21. Charles Hymas, "Efforts to Combat Extremism Failing Because of Way Government Has Defined It, Commissioner Says", *The Telegraph*, 6 October 2019: https://www.telegraph.co.uk/politics/2019/10/06/efforts-combat-terrorism-failing-governments-definition-extremism/, last accessed 27 July 2023.

22. Commission for Countering Extremism, "Three Years On: Achievements and Reflections" (March 2021), 2: https://assets.publishing.service.gov.uk/government/uploads/system/uploads/attachment_data/file/973636/CCE_End_of_year_report_2021_Accessible.pdf, last accessed 27 July 2023.

23. Commission for Countering Extremism, "Challenging Hateful Extremism" (October 2019), 1: https://assets.publishing.service.gov.uk/government/uploads/system/uploads/attachment_data/file/874101/200320_Challenging_Hateful_Extremism.pdf, last accessed 27 July 2023.

24. Michael Kenney, *The Islamic State in Britain: Radicalization and Resilience in an Activist Network* (Cambridge: Cambridge University Press, 2018), 147.

25. USAID, "Guide to the Drivers of Violent Extremism" (*USAID*, 2009), 86: https://www.cvereferenceguide.org/sites/default/files/resources/USAID%20Guide%20to%20the%20Drivers%20of%20Violent%20Extremism%20%281%29.pdf, last accessed 16 August 2023.

26. Thomas Hegghammer, *Jihad in Saudi Arabia: Violence and Pan-Islamism since 1979* (Cambridge; New York, NY: Cambridge University Press, 2011), 3.

27. Quintan Wiktorowicz, "Anatomy of the Salafi Movement", *Studies in Conflict & Terrorism* vol. 29, no. 3 (2006): 207–39.

28. Jeffrey M. Bale, "Islamism and Totalitarianism", *Totalitarian Movements and Political Religions* vol. 10, no. 2 (2009): 73–96; Lorenzo Vidino, "Islamism in Europe" (World Watch Research Unit of Open Doors International, 2015): http://opendoorsanalytical.org/wp-content/uploads/2014/10/Islamism-in-Europe-2015.pdf, last accessed 16 August 2023.

29. Robinson regained a Twitter profile late in 2022 but was again suspended in January 2023.

30. Hope Not Hate, "State of Hate 2022: On The March Again" (March 2022), 93: https://hopenothate.org.uk/wp-content/uploads/2022/03/state-of-hate-2022-v1_17-March-update.pdf, last accessed 27 July 2023.

31. Hope Not Hate, "State of Hate Report 2023".

32. Luke March notes that the far left is "to", not "on", the left of social democracy. The far left can be further classified as "radical" or "extreme", according to the stance on the action that needs to be taken to counter capitalism. Luke March, "Contemporary Far Left Parties in Europe: From Marxism to the Mainstream?" (Friedrich Ebert Stiftung, 2009), 3: https://library.fes.de/pdf-files/id/ipa/05818.pdf, last accessed 27 July 2023.

33. Kylie MacLellan, "Radical UK Islamist preacher Anjem Choudary charged with three terrorist offences ", Reuters, 24 July 2023: https://www.reuters.com/world/uk/radical-uk-islamist-preacher-anjem-choudary-charged-with-three-terrorist-2023-07-24/.

34. "Anjem Choudary: Radical Preacher's Public Speaking Ban to Be Lifted", BBC News, 18 July 2021: https://www.bbc.com/news/uk-england-london-57878910, last accessed 27 July 2023.

35. Douglas Weeks, "Doing Derad: An Analysis of the U.K. System", *Studies in Conflict & Terrorism* vol. 41, no. 7 (2017): 523–40. ASBOs have now been replaced with Criminal Behaviour Orders and Civil Injunctions.

36. Kenney, *The Islamic State in Britain*.

37. Graham Macklin and Joel Busher, "The Missing Spirals of Violence: Four Waves of Movement–Countermovement Contest in Post-War Britain", *Behavioral Sciences of Terrorism and Political Aggression* vol. 7, no. 1 (2015): 53–68 (53–54).

38. Jamie Bartlett and Jonathan Birdwell, "Cumulative Radicalisation Between the Far-Right and Islamist Groups in the UK: A Review of Evidence" (Demos, November 2013), 5; 8; 12: https://demos.co.uk/wp-content/uploads/files/Demos%20-%20Cumulative%20Radicalisation%20-%205%20Nov%202013.pdf, last accessed 27 July 2023.

39. Simone de Beauvoir, *The Second Sex*, trans. H. M. Parshley, 1949 (London: Vintage Classics, 1997), 295; Judith Butler, *Gender Trouble: Feminism and the Subversion of Identity*, 1990 (New York, NY: Routledge, 2006), 34.

40. UN Women, "Concepts and Definitions": https://www.un.org/womenwatch/osagi/conceptsandefinitions.htm, last accessed 22 August 2023.

41. Laura Sjoberg, Grace D. Cooke and Stacy Reiter Neal, "Introduction", in *Women, Gender, and Terrorism*, eds Laura Sjoberg and Caron E. Gentry (Athens, GA: University of Georgia Press, 2011), 1–26 (6).

42. Butler, *Gender Trouble*.

43. R. W. Connell, *Masculinities* (Cambridge: Polity Press, 1995), 71.

44. Kimberly Hutchings, "Making Sense of Masculinity and War", *Men and Masculinities* vol. 10, no. 4 (2007): 389–404 (390).

45. Joan W. Scott, "Gender: A Useful Category of Historical Analysis", *The American Historical Review* vol. 91, no. 5 (1986): 1053–75 (1057; 1069).
46. Laura Sjoberg, *Gendering Global Conflict: Toward a Feminist Theory of War* (New York, NY: Columbia University Press, 2013); Gentry, "Misogynistic Terrorism".
47. Edwin Bakker, "Jihadi Terrorists in Europe: Their Characteristics and the Circumstances in Which They Joined the Jihad: An Exploratory Study" (Clingendael Institute, 2006), 36: https://www.clingendael.org/sites/default/files/pdfs/20061200_cscp_csp_bakker.pdf, last accessed 27 July 2023.
48. Marc Sageman, *Understanding Terror Networks* (Philadelphia, PA: University of Pennsylvania Press, 2004); Daveed Gartenstein-Ross and Laura Grossman, *Homegrown Terrorists in the US and UK: An Empirical Examination of the Radicalization Process* (Washington, DC: FDD Press, 2009).
49. Robert Ford and Matthew J. Goodwin, *Revolt on the Right: Explaining Support for the Radical Right in Britain* (Abingdon; New York, NY: Routledge, 2014), 79.
50. Jamie Bartlett and Mark Littler, "Inside the EDL" (Demos, 2011), 14: https://www.demos.co.uk/files/Inside_the_edl_WEB.pdf, last accessed 27 July 2023; Hilary Pilkington, "'EDL Angels Stand Beside Their Men… Not Behind Them': The Politics of Gender and Sexuality in an Anti-Islam(ist) Movement", *Gender and Education* vol. 29, no. 2 (2017): 238–57 (253).
51. Nigel Copsey, "The English Defence League: Challenging Our Country and Our Values of Social Inclusion, Fairness and Equality" (Faith Matters, November 2010), 29: https://www.faith-matters.org/wp-content/uploads/2010/11/english-defense-league-report.pdf, last accessed 28 July 2023; Matthew Goodwin, "The Roots of Extremism: The English Defence League and the Counter-Jihad Challenge" (Chatham House, 2013), 6: https://www.chathamhouse.org/sites/default/files/public/Research/Europe/0313bp_goodwin.pdf, last accessed 28 July 2023; James Treadwell and Jon Garland, "Masculinity, Marginalization and Violence: A Case Study of the English Defence League", *British Journal of Criminology* vol. 51, no. 4 (2011): 621–34; Robert Ford and Matthew J. Goodwin, "Angry White Men: Individual and Contextual Predictors of Support for the British National Party", *Political Studies* vol. 58, no. 1 (2010): 1–25.
52. Eelco Harteveld and Elisabeth Ivarsflaten, 'Why Women Avoid the Radical Right: Internalized Norms and Party Reputations', *British Journal of Political Science* vol. 48, no. 2 (2016): 1–16; Kai Arzheimer and Elisabeth Carter, "Political Opportunity Structures and Right-Wing Extremist Party Success", *European Journal of Political Research* vol. 45, no. 3 (2006): 419–43 (428).
53. Quintan Wiktorowicz, *Radical Islam Rising: Muslim Extremism in the West* (Lanham, MD: Rowman & Littlefield, 2005), 115–17.
54. Douglas Weeks, *Al Muhajiroun: A Case Study in Contemporary Islamic Activism* (Basingstoke: Palgrave Macmillan, 2020); Kenney, *The Islamic State in Britain*.
55. Bakker, "Jihadi Terrorists in Europe"; Gartenstein-Ross and Grossman, *Homegrown Terrorists in the US and UK*; Janny Groen and Annieke Kranenberg, *Women Warriors for Allah: An Islamist Network in the Netherlands*, trans. Robert Naborn (Philadelphia, PA: University of Pennsylvania Press, 2010).

56. Ashley A. Mattheis and Charlie Winter, "'The Greatness of Her Position': Comparing Identitarian and Jihadi Discourses on Women" (International Centre for the Study of Radicalisation and Political Violence, 2019): https://icsr.info/wp-content/uploads/2019/05/ICSR-Report-'The-Greatness-of-Her-Position'-Comparing-Identitarian-and-Jihadi-Discourses-on-Women. pdf, last accessed 29 July 2023; Elizabeth Pearson, "Wilayat Shahidat: Boko Haram, the Islamic State, and the Question of the Female Suicide Bomber", in *Boko Haram: Behind the Headlines*, eds Jason Warner and Jacob Zenn (West Point, NY: CTC Sentinel, 2018), 33–52.

57. Charlie Winter, "Women of the Islamic State: A Manifesto on Women by the Al-Khanssaa Brigade" (London: The Quilliam Foundation, 2015), 7.

58. V. Spike Peterson, "Gendered Nationalism", *Peace Review* vol. 6, no. 1 (1994): 77–83; Cynthia Cockburn and Cynthia Enloe, "Militarism, Patriarchy and Peace Movements", *International Feminist Journal of Militarism* vol. 14, no. 4 (2012): 550–57; Wendy Brown, "The Impossibility of Women's Studies", in *Women's Studies on the Edge*, ed. Joan Wallach Scott (Durham, NC: Duke University Press, 2008), 17–38.

59. For a definition of the term 'hypermasculinity', see Andrew Childs, "Hyper or Hypo-Masculine? Re-Conceptualizing 'Hyper-Masculinity' through Seattle's Gay, Leather Community", *Gender, Place & Culture* vol. 23, no. 9 (2016): 1315–28; Childs notes that, instead of being understood as contextually dependent, it is frequently essentialised to represent violence and machismo. This meaning is common in terrorism studies. The term is further discussed in Chapter One.

60. Nira Yuval-Davis, "Women and the Biological Reproduction of 'The Nation'", *Women's Studies International Forum* vol. 19, no. 1/2 (1996): 17–24 (22).

61. Gentry, "Misogynistic Terrorism"; Joshua M. Roose and Joana Cook, "Supreme Men, Subjected Women: Gender Inequality and Violence in Jihadist, Far Right and Male Supremacist Ideologies", *Studies in Conflict & Terrorism* (2022): 1–29.

62. Kathleen M. Blee, "Next Steps in Gender Analysis of Far-Right Extremism" (Keynote Lecture, University of Oslo, 14 May 2018).

63. Kimmel, *Healing From Hate*.

64. Jean Bethke Elshtain, *Women and War* (Chicago, IL: University of Chicago Press, 1987).

65. Gentry writes that incels are "men who are lonely with no dating nor sex life. They believe this is owed to women's shallow and vain nature, leading them to be only attracted to physically attractive men." See Gentry, "Misogynistic Terrorism", 221.

66. Julia R. DeCook and Megan Kelly, "Interrogating the 'Incel Menace': Assessing the Threat of Male Supremacy in Terrorism Studies", *Critical Studies on Terrorism* vol. 15, no. 3 (2022): 706–26.

67. United States Department of State, "Country Reports on Human Rights Practices for 2016: Iraq" (Bureau of Democracy, Human Rights and Labor, March 2017): https://web.archive.org/web/20170307090250/https://www.state.gov/documents/organization/265710.pdf, last accessed 29 July 2023.

68. United Nations Security Council, Resolution 2242 (2015), 6: https://www. securitycouncilreport.org/atf/cf/%7B65BFCF9B-6D27-4E9C-8CD3-CF6E4FF96FF9%7D/s_res_2242.pdf, last accessed 29 July 2023.

69. Connell, *Masculinities*, 1st revised edition (Cambridge: Polity Press, 2005).

70. Richards, "Conceptualizing Terrorism".

71. See two books from 2020: Elizabeth Pearson, Emily Winterbotham and Katherine E. Brown, *Countering Violent Extremism: Making Gender Matter* (Basingstoke: Palgrave Macmillan, 2020); and Caron E. Gentry, *Disordered Violence: How Gender, Race and Heteronormativity Structure Terrorism* (Edinburgh: Edinburgh University Press, 2020).

72. Marc Sageman, *Misunderstanding Terrorism* (Philadelphia, PA: University of Pennsylvania Press, 2016), 20.

73. Kenney, *The Islamic State in Britain*, 10.

74. Sageman, *Misunderstanding Terrorism*, 90; Neumann, "The Trouble with Radicalization", 873.

75. Eve Kosofsky Sedgwick, "Gosh, Boy George, You Must Be Awfully Secure in Your Masculinity", in *Constructing Masculinity*, eds Maurice Berger, Brian Wallis and Simon Watson (London; New York, NY: Routledge, 1995), 11–20.

76. Magnus Ranstorp, "Introduction: Mapping Terrorism Research – Challenges and Priorities", in *Mapping Terrorism Research: State of the Art, Gaps and Future Direction*, ed. Magnus Ranstorp (London; New York, NY: Routledge, 2007), 1–28 (7).

77. Maria Stern, "Security Outsourcing and Critical Feminist Inquiry: Taking Stock and Looking Forward", in *The Routledge Research Companion to Security Outsourcing*, eds Joakim Berndtsson and Christopher Kinsey (London: Routledge, 2016), 282–92 (289).

78. Cas Mudde, "The War of Words Defining the Extreme Right Party Family", *West European Politics* vol. 19, no. 2 (1996): 225–48 (226).

79. Michel Foucault, *Power/Knowledge: Selected Interviews and Other Writings, 1972–1977*, ed. Colin Gordon (New York, NY: Vintage, 1980), 73; Michel Foucault, *The Foucault Reader: An Introduction to Foucault's Thought*, ed. Paul Rabinow (London: Penguin, 1991), 383–86.

1.   THEORY: MASCULINITIES AND EXTREMISM

1. Strictly, a *mahram* is a family member whom it is unlawful to marry; in this context it means a public companion of an otherwise unaccompanied woman, for reasons of propriety.

2. Vikram Dodd, "Anjem Choudary Jailed for Five-and-a-Half Years for Urging Support of Isis", *The Guardian*, 6 September 2016: https://www.theguardian. com/uk-news/2016/sep/06/anjem-choudary-jailed-for-five-years-and-six-months-for-urging-support-of-isis, last accessed 30 July 2023.

3. Commission for Countering Extremism, "Challenging Hateful Extremism" (October 2019), 1: https://assets.publishing.service.gov.uk/government/uploads/system/uploads/attachment_data/file/874101/200320_

Challenging_Hateful_Extremism.pdf, last accessed 27 July 2023; Sara Khan and Tony McMahon, *The Battle for British Islam: Reclaiming Muslim Identity from Extremism* (London: Saqi Books, 2016).

4. Raffaello Pantucci, *"We Love Death as You Love Life": Britain's Suburban Terrorists* (London: C. Hurst & Co., 2015), 116–17; Quintan Wiktorowicz, *Radical Islam Rising: Muslim Extremism in the West* (Lanham, MD: Rowman & Littlefield, 2005), 61; Petter Nesser, *Islamist Terrorism in Europe: A History* (London: C. Hurst & Co., 2016), 43.

5. Kylie Connor, "'Islamism' in the West? The Life-Span of the Al-Muhajiroun in the United Kingdom", *Journal of Muslim Minority Affairs* vol. 25, no. 1 (2005): 117–33 (119).

6. Alan Travis, "Extremist Islamist Groups to Be Banned Under New Terror Laws", *The Guardian*, 11 January 2010: http://www.theguardian.com/politics/2010/jan/11/islam4uk-al-muhajiroun-ban-laws, last accessed 30 July 2023; James Slack, "Banned Terror Group Al Muhajiroun Exploits Government Loophole to Reform Under New Hate-Filled Guise", *Daily Mail*, 17 June 2009: http://www.dailymail.co.uk/news/article-1193706/Banned-terror-group-Al-Muhajiroun-exploits-government-loophole-reform-new-hate-filled-guise.html, last accessed 30 July 2023.

7. Home Office, "CONTEST: The United Kingdom's Strategy for Countering Terrorism" (June 2018), 19: https://assets.publishing.service.gov.uk/government/uploads/system/uploads/attachment_data/file/716907/140618_CCS207_CCS0218929798-1_CONTEST_3.0_WEB.pdf, last accessed 26 July 2023.

8. In the UK the poppy is a symbol of honour for veterans, worn in the period before Armistice Day.

9. Tommy Robinson, *Enemy of the State* (Batley: The Press News Ltd, 2015), 99–110.

10. Hilary Pilkington, *Loud and Proud: Passion and Politics in the English Defence League* (Manchester: Manchester University Press, 2016), 37–38; 152.

11. EDL Media Team, "English Defence League – The Official English Defence League Website", 2016: http://www.englishdefenceleague.org.uk/, last accessed 20 March 2018; 'counter-jihad' is a term used to describe actors opposed to Muslim immigration and its perceived detrimental effects to Western culture.

12. "Statement from Jayda Fransen": http://jaydafransen.online/, last accessed 26 January 2019.

13. Britain First news update, 11 May 2018; Telegraph Reporting Team, "Britain First Leader and Deputy Jailed for Religiously-Aggravated Harassment over 'Hostility' Towards Muslims", *The Telegraph*, 7 March 2018: https://www.telegraph.co.uk/news/2018/03/07/britain-first-leader-deputy-guilty-religiously-aggravated-harassment/, last accessed 30 July 2023.

14. Telegraph Reporting Team, "Britain First Leader and Deputy Jailed".

15. Britain First newspaper, 2016, 3.

16. "Digging Deeper with DD Denslow", *TNT Radio*, 16 April 2023: https://tntradio.live/shows/digging-deeper-with-dd-denslow/, last accessed 31 July 2023.

17. Chris Allen, "Britain First: The 'Frontline Resistance' to the Islamification of Britain", *The Political Quarterly* vol. 85, no. 3 (2014): 354–61.

18. Hope Not Hate, "Britain First: Army of the Right": https://hopenothate.org.uk/wp-content/uploads/2017/11/Britain-First-Army-of-the-Right.pdf, last accessed 31 July 2023.

19. Anne Marie Waters, "Announcement From Anne Marie Waters", For Britain (blog), 13 July 2022: https://www.forbritain.uk/2022/07/13/announcement-from-anne-marie-waters/, last accessed 13 July 2022.

20. Hope Not Hate, "State of Hate Report 2023" (February 2023): https://hopenothate.org.uk/wp-content/uploads/2023/02/state-of-hate-2023-v7-1.pdf, last accessed 23 July 2023.

21. Sean O'Driscoll, "Ukip Reject Anne Marie Waters Founds Own Far-Right Party", *The Times*, 10 October 2017: https://www.thetimes.co.uk/article/ukip-reject-anne-marie-waters-founds-own-far-right-party-95wmr6wrh, last accessed 31 July 2023. *Pegida* is an acronym for the German for Patriotic Europeans Against the Islamisation of the West.

22. Katherine E. Brown, "Gender and Counter-Radicalization: Women and Emerging Counter-Terror Measures", in *Gender, National Security and Counter-Terrorism*, eds Jayne Huckerby and Margaret L. Satterthwaite (Abingdon; New York, NY: Routledge, 2013), 36–59.

23. Jane L. Parpart and Marysia Zalewski, "Introduction: Rethinking the Man Question", in *Rethinking the Man Question: Sex, Gender and Violence in International Relations*, eds Jane L. Parpart and Marysia Zalewski (London; New York, NY: Zed Books, 2008), 1–22; Charlotte Hooper, *Manly States: Masculinities, International Relations, and Gender Politics* (New York, NY: Columbia University Press, 2001); Christine Beasley, "Rethinking Hegemonic Masculinity in a Globalizing World", *Men and Masculinities* vol. 11, no. 1 (2008): 86–103; Paul Kirby and Marsha Henry, "Rethinking Masculinity and Practices of Violence in Conflict Settings", *International Feminist Journal of Politics* vol. 14, no. 4 (2012): 445–49.

24. Marc Sageman, *Understanding Terror Networks* (Philadelphia, PA: University of Pennsylvania Press, 2004), 115; this theory suggested that the social aspect of radicalisation precedes its ideological aspect.

25. Bruce Hoffman, Jacob Ware and Ezra Shapiro, "Assessing the Threat of Incel Violence", *Studies in Conflict & Terrorism* vol. 43, no. 7 (2020): 565–87; Mia M. Bloom, "The First Incel? The Legacy of Marc Lépine", *The Journal of Intelligence, Conflict, and Warfare* vol. 5, no. 1 (2022): 39–74.

26. Susanne Kaiser, *Political Masculinity: How Incels, Fundamentalists and Authoritarians Mobilise for Patriarchy*, trans. Valentine A. Pakis (Cambridge; Medford, MA: Polity Press, 2022); Michael Kimmel, *Angry White Men: American Masculinity at the End of an Era* (New York, NY: Bold Type Books, 2017).

27. Jacqui True and Melissa Johnston, "Misogyny & Violent Extremism: Implications for Preventing Violent Extremism" (UN Women, September 2019): https://asiapacific.unwomen.org/en/digital-library/publications/2019/10/misogyny-violent-extremism, last accessed 31 July 2023.

28. Jacob Zenn and Elizabeth Pearson, "Women, Gender and the Evolving Tactics of Boko Haram", *Journal of Terrorism Research* vol. 5, no. 1 (2014): 46–57; Elizabeth Pearson, "Gendered Reflections? Extremism in the UK's Radical Right and al-Muhajiroun Networks", *Studies in Conflict & Terrorism* vol. 46, no. 4 (2023): 489–512; Elizabeth Pearson, "Why Men Fight and Women Don't: Masculinity and Extremist Violence" (Tony Blair Institute for Global Change, September 2018): https://www.institute.global/insights/geopolitics-and-security/why-men-fight-and-women-dont-masculinity-and-extremist-violence, last accessed 31 July 2023.

29. Joshua M. Roose et al., *Masculinity and Violent Extremism* (Basingstoke: Palgrave Macmillan, 2022); True and Johnston, "Misogyny & Violent Extremism"; Alex DiBranco, "Mobilizing Misogyny", in *Male Supremacism in the United States: From Patriarchal Traditionalism to Misogynist Incels and the Alt-Right*, eds Emily K. Carian, Alex DiBranco and Chelsea Ebin (Abingdon; New York, NY: Routledge, 2022), 3–20.

30. Sanam Naraghi-Anderlini, "Challenging Conventional Wisdom, Transforming Current Practices: A Gendered Lens on PVE" (Berghof Foundation, May 2018), 34: https://berghof-foundation.org/library/challenging-conventional-wisdom-transforming-current-practices-a-gendered-lens-on-pve, last accessed 31 July 2023.

31. Caron E. Gentry, "Misogynistic Terrorism: It Has Always Been Here", *Critical Studies on Terrorism* vol. 15, no. 1 (2022): 209–24.

32. True and Johnston, "Misogyny & Violent Extremism"; Jacqui True, "Setting the Scene for Preventing Violent Extremism in South East and South Asia: A Way Forward for Women's Engagement in Indonesia and Bangladesh" (Monash Gender, Peace and Security Centre, 2019): https://asiapacific.unwomen.org/sites/default/files/2023-03/ap-Monash-Policy-Brief_WEB-re.PDF, last accessed 31 July 2023; Shannon Zimmerman, Luisa Ryan and David Duriesmith, "Recognizing the Violent Extremist Ideology of 'Incels'" (Women in International Security, 2018): https://www.wiisglobal.org/wp-content/uploads/2018/09/Policybrief-Violent-Extremists-Incels.pdf, last accessed 31 July 2023; as cited in Roose et al., *Masculinity and Violent Extremism*, 27–28.

33. Joan Smith, "How Toxic Masculinity Is Tied to Terrorism", UnHerd, 16 May 2019: https://unherd.com/2019/05/how-toxic-masculinity-is-tied-to-terrorism/, last accessed 31 July 2023.

34. Gina Vale, "Liberated, Not Free: Yazidi Women after Islamic State Captivity", *Small Wars & Insurgencies* vol. 31, no. 3 (2020): 511–39; "UN Human Rights Panel Concludes ISIL Is Committing Genocide against Yazidis", UN News, 16 June 2016: https://news.un.org/en/story/2016/06/532312, last accessed 31 July 2023.

35. Elizabeth Pearson and Jacob Zenn, "#BringBackOurGirls? Two Years After the Chibok Girls Were Taken, What Do We Know?", War on the Rocks, 14 April 2016: http://warontherocks.com/2016/04/bringbackourgirls-two-years-after-the-chibok-girls-were-taken-what-do-we-know/, last accessed 31 July 2023.

36. Aage Borchgrevink, *A Norwegian Tragedy: Anders Behring Breivik and the Massacre on Utoya*, trans. Guy Puzey (Cambridge: Polity Press, 2013); Asne Seierstad, *One of Us: The Story of Anders Breivik and the Massacre in Norway*, trans. Sarah Death (London: Virago, 2015).

37. Christine Chinkin and Madeleine Rees, "Commentary on Security Council Resolution 2467: Continued State Obligation and Civil Society Action on Sexual Violence in Conflict" (Centre for Women, Peace and Security, London School of Economics, 2019), 36: https://www.un.org/sexualviolenceinconflict/wp-content/uploads/2019/09/report/commentary-on-security-council-resolution-2467/19_0496_WPS_Commentary_Report_online.pdf, last accessed 31 July 2023.

38. Doris Asante et al., "UN Security Council Resolution 2242 and the Women, Peace, and Security Agenda", Australian Institute of International Affairs (blog), 7 July 2021: https://www.internationalaffairs.org.au/australianoutlook/un-security-council-resolution-2242-and-the-women-peace-and-security-agenda/, last accessed 31 July 2023.

39. Chinkin and Rees, "Commentary on Security Council Resolution 2467".

40. Jayne Huckerby, "Women, Gender and the U.K. Government's CVE Efforts: Looking Back and Forward", in *A Man's World? Exploring the Roles of Women in Countering Terrorism and Violent Extremism*, eds Naureen Chowdhury Fink, Sara Zeiger and Rafia Bhulai (Hedayah and The Global Center on Cooperative Security, 2016), 76–99; Jayne Huckerby, "In Harm's Way: Gender and Human Rights in National Security", *Duke Journal of Gender Law & Policy* vol. 27, no. 1 (2020): 179–202; Naaz Rashid, "Giving the Silent Majority a Stronger Voice? Initiatives to Empower Muslim Women as Part of the UK's 'War on Terror'", *Ethnic and Racial Studies* vol. 37, no. 4 (2014): 589–604.

41. Elizabeth Pearson and Chitra Nagarajan, "Gendered Security Harms: State Policy and the Counterinsurgency Against Boko Haram", *African Conflict and Peacebuilding Review* vol. 10, no. 2 (2020): 108–40; "Abubakar Shekau: Nigeria's Boko Haram Leader Is Dead, Say Rival Militants", BBC News, 7 June 2021, https://www.bbc.com/news/world-africa-57378493, last accessed 31 July 2023.

42. United States Department of State, "Country Reports on Human Rights Practices for 2016: Iraq" (Bureau of Democracy, Human Rights and Labor, March 2017): https://web.archive.org/web/20170307090250/https://www.state.gov/documents/organization/265710.pdf, last accessed 29 July 2023.

43. Tracie Farrell et al., "Exploring Misogyny across the Manosphere in Reddit", in *WebSci '19: Proceedings of the 10ᵗʰ ACM Conference on Web Science* (New York, NY: Association for Computing Machinery, 2019), 87–96.

44. Kaiser, *Political Masculinity*; Judith A. Allen, "Men Interminably in Crisis? Historians on Masculinity, Sexual Boundaries, and Manhood", *Radical History Review* vol. 82, no. 1 (2002): 191–207; John MacInnes, "The Crisis of Masculinity and the Politics of Identity", in *The Masculinities Reader*, eds Stephen M. Whitehead and Frank J. Barrett (Cambridge: Polity Press, 2001), 311–29.

45. Michael Flood, "'Toxic Masculinity': What Does It Mean, Where Did It Come from – and Is the Term Useful or Harmful?", The Conversation, 21 September 2022: http://theconversation.com/toxic-masculinity-what-does-it-mean-where-did-it-come-from-and-is-the-term-useful-or-harmful-189298, last accessed 31 July 2023; Michael Salter, "The Problem With a Fight Against Toxic Masculinity", The Atlantic, 27 February 2019: https://www.theatlantic.com/health/archive/2019/02/toxic-masculinity-history/583411/, last accessed 31 July 2023; Drew Brown, "Toxic Masculinity Is at the Heart of This Darkness", Vice, 25 April 2018: https://www.vice.com/en_uk/article/8xkjbx/toxic-masculinity-is-at-the-heart-of-this-darkness, last accessed 31 July 2023; Elizabeth Pearson, "Extremism and Toxic Masculinity: The Man Question Re-Posed", International Affairs vol. 95, no. 6 (2019): 1251–70.

46. Terry A. Kupers, "Toxic Masculinity as a Barrier to Mental Health Treatment in Prison", Journal of Clinical Psychology vol. 61, no. 6 (2005): 713–24 (714).

47. Paul Amar, "Middle East Masculinity Studies: Discourses of 'Men in Crisis', Industries of Gender in Revolution", Journal of Middle East Women's Studies vol. 7, no. 3 (2011): 36–70.

48. Bruce Hoffman, Inside Terrorism (New York, NY: Columbia University Press, 2006); Isabelle Duyvesteyn, "How New Is the New Terrorism?", Studies in Conflict & Terrorism vol. 27, no. 5 (2004): 439–54; Martha Crenshaw, ed., Terrorism in Context (University Park, PA: Pennsylvania State University Press, 2010).

49. Zillah Eisenstein, Against Empire: Feminisms, Racism and the West (London: Zed Books, 2004), 161.

50. Mariam Durrani, "The Gendered Muslim Subject", in The Oxford Handbook of Language and Race, eds H. Samy Alim, Angela Reyes and Paul V. Kroskrity (Oxford: Oxford University Press, 2020); Gargi Bhattacharyya, Dangerous Brown Men: Exploiting Sex, Violence and Feminism in the War on Terror (London: Zed Books, 2008).

51. Rachel Briggs, "Community Engagement for Counterterrorism: Lessons from the United Kingdom", International Affairs vol. 89, no. 4 (2010): 971–81.

52. Charlotte Heath-Kelly, "Counter-Terrorism and the Counterfactual: Producing the 'Radicalisation' Discourse and the UK PREVENT Strategy", The British Journal of Politics & International Relations vol. 15, no. 3 (2013): 394–415; Imran Awan, "'I Am a Muslim Not an Extremist': How the Prevent Strategy Has Constructed a 'Suspect' Community", Politics & Policy vol. 40, no. 6 (2012): 1158–85.

53. David Lammy, "Islamists, Gangs, the EDL – All Target Alienated Young Men", The Guardian, 24 May 2013: http://www.theguardian.com/uk/2013/may/24/islamists-gangs-edl-target-young-men, last accessed 31 July 2023; Smith, "How Toxic Masculinity Is Tied to Terrorism".

54. Diane Abbott, "Britain's Crisis of Masculinity", 16 May 2013: https://www.dianeabbott.org.uk/news/articles/item915, last accessed 31 July 2023.

55. Roose et al., Masculinity and Violent Extremism, 20–23.

56. Brown, "Gender and Counter-Radicalization", 41.

57. Awan, "'I Am a Muslim Not an Extremist'"; Katherine Brown, "The Promise and

Perils of Women's Participation in UK Mosques: The Impact of Securitisation Agendas on Identity, Gender and Community", *The British Journal of Politics & International Relations* vol. 10, no. 3 (2008): 472–91; Arun Kundnani, *Spooked! How Not to Prevent Violent Extremism* (London: Institute of Race Relations, 2009); Rashid, "Giving the Silent Majority a Stronger Voice?".

58. Katherine E. Brown, "Gender and Counter-Terrorism: UK Prevent and De-Radicalisation Strategies" (Washington, DC: British Politics Group, 2010); Laura J. Shepherd, "Veiled References: Constructions of Gender in the Bush Administration Discourse on the Attacks on Afghanistan Post-9/11", *International Feminist Journal of Politics* vol. 8, no. 1 (2006): 19–41; Elizabeth Pearson, Emily Winterbotham and Katherine E. Brown, *Countering Violent Extremism: Making Gender Matter* (Basingstoke: Palgrave Macmillan, 2020).

59. Amar, "Middle East Masculinity Studies"; Durrani, "The Gendered Muslim Subject".

60. Home Office, "Prevent Strategy" (2011), 21: https://www.gov.uk/government/uploads/system/uploads/attachment_data/file/97976/prevent-strategy-review.pdf, last accessed 26 July 2023.

61. Amar, "Middle East Masculinity Studies", 43.

62. David Duriesmith, "Hybrid Warriors and the Formation of New War Masculinities: A Case Study of Indonesian Foreign Fighters", *Stability: International Journal of Security and Development* vol. 7, no. 1 (2018): 1–16 (6).

63. Peter R. Neumann, "The Trouble with Radicalization", *International Affairs* vol. 89, no. 4 (2013): 873–93; Peter Neumann and Scott Kleinmann, "How Rigorous Is Radicalization Research?", *Democracy and Security* vol. 9, no. 4 (2013): 360–82.

64. Lisa Stampnitzky, *Disciplining Terror: How Experts Invented "Terrorism"* (Cambridge; New York, NY: Cambridge University Press, 2013).

65. John Horgan, "Discussion Point: The End of Radicalization?", START: National Consortium for the Study of Terrorism and Responses to Terrorism, 28 September 2012: http://www.start.umd.edu/news/discussion-point-end-radicalization, last accessed 31 July 2023; Arun Kundnani, "Radicalisation: The Journey of a Concept", *Race & Class* vol. 54, no. 2 (2012): 3–25; Katherine E. Brown, *Gender, Religion, Extremism: Finding Women in Anti-Radicalization* (Oxford: Oxford University Press, 2020).

66. Marc Sageman, "The Stagnation in Terrorism Research", *Terrorism and Political Violence* vol. 26, no. 4 (2014): 565–80; Neumann, "The Trouble with Radicalization".

67. Andrew Silke, ed., *Terrorists, Victims and Society: Psychological Perspectives on Terrorism and Its Consequences* (Chichester; Hoboken, NJ: Wiley-Blackwell, 2003); Sageman, "The Stagnation in Terrorism Research"; Neumann and Kleinmann, "How Rigorous Is Radicalization Research?"; Anja Dalgaard-Nielsen, "Violent Radicalization in Europe: What We Know and What We Do Not Know", *Studies in Conflict & Terrorism* vol. 33, no. 9 (2010): 797–814.

68. Michael Kimmel, *Healing from Hate: How Young Men Get Into—and Out of—Violent Extremism* (Oakland, CA: University of California Press, 2018); Sune Qvotrup

Jensen and Jeppe Fuglsang Larsen, "Sociological Perspectives on Islamist Radicalization – Bridging the Micro/Macro Gap", *European Journal of Criminology* vol. 18, no. 3 (2019): 426–43.

69. See Cynthia Enloe, *Nimo's War, Emma's War: Making Feminist Sense of the Iraq War* (Berkeley, CA; London: University of California Press, 2010).

70. Elizabeth Pearson, "The Case of Roshonara Choudhry: Implications for Theory on Online Radicalization, ISIS Women, and the Gendered Jihad", *Policy & Internet* vol. 8, no. 1 (2015): 5–33.

71. Adam Bermingham et al., "Combining Social Network Analysis and Sentiment Analysis to Explore the Potential for Online Radicalisation", in *IEEE International Conference on Advances in Social Network Analysis and Mining* (Athens, Greece: IEEE, 2009), 231–36; Peter R. Neumann, "Chapter Two: Recruitment Grounds", *The Adelphi Papers* vol. 48, no. 399 (2008): 21–30; "Quilliam Briefing Paper: The Threat of Radicalisation on British University Campuses" (London: Quilliam, 2010).

72. Stefan Malthaner and Peter Waldmann, "The Radical Milieu: Conceptualizing the Supportive Social Environment of Terrorist Groups", *Studies in Conflict & Terrorism* vol. 37, no. 12 (2014): 979–98.

73. Stefan Malthaner, "Radicalization: The Evolution of an Analytical Paradigm", *European Journal of Sociology / Archives Européennes de Sociologie* vol. 58, no. 3 (2017): 369–401; Donatella della Porta and Mario Diani, *Social Movements: An Introduction* (Malden, MA: Wiley-Blackwell, 2005); Donatella della Porta and Heinz-Gerhard Haupt, "Patterns of Radicalization in Political Activism: An Introduction", *Social Science History* vol. 36, no. 3 (2012): 311–20.

74. Fathali M. Moghaddam, "The Staircase to Terrorism: A Psychological Exploration", *American Psychologist* vol. 60, no. 2 (2005): 161–69; Dalgaard-Nielsen, "Violent Radicalization in Europe".

75. Dalgaard-Nielsen, "Violent Radicalization in Europe".

76. Sageman, *Understanding Terror Networks*; Wiktorowicz, *Radical Islam Rising*.

77. Sageman, *Understanding Terror Networks*; Janny Groen and Annieke Kranenberg, *Women Warriors for Allah: An Islamist Network in the Netherlands*, trans. Robert Naborn (Philadelphia, PA: University of Pennsylvania Press, 2010).

78. Marc Sageman, *Leaderless Jihad: Terror Networks in the Twenty-First Century* (Philadelphia, PA: University of Pennsylvania Press, 2008), 81; 111.

79. Thomas Hegghammer, "Introduction: What Is Jihadi Culture and Why Should We Study It?", in *Jihadi Culture: The Art and Social Practices of Militant Islamists*, ed. Thomas Hegghammer (Cambridge: Cambridge University Press, 2017), 1–21.

80. See, for instance, Awan, A. (2014). Spurning "This Worldly Life": Terrorism and Martydom in Contemporary Britain. In D. Janes, & A. Houen (Eds.), *Martyrdom and Terrorism: Pre-Modern to Contemporary Perspectives* (Oxford University Press). https://doi.org/10.1093/acprof:oso/9780199959853.003.0011; Sageman, *Understanding Terror Networks*; Sageman, *Leaderless Jihad*.

81. Olivier Roy, *Jihad and Death: The Global Appeal of Islamic State* (London: C. Hurst & Co., 2017), 51–52; 44.

82. Edwin Bakker, "Jihadi Terrorists in Europe: Their Characteristics and the Circumstances in Which They Joined the Jihad: An Exploratory Study" (Clingendael Institute, 2006): https://www.clingendael.org/sites/default/files/pdfs/20061200_cscp_csp_bakker.pdf, last accessed 27 July 2023; Daveed Gartenstein-Ross and Laura Grossman, *Homegrown Terrorists in the US and UK: An Empirical Examination of the Radicalization Process* (Washington, DC: FDD Press, 2009); Sageman, *Understanding Terror Networks*.

83. Malthaner, "Radicalization".

84. Olivier Roy, "Islamic Terrorist Radicalisation in Europe", in *European Islam: The Challenges for Society and Public Policy*, eds Samir Amghar, Amel Boubekeur and Michael Emerson (Brussels: Centre for European Policy Studies, 2007), 55–56: https://www.ceps.eu/wp-content/uploads/2013/02/1556.pdf, last accessed 1 August 2023.

85. Wiktorowicz, *Radical Islam Rising*, 92–98.

86. OSCE, "Women and Terrorist Radicalization" (2011): https://www.osce.org/files/f/documents/4/a/99919.pdf, last accessed 27 July 2023; Caron E. Gentry and Laura Sjoberg, *Mothers, Monsters, Whores: Women's Violence in Global Politics* (New York, NY: Zed Books, 2007); Laura Sjoberg, *Gendering Global Conflict: Toward a Feminist Theory of War* (New York, NY: Columbia University Press, 2013).

87. OSCE, "Women and Terrorist Radicalization"; Parpart and Zalewski, "Introduction"; J. Ann Tickner, "You Just Don't Understand: Troubled Engagements between Feminists and IR Theorists", *International Studies Quarterly* vol. 41, no. 4 (1997): 611–32; Cynthia Enloe, *Bananas, Beaches and Bases: Making Feminist Sense of International Politics* (Berkeley, CA: University of California Press, 2001).

88. See Joana Cook and Gina Vale, "From Daesh to 'Diaspora': Tracing the Women and Minors of Islamic State" (International Centre for the Study of Radicalisation and Political Violence, July 2018): https://icsr.info/wp-content/uploads/2018/07/ICSR-Report-From-Daesh-to-'Diaspora'-Tracing-the-Women-and-Minors-of-Islamic-State.pdf, last accessed 1 August 2023, for a sense of the scale of recruitment.

89. Cook and Vale, "From Daesh to 'Diaspora'".

90. Sjoberg, *Gendering Global Conflict*, 84.

91. Sue Clegg, "The Problem of Agency in Feminism: A Critical Realist Approach", *Gender and Education* vol. 18, no. 3 (2006): 309–24; Chandra T. Mohanty and Satya P. Mohanty, "Contradictions of Colonialism", *Women's Review of Books*, 1990, 19–21; Brown, "Gender and Counter-Radicalization"; Brown, *Gender, Religion, Extremism*.

92. Karen Jacques and Paul J. Taylor, "Female Terrorism: A Review", *Terrorism and Political Violence* vol. 21, no. 3 (2009): 499–515 (505).

93. Miranda Alison, "Women as Agents of Political Violence: Gendering Security", *Security Dialogue* vol. 35, no. 4 (2004): 447–63.

94. Sophie Giscard d'Estaing, "Engaging Women in Countering Violent Extremism: Avoiding Instrumentalisation and Furthering Agency", *Gender & Development* vol. 25, no. 1 (2017): 103–18; Devorah Margolin, "Neither Feminists nor Victims:

How Women's Agency Has Shaped Palestinian Violence" (Tony Blair Institute for Global Change, 2018): https://institute.global/policy/neither-feminists-nor-victims-how-womens-agency-has-shaped-palestinian-violence, last accessed 1 August 2023; Lori Poloni-Staudinger and Candice D. Ortbals, *Terrorism and Violent Conflict: Women's Agency, Leadership, and Responses* (New York, NY: Springer, 2013); Linda Åhäll, "Motherhood, Myth and Gendered Agency in Political Violence", *International Feminist Journal of Politics* vol. 14, no. 1 (2012): 103–20; Gentry and Sjoberg, *Mothers, Monsters, Whores.*

95. United Nations Security Council, Resolution 2242 (2015), 6: https://www.securitycouncilreport.org/atf/cf/%7B65BFCF9B-6D27-4E9C-8CD3-CF6E4FF96FF9%7D/s_res_2242.pdf, last accessed 29 July 2023.

96. Swati Parashar, "Gender, Jihad, and Jingoism: Women as Perpetrators, Planners, and Patrons of Militancy in Kashmir", *Studies in Conflict & Terrorism* vol. 34, no. 4 (2011): 295–317; Kathleen M. Blee, "Women and Organized Racial Terrorism in the United States", in *Female Terrorism and Militancy: Agency, Utility, and Organization*, ed. Cindy D. Ness (London; New York, NY: Routledge, 2008), 201–16; Mia Bloom, *Bombshell: The Many Faces of Women Terrorists* (London: C. Hurst & Co., 2011); Jessica Davis, "Evolution of the Global Jihad: Female Suicide Bombers in Iraq", *Studies in Conflict & Terrorism* vol. 36, no. 4 (2013): 279–91; Jessica Davis, *Women and Radical Islamic Terrorism: Planners, Perpetrators, Patrons?* (Toronto, ON: Canadian Institute of Strategic Studies, 2006); Philippa Eggert, "Women Fighters in the 'Islamic State' and Al-Qaida in Iraq: A Comparative Analysis", *Die Friedens-Warte* vol. 90, no. 3/4 (2015): 363–80; Akanksha Mehta, "The Aesthetics of 'Everyday' Violence: Narratives of Violence and Hindu Right-Wing Women", *Critical Studies on Terrorism* vol. 8, no. 3 (2015): 416–38.

97. Ashley A. Mattheis and Charlie Winter, "'The Greatness of Her Position': Comparing Identitarian and Jihadi Discourses on Women" (International Centre for the Study of Radicalisation and Political Violence, 2019): https://icsr.info/wp-content/uploads/2019/05/ICSR-Report-'The-Greatness-of-Her-Position'-Comparing-Identitarian-and-Jihadi-Discourses-on-Women.pdf, last accessed 29 July 2023; Groen and Kranenberg, *Women Warriors for Allah*; Wiktorowicz, *Radical Islam Rising.*

98. Pearson, Winterbotham and Brown, *Countering Violent Extremism*; Spike V. Peterson, "How (the Meaning of) Gender Matters in Political Economy", *New Political Economy* vol. 10, no. 4 (2005): 499–521.

99. Marysia Zalewski, "Introduction", in *The 'Man' Question in International Relations*, eds Marysia Zalewski and Jane L. Parpart (Boulder, CO: Routledge, 1997), 1–13.

100. Stephen M. Whitehead and Frank J. Barrett, "The Sociology of Masculinity", in *The Masculinities Reader*, eds Stephen M. Whitehead and Frank J. Barrett (Cambridge: Polity Press, 2001), 1–26 (15); Chris Beasley, *Gender and Sexuality: Critical Theories, Critical Thinkers* (London; Thousand Oaks, CA: SAGE Publications, 2005), 179.

101. See Tim Carrigan, Bob Connell and John Lee, "Toward a New Sociology of Masculinity", *Theory and Society* vol. 14, no. 5 (1985): 551–604.

102. R. W. Connell, *Masculinities* (Cambridge: Polity Press, 1995), 71.
103. R. W. Connell and James W. Messerschmidt, "Hegemonic Masculinity: Rethinking the Concept", *Gender & Society* vol. 19, no. 6 (2005): 829–59.
104. Rachel Jewkes et al., "Hegemonic Masculinity: Combining Theory and Practice in Gender Interventions", *Culture, Health & Sexuality* vol. 17, no. sup2 (2015): 112–27.
105. Christopher Mullins, *Holding Your Square: Masculinities, Streetlife and Violence* (Cullompton: Willan, 2006).
106. R. W. Connell, *Masculinities*, 1st revised edition (Cambridge: Polity Press, 2005).
107. Hooper, *Manly States*.
108. Christoffer Carlsson, "Masculinities, Persistence, and Desistance", *Criminology* vol. 51, no. 3 (2013): 661–93.
109. Candace West and Sarah Fenstermaker, "Doing Difference", *Gender & Society* vol. 9, no. 1 (1995): 8–37 (21), cited in Mullins, *Holding Your Square*, 7.
110. R. W. Connell, "The Social Organization of Masculinity", in *The Masculinities Reader*, eds Stephen M. Whitehead and Frank J. Barrett (Cambridge: Polity Press, 2001), 30–51 (38–41); R. W. Connell, *Gender and Power: Society, the Person and Sexual Politics* (Cambridge: Polity Press, 1987).
111. Connell, *Masculinities*, 1995; Victoria Foster, Michael Kimmel and Christine Skelton, "'What About the Boys?': An Overview of the Debates", in *What About the Boys? Issues of Masculinity in Schools*, eds Wayne Martino and Bob Meyenn (Buckingham; Philadelphia, PA: Open University Press, 2001).
112. Michael Kimmel, "Integrating Men into the Curriculum", *Duke Journal of Gender Law & Policy* vol. 4, no. 1 (1997): 181–96.
113. Connell, *Masculinities*, 1995, 77.
114. Connell, *Gender and Power*, 183.
115. James W. Messerschmidt and Achim Rohde, "Osama Bin Laden and His Jihadist Global Hegemonic Masculinity", *Gender & Society* vol. 32, no. 5 (2018): 663–85.
116. David Buchbinder, *Studying Men and Masculinities* (London: Routledge, 2013).
117. Mimi Schippers, "Recovering the Feminine Other: Masculinity, Femininity, and Gender Hegemony", *Theory and Society* vol. 36, no. 1 (2007): 85–102.
118. Connell, *Gender and Power*.
119. James W. Messerschmidt, *Masculinities and Crime: Critique and Reconceptualization of Theory* (Lanham, MD: Rowman & Littlefield, 1993), 17.
120. Amar, "Middle East Masculinity Studies".
121. Beasley, "Rethinking Hegemonic Masculinity in a Globalizing World"; Beasley, *Gender and Sexuality*.
122. Connell and Messerschmidt, "Hegemonic Masculinity: Rethinking the Concept", 848.
123. Connell and Messerschmidt, "Hegemonic Masculinity: Rethinking the Concept".
124. Schippers, "Recovering the Feminine Other", 95.
125. Mullins, *Holding Your Square*, 7.
126. Connell, *Gender and Power*, 187.
127. Salter, "The Problem With a Fight Against Toxic Masculinity".

128. David Rapoport, "The Fourth Wave: September 11 in the History of Terrorism", *Current History* vol. 100, no. 650 (2001): 419–24.
129. Connell, "The Social Organization of Masculinity", 45.
130. Tahir Abbas, "Muslim Minorities in Britain: Integration, Multiculturalism and Radicalism in the Post-7/7 Period", *Journal of Intercultural Studies* vol. 28, no. 3 (2007): 287–300.
131. Allen, "Men Interminably in Crisis?"; Rebecca Asher, *Man Up: Boys, Men and Breaking the Male Rules* (London: Harvill Secker, 2016); Francis Dupuis-Déri, "The Bogus 'Crisis' of Masculinity", The Conversation, 14 May 2018: http://theconversation.com/the-bogus-crisis-of-masculinity-96558, last accessed 2 August 2023; Whitehead and Barrett, "The Sociology of Masculinity".
132. Asher, *Man Up*, 113.
133. Mary Louise Roberts, "Beyond 'Crisis' in Understanding Gender Transformation", *Gender & History* vol. 28, no. 2 (2016): 358–66.
134. Pearson, "Extremism and Toxic Masculinity".
135. James Treadwell and Jon Garland, "Masculinity, Marginalization and Violence: A Case Study of the English Defence League", *British Journal of Criminology* vol. 51, no. 4 (2011): 621–34.
136. Tea Torbenfeldt Bengtsson, "Performing Hypermasculinity: Experiences with Confined Young Offenders", *Men and Masculinities* vol. 19, no. 4 (2016): 410–28 (412).
137. Sjoberg, *Gendering Global Conflict*.
138. Jack Halberstam, *Female Masculinity* (Durham, NC: Duke University Press, 1998).
139. Amar, "Middle East Masculinity Studies", 45.
140. Mullins, *Holding Your Square*.
141. Bengtsson, "Performing Hypermasculinity".
142. Connell and Messerschmidt, "Hegemonic Masculinity: Rethinking the Concept".
143. Michael S. Kimmel, "Globalization and Its Mal(e)Contents: The Gendered Moral and Political Economy of Terrorism", *International Sociology* vol. 18, no. 3 (2003): 603–20; R. W. Connell, "Globalisation, Imperialism and Masculinities", in *Handbook of Studies on Men and Masculinities*, eds Michael S. Kimmel, Jeff R. Hearn and R. W. Connell (Thousand Oaks, CA; London: SAGE Publications, 2004), 71–89; Raewyn Connell, "Masculinity Research and Global Society", in *Analyzing Gender, Intersectionality, and Multiple Inequalities: Global, Transnational and Local Contexts*, eds Esther Ngan-Ling Chow, Marcia Texler Segal and Lin Tan, vol. 15 (Bingley: Emerald Group Publishing Limited, 2011), 51–72; Michael Kimmel and Abby L. Ferber, "'White Men Are This Nation': Right-Wing Militias and the Restoration of Rural American Masculinity", *Rural Sociology* vol. 65, no. 4 (2000): 582–604; Kimmel, *Healing from Hate*; Kimmel, *Angry White Men*.
144. Philippe Bourgois, "In Search of Masculinity: Violence, Respect and Sexuality Among Puerto Rican Crack Dealers in East Harlem", *The British Journal of Criminology* vol. 36, no. 3 (1996): 412–27.
145. Mullins, *Holding Your Square*, 8.

146. Connell and Messerschmidt, "Hegemonic Masculinity: Rethinking the Concept".

147. James W. Messerschmidt, "Becoming 'Real Men': Adolescent Masculinity Challenges and Sexual Violence", *Men and Masculinities* vol. 2, no. 3 (2000): 286–307.

148. Mullins, *Holding Your Square*, 77.

149. Jean Bethke Elshtain, *Women and War* (Chicago, IL: University of Chicago Press, 1987).

150. Pierre Bourdieu, *Masculine Domination*, trans. Richard Nice (Stanford, CA: Stanford University Press, 2001), 51.

151. Bengtsson, "Performing Hypermasculinity", 412.

152. See Rod Earle, "Boys' Zone Stories: Perspectives from a Young Men's Prison", *Criminology & Criminal Justice* vol. 11, no. 2 (2011): 129–43 (138).

153. See Erving Goffman, *The Presentation of Self in Everyday Life* (London: Penguin, 1990).

154. Bengtsson, "Performing Hypermasculinity", 412.

155. Peter Hopkins, *The Issue of Masculine Identities for British Muslims After 9/11:A Social Analysis* (Lewiston, NY: Edwin Mellen Press Ltd, 2008).

156. James M. Jasper, "The Emotions of Protest: Affective and Reactive Emotions in and Around Social Movements", *Sociological Forum* vol. 13, no. 3 (1998): 397–424 (398).

157. Carlsson, "Masculinities, Persistence, and Desistance".

158. Carlsson, "Masculinities, Persistence, and Desistance".

159. Cliff Leek and Michael Kimmel, "Conceptualizing Intersectionality in Superordination: Masculinities, Whitenesses, and Dominant Classes", in *Routledge International Handbook of Race, Class, and Gender*, ed. Shirley A. Jackson (Oxford; New York, NY: Routledge, 2014), 3–9.

160. Sandra Harding, "Introduction: Is There a Feminist Method?", in *Feminism & Methodology*, ed. Sandra Harding (Bloomington, IN: Indiana University Press, 1987), 1–14 (8).

161. Carlsson, "Masculinities, Persistence, and Desistance".

162. Erving Goffman, *Frame Analysis* (New York, NY: Harper and Row, 1974), cited in Chris Brickell, "Masculinities, Performativity, and Subversion: A Sociological Reappraisal", *Men and Masculinities* vol. 8, no. 1 (2005): 24–43 (30).

163. Brickell, "Masculinities, Performativity, and Subversion".

164. Brickell, "Masculinities, Performativity, and Subversion", 32.

165. Devon Carbado and Mitu Gulati, "Working Identity", *Cornell Law Review* vol. 85, no. 5 (2000): 1259–1308.

166. Pearson, Winterbotham and Brown, *Countering Violent Extremism*.

167. Peterson, "How (the Meaning of) Gender Matters in Political Economy", 499.

168. Jody Miller, "The Strengths and Limits of 'Doing Gender' for Understanding Street Crime", *Theoretical Criminology* vol. 6, no. 4 (2002): 433–60.

169. Kathleen M. Blee, "Becoming A Racist: Women in Contemporary Ku Klux Klan and Neo-Nazi Groups", *Gender & Society* vol. 10, no. 6 (1996): 680–702; Ashley Mattheis, "Shieldmaidens of Whiteness: (Alt) Maternalism and Women

Recruiting for the Far/Alt-Right", *Journal for Deradicalization* no. 17 (2018): 128–62; Nelly Lahoud, "Empowerment or Subjugation: An Analysis of ISIL's Gendered Messaging" (UN Women, 2018): https://arabstates.unwomen. org/sites/default/files/Field%20Office%20Arab%20States/Attachments/ Publications/Lahoud-Fin-Web-rev.pdf, last accessed 2 August 2023; Hilary Matfess, *Women and the War on Boko Haram: Wives, Weapons, Witnesses* (London: Zed Books, 2017).

170. Jensen and Larsen, "Sociological Perspectives on Islamist Radicalization".

171. Michael Kimmel, "Racism as Adolescent Male Rite of Passage: Ex-Nazis in Scandinavia", *Journal of Contemporary Ethnography* vol. 36, no. 2 (2007): 202–18; Messerschmidt and Rohde, "Osama Bin Laden and His Jihadist Global Hegemonic Masculinity"; Jensen and Larsen, "Sociological Perspectives on Islamist Radicalization".

172. Miller, "The Strengths and Limits of 'Doing Gender' for Understanding Street Crime", 439.

173. Bourdieu, *Masculine Domination*, 8.

174. Miller, "The Strengths and Limits of 'Doing Gender' for Understanding Street Crime".

175. Carbado and Gulati, "Working Identity", 1288.

176. Bourdieu cited in King, "Thinking with Bourdieu Against Bourdieu", 419–20; 424.

177. David Duriesmith and Noor Huda Ismail, "Masculinities and Disengagement from Jihadi Networks: The Case of Indonesian Militant Islamists", *Studies in Conflict & Terrorism* (2022), 1–21: https://doi.org/10.1080/1057610X.2022.2034220, last accessed 2 August 2023; Kimmel, *Healing from Hate*; Messerschmidt and Rohde, "Osama Bin Laden and His Jihadist Global Hegemonic Masculinity".

178. See, for instance, Duriesmith and Ismail, "Masculinities and Disengagement from Jihadi Networks", 2.

179. Fairlie Chappuis and Jana Krause, "Research Dilemmas in Dangerous Places", in *Secrecy and Methods in Security Research: A Guide to Qualitative Fieldwork*, eds Marieke de Goede, Esmé Bosma and Polly Pallister-Wilkins (London: Routledge, 2019), 112–25; Adam Dolnik, ed., *Conducting Terrorism Field Research: A Guide* (Abingdon; New York, NY: Routledge, 2013); Sageman, "The Stagnation in Terrorism Research".

180. Gentry, "Misogynistic Terrorism".

181. Joan Smith, *Home Grown: How Domestic Violence Turns Men Into Terrorists* (London: riverrun, 2019); Kaiser, *Political Masculinity*.

2.   METHODOLOGY: IS IT OK TO TALK TO EXTREMISTS?

1. Tea Torbenfeldt Bengtsson, "Performing Hypermasculinity: Experiences with Confined Young Offenders", *Men and Masculinities* vol. 19, no. 4 (2016): 410–28; R. W. Connell, *Masculinities* (Cambridge: Polity Press, 1995); Rachel Jewkes et al., "Hegemonic Masculinity: Combining Theory and Practice in Gender

Interventions", *Culture, Health & Sexuality* vol. 17, no. sup2 (2015): 112–27; Christoffer Carlsson, "Masculinities, Persistence, and Desistance", *Criminology* vol. 51, no. 3 (2013): 661–93.

2. Pierre Bourdieu, *Masculine Domination*, trans. Richard Nice (Stanford, CA: Stanford University Press, 2001); Pierre Bourdieu, *Outline of a Theory of Practice*, trans. Richard Nice (Cambridge: Cambridge University Press, 1977); Erving Goffman, *The Presentation of Self in Everyday Life* (London: Penguin, 1990), 78–79.

3. Harmonie Toros, "Better Researchers, Better People? The Dangers of Empathetic Research on the Extreme Right", *Critical Studies on Terrorism* vol. 15, no. 1 (2022): 225–31.

4. Nicholas J. Wheeler, "Investigating Diplomatic Transformations", *International Affairs* vol. 89, no. 2 (2013): 477–96.

5. Konrad Kellen, "Ideology and Rebellion: Terrorism in West Germany", in *Origins of Terrorism: Psychologies, Ideologies, Theologies, States of Mind*, eds Walter Reich and Walter Laquer (Washington, DC; Baltimore; London: Woodrow Wilson Center Press, 1998), 43–58 (47).

6. Bourdieu, *Masculine Domination*, 115.

7. John Morrison, Andrew Silke and Eke Bont, "The Development of the Framework for Research Ethics in Terrorism Studies (FRETS)", *Terrorism and Political Violence* vol. 33, no. 2 (2021): 271–89 (272).

8. See, for instance, Rae Jereza, "Inheritance as Alternative to Ethnographic Empathy with the Far Right", C-REX – Center for Research on Extremism, RightNow! (blog), November 2022, https://www.sv.uio.no/c-rex/english/news-and-events/right-now/2022/inheritance-as-alternative-to-ethnographic-empathy.html, last accessed 3 August 2023.

9. John Horgan, "The Case for First-Hand Research", in *Research on Terrorism: Trends, Achievements and Failures*, ed. Andrew Silke (London; Portland, OR: Routledge, 2004), 30–57; Peter Neumann and Scott Kleinmann, "How Rigorous Is Radicalization Research?", *Democracy and Security* vol. 9, no. 4 (2013): 360–82; Andrew Silke, "The Devil You Know: Continuing Problems with Research on Terrorism", *Terrorism and Political Violence* vol. 13, no. 4 (2001): 1–14.

10. Adam Dolnik, "Conducting Field Research on Terrorism: A Brief Primer", *Perspectives on Terrorism* vol. 5, no. 2 (2011), 3–35; Roger Eatwell, "Community Cohesion and Cumulative Extremism in Contemporary Britain", *The Political Quarterly* vol. 77, no. 2 (2006): 204–16 (209).

11. Katrine Fangen, "An Observational Study of the Norwegian Far Right: Some Reflections", in *Researching the Far Right: Theory, Method and Practice*, eds Stephen D. Ashe et al. (London: Routledge, 2020), 241–53.

12. Virinder S. Kalra and Nisha Kapoor, "Interrogating Segregation, Integration and the Community Cohesion Agenda", *Journal of Ethnic and Migration Studies* vol. 35, no. 9 (2009): 1397–415 (1404). Interviewees for the research underpinning this book were generally working class, but extremists come from a range of class, socio-economic and educational backgrounds.

13. Toros, "Better Researchers, Better People?", 226.

NOTES pp. [53–55]

14. Dave Mearns, Brian Thorne and John McLeod, *Person-Centred Counselling in Action* (London: SAGE Publications, 2013), 13, cited in Toros, "Better Researchers, Better People?", 226.
15. Joel Busher, "Negotiating Ethical Dilemmas during an Ethnographic Study of Anti-Minority Activism: A Personal Reflection on the Adoption of a 'Non-Dehumanization' Principle", in *Researching the Far Right: Theory, Method and Practice*, eds Stephen D. Ashe et al. (London: Routledge, 2020), 271–83 (271).
16. Carolyn Ellis, "Emotional and Ethical Quagmires in Returning to the Field", *Journal of Contemporary Ethnography* vol. 24, no. 1 (1995): 68–98 (88–89).
17. Paul Amar, "Middle East Masculinity Studies: Discourses of 'Men in Crisis', Industries of Gender in Revolution", *Journal of Middle East Women's Studies* vol. 7, no. 3 (2011): 36–70; Caron E. Gentry and Laura Sjoberg, *Mothers, Monsters, Whores: Women's Violence in Global Politics* (New York, NY: Zed Books, 2007); Jasbir K. Puar and Amit S. Rai, "Monster, Terrorist, Fag: The War on Terrorism and the Production of Docile Patriots", *Social Text* vol. 20, no. 3 (2002): 117–48.
18. Andrew Silke, "Cheshire-Cat Logic: The Recurring Theme of Terrorist Abnormality in Psychological Research", *Psychology, Crime & Law* vol. 4, no. 1 (1998): 51–69; Jeff Victoroff, "The Mind of the Terrorist: A Review and Critique of Psychological Approaches", *Journal of Conflict Resolution* vol. 49, no. 1 (2005): 3–42.
19. Paul Gill and Emily Corner, "There and Back Again: The Study of Mental Disorder and Terrorist Involvement", *American Psychologist* vol. 72, no. 3 (2017): 231–41; John Horgan, *The Psychology of Terrorism* (London; New York, NY: Routledge, 2002); there are exceptions, predominantly when considering the lone actor terrorist population.
20. Fiona Robinson, "Stop Talking and Listen: Discourse Ethics and Feminist Care Ethics in International Political Theory", *Millennium – Journal of International Studies* vol. 39, no. 3 (2011): 845–60; Toros, "Better Researchers, Better People?".
21. Christine Sylvester, "Empathetic Cooperation: A Feminist Method For IR", *Millennium – Journal of International Studies* vol. 23, no. 2 (1994): 315–34 (326).
22. Sylvester, "Empathetic Cooperation", 326.
23. Toros, "Better Researchers, Better People?".
24. Margaret R. Somers, "The Narrative Constitution of Identity: A Relational and Network Approach", *Theory and Society* vol. 23, no. 5 (1994): 605–49 (619).
25. Somers, "The Narrative Constitution of Identity".
26. Annica Kronsell, "Gendered Practices in Institutions of Hegemonic Masculinity", *International Feminist Journal of Politics* vol. 7, no. 2 (2005): 280–98.
27. Sylvester, "Empathetic Cooperation", 323.
28. María C. Lugones and Elizabeth V. Spelman, "Have We Got a Theory for You! Feminist Theory, Cultural Imperialism and the Demand for 'the Woman's Voice'", *Women's Studies International Forum* vol. 6, no. 6 (1983): 573–81 (581).
29. Simon Cottee, "Judging Offenders: The Moral Implications of Criminological Theories", in *Values in Criminology and Community Justice*, eds Malcolm Cowburn et al. (Bristol: Policy Press, 2013), 5–20.
30. Stuart Croft, *Securitizing Islam: Identity and the Search for Security* (Cambridge;

304

New York, NY: Cambridge University Press, 2012); Anthony Richards, "From Terrorism to 'Radicalization' to 'Extremism': Counterterrorism Imperative or Loss of Focus?", *International Affairs* vol. 91, no. 2 (2015): 371–80; Quassim Cassam, *Extremism: A Philosophical Analysis* (London: Routledge, 2022).

31. Busher, "Negotiating Ethical Dilemmas".

32. Stephen D. Ashe, "Whiteness, Class and the 'Communicative Community': A Doctoral Researcher's Journey to a Local Political Ethnography", in *Researching the Far Right: Theory, Method and Practice*, eds Stephen D. Ashe et al. (London: Routledge, 2020), 284–306.

33. Ashe, "Whiteness, Class and the 'Communicative Community'"; Aurelien Mondon and Aaron Winter, *Reactionary Democracy: How Racism and the Populist Far Right Became Mainstream* (London: Verso Books, 2020); Lisa Stampnitzky, *Disciplining Terror: How Experts Invented "Terrorism"* (Cambridge; New York, NY: Cambridge University Press, 2013).

34. Stampnitzky, *Disciplining Terror*.

35. Vidhya Ramalingam, "Old Threat, New Approach: Tackling the Far Right Across Europe" (London: Institute for Strategic Dialogue, 2014): https://www. isdglobal.org/wp-content/uploads/2016/03/OldThreatNewApproach_2014. pdf, last accessed 6 August 2023; Mondon and Winter, *Reactionary Democracy*.

36. Jereza, "Inheritance as Alternative to Ethnographic Empathy with the Far Right".

37. Jereza, "Inheritance as Alternative to Ethnographic Empathy with the Far Right".

38. Cynthia Miller-Idriss, *The Extreme Gone Mainstream: Commercialization and Far Right Youth Culture in Germany* (Princeton, NJ: Princeton University Press, 2017); Mondon and Winter, *Reactionary Democracy*.

39. Richard Hugman, Eileen Pittaway and Linda Bartolomei, "When 'Do No Harm' Is Not Enough: The Ethics of Research With Refugees and Other Vulnerable Groups", *The British Journal of Social Work* vol. 41, no. 7 (2011): 1271–87.

40. Mondon and Winter, *Reactionary Democracy*; Jordan Kyle and Limor Gultchin, "Populists in Power Around the World" (Tony Blair Institute for Global Change, November 2018): https://institute.global/policy/populists-power-around-world, last accessed 6 August 2023.

41. Peggy McIntosh, "White Privilege: Unpacking the Invisible Knapsack (1989)", in *On Privilege, Fraudulence, and Teaching as Learning: Selected Essays 1981–2019* (New York: Routledge, 2019), 29–34.

42. Peggy McIntosh, "White Privilege and Male Privilege: A Personal Account of Coming to See Correspondences Through Work in Women's Studies (1988)", in *On Privilege, Fraudulence, and Teaching as Learning: Selected Essays 1981–2019* (New York: Routledge, 2019), 17–28.

43. Dolnik, "Conducting Field Research on Terrorism"; Eatwell, "Community Cohesion and Cumulative Extremism in Contemporary Britain".

44. Kalra and Kapoor, "Interrogating Segregation, Integration and the Community Cohesion Agenda".

45. Gavin Bailey, "Extremism, Community and Stigma: Researching the Far Right and Radical Islam in Their Context", in *Researching Marginalized Groups*, eds

pp. [58–62]

Kalwant Bhopal and Ross Deuchar (New York, NY: Routledge, 2015), 22–35; Gavin Bailey, "We Can All Be a Little Radicalised: Recognising This Will Help Tackle Extremism", The Conversation, 17 August 2016, http://theconversation.com/we-can-all-be-a-little-radicalised-recognising-this-will-help-tackle-extremism-63144, last accessed 6 August 2023.

46. Tim Bale, "Supplying the Insatiable Demand: Europe's Populist Radical Right", *Government and Opposition* vol. 47, no. 2 (2012): 256–74; Bailey, "Extremism, Community and Stigma".

47. Busher, "Negotiating Ethical Dilemmas During an Ethnographic Study of Anti-Minority Activism", 276.

48. Margaret Wetherell, *Affect and Emotion: A New Social Science Understanding* (Los Angeles, CA; London: SAGE Publications, 2012).

49. Hilary Pilkington, *Loud and Proud: Passion and Politics in the English Defence League* (Manchester: Manchester University Press, 2016).

50. A3M, personal communication, July 2016.

51. Cas Mudde, "The War of Words Defining the Extreme Right Party Family", *West European Politics* vol. 19, no. 2 (1996): 225–48.

52. Bailey, "Extremism, Community and Stigma"; Pilkington, *Loud and Proud*, 1.

53. Kathleen M. Blee, "White-Knuckle Research: Emotional Dynamics in Fieldwork with Racist Activists", *Qualitative Sociology* vol. 21, no. 4 (1998): 381–99 (388).

54. Joel Busher, *The Making of Anti-Muslim Protest: Grassroots Activism in the English Defence League* (London; New York, NY: Routledge, 2015) [online].

55. Busher, *The Making of Anti-Muslim Protest*.

56. Katie Boyden, "Jayda Fransen Has Confirmed Her Britain First Exit in an Eerie New Video", KentLive, 19 January 2019: https://www.kentlive.news/news/kent-news/jayda-fransen-confirmed-britain-first-2447847, last accessed 6 August 2023.

57. A full list of demonstrations and events attended can be found in the Appendix.

58. One incident of overt hostility after an evening in the pub suggested I was regarded as competition for male attention in what was a distinctly masculine space.

59. For more on this issue see Fatima Ahdash, "Should the Law Facilitate the Removal of the Children of Terrorists and Extremists from Their Care?", British Politics and Policy at LSE (blog), 9 March 2018: https://blogs.lse.ac.uk/politicsandpolicy/should-the-law-facilitate-the-removal-of-the-children-of-convicted-terrorists/, last accessed 6 August 2023.

60. Jane L. Parpart and Marysia Zalewski, "Introduction: Rethinking the Man Question", in *Rethinking the Man Question: Sex, Gender and Violence in International Relations*, eds Jane L. Parpart and Marysia Zalewski (London; New York, NY: Zed Books, 2008), 1–22.

61. R. W. Connell, *Masculinities*, 1st revised edition (Cambridge: Polity Press, 2005), 89–92.

62. Connell, *Masculinities*, 2005, 89.

63. Kirin Narayan, "How Native Is a 'Native' Anthropologist?", *American Anthropologist*, New Series, vol. 95, no. 3 (1993): 671–86 (672).

64. See, for instance, Blee, "White-Knuckle Research"; Mia Bloom, *Bombshell: The Many Faces of Women Terrorists* (London: C. Hurst & Co., 2011); John Horgan, "Interviewing the Terrorists: Reflections on Fieldwork and Implications for Psychological Research", *Behavioral Sciences of Terrorism and Political Aggression* vol. 4, no. 3 (2012): 195–211; Anne Speckhard, *Talking to Terrorists: Understanding the Psycho-Social Motivations of Militant Jihadi Terrorists, Mass Hostage Takers, Suicide Bombers & "Martyrs"* (McLean, VA: Advances Press, 2012); Douglas Weeks, *Al Muhajiroun: A Case Study in Contemporary Islamic Activism* (Basingstoke: Palgrave Macmillan, 2020); Quintan Wiktorowicz, *Radical Islam Rising: Muslim Extremism in the West* (Lanham, MD: Rowman & Littlefield, 2005).

65. John Myles, "From Habitus to Mouth: Language and Class in Bourdieu's Sociology of Language", *Theory and Society* vol. 28, no. 6 (1999): 879–901 (885).

66. Interview, Jane, 1 September 2016.

67. Interview, Jane, 1 September 2016.

68. Interview, Rifat, 16 July 2017.

69. Lugones and Spelman, "Have We Got a Theory for You!", 581.

70. Busher, "Negotiating Ethical Dilemmas During an Ethnographic Study of Anti-Minority Activism".

71. Enloe in Carol Cohn and Cynthia Enloe, "A Conversation with Cynthia Enloe: Feminists Look at Masculinity and the Men Who Wage War", *Signs: Journal of Women in Culture and Society* vol. 28, no. 4 (2003): 1187–207 (1189).

72. Marta Bolognani, "Islam, Ethnography and Politics: Methodological Issues in Researching amongst West Yorkshire Pakistanis in 2005", *International Journal of Social Research Methodology* vol. 10, no. 4 (2007): 279–93 (282); see also the experiences of Fangen, "An Observational Study of the Norwegian Far Right".

73. Emily Winterbotham and Elizabeth Pearson, "Different Cities, Shared Stories: A Five-Country Study Challenging Assumptions Around Muslim Women and CVE Interventions", *RUSI Journal* vol. 161, no. 5 (2016): 54–65.

74. Bolognani, "Islam, Ethnography and Politics", 283.

75. Hugman, Pittaway and Bartolomei, "When 'Do No Harm' Is Not Enough".

76. Blee, "White-Knuckle Research", 392.

77. Carolyn Gallaher, "Researching Repellent Groups: Some Methodological Considerations on How to Represent Militants, Radicals, and Other Belligerents", in *Surviving Field Research: Working in Violent and Difficult Situations*, eds Chandra Lekha Sriram et al. (London: Routledge, 2009), 139–58.

78. Lugones and Spelman, "Have We Got a Theory for You!", 580.

79. Howard Becker, "Problems of Inference and Proof in Interviewee Observation", *American Sociological Review* vol. 23, no. 6 (1958): 652–60 (654–55).

80. Robinson, "Stop Talking and Listen", 849.

81. Somers, "The Narrative Constitution of Identity"; Lugones and Spelman, "Have We Got a Theory for You!", 573.

82. Kristina Rolin, "Standpoint Theory as a Methodology for the Study of Power Relations", *Hypatia* vol. 24, no. 4 (2009): 218–26 (223).

83. Interview, Jason, 6 November 2016
84. Interview, Hel Gower, 2 November 2016.
85. Bolognani, "Islam, Ethnography and Politics", 369.

3. THE RADICAL RIGHT: SITUATING MASCULINITIES

1. J. M. Berger, *Extremism* (Cambridge, MA: MIT Press, 2018).
2. Christopher Mullins, *Holding Your Square: Masculinities, Streetlife and Violence* (Cullompton: Willan, 2006), 7.
3. Pietro Castelli Gattinara and A. L. P. Pirro, "Extremist and far right narratives in Europe: a research overview" (Radicalisation Awareness Network, 2017), 1; Cas Mudde, "Right-Wing Extremism Analyzed: A Comparative Analysis of the Ideologies of Three Alleged Right-Wing Extremist Parties (NPD, NDP, CP'86)", *European Journal of Political Research* vol. 27, no. 2 (1995): 203–24.
4. Matthew Goodwin, "The Roots of Extremism: The English Defence League and the Counter-Jihad Challenge" (Chatham House, 2013), 3: https://www.chathamhouse.org/sites/default/files/public/Research/Europe/0313bp_goodwin.pdf, last accessed 28 July 2023.
5. Cas Mudde, "The War of Words Defining the Extreme Right Party Family", *West European Politics* vol. 19, no. 2 (1996): 225–48 (226; 243); Mudde, "Right-Wing Extremism Analyzed", 204.
6. See, for instance, Matthew Feldman, "Introduction", in Paul Jackson et al., *The EDL: Britain's 'New Far Right' Social Movement* (Northampton: University of Northampton, 2011), 3–4; and Matthew Feldman and Paul Stocker, "The Post-Brexit Far-Right in Britain", in *Violent Radicalisation & Far-Right Extremism in Europe*, eds Aristotle Kallis, Sara Zeiger and Bilgehan Öztürk (Ankara: SETA Publications, 2018), 123–72.
7. See "State of Hate 2018" (London: Hope Not Hate, February 2018), 10–11: https://hopenothate.org.uk/wp-content/uploads/2021/09/State-of-Hate-2018.pdf, last accessed 7 August 2023; "International Counter-Jihad Organisations", HOPE Not Hate (blog), 11 January 2018: https://hopenothate.org.uk/2018/01/11/what-is-counter-jihadism/, last accessed 7 August 2023; and Alexander Meleagrou-Hitchens and Hans Brun, "A Neo-Nationalist Network: The English Defence League and Europe's Counter-Jihad Movement" (London: International Centre for the Study of Radicalisation and Political Violence, 2013): https://www.diva-portal.org/smash/get/diva2:1235939/FULLTEXT01.pdf, last accessed 7 August 2023.
8. Joel Busher, *The Making of Anti-Muslim Protest: Grassroots Activism in the English Defence League* (London; New York, NY: Routledge, 2015), para. 86 [online]. In response, some participants in this book countered that they were not 'anti-Muslim' as they had Muslim friends.
9. Hilary Pilkington, *Loud and Proud: Passion and Politics in the English Defence League* (Manchester: Manchester University Press, 2016), 4.

10. Tore Bjørgo, "Introduction", *Terrorism and Political Violence* vol. 7, no. 1 (1995): 1–16 (2).
11. Roger Griffin, *The Nature of Fascism* (London: Psychology Press, 1991), 6.
12. Matthew Feldman, "From Radical-Right Islamophobia to 'Cumulative Extremism'" (Faith Matters, 2012), 10: https://tellmamauk.org/wp-content/uploads/2013/02/islamophobia.pdf, last accessed 7 August 2023.
13. Paul Jackson et al., *The EDL: Britain's 'New Far Right' Social Movement* (Northampton: University of Northampton, 2011); Feldman, "From Radical-Right Islamophobia to 'Cumulative Extremism'"; Martin Barker, *New Racism: Conservatives and the Ideology of the Tribe* (London: Junction Books, 1981), 23–24.
14. Donald Holbrook and Max Taylor, "Introduction", in *Extreme Right-Wing Political Violence and Terrorism*, eds Donald Holbrook, Max Taylor and P. M. Currie (London; New York, NY: Bloomsbury, 2013), 1–14 (2).
15. John Meadowcroft and Elizabeth A. Morrow, "Violence, Self-Worth, Solidarity and Stigma: How a Dissident, Far-Right Group Solves the Collective Action Problem", *Political Studies* vol. 65, no. 2 (2017): 373–90 (375).
16. Gattinara, "Research Overview of Far Right Narratives", 3.
17. Feldman, "From Radical-Right Islamophobia to 'Cumulative Extremism'", 10. Fransen asserts that her 2019 party of the same name is not related to the earlier British Freedom Party.
18. Cas Mudde, "Right-wing extremism analyzed", *European Journal of Political Research* vol. 27, no. 2 (1995): 203–21 (218).
19. Cas Mudde, *The Far Right Today* (Cambridge: Polity Press, 2019), p. 23.
20. Paul Austin Murphy, "COUNTER-JIHAD: BEYOND THE EDL: The EDL's Tommy Robinson in Amsterdam [Video]", 2010: http://theenglishdefenceleagueextra.blogspot.co.uk/2010/10/edls-tommy-robinson-in-amsterdam-video.html, last accessed 2 July 2015.
21. "About Us", English Defence League website: http://www.englishdefenceleague.org.uk/mission-statement/, last accessed 20 March 2018.
22. Meleagrou-Hitchens and Brun, "A Neo-Nationalist Network", 7.
23. Meleagrou-Hitchens and Brun, "A Neo-Nationalist Network", 7; Nigel Copsey, "The English Defence League: Challenging Our Country and Our Values of Social Inclusion, Fairness and Equality" (Faith Matters, November 2010), 24: https://www.faith-matters.org/wp-content/uploads/2010/11/english-defense-league-report.pdf, last accessed 28 July 2023 .
24. Hayley Tsukayama and Craig Timberg, "'Twitter Purge' Suspends Account of Far-Right Leader Who Was Retweeted by Trump", *Washington Post*, 5 December 2021: https://www.washingtonpost.com/news/the-switch/wp/2017/12/18/twitter-purge-suspends-account-of-far-right-leader-who-was-retweeted-by-trump/, last accessed 8 August 2023.
25. Michael Kimmel, "Racism as Adolescent Male Rite of Passage: Ex-Nazis in Scandinavia", *Journal of Contemporary Ethnography* vol. 36, no. 2 (2007): 202–18; Michael Kimmel and Abby L. Ferber, "'White Men Are This Nation': Right-Wing

Militias and the Restoration of Rural American Masculinity", *Rural Sociology* vol. 65, no. 4 (2000): 582–604.

26. Arshy Mann, "The Misogynist Ideology Behind Toronto's Incel Terror Attack Must Be Confronted", Xtra, 26 April 2018: https://www.dailyxtra.com/the-misogynist-ideology-behind-torontos-incel-terror-attack-must-be-confronted-86222, last accessed 8 August 2023; Susanne Kaiser, *Political Masculinity: How Incels, Fundamentalists and Authoritarians Mobilise for Patriarchy*, trans. Valentine A. Pakis (Cambridge; Medford, MA: Polity Press, 2022); Julia R. DeCook and Megan Kelly, "Interrogating the 'Incel Menace': Assessing the Threat of Male Supremacy in Terrorism Studies", *Critical Studies on Terrorism* vol. 15, no. 3 (2022): 706–26.

27. James Treadwell and Jon Garland, "Masculinity, Marginalization and Violence: A Case Study of the English Defence League", *British Journal of Criminology* vol. 51, no. 4 (2011): 621–34 (621).

28. Jon Garland and James Treadwell, "'No Surrender to the Taliban': Football Hooliganism, Islamophobia and the Rise of the English Defence League", in *Papers from the British Criminology Conference* vol. 10 (2010): 19–35: https://www.britsoccrim.org/volume10/2010_Garland_Treadwell.pdf, last accessed 11 August 2023.

29. Treadwell and Garland, "Masculinity, Marginalization and Violence", 624.

30. Steve Hall, "Daubing the Drudges of Fury: Men, Violence and the Piety of the 'Hegemonic Masculinity' Thesis", *Theoretical Criminology* vol. 6, no. 1 (2002): 35–61; Antony Whitehead, "Man to Man Violence: How Masculinity May Work as a Dynamic Risk Factor", *The Howard Journal of Criminal Justice* vol. 44, no. 4 (2005): 411–22.

31. Treadwell and Garland, "Masculinity, Marginalization and Violence", 627–32; James Treadwell, "White Riot: The English Defence League and the 2011 English Riots", *Criminal Justice Matters* vol. 87, no. 1 (2012): 36–37 (37).

32. Busher, *The Making of Anti-Muslim Protest*, paras 51–52 [online].

33. Laura Sjoberg, *Gendering Global Conflict: Toward a Feminist Theory of War* (New York, NY: Columbia University Press, 2013), 47.

34. Eric Dunning, "Towards a Sociological Understanding of Football Hooliganism as a World Phenomenon", *European Journal on Criminal Policy and Research* vol. 8, no. 2 (2000): 141–62 (151).

35. Mark Hamm, "Apocalyptic Violence: The Seduction of Terrorist Subcultures", *Theoretical Criminology* vol. 8, no. 3 (2004): 323–39 (327).

36. Hamm, "Apocalyptic Violence", 337.

37. Anoop Nayak, "White Lives", in *Racialization: Studies in Theory and Practice*, eds Karim Murjil and John Solomos (Oxford: Oxford University Press, 2005), 152.

38. Cynthia Miller-Idriss, *The Extreme Gone Mainstream: Commercialization and Far Right Youth Culture in Germany* (Princeton, NJ: Princeton University Press, 2017), 162.

39. Beth Windisch, "A Downward Spiral: The Role of Hegemonic Masculinity in Lone Actor Terrorism", *Studies in Conflict & Terrorism* (2021): 1–18.

40. See also the Appendix for a list of participants. All participants with pseudonyms

are shown here with first name only. Leadership figures are named with both first name and surname.

41. Pilkington, *Loud and Proud*, 42.

42. "Football Lads Alliance (FLA) Founder Quits, but FLA Is Still a Growing Danger", Stand Up To Racism, 17 April 2018: http://www.standuptoracism.org.uk/football-lads-alliance-fla-founder-quits-but-fla-is-still-a-growing-danger/, last accessed 11 August 2023.

43. For Britain, "For Britain Manifesto", 2017: https://d3n8a8pro7vhmx.cloudfront.net/forbritain/pages/113/attachments/original/1519030879/ Manfiesto_2.pdf?1519030879, last accessed 20 March 2018.

44. For Britain, "For Britain Manifesto".

45. For Britain, "For Britain Manifesto".

46. For Britain, "For Britain Manifesto".

47. Searchlight Team, "Anne-Marie Waters Announces that For Britain Has Folded", 13 July 2022: https://www.searchlightmagazine.com/2022/07/anne-marie-waters-announces-that-for-britain-has-folded/#, last accessed 19 September 2023.

48. White Lives Matter is a US-based movement, formed in 2015 by white supremacists in response to the Black Lives Matter social movement. See https://www.splcenter.org/fighting-hate/extremist-files/group/white-lives-matter, last accessed 11 August 2023. A UK-based movement using the same name has, however, had little traction.

49. "Briefing: National Action", Hope Not Hate: https://hopenothate.org.uk/research-old/investigations/briefing-national-action/, last accessed 11 August 2023.

50. Nick Lowles, "State of Hate 2018" (Hope Not Hate, February 2018), 54–55: https://hopenothate.org.uk/wp-content/uploads/2021/09/State-of-Hate-2018.pdf, last accessed 11 August 2023.

51. Busher, *The Making of Anti-Muslim Protest*, para. 362 [online].

52. Busher, *The Making of Anti-Muslim Protest*; Lowles, "State of Hate 2018".

53. Interview, Iain, 10 December 2016.

54. Mullins, *Holding Your Square*; Elijah Anderson, *Streetwise: Race, Class, and Change in an Urban Community* (Chicago, IL: University of Chicago Press, 1992).

55. Selina Todd, *The People: The Rise and Fall of the Working Class, 1910–2010* (London: John Murray, 2014), 326–27.

56. Mimi Schippers, "Recovering the Feminine Other: Masculinity, Femininity, and Gender Hegemony", *Theory and Society* vol. 36, no. 1 (2007): 85–102.

57. Interview, Hel Gower, 2 November 2016.

58. V. Spike Peterson, "Gendered Nationalism", *Peace Review* vol. 6, no. 1 (1994): 77–83 (83).

59. Véronique Pin-Fat and Maria Stern, "The Scripting of Private Jessica Lynch: Biopolitics, Gender, and the 'Feminization' of the U.S. Military", *Alternatives: Global, Local, Political* vol. 30, no. 1 (2005): 25–53 (30); Anne McClintock, "'No Longer in a Future Heaven': Woman and Nationalism in South Africa", *Transition*

vol. 51 (1991): 104–23, cited in Joane Nagel, "Masculinity and Nationalism: Gender and Sexuality in the Making of Nations", *Ethnic and Racial Studies* vol. 21, no. 2 (1998): 242–69 (254).

60. Interview, Darren, 4 August 2016.
61. Mullins, *Holding Your Square*, 8.
62. Demetrakis Z. Demetriou, "Connell's Concept of Hegemonic Masculinity: A Critique", *Theory and Society* vol. 30, no. 3 (2001): 337–61.
63. R. W. Connell and James W. Messerschmidt, "Hegemonic Masculinity: Rethinking the Concept", *Gender & Society* vol. 19, no. 6 (2005): 829–59.
64. See, for instance, Anderson, *Streetwise*; Jack Katz, *Seductions of Crime: Moral and Sensual Attractions in Doing Evil* (New York, NY: Basic Books, 1988).
65. R. W. Connell, *Masculinities* (Cambridge: Polity Press, 1995), 53.
66. Ramón Spaaij, "Men Like Us, Boys Like Them: Violence, Masculinity, and Collective Identity in Football Hooliganism", *Journal of Sport and Social Issues* vol. 32, no. 4 (2008): 369–92 (380); James W. Messerschmidt, "Becoming 'Real Men': Adolescent Masculinity Challenges and Sexual Violence", *Men and Masculinities* vol. 2, no. 3 (2000): 286–307.
67. Nicola Ingram, "Working-Class Boys, Educational Success and the Misrecognition of Working-Class Culture", *British Journal of Sociology of Education* vol. 30, no. 4 (2009): 421–34 (442).
68. Interview, Darren, 4 August 2016.
69. Held in 2018.
70. Interview, Darren, 4 August 2016.
71. Spaaij, "Men Like Us, Boys Like Them", 374.
72. Miller-Idriss, *The Extreme Gone Mainstream*, 162.
73. Interview, Alex, 25 August 2016.
74. Interview, Tommy Robinson, 26 September 2016.
75. Interview, Tommy Robinson, 26 September 2016.
76. Interview, Iain, 25 August 2016.
77. Participants use the term 'liberal' frequently, and generally to imply the opposite.
78. Louise Casey, "The Casey Review: A Review into Opportunity and Integration" (Department for Communities and Local Government, December 2016), 16: https://www.gov.uk/government/publications/the-casey-review-a-review-into-opportunity-and-integration, last accessed 11 August 2023.
79. Casey, "The Casey Review", 15.
80. Todd, *The People*, 354.
81. Paul Amar, "Middle East Masculinity Studies: Discourses of 'Men in Crisis', Industries of Gender in Revolution", *Journal of Middle East Women's Studies* vol. 7, no. 3 (2011): 36–70 (42).
82. Ingram, "Working-Class Boys, Educational Success and the Misrecognition of Working-Class Culture".
83. Paul Connolly and Julie Healy, "Symbolic Violence, Locality and Social Class: The Educational and Career Aspirations of 10–11-Year-Old Boys in Belfast", *Pedagogy,*

Culture and Society vol. 12, no. 1 (2004): 15–33, cited in Ingram, "Working-Class Boys, Educational Success and the Misrecognition of Working-Class Culture", 422.

84. Rod Earle, "Boys' Zone Stories: Perspectives from a Young Men's Prison", *Criminology & Criminal Justice* vol. 11, no. 2 (2011): 129–43.

85. Interview, Georgey, 17 October 2016.

86. Amar, "Middle East Masculinity Studies", 43; see also Katherine E. Brown, "Gender and Counter-Radicalization: Women and Emerging Counter-Terror Measures", in *Gender, National Security and Counter-Terrorism*, eds Jayne Huckerby and Margaret L. Satterthwaite (Abingdon; New York, NY: Routledge, 2013), 36–59, and the use of these discourses in counter-terrorism measures.

87. Interview, Lydia, 19 August 2017.

88. Nira Yuval-Davis, Floya Anthias and Eleonore Kofman, "Secure Borders and Safe Haven and the Gendered Politics of Belonging: Beyond Social Cohesion", *Ethnic and Racial Studies* vol. 28, no. 3 (2005): 513–35.

89. Jayne Huckerby, "Women and Preventing Violent Extremism: The U.S. and U.K. Experiences" (NYU School of Law, Center for Human Rights and Global Justice, 2011): https://chrgj.org/wp-content/uploads/2016/09/Women-and-Violent-Extremism-The-US-and-UK-Experiences.pdf, last accessed 11 August 2023; Naaz Rashid, "Giving the Silent Majority a Stronger Voice? Initiatives to Empower Muslim Women as Part of the UK's 'War on Terror'", *Ethnic and Racial Studies* vol. 37, no. 4 (2014): 589–604.

90. Ben Quinn, "French Police Make Women Remove Clothing on Nice Beach Following Burkini Ban", *The Guardian*, 24 August 2016: https://www.theguardian.com/world/2016/aug/24/french-police-make-woman-remove-burkini-on-nice-beach, last accessed 10 August 2023.

91. Interview, Jane, 1 September 2016.

92. Interview, Anne Marie Waters, 16 October 2016.

93. See, for instance, June Edmunds, "The Limits of Post-National Citizenship: European Muslims, Human Rights and the Hijab", *Ethnic and Racial Studies* vol. 35, no. 7 (2012): 1181–99; Eoin Daly, "Political Liberalism and French National Identity in the Wake of the Face-Veiling Law", *International Journal of Law in Context* vol. 9, no. 3 (2013): 366–85; Antonia Zerbisias, "Canada Hijab Row Is All about the Anti-Terror Act", Al Jazeera, 5 March 2015: http://www.aljazeera.com/indepth/opinion/2015/03/canada-hijab-row-anti-terror-act-150303085632396.html, last accessed 11 August 2023.

94. Interview, Tommy Robinson, 26 September 2016; this is rhetoric he has reproduced with other researchers, and a version of this appears in Hsiao-Hung Pai, *Angry White People: Coming Face-to-Face with the British Far Right* (London: Zed Books, 2016), 143.

95. Goodwin, "The Roots of Extremism"; Jamie Bartlett and Mark Littler, "Inside the EDL" (Demos, 2011), 14: https://www.demos.co.uk/files/Inside_the_edl_WEB.pdf, last accessed 27 July 2023.

96. Bartlett and Littler, "Inside the EDL", 5.

97. Interview, Iain, 10 December 2016.

98. See Owen Jones, Twitter, 10 September 2016: https://twitter.com/owenjones84/status/774559722296967168, last accessed 11 August 2023.

99. Interview, Jason, 9 August 2016. The chance to disseminate their views was a key reason cited by participants for talking to me. Other reasons included liking me, trying to arrange a date and being curious about my views.

100. Interview, Darren, 4 August 2016.

101. Interview, Darren, 4 August 2016.

102. Interview, Darren, 4 August 2016.

103. Interview, Georgey, 17 October 2016.

104. Interview, Iain, 10 December 2016.

105. Although the focus was on Muslim CSE, I also heard criticism of widespread sexual abuse in football clubs and by one former EDL leader in speeches at demonstrations.

106. Interview, Iain, 5 November 2016.

107. Interview, Iain, 25 August 2016. It is true that his town and the wider area had seen and continue to see press reports on the failure of the police to prosecute grooming gangs and protect victims.

108. Interview, Iain, 10 December 2016.

109. Interview, Daniel, 25 August 2016.

110. Jack Halberstam, *Female Masculinity* (Durham, NC: Duke University Press, 1998), 2.

111. Interview, Jason, 6 November 2016.

112. Todd, *The People*, 358.

113. Interview, Jason, 6 November 2016.

114. Interview, Jason, 6 November 2016.

115. Interview, Jason, 6 November 2016.

116. Interview, Jason, 9 August 2016.

117. Interview, Jason, 6 November 2016.

118. William Ian Miller, *The Anatomy of Disgust* (Cambridge, MA: Harvard University Press, 1997).

119. Albert Memmi, *Racism* (Minneapolis, MN: University of Minnesota Press, 1999); Aurelien Mondon and Aaron Winter, *Reactionary Democracy: How Racism and the Populist Far Right Became Mainstream* (London: Verso Books, 2020).

120. Adam Rutherford, *How to Argue with a Racist: History, Science, Race and Reality* (London: Weidenfeld & Nicolson, 2020).

121. Anoop Nayak, "After Race: Ethnography, Race and Post-Race Theory", *Ethnic and Racial Studies* vol. 29, no. 3 (2006): 411–30; Mondon and Winter, *Reactionary Democracy*.

122. Judith Frankenberg, *White Women, Race Matters: The Social Construction of Whiteness* (Minneapolis, MN: University of Minnesota Press, 1993), 1.

123. Osamudia James, "White Like Me: The Negative Impact of the Diversity

Rationale on White Identity Formation", *New York University Law Review* vol. 89, no. 2 (2014), 425–512.

124. James, "White Like Me", 425–26.

125. James, "White Like Me".

126. Camille Gear Rich, "Marginal Whiteness", *California Law Review* vol. 98, no. 5 (2010): 1497–1593.

127. James, "White Like Me".

128. Roger Hewitt, *White Backlash and the Politics of Multiculturalism* (Cambridge: Cambridge University Press, 2005), 4.

129. Cliff Leek and Michael Kimmel, "Conceptualizing Intersectionality in Superordination: Masculinities, Whitenesses, and Dominant Classes", in *Routledge International Handbook of Race, Class, and Gender*, ed. Shirley A. Jackson (Oxford; New York, NY: Routledge, 2014), 3–9 (5).

130. Rich, "Marginal Whiteness", 1497.

131. Interview, Anne Marie Waters, 14 October 2016.

132. Hugo Gye, "Outrage After Irish Bar in Luton Refuses to Serve People Wearing Poppies", Mail Online, 9 November 2015: http://www.dailymail.co.uk/news/article-3310209/Outrage-Irish-bar-refuses-serve-people-wearing-poppies.html, last accessed 12 August 2023.

133. Interview, Tommy Robinson, 26 September 2016.

134. Mullins, *Holding Your Square*, 7.

135. Quintan Wiktorowicz, *Radical Islam Rising: Muslim Extremism in the West* (Lanham, MD: Rowman & Littlefield, 2005); Joel Busher, "Grassroots Activism in the English Defence League: Discourse and Public (Dis)Order", in *Extreme Right Wing Political Violence and Terrorism*, eds Max Taylor, P. M. Currie and Donald Holbrook (London: Bloomsbury Academic, 2013), 65–84; Mitchell D. Silber and Arvin Bhatt, "Radicalization in the West: The Homegrown Threat" (New York Police Department, 2007): https://info.publicintelligence.net/NYPDradicalization.pdf, last accessed 12 August 2023.

136. Ted Cantle, "Community Cohesion: Report of the Independent Review Team" (London: The Home Office, 2001); Busher, *The Making of Anti-Muslim Protest*, paras 153–223 [online]; Ray Forrest and Ade Kearns, "Social Cohesion, Social Capital and the Neighbourhood", *Urban Studies* vol. 38, no. 12 (2001): 2125–43.

137. See also Amar, "Middle East Masculinity Studies"; Michael S. Kimmel, Jeff R. Hearn and R. W. Connell, eds, *Handbook of Studies on Men and Masculinities* (Thousand Oaks, CA; London: SAGE Publications, 2004).

138. Cantle, "Community Cohesion"; Derek McGhee, *The End of Multiculturalism? Terrorism, Integration and Human Rights* (Maidenhead: Open University Press, 2008).

139. Treadwell and Garland, "Masculinity, Marginalization and Violence".

4.   THE RADICAL RIGHT: MOBILISING MASCULINITIES

1. R. W. Connell, *Masculinities*, 1st revised edition (Cambridge: Polity Press, 2005), 64.

2. Clare Hemmings, "Invoking Affect: Cultural Theory and the Ontological Turn", *Cultural Studies* vol. 19, no. 5 (2005): 548–67 (551).

3. Federica Giardini, "Public Affects: Clues towards a Political Practice of Singularity", *European Journal of Women's Studies* vol. 6, no. 2 (1999): 149–59 (150).

4. Margaret Wetherell, *Affect and Emotion: A New Social Science Understanding* (Los Angeles, CA; London: SAGE Publications, 2012), 141–43.

5. Pierre Bourdieu, *Masculine Domination*, trans. Richard Nice (Stanford, CA: Stanford University Press, 2001), 2.

6. Hannah Arendt, "Ideology and Terror: A Novel Form of Government", *The Review of Politics* vol. 15, no. 3 (1953): 303–27 (317).

7. Joseph Schull, "What Is Ideology? Theoretical Problems and Lessons from Soviet-Type Societies", *Political Studies* vol. 40, no. 4 (1992): 728–41 (729).

8. Peter Stearns, "History of Emotions: Issues of Change and Impact", in *Handbook of Emotions, 3rd edition*, eds Michael Lewis, Jeannette M. Haviland-Jones and Lisa Feldman Barrett (London: Guilford Press, 2008), 17–31 (18); James R. Averill, "The Social Construction of Emotion: With Special Reference to Love", in *The Social Construction of the Person*, eds Kenneth J. Gergen and Keith E. Davis (New York, NY: Springer New York, 1985), 89–109 (90).

9. Randall Collins, "Stratification, Emotional Energy, and the Transient Emotions", in *Research Agendas in the Sociology of Emotions*, ed. Theodore D. Kemper (Albany, NY: SUNY Press, 1990), 27–57 (27–28).

10. Émile Durkheim, *The Elementary Forms of the Religious Life*, trans. Karen E. Fields , 1912 (New York, NY: The Free Press, 1995), cited in Randall Collins, "Social Movements and the Focus of Emotional Attention", in *Passionate Politics: Emotions and Social Movements*, eds Jeff Goodwin, James M. Jasper and Francesca Polletta (Chicago, IL: University of Chicago Press, 2001), 27–44 (33).

11. Sara Ahmed, *The Cultural Politics of Emotion* (Edinburgh: Edinburgh University Press, 2004), 171.

12. Ahmed, *The Cultural Politics of Emotion*, 2004, 170–73.

13. Sara Ahmed, *The Cultural Politics of Emotion*, 2nd revised edition (Edinburgh: Edinburgh University Press, 2014); James M. Jasper, "The Emotions of Protest: Affective and Reactive Emotions in and Around Social Movements", *Sociological Forum* vol. 13, no. 3 (1998): 397–424 (398); Mabel Berezin, "Emotions and Political Identity: Mobilizing Affection for the Polity", in *Passionate Politics: Emotions and Social Movements*, eds Jeff Goodwin, James M. Jasper and Francesca Polletta (Chicago, IL: University of Chicago Press, 2001), 83–98 (97).

14. Mary Holmes, "The Emotionalization of Reflexivity", *Sociology* vol. 44, no. 1 (2010): 139–54 (140).

15. Jasper, "The Emotions of Protest", 398.

16. Collins, "Stratification, Emotional Energy, and the Transient Emotions", 27.

17. Randall Collins, "Emotional Energy as the Common Denominator of Rational Action", *Rationality and Society* vol. 5, no. 2 (1993): 203–30 (205).

18. Joel Busher, *The Making of Anti-Muslim Protest: Grassroots Activism in the English Defence League* (London; New York, NY: Routledge, 2015) [online].

19. "Tommy Robinson: 'I Left the EDL to Work With Muslims and Defeat Islamist Ideology", *Daily Express*, 8 October 2013: http://www.express.co.uk/news/uk/435321/Tommy-Robinson-I-left-the-EDL-to-work-with-Muslims-and-defeat-Islamist-ideology, last accessed 13 August 2023.

20. Peter McLaughlin and Tommy Robinson, *Mohammed's Koran: Why Muslims Kill for Islam* (Peter McLaughlin, 2017).

21. "Tommy Robinson Publishes Book on the Holy Quran", 5Pillars (blog), 2017: http://5pillarsuk.com/2017/07/22/tommy-robinson-publishes-book-on-the-holy-quran/, last accessed 13 August 2023.

22. Interview, Tommy Robinson, 16 September 2016.

23. Albert Ward, "Parliament and Government Have a Class Problem", British Politics and Policy at LSE (blog), 27 October 2022: https://blogs.lse.ac.uk/politicsandpolicy/parliament-and-government-have-a-class-problem/, last accessed 13 August 2023; Cassie Barton et al., "Social Background of Members of Parliament 1979–2019", House of Commons Library, 10 April 2023: https://commonslibrary.parliament.uk/research-briefings/cbp-7483/, last accessed 13 August 2023.

24. This was a 2017 van attack by a far-right extremist on worshippers outside the mosque which led to the death of one man and the injury of several others. See Lizzie Dearden, "Finsbury Park Terror Suspect Darren Osborne Read Messages from Tommy Robinson Days Before Attack, Court Hears", *The Independent*, 23 January 2018: https://www.independent.co.uk/news/uk/crime/tommy-robinson-darren-osborne-messages-finsbury-park-attack-mosque-van-latest-court-trial-muslims-a8174086.html, last accessed 13 August 2023; "Finsbury Park Terror Attack: Five Years On", Muslim Council of Britain, 18 June 2022: https://mcb.org.uk/finsbury-park-terror-attack-five-years-on/, last accessed 13 August 2023.

25. Interview, John Meighan, 5 July 2017.

26. BBC News, "Birmingham Football Lads Alliance Demo: Thousands March in City", BBC News, 24 March 2018: http://www.bbc.co.uk/news/uk-england-birmingham-43527109, last accessed 13 August 2023.

27. "Football Lads Alliance (FLA) Founder Quits, but FLA Is Still a Growing Danger", Stand Up To Racism, 17 April 2018, http://www.standuptoracism.org.uk/football-lads-alliance-fla-founder-quits-but-fla-is-still-a-growing-danger/, last accessed 11 August 2023.

28. Interview, Darren, 4 August 2016.

29. Interview, Jason, 9 August 2016.

30. The Bell Curve suggests that intelligence in people of colour and women is lower in general than in whites and men, noting the possibility, however, of intelligent outliers. It has been widely critiqued.

31. Interview translated from German, Henryk, 22 July 2017.

32. Field notes, Telford, EDL demonstration, 5 November 2016.

33. Joel Busher, "Grassroots Activism in the English Defence League: Discourse and Public (Dis)Order", in *Extreme Right Wing Political Violence and Terrorism*, eds Max Taylor, P. M. Currie and Donald Holbrook (London: Bloomsbury Academic, 2013), 65–84.

34. Charlotte Hooper, *Manly States: Masculinities, International Relations, and Gender Politics* (New York, NY: Columbia University Press, 2001), 32.

35. Busher, *The Making of Anti-Muslim Protest*, para. 79 [online].

36. Text message, Jayda Fransen, 30 May 2017.

37. Interview, Tommy Robinson, 10 March 2017.

38. David Maddox, "'Defund the BBC!' New Prime Minister Told to Abolish Licence Fee as Fury Grows at Broadcaster", *Daily Express*, 14 July 2022: https://www.express.co.uk/news/politics/1639932/BBC-licence-fee-Tory-leadership-hopefuls-campaign-group-defund-update, last accessed 13 August 2023.

39. Mark Sweney, "'Proud to Be a Disruptor': GB News Faces Growing Pains as It Tries to Clean Up Image", *The Guardian*, 17 January 2023: https://www.theguardian.com/media/2023/jan/17/gb-news-rightwing-tv-channel, last accessed 13 August 2023; Andy Gregory, "Who Is Behind GB News and What Is Channel's Agenda?", *The Independent*, 15 June 2021: https://www.independent.co.uk/news/uk/home-news/gb-news-channel-launch-andrew-neil-b1864268.html, last accessed 13 August 2023.

40. Interview, Jason, 11 December 2016.

41. Interview, Henryk, 22 July 2017.

42. Interview, Darren, 4 August 2016.

43. Interview, Darren, 4 August 2016.

44. His last book is titled *Silenced*.

45. Dominic Casciani, "Ex-EDL Leader Tommy Robinson Jailed at Leeds Court", BBC News, 29 May 2018: https://www.bbc.co.uk/news/uk-england-leeds-44287640, last accessed 13 August 2023; Tom Powell, "Hundreds of Protesters Descend on Whitehall after Tommy Robinson Arrested for 'Breaching the Peace'", *Evening Standard*, 26 May 2018: https://www.standard.co.uk/news/london/hundreds-of-protesters-descend-on-whitehall-after-tommy-robinson-arrested-for-breaching-the-peace-a3849046.html, last accessed 13 August 2023.

46. Interview, Iain, 10 December 2016.

47. Ben Quinn, "Tommy Robinson Link With Quilliam Foundation Raises Questions", *The Guardian*, 12 October 2013: https://www.theguardian.com/uk-news/2013/oct/12/tommy-robinson-quilliam-foundation-questions-motivation, last accessed 13 August 2023; Steven Hopkins, "Tommy Robinson Claims He Was Paid Thousands to Leave EDL", HuffPost UK, 4 December 2015: http://www.huffingtonpost.co.uk/2015/12/03/tommy-robinson-claims-quilliam-paid-him-to-leave-edl_n_8710834.html, last accessed 13 August 2023.

48. Hilary Pilkington, *Loud and Proud: Passion and Politics in the English Defence League* (Manchester: Manchester University Press, 2016), 45.

49. Hope Not Hate, "State of Hate 2019: People Vs the Elite?" (February 2019),

3: https://hopenothate.org.uk/wp-content/uploads/2019/02/state-of-hate-2019-final-1.pdf, last accessed 13 August 2023.

50. Hope Not Hate, "State of Hate Report 2023" (February 2023), 7: https://hopenothate.org.uk/wp-content/uploads/2023/02/state-of-hate-2023-v7-1.pdf, last accessed 23 July 2023.

51. Interview, Jayda Fransen, 27 April 2023.

52. Interview, Iain, 25 August 2016.

53. Jon Garland and James Treadwell, "'No Surrender to the Taliban': Football Hooliganism, Islamophobia and the Rise of the English Defence League", in *Papers from the British Criminology Conference* vol. 10 (2010): 19–35: https://www.britsoccrim.org/volume10/2010_Garland_Treadwell.pdf, last accessed 11 August 2023.

54. Interview, Darren, 4 August 2016.

55. Interview, Alex, 25 August 2016.

56. Rajan Basra, Peter R. Neumann and Claudia Brunner, "Criminal Pasts, Terrorist Futures: European Jihadists and the New Crime–Terror Nexus" (King's College London, International Centre for the Study of Radicalisation and Political Violence, May 2016), 28: https://icsr.info/wp-content/uploads/2016/10/ICSR-Report-Criminal-Pasts-Terrorist-Futures-European-Jihadists-and-the-New-Crime-Terror-Nexus.pdf, last accessed 14 August 2023.

57. Christoffer Carlsson, "Masculinities, Persistence, and Desistance", *Criminology* vol. 51, no. 3 (2013): 661–93.

58. Interview, Alex, 25 August 2016.

59. Stephen Stewart, "Football Hooligan Heads to Scotland in Recruitment Drive for Far-Right Group", *Daily Record*, 28 October 2017: http://www.dailyrecord.co.uk/news/scottish-news/football-hooligan-heads-scotland-recruitment-11422487, last accessed 14 August 2023.

60. Louis Emanuel, "Heavy Police Presence in London as Football Lads Alliance and EDL March", *The Times*, 24 June 2017: https://www.thetimes.co.uk/article/heavy-police-presence-in-the-capital-as-football-lads-alliance-and-edl-march-xtcprkrw7, last accessed 14 August 2023; interview, John Meighan, 5 July 2017.

61. Vikram Dodd et al., "London Bridge Attackers Were Regulars at Sunday Afternoon Pool Sessions", *The Guardian*, 7 June 2017: https://www.theguardian.com/uk-news/2017/jun/07/london-bridge-attackers-were-regulars-at-sunday-afternoon-pool-sessions, last accessed 14 August 2023.

62. Interview, Alex, 25 August 2016.

63. Interview, demonstrator, 26 October 2016.

64. Thomas Hegghammer, "Introduction: What Is Jihadi Culture and Why Should We Study It?", in *Jihadi Culture: The Art and Social Practices of Militant Islamists*, ed. Thomas Hegghammer (Cambridge: Cambridge University Press, 2017), 1–21 (2).

65. Berezin, "Emotions and Political Identity: Mobilizing Affection for the Polity".

66. Wetherell, *Affect and Emotion*.

67. Fabian Virchow cited in Cynthia Miller-Idriss, *The Extreme Gone Mainstream: Commercialization and Far Right Youth Culture in Germany* (Princeton, NJ: Princeton University Press, 2017), 168.

68. Ahmed, *The Cultural Politics of Emotion*, 2014.

69. Jeff Goodwin, James M. Jasper and Francesca Polletta, "Introduction: Why Emotions Matter", in *Passionate Politics: Emotions and Social Movements*, eds Jeff Goodwin, James M. Jasper and Francesca Polletta (Chicago, IL: University of Chicago Press, 2001), 1–26 (20).

70. Ramón Spaaij, "Men Like Us, Boys Like Them: Violence, Masculinity, and Collective Identity in Football Hooliganism", *Journal of Sport and Social Issues* vol. 32, no. 4 (2008): 369–92.

71. Nick Lowles, "Racist Terrorism on Rise, Businessman Bankrolls 'Street Army'", Turkish Forum English (blog), 19 November 2009: https://www.turkishnews.com/en/content/2009/11/19/racist-terrorism-on-rise-businessman-bankrolls-%e2%80%98street-army%e2%80%99/, last accessed 14 August 2023.

72. Robinson denied the EDL had formal funding or any involvement with Lake. Interview, Tommy Robinson, March 2017.

73. Wetherell, *Affect and Emotion*, 4.

74. Sara Ahmed, "Atmospheric Walls", feministkilljoys (blog), 15 September 2014: https://feministkilljoys.com/2014/09/15/atmospheric-walls/, last accessed 14 August 2023.

75. Pilkington, *Loud and Proud*, 177; Fabian Virchow, "Performance, Emotion, and Ideology: On the Creation of 'Collectives of Emotion' and Worldview in the Contemporary German Far Right", *Journal of Contemporary Ethnography* vol. 36, no. 2 (2007): 147–64 (147).

76. Goodwin, Jasper and Polletta, "Introduction", 20.

77. Interview, Iain and David, 25 August 2016.

78. Pilkington, *Loud and Proud*.

79. Interview, Tommy Robinson, 26 September 2016.

80. Alex and the Bandits, "Alex and The Bandits – About", Facebook: https://www.facebook.com/pg/Alex-And-The-Bandits-121068861335907/about/?ref=page_internal, last accessed 17 April 2017.

81. ICHOR Trust Team, "I.C.H.O.R. Trust Home": http://www.ichortrust.co.uk/index.php, last accessed 17 April 2017.

82. Pilkington, *Loud and Proud*, 79.

83. Anoop Nayak, "Displaced Masculinities: Chavs, Youth and Class in the Post-Industrial City", *Sociology* vol. 40, no. 5 (2006): 813–31 (828).

84. Ahmed, *The Cultural Politics of Emotion*, 2014, 171.

85. Chris Walton, Adrian Coyle and Evanthia Lyons, "Death and Football: An Analysis of Men's Talk about Emotions", *The British Journal of Social Psychology* vol. 43, no. 3 (September 2004): 401–16 (406; 412).

86. Nayak, "Displaced Masculinities", 819.

87. See the other Tommy Robinson's retelling of his violent career in Tommy

Robinson, *MIG Crew: The Story of Luton's MIG Crew As Told From the Sharp End of Football's Frontline* (Hove: Pennant Books Ltd, 2007).

88. Interview, Darren, 4 August 2016.
89. Interview, Darren, 4 August 2016.
90. Eric Dunning, "Towards a Sociological Understanding of Football Hooliganism as a World Phenomenon", *European Journal on Criminal Policy and Research* vol. 8, no. 2 (2000): 141–62 (157).
91. Interview, Darren, 4 August 2016.
92. Interview, Darren, 4 August 2016.
93. At the White Lives Matter demonstration in Margate, I was filmed by police who thought I was an Antifa leader, as I was wearing all black, seen running and with a similarly dressed man carrying a rolled-up banner.
94. James Treadwell and Jon Garland, "Masculinity, Marginalization and Violence: A Case Study of the English Defence League", *British Journal of Criminology* vol. 51, no. 4 (2011): 621–34.
95. Spaaij, "Men Like Us, Boys Like Them", 387.
96. Pilkington, *Loud and Proud*, 196.
97. Busher, "Grassroots Activism in the English Defence League", 8.
98. Jack Katz, *Seductions of Crime: Moral and Sensual Attractions in Doing Evil* (New York, NY: Basic Books, 1988), 142, cited in Louis Kontos and David Brotherton, *Encyclopedia of Gangs* (Westport, CT; Oxford: Greenwood Press, 2008), 68.
99. Henri Lefebvre, *The Production of Space*, trans. Donald Nicholson-Smith (Malden, MA: Wiley-Blackwell, 1991), 73–75.
100. Conal Urquhart and Mark Townsend, "EDL Marchers Scuffle with Anti-Racist Protesters Near East London Mosque", *The Guardian*, 7 September 2013: https://www.theguardian.com/uk-news/2013/sep/07/edl-marchers-east-london-mosque, last accessed 14 August 2023; Chris York, "EDL in Birmingham Shown Where to Go by Mosque and Residents", *The Huffington Post*, 6 April 2017: http://www.huffingtonpost.co.uk/entry/edl-in-birmingham_uk_58e93ffee4b05413bfe36c87, last accessed 14 August 2023.
101. Pilkington, *Loud and Proud*, 196; Garland and Treadwell, "'No Surrender to the Taliban'".
102. Dunning, "Towards a Sociological Understanding of Football Hooliganism as a World Phenomenon", 153; 157–61.
103. Richard Giulianotti and Gary Armstrong, "Avenues of Contestation: Football Hooligans Running and Ruling Urban Spaces", *Social Anthropology* vol. 10, no. 2 (2002): 211–38 (218).
104. Interview, Jacek, 7 September 2016.
105. Jeffrey S. Juris, "Performing Politics: Image, Embodiment, and Affective Solidarity During Anti-Corporate Globalization Protests", *Ethnography* vol. 9, no. 1 (2008): 61–97 (66).
106. Pie and Mash are an anti-Islam group linked to football hooliganism and supportive of the EDL. James Poulter, "The English Far-Right's War on Anti-Fascist Football Ultras", Vice, 13 February 2015: https://www.vice.com/en/

article/4wm3jb/is-english-far-right-hooligans-war-on-left-wing-football-ultras-spreading-to-the-premier-league-181, last accessed 16 September 2023.

107. Field notes, Telford, 5 November 2016.
108. Interview, Iain, 10 December 2016.
109. Field notes, Britain First demonstration, Telford, 25 February 2017.
110. Steve Hall, "Daubing the Drudges of Fury: The Piety of the Hegemonic Masculinity Thesis", *Theoretical Criminology* vol. 6, no. 1 (2002): 35–61.
111. Linda McDowell, *Redundant Masculinities? Employment Change and White Working-Class Youth* (New York, NY: John Wiley & Sons, 2011); Michael S. Kimmel, "Globalization and Its Mal(e)Contents: The Gendered Moral and Political Economy of Terrorism", *International Sociology* vol. 18, no. 3 (2003): 603–20.
112. Nicola Ingram, "Working-Class Boys, Educational Success and the Misrecognition of Working-Class Culture", *British Journal of Sociology of Education* vol. 30, no. 4 (2009): 421–34 (423).
113. Field notes, Telford, 5 November 2016.
114. Wetherell, *Affect and Emotion*, 117; Ahmed, *The Cultural Politics of Emotion*, 2004, 176.
115. Ahmed, *The Cultural Politics of Emotion*, 2014, 176–77.
116. Sara Ahmed, "Multiculturalism and the Promise of Happiness", in *Feminist Theory Reader: Local and Global Perspectives*, eds Carole McCann, Seung-Kyung Kim and Emek Ergun (New York, NY: Routledge, 2013), 517–32 (531); Bev Skeggs, "The Making of Class and Gender Through Visualizing Moral Subject Formation", *Sociology* vol. 39, no. 5 (2005): 965–82.
117. Field notes, EDL demonstration, Telford, 5 November 2016.
118. Interview, Georgey, 17 October 2016.
119. Interview, Georgey, 17 October 2016.
120. Interview, Georgey, 17 October 2016.
121. Interview, Tommy Robinson, 10 March 2017.
122. Interview, Iain, 10 December 2016.
123. Interview, Hel Gower, 2 November 2016.
124. Pilkington, *Loud and Proud*.
125. Elizabeth Ralph-Morrow, "Vigilantism in the United Kingdom: Britain First and 'Operation Fightback'", in *Vigilantism Against Migrants and Minorities*, eds Tore Bjørgo and Miroslav Mareš (Abingdon; New York, NY: Routledge, 2019), 228–40.
126. Interview, Jayda Fransen, 5 April 2017.
127. "JAYDA FRANSEN EPIC RANT ON LONDON TERROR ATTACK!", YouTube, 2017: https://www.youtube.com/watch?v=flX11KVNj5Y, last accessed 14 August 2023.
128. Wetherell, *Affect and Emotion*.
129. A Britain First security guard told me he ensures two flags for each protestor, for this reason.
130. Owen Jones, *Chavs: The Demonization of the Working Class* (London: Verso Books, 2012).

131. Interview, Daniel, 25 August 2016.
132. Interview, Iain, 10 December 2016.
133. Interview, Jacek, 7 September 2016.
134. Garland and Treadwell, "'No Surrender to the Taliban'", 29.
135. Britain First, "#BritishHistory #OnThisDay 21st January: English Army Raised for Third Crusade", Britain First – Taking Our Country Back! (blog), 21 January 2016: http://www.britainfirst.org/britishhistory-onthisday-21st-january-english-army-raised-for-third-crusade/, last accessed 18 April 2017.
136. Interview, Jayda Fransen, 3 December 2016.
137. Nira Yuval-Davis, "Women and the Biological Reproduction of 'The Nation'", *Women's Studies International Forum* vol. 19, no. 1/2 (1996): 17–24; Vron Ware, "Whiteness in the Glare of War: Soldiers, Migrants and Citizenship", *Ethnicities* vol. 10, no. 3 (2010): 313–30; Amanda Chisholm, "Marketing Militarized Masculinities: An Ethnographic Account of Racial and Gendered Practices in Private Security Contractors in Afghanistan" Paper presented to the International Studies Association Annual Conference, Montreal, Canada, 2011, cited in Paul Higate, "'Cowboys and Professionals': The Politics of Identity Work in the Private and Military Security Company", *Millennium – Journal of International Studies* vol. 40, no. 2 (2012): 321–41; Bolette B. Blaagaard, "Workings of Whiteness: Interview with Vron Ware", *Social Identities* vol. 17, no. 1 (2011): 153–61; Jamie Cleland, "Racism, Football Fans, and Online Message Boards: How Social Media Has Added a New Dimension to Racist Discourse in English Football", *Journal of Sport and Social Issues* vol. 38, no. 5 (2014): 415–31; Les Back, Tim Crabbe and John Solomos, "Beyond the Racist/Hooligan Couplet: Race, Social Theory and Football Culture", *The British Journal of Sociology* vol. 50, no. 3 (1999): 419–42.
138. Jon Burnett, "Racial Violence and the Brexit State", *Race & Class* vol. 58, no. 4 (2017): 85–97; Aurelien Mondon and Aaron Winter, *Reactionary Democracy: How Racism and the Populist Far Right Became Mainstream* (London: Verso Books, 2020); Albert Memmi, *Racism* (Minneapolis, MN: University of Minnesota Press, 1999).
139. Vidhya Ramalingam, "Old Threat, New Approach: Tackling the Far Right Across Europe" (London: Institute for Strategic Dialogue, 2014), 8: https://www.isdglobal.org/wp-content/uploads/2016/03/OldThreatNewApproach_2014.pdf, last accessed 6 August 2023.
140. Tahir Abbas, "Ethnicity and Politics in Contextualising Far Right and Islamist Extremism", *Perspectives on Terrorism* vol. 11, no. 3 (2017): 54–61; Anna A. Meier, "The Idea of Terror: Institutional Reproduction in Government Responses to Political Violence", *International Studies Quarterly* vol. 64, no. 3 (2020): 499–509; Imran Awan and Irene Zempi, "'I Will Blow Your Face Off'—Virtual and Physical World Anti-Muslim Hate Crime", *British Journal of Criminology* vol. 57, no. 2 (2017): 362–80.
141. David Duriesmith, "Hybrid Warriors and the Formation of New War Masculinities: A Case Study of Indonesian Foreign Fighters", *Stability: International Journal of Security and Development* vol. 7, no. 1 (2018): 1–16 (2).

142. Miller-Idriss, *The Extreme Gone Mainstream*, 163.

143. Syed Haider, "The Shooting in Orlando: Terrorism or Toxic Masculinity (or Both?)", *Men and Masculinities* vol. 19, no. 5 (2016): 555–65 (558).

144. Interview, Tommy Robinson, 10 March 2017.

145. Interview, Tommy Robinson, 20 May 2018.

146. Hegghammer, "Introduction", 2.

5. THE RADICAL RIGHT: MISOGYNY, MASCULINITIES AND WOMEN'S LEADERSHIP

1. "Digging Deeper with DD Denslow", *TNT Radio*, 16 April 2023: https://tntradio.live/shows/digging-deeper-with-dd-denslow/, last accessed 31 July 2023.

2. Kathleen M. Blee and Sandra McGee Deutsch, "Introduction", in *Women of the Right: Comparisons and Interplay Across Borders* (University Park, PA: Penn State University Press, 2012), 1–17 (1).

3. Charlotte Hooper, *Manly States: Masculinities, International Relations, and Gender Politics* (New York, NY: Columbia University Press, 2001), 230–31.

4. Laura Sjoberg, *Gendering Global Conflict: Toward a Feminist Theory of War* (New York, NY: Columbia University Press, 2013), 265.

5. Joshua S. Goldstein, *War and Gender: How Gender Shapes the War System and Vice Versa* (Cambridge: Cambridge University Press, 2003).

6. Deniz Kandiyoti, "Bargaining with Patriarchy", *Gender and Society* vol. 2, no. 3 (1988): 274–90 (274; 286).

7. Kate Manne, *Down Girl: The Logic of Misogyny* (London: Penguin, 2019), 52.

8. Manne, *Down Girl*, 27.

9. Caron E. Gentry, "Misogynistic Terrorism: It Has Always Been Here", *Critical Studies on Terrorism* vol. 15, no. 1 (2022): 209–24 (216).

10. R. W. Connell, *Masculinities* (Cambridge: Polity Press, 1995), 74.

11. Sylvia Walby, "Theorising Patriarchy", *Sociology* vol. 23, no. 2 (1989): 213–34 (214).

12. Catharine A. MacKinnon, "Feminism, Marxism, Method, and the State: An Agenda for Theory", *Feminist Theory* vol. 7, no. 3 (1982): 515–44; Sylvia Walby, *Theorising Patriarchy* (Oxford: Basil Blackwell, 1990).

13. Tim Carrigan, Bob Connell and John Lee, "Toward a New Sociology of Masculinity", *Theory and Society* vol. 14, no. 5 (1985): 551–604.

14. Jack Halberstam, *Female Masculinity* (Durham, NC: Duke University Press, 1998).

15. Christoffer Carlsson, "Masculinities, Persistence, and Desistance", *Criminology* vol. 51, no. 3 (2013): 661–93; Finn MacKay, *Female Masculinities and the Gender Wars: The Politics of Sex* (London: IB Tauris Bloomsbury, 2021); Halberstam, *Female Masculinity*; R. W. Connell, *The Men and the Boys* (Queensland: Allen and Unwin, 2000), 29, cited in MacKay, *Female Masculinities and the Gender Wars*, 129.

16. Eve Kosofsky Sedgwick, "Gosh, Boy George, You Must Be Awfully Secure in Your Masculinity", in *Constructing Masculinity*, eds Maurice Berger, Brian Wallis and Simon Watson (London; New York, NY: Routledge, 1995), 11–20.

17. Halberstam, *Female Masculinity*.

18. Paul Amar, "Middle East Masculinity Studies: Discourses of 'Men in Crisis', Industries of Gender in Revolution", *Journal of Middle East Women's Studies* vol. 7, no. 3 (2011): 36–70 (41).

19. Katherine E. Brown, "Gender and Counter-Radicalization: Women and Emerging Counter-Terror Measures", in *Gender, National Security and Counter-Terrorism*, eds Jayne Huckerby and Margaret L. Satterthwaite (Abingdon; New York, NY: Routledge, 2013), 36–59 (50).

20. Karen D. Pyke and Denise L. Johnson, "Asian American Women and Racialized Femininities: 'Doing' Gender Across Cultural Worlds", *Gender and Society* vol. 17, no. 1 (2003): 33–53.

21. Mimi Schippers, "Recovering the Feminine Other: Masculinity, Femininity, and Gender Hegemony", *Theory and Society* vol. 36, no. 1 (2007): 85–102 (95).

22. Athena Nguyen, "Patriarchy, Power, and Female Masculinity", *Journal of Homosexuality* vol. 55, no. 4 (2008): 665–83.

23. "We must secure the existence of our people and a future for white children."

24. Jean Bethke Elshtain, *Women and War* (Chicago, IL: University of Chicago Press, 1987), 9.

25. Kimberly Hutchings, "Making Sense of Masculinity and War", *Men and Masculinities* vol. 10, no. 4 (2007): 389–404 (389); Elshtain, *Women and War*, 9; Véronique Pin-Fat and Maria Stern, "The Scripting of Private Jessica Lynch: Biopolitics, Gender, and the 'Feminization' of the U.S. Military", *Alternatives: Global, Local, Political* vol. 30, no. 1 (2005): 25–53 (45); Goldstein, *War and Gender*, 262–66.

26. Floya Anthias and Nira Yuval-Davis, *Racialized Boundaries: Race, Nation, Gender, Colour and Class and the Anti-Racist Struggle* (London: Routledge, 1992).

27. Kathleen M. Blee, "Becoming A Racist: Women in Contemporary Ku Klux Klan and Neo-Nazi Groups", *Gender & Society* vol. 10, no. 6 (1996): 680–702 (682); Kathleen M. Blee, "Women and Organized Racial Terrorism in the United States", in *Female Terrorism and Militancy: Agency, Utility, and Organization*, ed. Cindy D. Ness (London; New York, NY: Routledge, 2008), 201–16.

28. Nira Yuval-Davis, "Women and the Biological Reproduction of 'The Nation'", *Women's Studies International Forum* vol. 19, no. 1/2 (1996): 17–24 (22–23).

29. Daniella Sarnoff, "Domesticating Fascism: Family and Gender in French Fascist Leagues", in *Women of the Right: Comparisons and Interplay Across Borders*, eds Kathleen M. Blee and Sandra McGee Deutsch (University Park, PA: Penn State University Press, 2012), 163–76 (164); Meera Seghal, "Mothering the Nation: Maternalist Frames in the Hindu Nationalist Movement in India", in *Women of the Right: Comparisons and Interplay Across Borders*, eds Kathleen M. Blee and Sandra McGee Deutsch (University Park, PA: Penn State University Press, 2012), 192–207 (198).

30. Kathleen M. Blee and Kimberly A. Creasap, "Conservative and Right-Wing Movements", *Annual Review of Sociology* vol. 36, no. 1 (2010): 269–86 (274); Jean Hardisty, ed., *Kitchen Table Backlash: The Antifeminist Women's Movement* (Boulder, CO: Westview, 2001), cited in Blee and Creasap, 274.

31. Barbara Perry and Ryan Scrivens, "Uneasy Alliances: A Look at the Right-Wing Extremist Movement in Canada", *Studies in Conflict & Terrorism* vol. 39, no. 9 (2016): 819–41; Ashley Mattheis, "Women and the Alt-Right", VOX – Pol Conference, Amsterdam, 2018; J. M. Berger, "The Alt-Right Twitter Census: Defining and Describing the Audience for Alt-Right Content on Twitter" (VOX-Pol, 2018): https://www.voxpol.eu/download/vox-pol_publication/AltRightTwitterCensus.pdf, last accessed 14 August 2023; Tina Askanius, "Women in the Nordic Resistance Movement and Their Online Media Practices: Between Internalised Misogyny and 'Embedded Feminism'", *Feminist Media Studies* vol. 22, no. 7 (2022): 1763–80.

32. Randy Blazak, "'Getting It': The Role of Women in Male Desistance From Hate Groups", in *Home-Grown Hate: Gender and Organized Racism*, ed. Abby L. Ferber (New York, NY; London: Routledge, 2004), 154–71.

33. Blee, "Becoming A Racist", 682; Blee, "Women and Organized Racial Terrorism in the United States".

34. Niels Spierings and Andrej Zaslove, "Gendering the Vote for Populist Radical-Right Parties", *Patterns of Prejudice* vol. 49, no. 1–2 (2015): 135–62 (143).

35. Sarah L. de Lange and Liza M. Mügge, "Gender and Right-Wing Populism in the Low Countries: Ideological Variations Across Parties and Time", *Patterns of Prejudice* vol. 49, no. 1–2 (2015): 61–80 (62; 79–80).

36. "About Us", English Defence League website: http://www.english defenceleague.org.uk/mission-statement/, last accessed 20 March 2018.

37. Joshua M. Roose et al., *Masculinity and Violent Extremism* (Basingstoke: Palgrave Macmillan, 2022), 58.

38. Tania Modleski, *Feminism Without Women: Culture and Criticism in a "Postfeminist" Age* (New York, NY: Routledge, 1991), 7.

39. Lange and Mügge, "Gender and Right-Wing Populism in the Low Countries", 62.

40. Hilary Pilkington, "'EDL Angels Stand Beside Their Men... Not Behind Them': The Politics of Gender and Sexuality in an Anti-Islam(ist) Movement", *Gender and Education* vol. 29, no. 2 (2017): 238–57 (240).

41. Pilkington, "'EDL Angels Stand Beside Their Men'", 253.

42. Askanius, "Women in the Nordic Resistance Movement and Their Online Media Practices"; Elizabeth Pearson, "Extremism and Toxic Masculinity: The Man Question Re-Posed", *International Affairs* vol. 95, no. 6 (2019): 1251–70.

43. Pilkington, "'EDL Angels Stand Beside Their Men'", 243; 253.

44. Jamie Bartlett and Mark Littler, "Inside the EDL" (Demos, 2011), 14: https://www.demos.co.uk/files/Inside_the_edl_WEB.pdf, last accessed 27 July 2023; Nigel Copsey, "The English Defence League: Challenging Our Country and Our Values of Social Inclusion, Fairness and Equality" (Faith Matters, November 2010),

29:   https://www.faith-matters.org/wp-content/uploads/2010/11/english-defense-league-report.pdf, last accessed 28 July 2023; Matthew Goodwin, "The Roots of Extremism: The English Defence League and the Counter-Jihad Challenge", (Chatham House, 2013), 6: https://www.chathamhouse.org/sites/default/files/public/Research/Europe/0313bp_goodwin.pdf, last accessed 28 July 2023; Pilkington, "'EDL Angels Stand Beside Their Men'"; Tommy Robinson, *Enemy of the State* (Batley: The Press News Ltd, 2015), 110; James Treadwell and Jon Garland, "Masculinity, Marginalization and Violence: A Case Study of the English Defence League", *British Journal of Criminology* vol. 51, no. 4 (2011): 621–34 (621).

45. Joel Busher, *The Making of Anti-Muslim Protest: Grassroots Activism in the English Defence League* (London; New York, NY: Routledge, 2015), paras 38–40 [online].

46. Interview, Jayda Fransen, 27 April 2023.

47. "Statement from Jayda Fransen": http://jaydafransen.online/, last accessed 26 January 2019.

48. "Digging Deeper with DD Denslow".

49. See her Twitter feed on 26 April 2023.

50. Jayda Fransen, "The Fake Right and The Whole Truth", Jayda Fransen Online, 28 July 2022: https://www.jaydafransen.online/the_fake_right_and_the_whole_truth, last accessed 15 August 2023.

51. Fransen, "The Fake Right and the Whole Truth".

52. Interview, Jayda Fransen, 5 December 2017.

53. Interview, Jayda Fransen, 26 April 2017.

54. Interview, Jayda Fransen, 26 April 2017.

55. "Digging Deeper with DD Denslow".

56. Kayleen Devlin, "The Anti-Immigration Party Trying to Recruit Immigrants", BBC News, 11 July 2017: https://www.bbc.com/news/blogs-trending-40509632, last accessed 15 August 2023.

57. James Fergusson, *Al-Britannia, My Country: A Journey Through Muslim Britain* (London: Bantam Press, 2017).

58. Jayda Fransen Online: https://www.jaydafransen.online/, last accessed 15 August 2023.

59. For other examples, see Ashley Mattheis, "Shieldmaidens of Whiteness: (Alt) Maternalism and Women Recruiting for the Far/Alt-Right", *Journal for Deradicalization* no. 17 (2018): 128–62; and Cynthia Miller-Idriss, *The Extreme Gone Mainstream: Commercialization and Far Right Youth Culture in Germany* (Princeton, NJ: Princeton University Press, 2017).

60. Caron E. Gentry and Laura Sjoberg, *Mothers, Monsters, Whores: Women's Violence in Global Politics* (New York, NY: Zed Books, 2007), p. 39.

61. Sara Correia, "Researching Gender and the Far/Alt-Right – Interview With Dr Ashley Mattheis", *Methods Café* (podcast), 23 March 2023: https://shows.acast.com/methods-cafe/episodes/s2e2-researching-gender-and-the-faraltright-ashley-mattheis, last accessed 15 August 2023.

62. "Digging Deeper with DD Denslow".
63. Caron E. Gentry and Laura Sjoberg, *Mothers, Monsters, Whores: Women's Violence in Global Politics* (New York, NY: Zed Books, 2007).
64. Interview, Jayda Fransen, 27 April 2023.
65. Sharia Watch Team and Anne Marie Waters, "Introduction to Sharia Watch", Sharia Watch UK Ltd: http://www.shariawatch.org.uk/?q=content/introduction-sharia-watch, last accessed 20 March 2018.
66. Jan Erk, "From Vlaams Blok to Vlaams Belang: The Belgian Far-Right Renames Itself", *West European Politics* vol. 28, no. 3 (2005): 493–502; Emilie van Haute and Teun Pauwels, "Caught Between Mainstreaming and Radicalisation: Tensions Inside the Populist Vlaams Belang in Belgium", EUROPP (blog), 11 January 2017: http://blogs.lse.ac.uk/europpblog/2017/01/11/tensions-inside-vlaams-belang-belgium/, last accessed 15 August 2023.
67. Coulter is an American conservative commentator who has been outspoken on Islam and immigration as threats.
68. Interview, Anne Marie Waters, 14 October 2016.
69. Halberstam, *Female Masculinity*.
70. Interview, Anne Marie Waters, 14 October 2016.
71. Sonya Michel, "Maternalism and Beyond", in *Maternalism Reconsidered: Motherhood, Welfare and Social Policy in the Twentieth Century*, eds Marian van der Klein et al. (New York, NY: Berghahn Books, 2012), 22–37.
72. Interview, Jane, 1 September 2016.
73. Interview, Iain, 10 December 2016.
74. Interview, Jacek, 7 September 2016.
75. Interview, Lydia, 19 August 2017.
76. Interview, Jason, 6 November 2016.
77. Pierre Bourdieu, *Masculine Domination*, trans. Richard Nice (Stanford, CA: Stanford University Press, 2001), 9.
78. Bourdieu, *Masculine Domination*, 8.
79. Interview, Jason, 6 November 2016.
80. Kandiyoti, "Bargaining with Patriarchy", 285.
81. Interview, Anne Marie Waters, 14 October 2016.
82. Selina Todd, *The People: The Rise and Fall of the Working Class, 1910–2010* (London: John Murray, 2014), 308.
83. Interview, Georgey, 17 October 2016.
84. Modleski, *Feminism Without Women*, 7.
85. Interview, Jacek, 7 September 2016.
86. Todd, *The People*, 384.
87. Interview, Jane, 1 September 2016.
88. Interview, Jane, 1 September 2016.
89. Interview, Jane, 23 August 2016.
90. Interview, Tommy Robinson, 26 September 2016.
91. Marshall Peter, "EDL Women Tell Cameron We're Not Sick", Demotix, 8 October 2011: https://web.archive.org/web/20111011144736/http://

www.demotix.com/news/863998/edl-women-tell-cameron-were-not-sick, last accessed 15 August 2023.

92. Francesca Scrinzi, "Caring for the Nation: Men and Women Activists in Radical Right Populist Parties", Final Research Report (European Research Council, 2014), 3: https://www.gla.ac.uk/media/Media_383799_smxx.pdf, last accessed 15 August 2023.

93. Interview, Hel Gower, 2 November 2016.

94. Field notes, 1 April 2017.

95. Interview, Jane, 1 September 2016.

96. See Jack Sommers, "Dover Protest Turns Violent as Far Right Clashes with Anti-Fascist Demonstrators", HuffPost UK, 30 January 2016: https://www.huffingtonpost.co.uk/2016/01/30/dover-protest-turns-violent-demonstrator-bloodied_n_9119604.html, last accessed 15 August 2023.

97. Interview, Jane, 1 September 2016.

98. Interview, Iain, 10 December 2016.

99. Interview, Hel Gower, 2 November 2016; interview, Jane, 1 September 2016.

100. Interview, Georgey, 17 October 2016.

101. Interview, Georgey, 17 October 2016.

102. Pin-Fat and Stern, "The Scripting of Private Jessica Lynch".

103. Interview, Hel Gower, 2 November 2016.

104. Interview, Hel Gower, 2 November 2016.

105. Manne, *Down Girl*, 27.

106. Interview, Hel Gower, 2 November 2016.

107. Bourdieu, *Masculine Domination*, 51.

108. Joane Nagel, "Masculinity and Nationalism: Gender and Sexuality in the Making of Nations", *Ethnic and Racial Studies* vol. 21, no. 2 (1998): 242–69 (248).

109. Interview, Georgey, 17 October 2016.

110. Interview, Darren, 4 August 2016.

111. Interview, Jane, 1 September 2016.

112. Interview, Iain, 10 December 2016.

113. Interview, Iain, 10 December 2016.

114. Interview, Jane, 1 September 2016.

115. Carlsson, "Masculinities, Persistence, and Desistance".

116. Hilary Pilkington, *Loud and Proud: Passion and Politics in the English Defence League* (Manchester: Manchester University Press, 2016).

117. Interview, Jane, 1 September 2016.

118. Interview, Georgey, 17 October 2016.

119. Margaret Wetherell, *Affect and Emotion: A New Social Science Understanding* (Los Angeles, CA; London: SAGE Publications, 2012), 141–43.

120. Sara Ahmed, *The Cultural Politics of Emotion*, 2nd revised edition (Edinburgh: Edinburgh University Press, 2014).

121. Wetherell, *Affect and Emotion*.

122. Sara Ahmed, "Multiculturalism and the Promise of Happiness", in *Feminist Theory*

Reader: Local and Global Perspectives, eds Carole McCann, Seung-Kyung Kim and Emek Ergun (New York, NY: Routledge, 2013), 517–32 (523).

123. William Ian Miller, *The Anatomy of Disgust* (Cambridge, MA: Harvard University Press, 1997), xiv.

124. Stephanie Lawler, "Disgusted Subjects: The Making of Middle-Class Identities", *The Sociological Review* vol. 53, no. 3 (2005): 429–46 (435).

125. Bev Skeggs, "The Making of Class and Gender Through Visualizing Moral Subject Formation", *Sociology* vol. 39, no. 5 (2005): 965–82 (966–68).

126. Peter Stearns, "History of Emotions: Issues of Change and Impact", in *Handbook of Emotions*, 3rd edition, eds Michael Lewis, Jeannette M. Haviland-Jones and Lisa Feldman Barrett (London: Guilford Press, 2008), 17–31 (18); James R. Averill, "The Social Construction of Emotion: With Special Reference to Love", in *The Social Construction of the Person*, eds Kenneth J. Gergen and Keith E. Davis (New York, NY: Springer New York, 1985), 89–109 (90); Imogen Tyler, "'Chav Mum Chav Scum': Class Disgust in Contemporary Britain", *Feminist Media Studies* vol. 8, no. 1 (2008): 17–34.

127. Helen Wilson and Annette Huntington, "Deviant (M)others: The Construction of Teenage Motherhood in Contemporary Discourse", *Journal of Social Policy* vol. 35, no. 1 (2006): 59–76 (69).

128. See, for instance, the anti-BF hashtag #JaydaFransenFacts, which followed her retweet by Donald Trump in November 2017: "Jayda Fransen has a poppy on her pyjamas for when she goes to ASDA"; "Jayda's tits dispense Carling to the faithful at Britain First rallies"; "Eds Fanny ajar is an anagram of Jayda Fransen"; "The only test Jayda has ever passed was the one for gonorrhea"; and so on.

129. Philip Slater, "On Social Regression", *American Sociological Review* vol. 28, no. 3 (1963): 339–64 (348), cited in Jeff Goodwin, "The Libidinal Constitution of a High-Risk Social Movement: Affectual Ties and Solidarity in the Huk Rebellion, 1946 to 1954", *American Sociological Review* vol. 62, no. 1 (1997): 53–69 (56).

130. Ahmed, *The Cultural Politics of Emotion*, 2014, 176.

131. Interview, Tommy Robinson, 10 March 2017.

132. Interview, Tommy Robinson, 26 September 2016.

133. Sjoberg, *Gendering Global Conflict*; Goldstein, *War and Gender*.

134. Kathleen M. Blee and Annette Linden, "Women in Extreme Right Parties and Movements: A Comparison of the Netherlands and the United States", in *Women of the Right: Comparisons and Interplay Across Borders*, eds Kathleen M. Blee and Sandra McGee Deutsch (University Park, PA: Penn State University Press, 2012), 98–114 (107).

135. Sjoberg, *Gendering Global Conflict*, 265.

6.   ALM: SITUATING MASCULINITIES

1. Interview, Aisha, 10 April 2017.

2. Hope Not Hate, "Al-Muhajiroun Network", Hope Not Hate: The Hate Files, 2013: http://www.hopenothate.org.uk/research/the-hate-files/al-muhajiroun-

network/, last accessed 15 August 2023; Tom Burgis, "The Network That Remains at the Heart of UK Islamist Extremism", *Financial Times*, 6 June 2017: https://www.ft.com/content/54eb9e5e-4ab7-11e7-a3f4-c742b9791d43, last accessed 15 August 2023.

3. Vikram Dodd, "Anjem Choudary: A Hate Preacher Who Spread Terror in UK and Europe", *The Guardian*, 16 August 2016: https://www.theguardian.com/uk-news/2016/aug/16/anjem-choudary-hate-preacher-spread-terror-uk-europe, last accessed 15 August 2023; Lizzie Dearden, "Abu Qatada to Walk Free After Being Cleared of Terrorism Plot Charges by Jordan Court", *The Independent*, 24 September 2014: http://www.independent.co.uk/news/world/middle-east/abu-qatada-to-walk-free-after-being-cleared-of-terrorism-plot-charges-by-jordan-court-9752346.html, last accessed 15 August 2023; Sara Khan and Tony McMahon, *The Battle for British Islam: Reclaiming Muslim Identity from Extremism* (London: Saqi Books, 2016), 53; Pantucci, *"We Love Death as You Love Life"*; Loulla-Mae Eleftheriou-Smith, "Radical Islamist Group Al-Muhajiroun Linked to Half of British Terror Attacks in Past 20 Years", *The Independent*, 23 March 2015: http://www.independent.co.uk/news/uk/crime/radical-islamist-group-al-muhajiroun-linked-to-half-of-british-terror-attacks-in-past-20-years-10128492.html, last accessed 15 August 2023.

4. Hannah McDonald, "Hate Preacher Anjem Choudary Arrested on Suspicion of Terrorism", *Mail Online*, 18 July 2023: https://www.dailymail.co.uk/news/article-12308877/Hate-preacher-Anjem-Choudary-arrested-suspicion-terrorism-offences-dawn-police-raid-home.html, last accessed 27 July 2023.

5. Shahin Gerami, "Islamist Masculinity and Muslim Masculinities", in *Handbook of Studies on Men and Masculinities*, eds Michael S. Kimmel, Jeff R. Hearn and R. W. Connell (Thousand Oaks, CA; London: SAGE Publications, 2004), 448–57.

6. Marcia Inhorn, *The New Arab Man: Emergent Masculinities, Technologies, and Islam in the Middle East* (Princeton, NJ: Princeton University Press, 2012), 50.

7. Gerami, "Islamist Masculinity and Muslim Masculinities".

8. Tufyal Choudhury, "The Role of Muslim Identity Politics in Radicalisation (a Study in Progress)" (Department for Communities and Local Government, 2007): https://webarchive.nationalarchives.gov.uk/ukgwa/20070506190701mp_/http://www.communities.gov.uk/pub/393/TheRoleofMuslimIdentityPoliticsinRadicalisationastudyinprogress_id1509393.pdf, last accessed 15 August 2023; Imran Awan, "'I Am a Muslim Not an Extremist': How the Prevent Strategy Has Constructed a 'Suspect' Community", *Politics & Policy* vol. 40, no. 6 (2012): 1158–85; Naaz Rashid, *Veiled Threats: Representing the Muslim Woman in Public Policy Discourses* (Bristol: Policy Press, 2008).

9. Peter Hopkins, *The Issue of Masculine Identities for British Muslims After 9/11: A Social Analysis* (Lewiston, NY: Edwin Mellen Press Ltd, 2008), 192.

10. Louise Archer and Hiromi Yamashita, "Theorising Inner-City Masculinities: 'Race', Class, Gender and Education", *Gender and Education* vol. 15, no. 2 (2003): 115–32; Mairtin Mac an Ghaill and Chris Haywood, "British-Born Pakistani and

BangladeshiYoung Men: Exploring Unstable Concepts of Muslim, Islamophobia and Racialization", *Critical Sociology* vol. 41, no. 1 (2015): 97–114.

11. Wiktorowicz, *Radical Islam Rising*.

12. Choudhury, "The Role of Muslim Identity Politics in Radicalisation", 21.

13. Choudhury, "The Role of Muslim Identity Politics in Radicalisation"; Awan, "'I Am a Muslim Not an Extremist'";Tahir Abbas, "After 9/11: British South Asian Muslims, Islamophobia, Multiculturalism, and the State", *American Journal of Islamic Social Sciences* vol. 21, no. 3 (2004): 26–38.

14. Margaret S. Archer, The Reflexive Imperative in Late Modernity (Cambridge: Cambridge University Press, 2012). Also see, for instance, Scott Lash, "Reflexive Modernization:The Aesthetic Dimension", *Theory, Culture & Society* vol. 10, no. 1 (1993): 1–23; John Urry, "The Global Complexities of September 11th", *Theory, Culture & Society* vol. 19, no. 4 (2002): 57–69; Ulrich Beck, Anthony Giddens and Scott Lash, *Reflexive Modernization: Politics,Tradition and Aesthetics in the Modern Social Order* (Cambridge: Polity Press, 1994); and Anthony Giddens, *Modernity and Self-Identity: Self and Society in the Late Modern Age* (Stanford, CA: Stanford University Press, 1991).

15. Margaret S. Archer, *The Reflexive Imperative in Late Modernity* (Cambridge: Cambridge University Press, 2012), 16, cited in Yasmin Hussain and Paul Bagguley, "Reflexive Ethnicities: Crisis, Diversity and Re-Composition", *Sociological Research Online* vol. 20, no. 3 (2015): 18: https://www.socresonline. org.uk/20/3/18.html, last accessed 15 August 2023.

16. Hussain and Bagguley, "Reflexive Ethnicities".

17. Mac an Ghaill and Haywood, "British-Born Pakistani and Bangladeshi Young Men".

18. Choudhury, "The Role of Muslim Identity Politics in Radicalisation".

19. Talal Asad, "Multiculturalism and British Identity in the Wake of the Rushdie Affair", *Politics & Society* vol. 18, no. 4 (1990): 455–80.

20. Tariq Modood, "British Asian Muslims and the Rushdie Affair", in *"Race", Culture and Difference*, eds James Donald and Au Rattansi (London: SAGE Publications, 1992), 260–77 (261), cited in Sarah Glynn, "Bengali Muslims:The New East End Radicals?", *Ethnic and Racial Studies* vol. 25, no. 6 (2002): 969–88 (977).

21. Paul Statham et al., "Resilient or Adaptable Islam? Multiculturalism, Religion and Migrants' Claims-Making for Group Demands in Britain, the Netherlands and France", *Ethnicities* vol. 5, no. 4 (2005): 427–59.

22. Hopkins, *The Issue of Masculine Identities for British Muslims After 9/11*, 71.

23. See, for instance, Rupert Sutton, "Preventing Prevent? Challenges to Counter-Radicalisaton Policy on Campus" (London: Henry Jackson Society, 2015): https://henryjacksonsociety.org/wp-content/uploads/2015/10/Preventing-Prevent_webversion3.pdf, last accessed 16 August 2023.

24. Home Affairs Select Committee, "Radicalisation: The Counter-Narrative and Identifying the Tipping Point" (House of Commons Home Affairs Select Committee, August 2016): http://www.publications.parliament.uk/pa/

cm201617/cmselect/cmhaff/135/135.pdf, last accessed 16 August 2023; Abbas, "After 9/11".

25. Gabe Mythen, Sandra Walklate and Fatima Khan, "'I'm a Muslim, but I'm Not a Terrorist': Victimization, Risky Identities and the Performance of Safety", *British Journal of Criminology* vol. 49, no. 6 (2009): 736–54; Awan, "'I Am a Muslim Not an Extremist'"; Katherine E. Brown, "Gender and Counter-Radicalization: Women and Emerging Counter-Terror Measures", in *Gender, National Security and Counter-Terrorism*, eds Jayne Huckerby and Margaret L. Satterthwaite (Abingdon; New York, NY: Routledge, 2013), 36–59.

26. Hopkins, *The Issue of Masculine Identities for British Muslims After 9/11*.

27. Stuart Croft, *Securitizing Islam: Identity and the Search for Security* (Cambridge; New York, NY: Cambridge University Press, 2012).

28. Choudhury, "The Role of Muslim Identity Politics in Radicalisation"; Katherine E. Brown, *Gender, Religion, Extremism: Finding Women in Anti-Radicalization* (Oxford: Oxford University Press, 2020).

29. Emily Winterbotham and Elizabeth Pearson, "Different Cities, Shared Stories: A Five-Country Study Challenging Assumptions Around Muslim Women and CVE Interventions", *RUSI Journal* vol. 161, no. 5 (2016): 54–65.

30. Brown, *Gender, Religion, Extremism*, 221.

31. Brown, *Gender, Religion, Extremism*.

32. Mac an Ghaill and Haywood, "British-Born Pakistani and Bangladeshi Young Men".

33. Mac an Ghaill and Haywood, "British-Born Pakistani and Bangladeshi Young Men".

34. Claire Dwyer, "Negotiating Diasporic Identities: Young British South Asian Muslim Women", *Women's Studies International Forum* vol. 23, no. 4 (2000): 475–86.

35. Katherine Brown, "The Promise and Perils of Women's Participation in UK Mosques: The Impact of Securitisation Agendas on Identity, Gender and Community", *The British Journal of Politics & International Relations* vol. 10, no. 3 (2008): 472–91.

36. Michael Kenney, Stephen Coulthart and Dominick Wright, "Structure and Performance in a Violent Extremist Network: The Small-World Solution", *Journal of Conflict Resolution* vol. 61, no. 10 (2016): 2208–34.

37. Bassam Alloni, "Interview: Sheikh Omar Bakri Mohammad", UPI, 14 September 2003: https://www.upi.com/Interview-Sheikh-Omar-Bakri-Mohammad/81231063546303/, last accessed 16 August 2023.

38. See Appendix.

39. Michael Kenney, *The Islamic State in Britain: Radicalization and Resilience in an Activist Network* (Cambridge: Cambridge University Press, 2018), 104.

40. Kenney, *The Islamic State in Britain*, 47.

41. Kenney, *The Islamic State in Britain*, 14.

42. 'Revert' is an alternative term for 'convert' preferred by Islamist participants in this study.

43. 'Tariq Modood, "A Defence of Multiculturalism", *Soundings* no. 29 (2005): 62–71 (63).
44. Interview, Adam, 28 March 2017.
45. Interview, Farhan, 24 August 2016.
46. Interview, Saleha, 20 July 2016.
47. Hopkins, *The Issue of Masculine Identities for British Muslims After 9/11*, 189.
48. Hopkins, *The Issue of Masculine Identities for British Muslims After 9/11*.
49. Louise Archer, "'Muslim Brothers, Black Lads, Traditional Asians': British Muslim Young Men's Constructions of Race, Religion and Masculinity", *Feminism & Psychology* vol. 11, no. 1 (2001): 79–105; Glynn, "Bengali Muslims".
50. Interview, Kate, 17 July 2016.
51. See more on the murder and attackers here: Paul Peachey, Jonathan Brown and Kim Sengupta, "Lee Rigby Murder: How Killers Michael Adebolajo and Michael Adebowale Became Ultra-Violent Radicals", *The Independent*, 19 December 2013: https://www.independent.co.uk/news/uk/crime/lee-rigby-murder-how-killers-michael-adebolajo-and-michael-adebowale-became-ultraviolent-radicals-9015743.html, last accessed 16 August 2023.
52. Interview, Adam, 12 July 2016.
53. Kenney, *The Islamic State in Britain*; Rajan Basra, Peter R. Neumann and Claudia Brunner, "Criminal Pasts, Terrorist Futures: European Jihadists and the New Crime–Terror Nexus" (King's College London, International Centre for the Study of Radicalisation and Political Violence, May 2016), 28: https://icsr.info/wp-content/uploads/2016/10/ICSR-Report-Criminal-Pasts-Terrorist-Futures-European-Jihadists-and-the-New-Crime-Terror-Nexus.pdf, last accessed 14 August 2023.
54. Interview, Akash, 29 March 2017.
55. Interview, Adam, 12 July 2016.
56. A fundamentalist strand of Islam; see Alastair Crooke, "You Can't Understand ISIS if You Don't Know the History of Wahhabism in Saudi Arabia", *New Perspectives Quarterly* vol. 32, no. 1 (2015): 56–70.
57. Choudhury, "The Role of Muslim Identity Politics in Radicalisation".
58. Interview, Akash, 1 November 2016.
59. Field notes, 2 December 2016.
60. Gavin Bailey and Phil Edwards, "Rethinking 'Radicalisation': Microradicalisations and Reciprocal Radicalisation as an Intertwined Process", *Journal for Deradicalization* no. 10 (2017): 255–81.
61. Mac an Ghaill and Haywood, "British-Born Pakistani and Bangladeshi Young Men".
62. Interview, Akash, 29 March 2017.
63. Maéva Clément, "Al-Muhajiroun in the United Kingdom: The Role of International Non-Recognition in Heightened Radicalization Dynamics", *Global Discourse* vol. 4, no. 4 (2014): 428–43.
64. Hussain and Bagguley, "Reflexive Ethnicities".
65. Messaging, Ahmed, 5 May 2016.

66. Wiktorowicz, *Radical Islam Rising*, 22–23.

67. Catherine Zara Raymond, "Al Muhajiroun and Islam4UK: The Group behind the Ban" (King's College London, International Centre for the Study of Radicalisation and Political Violence, May 2010), 20: https://icsr.info/wp-content/uploads/2010/06/ICSR-Feature-Al-Muhajiroun-and-Islam4UK-The-group-behind-the-ban.pdf, last accessed 16 August 2023.

68. Field notes, 5 October 2016.

69. Interview, Mo, 5 October 2016.

70. Brooke Rogers and Peter R. Neumann, "Recruitment and Mobilisation for the Islamist Militant Movement in Europe" (King's College London, International Centre for the Study of Radicalisation and Political Violence, 2007): https://icsr.info/wp-content/uploads/2008/10/1234516791ICSREUResearchReport_Proof1.pdf, last accessed 16 August 2023.

71. Interview, Aisha, 10 April 2017.

72. Interview, Aisha, 10 April 2017.

73. Interview, Aisha, 10 April 2017.

74. Olivier Roy, *Jihad and Death: The Global Appeal of Islamic State* (London: C. Hurst & Co., 2017), 27.

75. Roy, *Jihad and Death*, 8.

76. Khan and McMahon, *The Battle for British Islam*.

77. Choudhury, "The Role of Muslim Identity Politics in Radicalisation"; Marie Macey, "Class, Gender and Religious Influences on Changing Patterns of Pakistani Muslim Male Violence in Bradford", *Ethnic and Racial Studies* vol. 22, no. 5 (1999): 845–66.

78. Saleha is referring to publicity around a series of protests by the feminist group Femen, who demonstrated topless.

79. Interview, Saleha, 16 August 2016.

80. Tellmama, "Understanding Hate Incident Patterns After the Westminster Terrorist Attack of the 22nd of March 2017. Building a Pattern of Community Resilience Against Hate – What Worked?", TellMAMA (blog), 4 December 2018: https://tellmamauk.org/understanding-hate-incident-patterns-after-the-westminster-terrorist-attack-of-the-22nd-of-march-2017-building-a-pattern-of-community-resilience-against-hate-what-worked/, last accessed 16 August 2023.

81. Naaz Rashid, "Giving the Silent Majority a Stronger Voice? Initiatives to Empower Muslim Women as Part of the UK's 'War on Terror'", *Ethnic and Racial Studies* vol. 37, no. 4 (2014): 589–604.

82. Interview, Aisha, 10 April 2017.

83. Archer, "'Muslim Brothers, Black Lads, Traditional Asians'"; Khan and McMahon, *The Battle for British Islam*.

84. Interview, Aisha, 10 April 2017.

85. Hopkins, *The Issue of Masculine Identities for British Muslims After 9/11*, 112.

86. Interview, Aisha, 10 April 2017.

87. Hopkins, *The Issue of Masculine Identities for British Muslims After 9/11*.

88. Kate Manne, *Down Girl: The Logic of Misogyny* (London: Penguin, 2019).

89. Interview, Rifat, 16 July 2017.

90. Home Office, "Home | ENOUGH": https://enough.campaign.gov.uk/, last accessed 16 August 2023.

91. Steven Morris, "Wales launches campaign to help tackle misogyny and violence against women", *The Guardian*, 14 July 2023: https://www.theguardian.com/society/2023/jul/14/wales-launches-campaign-to-help-tackle-misogyny-and-violence-against-women, last accessed 3 October 2023; Mayor of London, "Mayor launches new campaign empowering men to challenge misogyny by saying 'maaate' to their mates when they cross the line", Mayoral Press Release, 21 July 2023:https://www.london.gov.uk/media-centre/mayors-press-release/mayor-launches-major-new-campaign-to-empower-men-and-boys-to-say-maaate-to-their-mates-and-challenge-sexism-and-misogyny#:~:text=This%20initiative%20aims%20to%20challenge,viewed%20over%2015%20million%20times, last accessed 3 October 2023.

92. Khan and McMahon, *The Battle for British Islam*.

93. Claire Dwyer, "Negotiating Diasporic Identities: Young British South Asian Muslim Women", *Women's Studies International Forum* vol. 23, no. 4 (2000): 475–86.

94. Hopkins, *The Issue of Masculine Identities for British Muslims After 9/11*, 105.

95. Interview, Rifat, 16 July 2017.

96. Interview, Adam, 28 March 2017.

97. Gerami, "Islamist Masculinity and Muslim Masculinities".

98. Hussain and Bagguley, "Reflexive Ethnicities". "[R]ules of the game" is a reference to Jürgen Habermas's *On the Pragmatics of Social Interaction: Preliminary Studies in the Theory of Communicative Action* (1976).

99. Interview, Saleha, 20 July 2016.

100. Interview, Rifat, 16 July 2017.

101. Wiktorowicz, *Radical Islam Rising*; Simon Cottee, "Jihadism as a Subcultural Response to Social Strain: Extending Marc Sageman's 'Bunch of Guys' Thesis", *Terrorism and Political Violence* vol. 23, no. 5 (2011): 730–51; Robert Agnew, "A General Strain Theory of Terrorism", *Theoretical Criminology* vol. 14, no. 2 (2010): 131–53.

102. Messaging, Ahmed, 6 May 2016.

103. Hussain and Bagguley, "Reflexive Ethnicities"; Brown, *Gender, Religion, Extremism*; Mac an Ghaill and Haywood, "British-Born Pakistani and Bangladeshi Young Men".

104. Interview, Akash, 29 March 2017.

105. Choudhury, "The Role of Muslim Identity Politics in Radicalisation", 16.

106. Floya Anthias and Nira Yuval-Davis, *Racialized Boundaries: Race, Nation, Gender, Colour and Class and the Anti-Racist Struggle* (London: Routledge, 1992).

107. Interview, Akash, 29 March 2017.

108. Choudhury, "The Role of Muslim Identity Politics in Radicalisation".

109. Christian Karner, *Ethnicity and Everyday Life* (London; New York, NY: Routledge, 2007).

110. Sallie A. Marston, "The Social Construction of Scale", *Progress in Human Geography* vol. 24, no. 2 (2000): 219–42.

111. Interview, Akash, 29 March 2017.

112. Zillah Eisenstein, *Against Empire: Feminisms, Racism and the West* (London: Zed Books, 2004).

113. Véronique Pin-Fat and Maria Stern, "The Scripting of Private Jessica Lynch: Biopolitics, Gender, and the 'Feminization' of the U.S. Military", *Alternatives: Global, Local, Political* vol. 30, no. 1 (2005): 25–53; Jasbir K. Puar and Amit S. Rai, "Monster, Terrorist, Fag: The War on Terrorism and the Production of Docile Patriots", *Social Text* vol. 20, no. 3 (2002): 117–48.

114. Charlotte Hooper, *Manly States: Masculinities, International Relations, and Gender Politics* (New York, NY: Columbia University Press, 2001), 39.

115. Wiktorowicz, *Radical Islam Rising*; Farhad Khosrokhavar, "Terrorism in Europe" (Centre for Studies in Islamism and Radicalisation at the Department of Political Science, University of Aarhus, 2008): https://ps.au.dk/fileadmin/site_files/filer_statskundskab/subsites/cir/pdf-filer/khosrokhavar.pdf, last accessed 16 August 2023.

116. Khan and McMahon, *The Battle for British Islam*, 53.

117. Kenney, *The Islamic State in Britain*, 69.

118. Archer and Yamashita, "Theorising Inner-City Masculinities", 116.

119. Wiktorowicz, *Radical Islam Rising*; Roy, *Jihad and Death*; Anja Dalgaard-Nielsen, "Violent Radicalization in Europe: What We Know and What We Do Not Know", *Studies in Conflict & Terrorism* vol. 33, no. 9 (2010): 797–814.

120. Roy, *Jihad and Death*, 67.

121. Kenney, *The Islamic State in Britain*, 216.

122. Roy, *Jihad and Death*, 31.

123. Kimberly Hutchings, "Making Sense of Masculinity and War", *Men and Masculinities* vol. 10, no. 4 (2007): 389–404.

7. ALM: MOBILISING MASCULINITIES

1. Michael Kenney, *The Islamic State in Britain: Radicalization and Resilience in an Activist Network* (Cambridge: Cambridge University Press, 2018), 101.

2. James W. Messerschmidt and Achim Rohde, "Osama Bin Laden and His Jihadist Global Hegemonic Masculinity", *Gender & Society* vol. 32, no. 5 (2018): 663–85; Elizabeth Pearson, "Online as the New Frontline: Affect, Gender, and ISIS Take-Down on Social Media", *Studies in Conflict & Terrorism* vol. 49, no. 11 (2017): 850–74; Rüdiger Lohlker, "Jihadi Masculinities: Another Masculinity in Crisis", in *Jihadi Thought and Ideology*, eds Rüdiger Lohlker and Tamara Abu-Hamdeh (Berlin: Logos, 2013), 138–64.

3. Cynthia Enloe, "Beyond 'Rambo': Women and the Varieties of Militarized Masculinity", in *Women and the Military System*, ed. Eva Isaksson (New York, NY: St. Martin's, 1988), 71–93 (91).

4. Stephen McVeigh and Nicola Cooper, "Introduction", in *Men After War*, eds Stephen McVeigh and Nicola Cooper (London: Routledge, 2013), 1–17 (3).

5. John Stoltenberg, "Andrea Dworkin Was a Trans Ally", *Boston Review*, 8 April 2020: https://www.bostonreview.net/articles/john-stoltenberg-andrew-dworkin-was-trans-ally/, last accessed 16 August 2023, cited in Finn MacKay, *Female Masculinities and the Gender Wars: The Politics of Sex* (London: IB Tauris Bloomsbury, 2021), 128.

6. Raewyn W. Connell and James W. Messerschmidt. "Hegemonic Masculinity: Rethinking the Concept", Gender and Society vol. 19, no. 6 (2005): 829–59 (829).

7. Lohlker, "Jihadi Masculinities".

8. Thomas Hegghammer, "Introduction: What Is Jihadi Culture and Why Should We Study It?", in *Jihadi Culture: The Art and Social Practices of Militant Islamists*, ed. Thomas Hegghammer (Cambridge: Cambridge University Press, 2017), 1–21.

9. Maleeha Aslam, *Gender-Based Explosions: The Nexus Between Muslim Masculinities, Jihadist Islamism and Terrorism* (Tokyo: United Nations University Press, 2012); Lahoucine Ouzgane, ed., *Islamic Masculinities* (London: Bloomsbury, 2006).

10. Duriesmith and Ismail, "Militarized Masculinities Beyond Methodological Nationalism".

11. Messerschmidt and Rohde, "Osama Bin Laden and His Jihadist Global Hegemonic Masculinity".

12. Tufyal Choudhury, "The Role of Muslim Identity Politics in Radicalisation (a Study in Progress)" (Department for Communities and Local Government, 2007), 10: https://webarchive.nationalarchives.gov.uk/ukgwa/20070506190701mp_/http://www.communities.gov.uk/pub/393/TheRoleofMuslimIdentityPoliticsinRadicalisationastudyinprogress_id1509393.pdf, last accessed 15 August 2023.

13. Literalism is instinctive to many Muslims, as a core principle of Islam is that the Arabic-language Quran is the literal word of God, delivered through the Prophet Mohammed.

14. Raffaello Pantucci, *"We Love Death as You Love Life": Britain's Suburban Terrorists* (London: C. Hurst & Co., 2015), 9. One example ALM members give of *bidah* is the Shia veneration of ancestors.

15. Shahin Gerami, "Islamist Masculinity and Muslim Masculinities", in *Handbook of Studies on Men and Masculinities*, eds Michael S. Kimmel, Jeff R. Hearn and R.W. Connell (Thousand Oaks, CA; London: SAGE Publications, 2004), 448–57.

16. Sayyid Qutb, *Milestones* (London: Islamic Book Service, 2006).

17. Olivier Roy, *Jihad and Death: The Global Appeal of Islamic State* (London: C. Hurst & Co., 2017), 50.

18. Qutb, *Milestones*, 6–7.

19. Charlie Winter, "Women of the Islamic State: A Manifesto on Women by the Al-Khanssaa Brigade" (London: The Quilliam Foundation, 2015); Thomas Hegghammer, "Non-Military Practices in Jihadi Groups", in *Jihadi Culture: The Art and Social Practices of Militant Islamists*, ed. Thomas Hegghammer (Cambridge:

Cambridge University Press, 2017), 171–201; European Union Agency for Law Enforcement Cooperation, "Online Jihadist Propaganda: 2020 in Review" (EU Publications Office, 2021): https://data.europa.eu/doi/10.2813/169367, last accessed 16 August 2023; Pearson, "Online as the New Frontline".

20. Hegghammer, "Non-Military Practices in Jihadi Groups"; Aslam, *Gender-Based Explosions*.

21. Qutb, *Milestones*, 91; 117.

22. Shiraz Maher, *Salafi-Jihadism: The History of an Idea* (London: C. Hurst & Co., 2016), 177.

23. John Calvert, "'The World Is an Undutiful Boy!': Sayyid Qutb's American Experience", *Islam and Christian–Muslim Relations* vol. 11, no. 1 (2000): 87–103 (88).

24. Qutb, *Milestones*, 53.

25. For Sheikh Abdullah Yusuf Azzam's call for fighters, see Abdullah Azzam, *Join The Caravan* (1987), Internet Archive: http://archive.org/details/JoinTheCaravan, last accessed 16 August 2023.

26. Nelly Lahoud, "The Neglected Sex: The Jihadis' Exclusion of Women from Jihad", *Terrorism and Political Violence*, vol. 26, no. 5 (2014): 780–802; Nelly Lahoud, "Can Women Be Soldiers of the Islamic State?", *Survival* vol. 59, no. 1 (2017): 61–78.

27. Lahoud, "The Neglected Sex"; Lahoud, "Can Women Be Soldiers of the Islamic State?"; Nelly Lahoud, "Empowerment or Subjugation: An Analysis of ISIL's Gendered Messaging" (UN Women, 2018): https://arabstates.unwomen.org/sites/default/files/Field%20Office%20Arab%20States/Attachments/Publications/Lahoud-Fin-Web-rev.pdf, last accessed 2 August 2023.

28. Shaun Best, "Liquid Terrorism: Altruistic Fundamentalism in the Context of Liquid Modernity", *Sociology* vol. 44, no. 4 (2010): 678–94; Ami Pedahzur, Arie Perliger and Leonard Weinberg, "Altruism and Fatalism: The Characteristics of Palestinian Suicide Terrorists", *Deviant Behavior* vol. 24, no. 4 (2003): 405–23.

29. Assaf Moghadam, "Motives for Martyrdom: Al-Qaida, Salafi Jihad, and the Spread of Suicide Attacks", *International Security* vol. 33, no. 3 (2008): 46–78; V. G. Julie Rajan, *Women Suicide Bombers: Narratives of Violence* (London: Routledge, 2012).

30. Jennie Stone and Katherine Pattillo, "Al-Qaeda's Use of Female Suicide Bombers in Iraq: A Case Study", in *Women, Gender, and Terrorism*, eds Laura Sjoberg and Caron E. Gentry (Athens, GA: University of Georgia Press, 2011); Caron Gentry, "The Relationship Between New Social Movement Theory and Terrorism Studies: The Role of Leadership, Membership, Ideology and Gender", *Terrorism and Political Violence* vol. 16, no. 2 (2004): 274–93; Hamoon Khelghat-Doost, "The Strategic Logic of Women in Jihadi Organizations", *Studies in Conflict & Terrorism* vol. 42, no. 10 (2019): 853–77; Lahoud, "The Neglected Sex".

31. Messerschmidt and Rohde, "Osama Bin Laden and His Jihadist Global Hegemonic Masculinity".

32. John G. Horgan et al., "From Cubs to Lions: A Six Stage Model of Child

Socialization into the Islamic State", *Studies in Conflict & Terrorism* vol. 40, no. 7 (2017): 645–64; Joana Cook and Gina Vale, "From Daesh to 'Diaspora': Tracing the Women and Minors of Islamic State" (International Centre for the Study of Radicalisation and Political Violence, July 2018): https://icsr.info/wp-content/uploads/2018/07/ICSR-Report-From-Daesh-to-'Diaspora'-Tracing-the-Women-and-Minors-of-Islamic-State.pdf, last accessed 1 August 2023.

33. Katherine E. Brown, "Gender and Counter-Radicalization: Women and Emerging Counter-Terror Measures", in *Gender, National Security and Counter-Terrorism*, eds Jayne Huckerby and Margaret L. Satterthwaite (Abingdon; New York, NY: Routledge, 2013), 36–59.

34. Louise Archer, "'Muslim Brothers, Black Lads, Traditional Asians': British Muslim Young Men's Constructions of Race, Religion and Masculinity", *Feminism & Psychology* vol. 11, no. 1 (2001): 79–105; Maleiha Malik, "'The Branch on Which We Sit': Multiculturalism, Minority Women and Family Law", in *Feminist Perspectives on Family Law*, eds Alison Diduck and Katherine O'Donovan (Abingdon; New York, NY: Routledge-Cavendish, 2006), 211–31.

35. Aslam, *Gender-Based Explosions*.

36. Aslam, *Gender-Based Explosions*.

37. Pearson, "Online as the New Frontline".

38. Jigmey Bhutia, "Isis's Al-Khansaa Brigade Kills Woman for Breast-Feeding Baby in Public in Raqqa", *International Business Times UK*, 28 December 2015: http://www.ibtimes.co.uk/isiss-al-khansaa-brigade-kills-woman-breast-feeding-baby-public-raqqa-1535110, last accessed 16 August 2023; Winter, "Women of the Islamic State"; Loulla-Mae Eleftheriou-Smith, "Escaped Isis Wives Describe Life in the All-Female al-Khansa Brigade Who Punish Women With 40 Lashes for Wearing Wrong Clothes", *The Independent*, 20 April 2015: http://www.independent.co.uk/news/world/middle-east/escaped-isis-wives-describe-life-in-the-allfemale-alkhansa-brigade-who-punish-women-with-40-lashes-for-wearing-wrong-clothes-10190317.html, last accessed 16 August 2023.

39. Interview, Akash, 29 March 2017.

40. Interview, Rifat, 16 July 2017.

41. Rajan Basra, Peter R. Neumann and Claudia Brunner, "Criminal Pasts, Terrorist Futures: European Jihadists and the New Crime–Terror Nexus" (King's College London, International Centre for the Study of Radicalisation and Political Violence, May 2016): https://icsr.info/wp-content/uploads/2016/10/ICSR-Report-Criminal-Pasts-Terrorist-Futures-European-Jihadists-and-the-New-Crime-Terror-Nexus.pdf, last accessed 14 August 2023.

42. Interview, Adam, 12 July 2016.

43. Dominic Kennedy, "Hate Preacher Abu Haleema Flees After Far-Right Fanatic Tommy Robinson Finds Him", *The Times*, 7 June 2017: https://www.thetimes.co.uk/article/hate-preacher-abu-haleema-flees-after-far-right-fanatic-tommy-robinson-finds-him-bjh0csdbf, last accessed 16 August 2023; "Abu Haleema", Counter Extremism Project, 19 September 2015: https://www.counterextremism.com/extremists/abu-haleema, last accessed 16 August 2023.

44. https://www.independent.co.uk/news/uk/crime/terror-attacker-shakil-chapra-jailed-video-b1877395.html

45. Interview, Mo, 5 October 2016.

46. HM Inspector of Prisons, "Muslim Prisoners' Experiences: A Thematic Review" (HM Government, 2010), 31: https://www.justiceinspectorates.gov.uk/hmiprisons/wp-content/uploads/sites/4/2014/04/Muslim_prisoners_2010_rps.pdf, last accessed 16 August 2023.

47. Tea Torbenfeldt Bengtsson, "Performing Hypermasculinity: Experiences with Confined Young Offenders", *Men and Masculinities* vol. 19, no. 4 (2016): 410–28.

48. Sara Khan and Tony McMahon, *The Battle for British Islam: Reclaiming Muslim Identity from Extremism* (London: Saqi Books, 2016), 147; Kylie Connor, "'Islamism' in the West? The Life-Span of the Al-Muhajiroun in the United Kingdom", *Journal of Muslim Minority Affairs* vol. 25, no. 1 (2005): 117–33 (123); Lorenzo Vidino, "Sharia4: From Confrontational Activism to Militancy", *Perspectives on Terrorism* vol. 9, no. 2 (2015): 2–16 (6).

49. Khan and McMahon, *The Battle for British Islam*, 147; Connor, "'Islamism' in the West?", 123; Quintan Wiktorowicz, *Radical Islam Rising: Muslim Extremism in the West* (Lanham, MD: Rowman & Littlefield, 2005), 150.

50. David Churchill, "Anjem Choudary Protest Sparks Fresh Call for Met to Prevent Rallies By Extremists", *Evening Standard*, 13 April 2015: http://www.standard.co.uk/news/london/anjem-choudary-protest-sparks-fresh-call-for-met-to-prevent-rallies-by-extremists-10172641.html, last accessed 16 August 2023.

51. Interview, Rifat, 16 July 2017.

52. CNN, "London's 'Muslim Patrol' Aims to Impose Sharia Law in East London", YouTube, 1 February 2013: https://www.youtube.com/watch?v=rcsG-u2GtZE, last accessed 16 August 2023; Alice Hutton, "Don't Vote, Radical Cleric Anjem Choudary Tells Muslims", *The Times*, 3 April 2015: https://www.thetimes.co.uk/article/dont-vote-radical-cleric-anjem-choudary-tells-muslims-vfsp57z5jzh, last accessed 16 August 2023.

53. Calvert, "'The World Is an Undutiful Boy!'", 98.

54. Qutb quoted in Calvert, "'The World Is an Undutiful Boy!'", 97–98; Lawrence Wright, *The Looming Tower: Al Qaeda's Road to 9/11* (London: Penguin, 2007).

55. Khan and McMahon, *The Battle for British Islam*, 52.

56. Interview, Mo, 8 October 2016.

57. Field notes, 8 October 2016.

58. Interview, Anjem Choudary, 18 July 2016.

59. Vidino, "Sharia4", 9.

60. Maéva Clément, "Al-Muhajiroun in the United Kingdom: The Role of International Non-Recognition in Heightened Radicalization Dynamics", *Global Discourse* vol. 4, no. 4 (2014): 428–43 (430).

61. Pantucci, *We Love Death as You Love Life*, 9.

62. Bakri Mohammed founded the first al-Muhajiroun in Saudi Arabia in 1983; Khan and McMahon, *The Battle for British Islam*, 53; Michael Kenney, Stephen Coulthart and Dominick Wright, "Structure and Performance in a Violent Extremist

Network: The Small-World Solution", *Journal of Conflict Resolution* vol. 61, no. 10 (2016): 2208–34 (2209); Vidino, "Sharia4", 3.

63. Innes Bowen, *Medina in Birmingham, Najaf in Brent: Inside British Islam* (London: C. Hurst & Co., 2014), 68.

64. Connor, "'Islamism' in the West?", 121.

65. Interview, Anjem Choudary, 18 July 2016.

66. Bassam Alloni, "Interview: Sheikh Omar Bakri Mohammad", UPI, 14 September 2003: https://www.upi.com/Interview-Sheikh-Omar-Bakri-Mohammad/81231063546303/, last accessed 16 August 2023.

67. Petter Nesser, *Islamist Terrorism in Europe: A History* (London: C. Hurst & Co., 2016), 269–70.

68. Interview, Anjem Choudary, 18 July 2016.

69. Kenney, *The Islamic State in Britain*, 23.

70. Home Office, "CONTEST: The United Kingdom's Strategy for Countering Terrorism" (June 2018), 19: https://assets.publishing.service.gov.uk/government/uploads/system/uploads/attachment_data/file/716907/140618_CCS207_CCS0218929798-1_CONTEST_3.0_WEB.pdf, last accessed 26 July 2023.

71. HM Government, "CONTEST 2023" (July 2023): https://assets.publishing.service.gov.uk/government/uploads/system/uploads/attachment_data/file/1171084/CONTEST_2023.pdf, last accessed 26 July 2023.

72. Interview, Anjem Choudary, 18 July 2016.

73. Interview, Anjem Choudary, 18 July 2016.

74. Wiktorowicz, *Radical Islam Rising*.

75. See Kenney, *The Islamic State in Britain*; and Douglas Weeks, *Al Muhajiroun: A Case Study in Contemporary Islamic Activism* (Basingstoke: Palgrave Macmillan, 2020) for more on the Covenant.

76. Messaging, Mo, 5 June 2017.

77. Interview, Adam, 12 July 2016.

78. Interview, Akash, 7 February 2017.

79. Messaging, Abu M., 10 October 2016.

80. Court notes, December 2016.

81. Interview, Aisha, 10 April 2017.

82. Interview, Mo, 8 October 2016.

83. Interview, Akash, 11 December 2016.

84. Messaging, Ahmed, 5 May 2016.

85. Interview, Rifat, 21 May 2017.

86. Kenney, *The Islamic State in Britain*, 101.

87. Imran Nazar Hosein, "Ten Major Signs of the Last Day – Has One Just Occurred?", 10 Rajab 1428: http://www.imranhosein.org/articles/signs-of-the-last-day/76-ten-major-signs-of-the-last-day-has-one-just-occurred.html, last accessed 3 August 2017.

88. Interview, Akash, 29 March 2017.

89. Kenney, *The Islamic State in Britain*, 102–12.

90. Interview, Adam, 12 July 2016.

91. Interview, Adam, 12 July 2016.
92. Hegghammer, "Introduction", 10; 15.
93. Interview, Adam, 12 July 2016.
94. Kenney, *The Islamic State in Britain*, 62; 93; 190.
95. Kenney, *The Islamic State in Britain*, 47.
96. Interview, Adam, 12 July 2016.
97. Interview, Rifat, 16 July 2017.
98. Field notes, December 2016.
99. Wiktorowicz, *Radical Islam Rising*, 92–93; Mohammed Ilyas, "Islamist Groups in the UK and Recruitment", *Journal of Terrorism Research* vol. 4, no. 2 (2013): https://jtr.st-andrews.ac.uk/articles/10.15664/jtr.631/, last accessed 16 August 2023; AIVD, "Jihadism on the Web: A Breeding Ground for Jihad in the Modern Age" (Dutch General Intelligence and Security Services, 2012); Ghaffar Hussain and Erin Marie Saltman, "Jihad Trending: A Comprehensive Analysis of Online Extremism and How to Counter It" (The Quilliam Foundation, 2014): https://preventviolentextremism.info/sites/default/files/Jihad%20Trending-%20A%20Comprehensive%20Analysis%20of%20Online%20Extremism%20and%20How%20to%20Counter%20it.pdf, last accessed 16 August 2023.
100. Social media, Oliver, August 2016.
101. Interview, Rifat, 16 July 2017.
102. Messaging, Oliver, 13 November 2016.
103. Interview, Umm M., 20 August 2016.
104. Roy, *Jihad and Death*, 44.
105. Messaging, Abu M., 2 October 2016.
106. Jytte Klausen et al., "The YouTube Jihadists: A Social Network Analysis of Al-Muhajiroun's Propaganda Campaign", *Perspectives on Terrorism* vol. 6, no. 1 (2012): 36–53 (39).
107. Khaled Fattah and K. M. Fierke, "A Clash of Emotions: The Politics of Humiliation and Political Violence in the Middle East", *European Journal of International Relations* vol. 15, no. 1 (2009): 67–93.
108. Judge summing up, Old Bailey, September 2016.
109. Pearson, "Online as the New Frontline".
110. Mohammed Ilyas, "The 'Al-Muhajiroun Brand' of Islamism", *Interface: A Journal for and about Social Movements* vol. 6, no. 1 (2014): 441–53.
111. Interview, Umm M., 20 August 2016.
112. Interview, Saleha, 20 July 2016.
113. Jytte Klausen et al., "Radicalization Trajectories: An Evidence-Based Computational Approach to Dynamic Risk Assessment of 'Homegrown' Jihadists", *Studies in Conflict & Terrorism* vol. 43, no. 7 (2020): 588–615.
114. Interview, Saleha, 20 July 2016.
115. Interview, Farhan, 24 August 2016.
116. Aslam, *Gender-Based Explosions*, 266.
117. Interview, Saleha, 20 July 2016.

118. Claire Dwyer, "Negotiating Diasporic Identities: Young British South Asian Muslim Women", *Women's Studies International Forum* vol. 23, no. 4 (2000): 475–86; Sarah Glynn, "Bengali Muslims: The New East End Radicals?", *Ethnic and Racial Studies* vol. 25, no. 6 (2002): 969–88; Elizabeth Pearson and Emily Winterbotham, "Women, Gender and Daesh Radicalisation: A Milieu Approach", *The RUSI Journal* vol. 162, no. 3 (2017): 60–72; Nimmi Gowrinathan, "The Women of ISIS: Understanding and Combating Female Extremism", *Foreign Affairs*, 21 August 2014: http://www.foreignaffairs.com/articles/141926/nimmi-gowrinathan/the-women-of-isis, last accessed 16 August 2023.

119. Interview, Saleha, 16 August 2016.

120. Interview, Aisha, 10 April 2017.

121. Basra, Neumann and Brunner, "Criminal Pasts, Terrorist Futures"; Jonathan Ilan and Sveinung Sandberg, "How 'Gangsters' Become Jihadists: Bourdieu, Criminology and the Crime–Terrorism Nexus", *European Journal of Criminology* vol. 16, no. 3 (2019): 278–94; Sveinung Sandberg, "How Gangsters Become Jihadists (And Why Most Don't): Bourdieu, Criminology, and the Crime–Terror Nexus", Faculty of Law Blogs, University of Oxford, 5 November 2018: https://blogs.law.ox.ac.uk/centres-institutes/centre-criminology/blog/2018/11/how-gangsters-become-jihadists-and-why-most-dont, last accessed 16 August 2023.

8. CONCLUSIONS

1. Katherine E. Brown, "Gender and Counter-Radicalization: Women and Emerging Counter-Terror Measures", in *Gender, National Security and Counter-Terrorism*, eds Jayne Huckerby and Margaret L. Satterthwaite (Abingdon; New York, NY: Routledge, 2013), 36–59.

2. Jack Halberstam, *Female Masculinity* (Durham, NC: Duke University Press, 1998), 2.

3. Nimmi Gowrinathan, *Radicalizing Her: Why Women Choose Violence* (London: Penguin Random House, 2022).

4. Laura Sjoberg, *Gendering Global Conflict: Toward a Feminist Theory of War* (New York, NY: Columbia University Press, 2013), 265.

5. Peter Hopkins, *The Issue of Masculine Identities for British Muslims After 9/11: A Social Analysis* (Lewiston, NY: Edwin Mellen Press Ltd, 2008), 75.

6. Hopkins, *The Issue of Masculine Identities for British Muslims After 9/11*, 92.

7. Joel Busher, *The Making of Anti-Muslim Protest: Grassroots Activism in the English Defence League* (London; New York, NY: Routledge, 2015), para. 612 [online].

8. Busher, *The Making of Anti-Muslim Protest*, para. 613 [online].

9. Gavin Bailey, "We Can All Be a Little Radicalised: Recognising This Will Help Tackle Extremism", The Conversation, 17 August 2016, http://theconversation.com/we-can-all-be-a-little-radicalised-recognising-this-will-help-tackle-extremism-63144, last accessed 6 August 2023.

10. J. M. Berger, *Extremism* (Cambridge, MA: MIT Press, 2018), 44; additions in italics are mine.

11. Jane L. Parpart and Marysia Zalewski, "Introduction: Rethinking the Man Question", in *Rethinking the Man Question: Sex, Gender and Violence in International Relations*, eds Jane L. Parpart and Marysia Zalewski (London; New York, NY: Zed Books, 2008), 1–22

12. Parpart and Zalewski, "Introduction", 3.

13. Joan W. Scott, "Gender: A Useful Category of Historical Analysis", *The American Historical Review* vol. 91, no. 5 (1986): 1053–75 (1053).

14. David Buchbinder, *Studying Men and Masculinities* (London: Routledge, 2013).

15. Marcia Inhorn, *The New Arab Man: Emergent Masculinities, Technologies, and Islam in the Middle East* (Princeton, NJ: Princeton University Press, 2012), 45.

16. David Duriesmith and Noor Huda Ismail, "Militarized Masculinities Beyond Methodological Nationalism: Charting the Multiple Masculinities of an Indonesian Jihadi", *International Theory* vol. 11, no. 2 (2019): 139–59 (155).

17. Eve Kosofsky Sedgwick, "Gosh, Boy George, You Must Be Awfully Secure in Your Masculinity", in *Constructing Masculinity*, eds Maurice Berger, Brian Wallis and Simon Watson (London; New York, NY: Routledge, 1995), 11–20 (16).

18. Terry A. Kupers, "Toxic Masculinity as a Barrier to Mental Health Treatment in Prison", *Journal of Clinical Psychology* vol. 61, no. 6 (2005): 713–24.

19. Fred Pfeil, *White Guys: Studies in Postmodern Domination and Difference* (London: Verso Books, 1995), 15.

20. Syed Haider, "The Shooting in Orlando: Terrorism or Toxic Masculinity (or Both?)", *Men and Masculinities* vol. 19, no. 5 (2016): 555–65 (558).

21. Sally Robinson, "Pedagogy of the Opaque: Teaching Masculinity Studies", in *Masculinity Studies and Feminist Theory*, ed. Judith Kegan Gardiner (New York, NY: Columbia University Press, 2002), 141–60.

22. Nikki Wedgwood, "Connell's Theory of Masculinity – Its Origins and Influences on the Study of Gender", *Journal of Gender Studies* vol. 18, no. 4 (2009): 329–39 (334).

23. Cynthia Weber, *International Relations Theory: A Critical Introduction* (New York, NY: Routledge, 2004), 89.

24. V. Spike Peterson, "Introduction", in *Gendered States: Feminist (Re)visions of International Relations Theory*, ed. V. Spike Peterson (Boulder, CO; London: Lynne Rienner, 1992), 1–30 (9), cited in Adam Jones, "Does 'Gender' Make the World Go Round? Feminist Critiques of International Relations", *Review of International Studies* vol. 22, no. 4 (October 1996): 405–29 (405).

25. Peterson, "Introduction", 7, cited in Jones, "Does 'Gender' Make the World Go Round?", 406.

26. Halberstam, *Female Masculinity*; Chris Beasley, *Gender and Sexuality: Critical Theories, Critical Thinkers* (London; Thousand Oaks, CA: SAGE Publications, 2005); Gayle S. Rubin, "Thinking Sex: Notes for a Radical Theory of the Politics of Sexuality", in *Deviations: A Gayle Rubin Reader* (Durham, NC: Duke University Press, 2011), 137–81.

27. Maria Stern and Marysia Zalewski, "Feminist Fatigue(s): Reflections on Feminism and Familiar Fables of Militarisation", *Review of International Studies* vol. 35, no. 3 (2009): 611–30 (621).
28. Christoffer Carlsson, "Masculinities, Persistence, and Desistance", *Criminology* vol. 51, no. 3 (2013): 661–93.
29. Paul Amar, "Middle East Masculinity Studies: Discourses of 'Men in Crisis', Industries of Gender in Revolution", *Journal of Middle East Women's Studies* vol. 7, no. 3 (2011): 36–70 (38).
30. R. W. Connell, "The Social Organization of Masculinity", in *The Masculinities Reader*, eds Stephen M. Whitehead and Frank J. Barrett (Cambridge: Polity Press, 2001), 30–51 (38).
31. Laura J. Shepherd, "White Feminism and the Governance of Violent Extremism", *Critical Studies on Terrorism* vol. 15, no. 3 (2022): 727–49.
32. See Douglas Weeks, "The Method", Usman Raja: https://www.usman-raja.com/the-method, last accessed 16 August 2023.
33. Amar, "Middle East Masculinity Studies", 39.
34. R. W. Connell, "Globalisation, Imperialism and Masculinities", in *Handbook of Studies on Men and Masculinities*, eds Michael S. Kimmel, Jeff R. Hearn and R. W. Connell (Thousand Oaks, CA; London: SAGE Publications, 2004), 71–89.
35. Claudia Fonseca, "Philanderers, Cuckolds, and Wily Women: A Reexamination of Gender Relations in a Brazilian Working-Class Neighborhood", *Men and Masculinities* vol. 3, no. 3 (2001): 261–77.
36. Enloe in Carol Cohn and Cynthia Enloe, "A Conversation with Cynthia Enloe: Feminists Look at Masculinity and the Men Who Wage War", *Signs: Journal of Women in Culture and Society* vol. 28, no. 4 (2003): 1187–207 (1198).
37. David Duriesmith, "Hybrid Warriors and the Formation of New War Masculinities: A Case Study of Indonesian Foreign Fighters", *Stability: International Journal of Security and Development* vol. 7, no. 1 (2018): 1–16 (8).
38. HM Government, "CONTEST 2023" (July 2023): https://assets.publishing.service.gov.uk/government/uploads/system/uploads/attachment_data/file/1171084/CONTEST_2023.pdf, last accessed 26 July 2023.
39. Linda McDowell, *Redundant Masculinities? Employment Change and White Working-Class Youth* (New York, NY: John Wiley & Sons, 2011); Amar, "Middle East Masculinity Studies".
40. See, for instance, Finn MacKay, *Female Masculinities and the Gender Wars: The Politics of Sex* (London: IB Tauris Bloomsbury, 2021).
41. Paul Kirby, "Refusing to Be a Man? Men's Responsibility for War Rape and the Problem of Social Structures in Feminist and Gender Theory", *Men and Masculinities* vol. 16, no. 1 (2013): 93–114; Charlotte Hooper, *Manly States: Masculinities, International Relations, and Gender Politics* (New York, NY: Columbia University Press, 2001); Duriesmith and Ismail, "Militarized Masculinities Beyond Methodological Nationalism".

BIBLIOGRAPHY

5Pillars. "Tommy Robinson Publishes Book on the Holy Quran". 5Pillars (blog). 2017. http://5pillarsuk.com/2017/07/22/tommy-robinson-publishes-book-on-the-holy-quran/. Last accessed 13 August 2023.

Abbas, Tahir. "After 9/11: British South Asian Muslims, Islamophobia, Multiculturalism, and the State". *American Journal of Islamic Social Sciences* vol. 21, no. 3 (2004): 26–38.

———. "Muslim Minorities in Britain: Integration, Multiculturalism and Radicalism in the Post-7/7 Period". *Journal of Intercultural Studies* vol. 28, no. 3 (2007): 287–300.

———. "Ethnicity and Politics in Contextualising Far Right and Islamist Extremism". *Perspectives on Terrorism* vol. 11, no. 3 (2017): 54–61.

Abbott, Diane. "Britain's Crisis of Masculinity". 16 May 2013. https://www.dianeabbott.org.uk/news/articles/item915. Last accessed 31 July 2023.

"About Us". English Defence League website. http://www.englishdefenceleague.org.uk/mission-statement/. Last accessed 20 March 2018.

Agnew, Robert. "A General Strain Theory of Terrorism". *Theoretical Criminology* vol. 14, no. 2 (2010): 131–53.

Åhäll, Linda. "Motherhood, Myth and Gendered Agency in Political Violence". *International Feminist Journal of Politics* vol. 14, no. 1 (2012): 103–20.

Ahdash, Fatima. "Should the Law Facilitate the Removal of the Children of Terrorists and Extremists from Their Care?". British Politics and Policy at LSE (blog). 9 March 2018. https://blogs.lse.ac.uk/politicsandpolicy/should-the-law-facilitate-the-removal-of-the-children-of-convicted-terrorists/. Last accessed 6 August 2023.

Ahmed, Sara. *The Cultural Politics of Emotion*. Edinburgh: Edinburgh University Press, 2004.

———. "Multiculturalism and the Promise of Happiness". In *Feminist Theory Reader: Local and Global Perspectives*. Eds Carole McCann, Seung-Kyung Kim and Emek Ergun. New York, NY: Routledge, 2013. 517–32.

———. *The Cultural Politics of Emotion*. 2nd revised edition. Edinburgh: Edinburgh University Press, 2014.

BIBLIOGRAPHY

————. "Atmospheric Walls". feministkilljoys (blog). 15 September 2014. https://feministkilljoys.com/2014/09/15/atmospheric-walls/. Last accessed 14 August 2023.

AIVD. "Jihadism on the Web: A Breeding Ground for Jihad in the Modern Age". Dutch General Intelligence and Security Services, 2012.

Alex and the Bandits. "Alex and The Bandits – About". Facebook. https://www.facebook.com/pg/Alex-And-The-Bandits-121068861335907/about/?ref=page_internal. Last accessed 17 April 2017.

Alison, Miranda. "Women as Agents of Political Violence: Gendering Security". *Security Dialogue* vol. 35, no. 4 (2004): 447–63.

Allen, Chris. "Britain First: The 'Frontline Resistance' to the Islamification of Britain". *The Political Quarterly* vol. 85, no. 3 (2014): 354–61.

Allen, Judith A. "Men Interminably in Crisis? Historians on Masculinity, Sexual Boundaries, and Manhood". *Radical History Review* vol. 82, no. 1 (2002): 191–207.

Alloni, Bassam. "Interview: Sheikh Omar Bakri Mohammad". UPI. 14 September 2003. https://www.upi.com/Interview-Sheikh-Omar-Bakri-Mohammad/81231063546303/. Last accessed 16 August 2023.

Amar, Paul. "Middle East Masculinity Studies: Discourses of 'Men in Crisis', Industries of Gender in Revolution". *Journal of Middle East Women's Studies* vol. 7, no. 3 (2011): 36–70.

Anderson, Elijah. *Streetwise: Race, Class, and Change in an Urban Community*. Chicago, IL: University of Chicago Press, 1992.

Anthias, Floya, and Nira Yuval-Davis. *Racialized Boundaries: Race, Nation, Gender, Colour and Class and the Anti-Racist Struggle*. London: Routledge, 1992.

Archer, Louise. "'Muslim Brothers, Black Lads, Traditional Asians': British Muslim Young Men's Constructions of Race, Religion and Masculinity". *Feminism & Psychology* vol. 11, no. 1 (2001): 79–105.

Archer, Louise, and Hiromi Yamashita. "Theorising Inner-City Masculinities: 'Race', Class, Gender and Education". *Gender and Education* vol. 15, no. 2 (2003): 115–32.

Archer, Margaret S. *The Reflexive Imperative in Late Modernity*. Cambridge: Cambridge University Press, 2012.

Arendt, Hannah. "Ideology and Terror: A Novel Form of Government". *The Review of Politics* vol. 15, no. 3 (1953): 303–27.

Arzheimer, Kai, and Elisabeth Carter. "Political Opportunity Structures and Right-Wing Extremist Party Success". *European Journal of Political Research* vol. 45, no. 3 (2006): 419–43.

Asad, Talal. "Multiculturalism and British Identity in the Wake of the Rushdie Affair". *Politics & Society* vol. 18, no. 4 (1990): 455–80.

Asante, Doris, Yasmin Chilmeran, Zoe Chiller and Laura J. Shepherd. "UN Security Council Resolution 2242 and the Women, Peace, and Security Agenda". Australian Institute of International Affairs (blog). 7 July 2021. https://www.internationalaffairs.org.au/australianoutlook/un-security-council-resolution-2242-and-the-women-peace-and-security-agenda/, last accessed 31 July 2023.

Ashe, Stephen D. "Whiteness, Class and the 'Communicative Community': A Doctoral

BIBLIOGRAPHY

Researcher's Journey to a Local Political Ethnography". In *Researching the Far Right: Theory, Method and Practice*. Eds Stephen D. Ashe, Joel Busher, Graham Macklin and Aaron Winter. London: Routledge, 2020. 284–306.

Asher, Rebecca. *Man Up: Boys, Men and Breaking the Male Rules*. London: Harvill Secker, 2016.

Askanius, Tina. "Women in the Nordic Resistance Movement and Their Online Media Practices: Between Internalised Misogyny and 'Embedded Feminism'". *Feminist Media Studies* vol. 22, no. 7 (2022): 1763–80.

Aslam, Maleeha. *Gender-Based Explosions: The Nexus Between Muslim Masculinities, Jihadist Islamism and Terrorism*. Tokyo: United Nations University Press, 2012.

Averill, James R. "The Social Construction of Emotion: With Special Reference to Love". In *The Social Construction of the Person*. Eds Kenneth J. Gergen and Keith E. Davis. New York, NY: Springer New York, 1985. 89–109.

Awan, Akil (2014). Spurning "This Worldly Life": Terrorism and Martydom in Contemporary Britain. In D. Janes, & A. Houen (Eds.), *Martyrdom and Terrorism: Pre-Modern to Contemporary Perspectives* (Oxford University Press). https://doi.org/10.1093/acprof:oso/9780199959853.003.0011

Awan, Imran. "'I Am a Muslim Not an Extremist': How the Prevent Strategy Has Constructed a 'Suspect' Community". *Politics & Policy* vol. 40, no. 6 (2012): 1158–85.

Awan, Imran, and Irene Zempi. "'I Will Blow Your Face Off'—Virtual and Physical World Anti-Muslim Hate Crime". *British Journal of Criminology* vol. 57, no. 2 (2017): 362–80.

Azzam, Abdullah. *Join The Caravan*, 1987. Internet Archive. http://archive.org/details/JoinTheCaravan. Last accessed 16 August 2023.

Back, Les, Tim Crabbe and John Solomos. "Beyond the Racist/Hooligan Couplet: Race, Social Theory and Football Culture". *The British Journal of Sociology* vol. 50, no. 3 (1999): 419–42.

Bailey, Gavin. "Extremism, Community and Stigma: Researching the Far Right and Radical Islam in Their Context". In *Researching Marginalized Groups*. Eds Kalwant Bhopal and Ross Deuchar. New York, NY: Routledge, 2015. ri22–35.

———. "We Can All Be a Little Radicalised: Recognising This Will Help Tackle Extremism". The Conversation. 17 August 2016. http://theconversation.com/we-can-all-be-a-little-radicalised-recognising-this-will-help-tackle-extremism-63144. Last accessed 6 August 2023.

Bailey, Gavin, and Phil Edwards. "Rethinking 'Radicalisation': Microradicalisations and Reciprocal Radicalisation as an Intertwined Process". *Journal for Deradicalization* no. 10 (2017): 255–81.

Bakker, Edwin. "Jihadi Terrorists in Europe: Their Characteristics and the Circumstances in Which They Joined the Jihad: An Exploratory Study". Clingendael Institute, 2006. http://www.clingendael.nl/sites/default/files/20061200_cscp_csp_bakker.pdf. Last accessed 27 July 2023.

Bale, Jeffrey M. "Islamism and Totalitarianism". *Totalitarian Movements and Political Religions* vol. 10, no. 2 (2009): 73–96.

Bale, Tim. "Supplying the Insatiable Demand: Europe's Populist Radical Right". *Government and Opposition* vol. 47, no. 2 (2012): 256–74.

Barker, Martin. *New Racism: Conservatives and the Ideology of the Tribe*. London: Junction Books, 1981.

Barkindo, Atta, Caroline K. Wesley and Benjamin Tyavkase Gudaku. "Our Bodies, Their Battleground: Boko Haram and Gender-Based Violence against Christian Women and Children in North-Eastern Nigeria since 1999". World Watch Research Unit of Open Doors International, the Netherlands. November 2013. https://www.worldwatchmonitor.org/research/3117403. Last accessed 27 July 2023.

Bartlett, Jamie, and Jonathan Birdwell. "Cumulative Radicalisation Between The Far-Right and Islamist Groups In The UK: A Review Of Evidence". Demos. November 2013. https://demos.co.uk/wp-content/uploads/files/Demos%20-%20 Cumulative%20Radicalisation%20-%205%20Nov%202013.pdf. Last accessed 27 July 2023.

Bartlett, Jamie and Mark Littler. "Inside the EDL". Demos. 2011. https://www.demos.co.uk/files/Inside_the_edl_WEB.pdf. Last accessed 27 July 2023.

Barton, Cassie, Lukas Audickas, Richard Cracknell and Richard Tunnicliffe. "Social Background of Members of Parliament 1979–2019". House of Commons Library. 10 April 2023. https://commonslibrary.parliament.uk/research-briefings/cbp-7483/. Last accessed 13 August 2023.

Basra, Rajan, Peter R. Neumann and Claudia Brunner. "Criminal Pasts, Terrorist Futures: European Jihadists and the New Crime–Terror Nexus". King's College London, International Centre for the Study of Radicalisation and Political Violence. May 2016. https://icsr.info/wp-content/uploads/2016/10/ICSR-Report-Criminal-Pasts-Terrorist-Futures-European-Jihadists-and-the-New-Crime-Terror-Nexus.pdf. Last accessed 14 August 2023.

BBC News. "Birmingham Football Lads Alliance Demo: Thousands March in City". BBC News. 24 March 2018. http://www.bbc.co.uk/news/uk-england-birmingham-43527109. Last accessed 13 August 2023.

———. "Abubakar Shekau: Nigeria's Boko Haram Leader Is Dead, Say Rival Militants". BBC News. 7 June 2021. https://www.bbc.com/news/world-africa-57378493. Last accessed 31 July 2023.

———. "Anjem Choudary: Radical Preacher's Public Speaking Ban to Be Lifted". BBC News. 18 July 2021. https://www.bbc.com/news/uk-england-london-57878910. Last accessed 27 July 2023.

Beasley, Chris. *Gender and Sexuality: Critical Theories, Critical Thinkers*. London; Thousand Oaks, CA: SAGE Publications, 2005.

Beasley, Christine. "Rethinking Hegemonic Masculinity in a Globalizing World". *Men and Masculinities* vol. 11, no. 1 (October 2008): 86–103.

Beauvoir, Simone de. *The Second Sex*. Trans. H. M. Parshley. 1949. London: Vintage Classics, 1997.

Beck, Ulrich, Anthony Giddens and Scott Lash. *Reflexive Modernization: Politics, Tradition and Aesthetics in the Modern Social Order*. Cambridge: Polity Press, 1994.

BIBLIOGRAPHY

Becker, Howard. "Problems of Inference and Proof in Participant Observation". *American Sociological Review* vol. 23, no. 6 (1958): 652–60.

Bengtsson, Tea Torbenfeldt. "Performing Hypermasculinity: Experiences with Confined Young Offenders". *Men and Masculinities* vol. 19, no. 4 (2016): 410–28.

Berezin, Mabel. "Emotions and Political Identity: Mobilizing Affection for the Polity". In *Passionate Politics: Emotions and Social Movements*. Eds Jeff Goodwin, James M. Jasper and Francesca Polletta. Chicago, IL: University of Chicago Press, 2001.

Berger, J. M. *Extremism*. Cambridge, MA: MIT Press, 2018.

―――. "The Alt-Right Twitter Census: Defining and Describing the Audience for Alt-Right Content on Twitter". VOX-Pol. 2018. https://www.voxpol.eu/download/vox-pol_publication/AltRightTwitterCensus.pdf. Last accessed 14 August 2023.

Bermingham, Adam, Maura Conway, Lisa Mcinerney, Neil O'Hare and Alan F. Smeaton. "Combining Social Network Analysis and Sentiment Analysis to Explore the Potential for Online Radicalisation". In *IEEE International Conference on Advances in Social Network Analysis and Mining*. Athens, Greece, 2009. 231–36.

Best, Shaun. "Liquid Terrorism: Altruistic Fundamentalism in the Context of Liquid Modernity". *Sociology* vol. 44, no. 4 (2010): 678–94.

Bhattacharyya, Gargi. *Dangerous Brown Men: Exploiting Sex, Violence and Feminism in the War on Terror*. London: Zed Books, 2008.

Bhutia, Jigmey. "Isis's Al-Khansaa Brigade Kills Woman for Breast-Feeding Baby in Public in Raqqa". *International Business Times UK*. 28 December 2015. http://www.ibtimes.co.uk/isiss-al-khansaa-brigade-kills-woman-breast-feeding-baby-public-raqqa-1535110. Last accessed 16 August 2023.

Bjørgo, Tore. "Introduction". *Terrorism and Political Violence* vol. 7, no. 1 (1995): 1–16.

Blaagaard, Bolette B. "Workings of Whiteness: Interview with Vron Ware". *Social Identities* vol. 17, no. 1 (2011): 153–61.

Blazak, Randy. "'Getting It': The Role of Women in Male Desistance from Hate Groups". In *Home-Grown Hate: Gender and Organized Racism*. Ed. Abby L. Ferber. New York, NY; London: Routledge, 2004. 154–71.

Blee, Kathleen M. "Becoming A Racist: Women in Contemporary Ku Klux Klan and Neo-Nazi Groups". *Gender & Society* vol. 10, no. 6 (1996): 680–702.

―――. "White-Knuckle Research: Emotional Dynamics in Fieldwork with Racist Activists". *Qualitative Sociology* vol. 21, no. 4 (1998): 381–99.

―――. "Women and Organized Racial Terrorism in the United States". In *Female Terrorism and Militancy: Agency, Utility, and Organization*. Ed. Cindy D. Ness. London; New York, NY: Routledge, 2008. 201–16.

―――. "Next Steps in Gender Analysis of Far-Right Extremism". Keynote Lecture, University of Oslo. 14 May 2018.

Blee, Kathleen M., and Kimberly A. Creasap. "Conservative and Right-Wing Movements". *Annual Review of Sociology* vol. 36, no. 1 (2010): 269–86.

Blee, Kathleen M., and Sandra McGee Deutsch. "Introduction". In *Women of the Right: Comparisons and Interplay Across Borders*. Eds Kathleen M. Blee and Sandra McGee Deutsch. University Park, PA: Penn State University Press, 2012. 1–17.

Blee, Kathleen M., and Annette Linden. "Women in Extreme Right Parties and

Movements: A Comparison of the Netherlands and the United States". In *Women of the Right: Comparisons and Interplay Across Borders*. Eds Kathleen M. Blee and Sandra McGee Deutsch. University Park, PA: Penn State University Press, 2012. 98–114.

Bloom, Mia. *Bombshell: The Many Faces of Women Terrorists*. London: C. Hurst & Co., 2011.

Bloom, Mia M. "The First Incel? The Legacy of Marc Lépine". *The Journal of Intelligence, Conflict, and Warfare* vol. 5, no. 1 (2022): 39–74.

Bloxham, Andy. "Muslims Clash with Police After Burning Poppy in Anti-Armistice Day Protest". *The Telegraph*. 11 November 2010. http://www.telegraph.co.uk/news/uknews/law-and-order/8126357/Muslims-clash-with-police-after-burning-poppy-in-anti-Armistice-Day-protest.html. Last accessed 16 August 2023.

Bolognani, Marta. "Islam, Ethnography and Politics: Methodological Issues in Researching Amongst West Yorkshire Pakistanis in 2005". *International Journal of Social Research Methodology* vol. 10, no. 4 (2007): 279–93.

Borchgrevink, Aage. *A Norwegian Tragedy: Anders Behring Breivik and the Massacre on Utoya*. Trans. Guy Puzey. Cambridge: Polity Press, 2013.

Bourdieu, Pierre. *Outline of a Theory of Practice*. Trans. Richard Nice. Cambridge: Cambridge University Press, 1977.

———. *Masculine Domination*. Trans. Richard Nice. Stanford, CA: Stanford University Press, 2001.

Bourgois, Philippe. "In Search of Masculinity: Violence, Respect and Sexuality Among Puerto Rican Crack Dealers in East Harlem". *The British Journal of Criminology* vol. 36, no. 3 (1996): 412–27.

Bowen, Innes. *Medina in Birmingham, Najaf in Brent: Inside British Islam*. London: C. Hurst & Co., 2014.

Boyden, Katie. "Jayda Fransen Has Confirmed Her Britain First Exit in an Eerie New Video". KentLive. 19 January 2019. https://www.kentlive.news/news/kent-news/jayda-fransen-confirmed-britain-first-2447847. Last accessed 6 August 2023.

Brickell, Chris. "Masculinities, Performativity, and Subversion: A Sociological Reappraisal". *Men and Masculinities* vol. 8, no. 1 (2005): 24–43.

Briggs, Rachel. "Community Engagement for Counterterrorism: Lessons from the United Kingdom". *International Affairs* vol. 89, no. 4 (2010): 971–81.

Britain First. "#BritishHistory #OnThisDay 21st January: English Army Raised for Third Crusade". Britain First – Taking Our Country Back! (blog). 21 January 2016. http://www.britainfirst.org/britishhistory-onthisday-21st-january-english-army-raised-for-third-crusade/.

Brown, Drew. "Toxic Masculinity Is at the Heart of This Darkness". Vice. 25 April 2018. https://www.vice.com/en_uk/article/8xkjbx/toxic-masculinity-is-at-the-heart-of-this-darkness. Last accessed 31 July 2023.

Brown, Katherine. "The Promise and Perils of Women's Participation in UK Mosques: The Impact of Securitisation Agendas on Identity, Gender and Community". *The British Journal of Politics & International Relations* vol. 10, no. 3 (2008): 472–91.

BIBLIOGRAPHY

Brown, Katherine E. "Gender and Counter-Terrorism: UK Prevent and De-Radicalisation Strategies". Washington, DC: British Politics Group, 2010.

————. "Gender and Counter-Radicalization: Women and Emerging Counter-Terror Measures". In *Gender, National Security and Counter-Terrorism*. Eds Jayne Huckerby and Margaret L. Satterthwaite. Abingdon; New York, NY: Routledge, 2013. 36–59.

————. *Gender, Religion, Extremism*. Oxford: Oxford University Press, 2020.

Brown, Wendy. "The Impossibility of Women's Studies". In *Women's Studies on the Edge*. Ed. Joan Wallach Scott. Durham, NC: Duke University Press, 2008. 17–38.

Buchbinder, David. *Studying Men and Masculinities*. London: Routledge, 2013.

Burgis, Tom. "The Network That Remains at the Heart of UK Islamist Extremism". *Financial Times*. 6 June 2017. https://www.ft.com/content/54eb9e5e-4ab7-11e7-a3f4-c742b9791d43. Last accessed 15 August 2023.

Burnett, Jon. "Racial Violence and the Brexit State". *Race & Class* vol. 58, no. 4 (2017): 85–97.

Busher, Joel. "Grassroots Activism in the English Defence League: Discourse and Public (Dis)Order". In *Extreme Right Wing Political Violence and Terrorism*. Eds Max Taylor, P. M. Currie and Donald Holbrook. London: Bloomsbury Academic, 2013. 65–84.

————. *The Making of Anti-Muslim Protest: Grassroots Activism in the English Defence League*. London; New York, NY: Routledge, 2015.

————. "Negotiating Ethical Dilemmas During an Ethnographic Study of Anti-Minority Activism: A Personal Reflection on the Adoption of a 'Non-Dehumanization' Principle". In *Researching the Far Right: Theory, Method and Practice*. Eds Stephen D. Ashe, Joel Busher, Graham Macklin and Aaron Winter. London: Routledge, 2020. 271–83.

Butler, Judith. *Gender Trouble: Feminism and the Subversion of Identity*. New York, NY: Routledge, 2006.

Calvert, John. "'The World Is an Undutiful Boy!': Sayyid Qutb's American Experience". *Islam and Christian–Muslim Relations* vol. 11, no. 1 (2000): 87–103.

Cantle, Ted. "Community Cohesion: Report of the Independent Review Team". London: The Home Office, 2001.

Carbado, Devon, and Mitu Gulati. "Working Identity". *Cornell Law Review* vol. 85, no. 5 (2000): 1259–308.

Carlsson, Christoffer. "Masculinities, Persistence, and Desistance'. *Criminology* vol. 51, no. 3 (2013): 661–93.

Carrigan, Tim, Bob Connell and John Lee. "Toward a New Sociology of Masculinity". *Theory and Society* vol. 14, no. 5 (1985): 551–604.

Casciani, Dominic. "Ex-EDL Leader Tommy Robinson Jailed at Leeds Court". BBC News. 29 May 2018. https://www.bbc.co.uk/news/uk-england-leeds-44287640. Last accessed 13 August 2023.

Casey, Louise. "The Casey Review: A Review into Opportunity and Integration". Department for Communities and Local Government. December 2016. https://www.gov.uk/government/publications/the-casey-review-a-review-into-opportunity-and-integration. Last accessed 11 August 2023.

BIBLIOGRAPHY

Cassam, Quassim. *Extremism: A Philosophical Analysis*. London: Routledge, 2022.

Chappuis, Fairlie, and Jana Krause. "Research Dilemmas in Dangerous Places". In *Secrecy and Methods in Security Research: A Guide to Qualitative Fieldwork*. Eds Marieke de Goede, Esmé Bosma and Polly Pallister-Wilkins. London: Routledge, 2019. 112–25.

Childs, Andrew. "Hyper or Hypo-Masculine? Re-Conceptualizing 'Hyper-Masculinity' Through Seattle's Gay, Leather Community". *Gender, Place & Culture* vol. 23, no. 9 (2016): 1315–28.

Chinkin, Christine, and Madeleine Rees. "Commentary On Security Council Resolution 2467: Continued State Obligation and Civil Society Action on Sexual Violence in Conflict". Centre for Women, Peace and Security, London School of Economics. https://www.un.org/sexualviolenceinconflict/wp-content/uploads/2019/09/report/commentary-on-security-council-resolution-2467/19_0496_WPS_Commentary_Report_online.pdf. Last accessed 31 July 2023.

Choudhury, Tufyal. "The Role of Muslim Identity Politics in Radicalisation (a Study in Progress)". Department for Communities and Local Government. 2007. https://webarchive.nationalarchives.gov.uk/ukgwa/20070506190701mp_/http://www.communities.gov.uk/pub/393/TheRoleofMuslimIdentityPoliticsin Radicalisationastudyinprogress_id1509393.pdf.

Churchill, David. "Anjem Choudary Protest Sparks Fresh Call for Met to Prevent Rallies By Extremists". *Evening Standard*. 13 April 2015. http://www.standard.co.uk/news/london/anjem-choudary-protest-sparks-fresh-call-for-met-to-prevent-rallies-by-extremists-10172641.html. Last accessed 16 August 2023.

Clegg, Sue. "The Problem of Agency in Feminism: A Critical Realist Approach". *Gender and Education* vol. 18, no. 3 (2006): 309–24.

Cleland, Jamie. "Racism, Football Fans, and Online Message Boards: How Social Media Has Added a New Dimension to Racist Discourse in English Football". *Journal of Sport and Social Issues* vol. 38, no. 5 (2014). 415–31.

Clément, Maéva. "Al-Muhajiroun in the United Kingdom: The Role of International Non-Recognition in Heightened Radicalization Dynamics". *Global Discourse* vol. 4, no. 4 (2014): 428–43.

CNN. "London's 'Muslim Patrol' Aims to Impose Sharia Law in East London". YouTube. 1 February 2013. https://www.youtube.com/watch?v=rcsG-u2GtZE. Last accessed 16 August 2023.

Cockburn, Cynthia, and Cynthia Enloe. "Militarism, Patriarchy and Peace Movements". *International Feminist Journal of Militarism* vol. 14, no. 4 (2012): 550–57.

Cohn, Carol, and Cynthia Enloe. "A Conversation with Cynthia Enloe: Feminists Look at Masculinity and the Men Who Wage War". *Signs: Journal of Women in Culture and Society* 28, no. 4 (June 2003): 1187–207.

Collins, Randall. "Stratification, Emotional Energy, and the Transient Emotions". In *Research Agendas in the Sociology of Emotions*. Ed. Theodore D. Kemper. Albany, NY: SUNY Press, 1990. 27–57.

———. "Emotional Energy as the Common Denominator of Rational Action". *Rationality and Society* vol. 5, no. 2 (1993): 203–30.

BIBLIOGRAPHY

————. "Social Movements and the Focus of Emotional Attention". *Passionate Politics: Emotions and Social Movements*. Eds Jeff Goodwin, James M. Jasper and Francesca Polletta. Chicago, IL: University of Chicago Press, 2001. 27–44.

Commission for Countering Extremism. "Challenging Hateful Extremism". London: CCE. October 2019. https://assets.publishing.service.gov.uk/government/uploads/system/uploads/attachment_data/file/874101/200320_Challenging_Hateful_Extremism.pdf. Last accessed 27 July 2023.

————. "Three Years on: Achievements and Reflections". March 2021. https://assets.publishing.service.gov.uk/government/uploads/system/uploads/attachment_data/file/973636/CCE_End_of_year_report_2021_Accessible.pdf. Last accessed 27 July 2023.

Connell, R. W. *Gender and Power: Society, the Person and Sexual Politics*. Cambridge: Polity Press, 1987.

————. *Masculinities*. Cambridge: Polity Press, 1995.

————. *The Men and the Boys*. Queensland: Allen and Unwin, 2000.

————. "The Social Organization of Masculinity". In *The Masculinities Reader*. Eds Stephen M. Whitehead and Frank J. Barrett. Cambridge: Polity Press, 2001. 30–51.

————. "Globalisation, Imperialism and Masculinities". In *Handbook of Studies on Men and Masculinities*. Eds Michael S. Kimmel, Jeff R. Hearn and R. W. Connell. Thousand Oaks, CA; London: SAGE Publications, 2004. 71–89.

————. *Masculinities*. 1st revised edition. Cambridge: Polity Press, 2005.

Connell, R. W. and James W. Messerschmidt. "Hegemonic Masculinity: Rethinking the Concept". *Gender & Society* vol. 19, no. 6 (2005): 829–59.

Connell, Raewyn. "Masculinity Research and Global Society". In *Analyzing Gender, Intersectionality, and Multiple Inequalities: Global, Transnational and Local Contexts*. Eds Esther Ngan-Ling Chow, Marcia Texler Segal and Lin Tan. Volume 15. Bingley: Emerald Group Publishing Limited, 2011. 51–72.

Connolly, Paul, and Julie Healy. "Symbolic Violence, Locality and Social Class: The Educational and Career Aspirations of 10–11-Year-Old Boys in Belfast". *Pedagogy, Culture and Society* vol. 12, no. 1 (2004): 15–33.

Connor, Kylie. "'Islamism' in the West? The Life-Span of the Al-Muhajiroun in the United Kingdom". *Journal of Muslim Minority Affairs* vol. 25, no. 1 (2005): 117–33.

Cook, Joana, and Gina Vale. "From Daesh to Diaspora: Tracing the Women and Minors of Islamic State". International Centre for the Study of Radicalisation and Political Violence. 23 July 2018. https://icsr.info/wp-content/uploads/2018/07/ICSR Report-From-Daesh-to-'Diaspora'-Tracing-the-Women-and-Minors-of-Islamic-State.pdf. Last accessed 1 August 2023.

Copsey, Nigel. "The English Defence League: Challenging Our Country and Our Values of Social Inclusion, Fairness and Equality". Faith Matters. November 2010. https://www.faith-matters.org/wp-content/uploads/2010/11/english-defense-league-report.pdf. Last accessed 28 July 2023.

Correia, Sara. "Researching Gender and the Far/Alt-Right – Interview With Dr Ashley Mattheis". *Methods Café* (podcast). 23 March 2023. https://shows.acast.

com/methods-cafe/episodes/s2e2-researching-gender-and-the-faraltright-ashley-mattheis. Last accessed 15 August 2023.

Cottee, Simon. "Jihadism as a Subcultural Response to Social Strain: Extending Marc Sageman's 'Bunch of Guys' Thesis". *Terrorism and Political Violence* vol. 23, no. 5 (2011): 730–51.

———. "Judging Offenders: The Moral Implications of Criminological Theories". In *Values in Criminology and Community Justice*. Eds Malcolm Cowburn, Marian Duggan, Anne Robinson and Paul Senior. Bristol: Policy Press, 2013. 5–20.

Counter Extremism Project. "Abu Haleema". 19 September 2015. https://www.counterextremism.com/extremists/abu-haleema. Last accessed 16 August 2023.

Crenshaw, Martha, ed. *Terrorism in Context*. University Park, PA: Penn State University Press, 2010.

Croft, Stuart. *Securitizing Islam: Identity and the Search for Security*. Cambridge; New York, NY: Cambridge University Press, 2012.

Crooke, Alastair. "You Can't Understand ISIS if You Don't Know the History of Wahhabism in Saudi Arabia". *New Perspectives Quarterly* vol. 32, no. 1 (2015): 56–70.

Dalgaard-Nielsen, Anja. "Violent Radicalization in Europe: What We Know and What We Do Not Know". *Studies in Conflict & Terrorism* vol. 33, no. 9 (2010): 797–814.

Daly, Eoin. "Political Liberalism and French National Identity in the Wake of the Face-Veiling Law". *International Journal of Law in Context* vol. 9, no. 3 (2013): 366–85.

Davis, Jessica. *Women and Radical Islamic Terrorism: Planners, Perpetrators, Patrons?*. Toronto, ON: Canadian Institute of Strategic Studies, 2006.

———. "Evolution of the Global Jihad: Female Suicide Bombers in Iraq". *Studies in Conflict & Terrorism* vol. 36, no. 4 (2013): 279–91.

Dearden, Lizzie. "Abu Qatada to Walk Free After Being Cleared of Terrorism Plot Charges by Jordan Court". *The Independent*. 24 September 2014. http://www.independent.co.uk/news/world/middle-east/abu-qatada-to-walk-free-after-being-cleared-of-terrorism-plot-charges-by-jordan-court-9752346.html. Last accessed 15 August 2023.

———. "Finsbury Park Terror Suspect Darren Osborne Read Messages from Tommy Robinson Days Before Attack, Court Hears". *The Independent*. 23 January 2018. https://www.independent.co.uk/news/uk/crime/tommy-robinson-darren-osborne-messages-finsbury-park-attack-mosque-van-latest-court-trial-muslims-a8174086.html. Last accessed 13 August 2023.

DeCook, Julia R., and Megan Kelly. "Interrogating the 'Incel Menace': Assessing the Threat of Male Supremacy in Terrorism Studies". *Critical Studies on Terrorism* vol. 15, no. 3 (2022): 706–26.

Demetriou, Demetrakis Z. "Connell's Concept of Hegemonic Masculinity: A Critique". *Theory and Society* vol. 30, no. 3 (2001): 337–61.

Devlin, Kayleen. "The Anti-Immigration Party Trying to Recruit Immigrants". BBC News. 11 July 2017. https://www.bbc.com/news/blogs-trending-40509632. Last accessed 15 August 2023.

DiBranco, Alex. "Mobilizing Misogyny". In *Male Supremacism in the United States: From Patriarchal Traditionalism to Misogynist Incels and the Alt-Right*. Eds Emily K. Carian,

Alex DiBranco and Chelsea Ebin. Abingdon; New York, NY: Routledge, 2022. 3–20.

"Digging Deeper with DD Denslow". TNT Radio. 16 April 2023. https://tntradio. live/shows/digging-deeper-with-dd-denslow/. Last accessed 31 July 2023.

Dodd, Vikram. "Anjem Choudary: A Hate Preacher Who Spread Terror in UK and Europe". *The Guardian*. 16 August 2016. https://www.theguardian.com/uk-news/2016/aug/16/anjem-choudary-hate-preacher-spread-terror-uk-europe. Last accessed 15 August 2023.

————. "Anjem Choudary Jailed for Five-and-a-Half Years for Urging Support of Isis". *The Guardian*. 6 September 2016. https://www.theguardian.com/uk-news/2016/sep/06/anjem-choudary-jailed-for-five-years-and-six-months-for-urging-support-of-isis. Last accessed 30 July 2023.

Dodd, Vikram, Matthew Taylor, Alice Ross and Jamie Grierson. "London Bridge Attackers Were Regulars at Sunday Afternoon Pool Sessions". *The Guardian*. 7 June 2017. https://www.theguardian.com/uk-news/2017/jun/07/london-bridge-attackers-were-regulars-at-sunday-afternoon-pool-sessions. Last accessed 14 August 2023.

Dolnik, Adam. "Conducting Field Research on Terrorism: A Brief Primer". *Perspectives on Terrorism* vol. 5, no. 2 (2011): 3–35.

————, ed. *Conducting Terrorism Field Research: A Guide*. Abingdon; New York, NY: Routledge, 2013.

Dunning, Eric. "Towards a Sociological Understanding of Football Hooliganism as a World Phenomenon". *European Journal on Criminal Policy and Research* vol. 8, no. 2 (2000): 141–62.

Dupuis-Déri, Francis. "The Bogus 'Crisis' of Masculinity". The Conversation. 14 May 2018. http://theconversation.com/the-bogus-crisis-of-masculinity-96558. Last accessed 2 August 2023.

Duriesmith, David. "Hybrid Warriors and the Formation of New War Masculinities: A Case Study of Indonesian Foreign Fighters". *Stability: International Journal of Security and Development* vol. 7, no. 1 (2018): 1–16.

Duriesmith, David, and Noor Huda Ismail. "Militarized Masculinities Beyond Methodological Nationalism: Charting the Multiple Masculinities of an Indonesian Jihadi". *International Theory* vol. 11, no. 2 (2019): 139–59.

————. "Masculinities and Disengagement From Jihadi Networks: The Case of Indonesian Militant Islamists". *Studies in Conflict & Terrorism* (2022): 1–21. https://doi.org/10.1080/1057610X.2022.2034220. Last accessed 2 August 2023.

Durkheim, Émile. *The Elementary Forms of the Religious Life*. Trans. Karen E. Fields. 1912. New York, NY: The Free Press, 1995.

Durrani, Mariam. "The Gendered Muslim Subject: At the Intersection of Race, Religion and Gender". In *The Oxford Handbook of Language and Race*. Eds H. Samy Alim, Angela Reyes and Paul V. Kroskrity. Oxford: Oxford University Press, 2020. 342–66.

Duyvesteyn, Isabelle. "How New Is the New Terrorism?" *Studies in Conflict & Terrorism* vol. 27, no. 5 (2004): 439–54.

BIBLIOGRAPHY

Dwyer, Claire. "Negotiating Diasporic Identities: Young British South Asian Muslim Women". *Women's Studies International Forum* vol. 23, no. 4 (2000): 475–86.

Earle, Rod. "Boys' Zone Stories: Perspectives from a Young Men's Prison". *Criminology & Criminal Justice* vol. 11, no. 2 (2011): 129–43.

Eatwell, Roger. "Community Cohesion and Cumulative Extremism in Contemporary Britain". *The Political Quarterly* vol. 77, no. 2 (2006): 204–16.

EDL Media Team. "English Defence League – The Official English Defence League Website". 2016. http://www.englishdefenceleague.org.uk/. Last accessed 20 March 2018.

Edmunds, June. "The Limits of Post-National Citizenship: European Muslims, Human Rights and the Hijab". *Ethnic and Racial Studies* vol. 35, no. 7 (2012): 1181–99.

Eggert, Philippa. "Women Fighters in the 'Islamic State' and Al-Qaida in Iraq: A Comparative Analysis". *Die Friedens-Warte* vol. 90, no. 3/4 (2015): 363–80.

Eisenstein, Zillah. *Against Empire: Feminisms, Racism and the West*. London: Zed Books, 2004.

Eleftheriou-Smith, Loulla-Mae. "Radical Islamist Group Al-Muhajiroun Linked to Half of British Terror Attacks in Past 20 Years". *The Independent*. 23 March 2015. http://www.independent.co.uk/news/uk/crime/radical-islamist-group-al-muhajiroun-linked-to-half-of-british-terror-attacks-in-past-20-years-10128492.html. Last accessed 15 August 2023.

———. "Escaped Isis Wives Describe Life in the All-Female al-Khansa Brigade Who Punish Women With 40 Lashes for Wearing Wrong Clothes". *The Independent*. 20 April 2015. http://www.independent.co.uk/news/world/middle-east/escaped-isis-wives-describe-life-in-the-allfemale-alkhansa-brigade-who-punish-women-with-40-lashes-for-wearing-wrong-clothes-10190317.html. Last accessed 16 August 2023.

Ellis, Carolyn. "Emotional and Ethical Quagmires in Returning to the Field". *Journal of Contemporary Ethnography* vol. 24, no. 1 (1995): 68–98.

Elshtain, Jean Bethke. *Women and War*. Chicago, IL: University of Chicago Press, 1987.

Emanuel, Louis. "Heavy Police Presence in London as Football Lads Alliance and EDL March". *The Times*. 24 June 2017. https://www.thetimes.co.uk/article/heavy-police-presence-in-the-capital-as-football-lads-alliance-and-edl-march-xtcprkrw7. Last accessed 14 August 2023.

Enloe, Cynthia. "Beyond 'Rambo': Women and the Varieties of Militarized Masculinity". In *Women and the Military System*. Ed. Eva Isaksson. New York, NY: St. Martin's, 1988. 71–93.

———. *Bananas, Beaches and Bases: Making Feminist Sense of International Politics*. Berkeley, CA: University of California Press, 2001.

———. *Nimo's War, Emma's War: Making Feminist Sense of the Iraq War*. Berkeley, CA: University of California Press, 2010.

Erk, Jan. "From Vlaams Blok to Vlaams Belang: The Belgian Far-Right Renames Itself". *West European Politics* vol. 28, no. 3 (2005): 493–502.

European Union Agency for Law Enforcement Cooperation. "Online Jihadist

Propaganda: 2020 in Review". EU Publications Office. 2021. https://data.
europa.eu/doi/10.2813/169367. Last accessed 16 August 2023.

Fangen, Katrine. "An Observational Study of the Norwegian Far Right: Some
Reflections". In *Researching the Far Right: Theory, Method and Practice*. Eds Stephen D.
Ashe, Joel Busher, Graham Macklin and Aaron Winter. London: Routledge, 2020.
241–53.

Farrell, Tracie, Miriam Fernandez, Jakub Novotny and Harith Alani. "Exploring
Misogyny Across the Manosphere in Reddit". In *WebSci '19: Proceedings of the
10th ACM Conference on Web Science*. New York, NY: Association for Computing
Machinery, 2019. 87–96.

Fattah, Khaled, and K. M. Fierke. "A Clash of Emotions: The Politics of Humiliation
and Political Violence in the Middle East". *European Journal of International Relations*
vol. 15, no. 1 (2009): 67–93.

Feldman, Matthew. "Introduction". In *The EDL: Britain's 'New Far Right' Social Movement*.
Northampton: University of Northampton, 2011. 3–4.

———. "From Radical-Right Islamophobia to 'Cumulative Extremism'". Faith
Matters. 2012. https://tellmamauk.org/wp-content/uploads/2013/02/
islamophobia.pdf. Last accessed 7 August 2023.

Feldman, Matthew, and Paul Stocker. "The Post-Brexit Far-Right in Britain". In *Violent
Radicalisation & Far-Right Extremism in Europe*. Eds Aristotle Kallis, Sara Zeiger and
Bilgehan Öztürk. Ankara: SETA Publications, 2018. 123–72.

Fergusson, James. *Al-Britannia, My Country: A Journey Through Muslim Britain*. London:
Bantam Press, 2017.

Flood, Michael. "'Toxic Masculinity': What Does It Mean, Where Did It Come From
– and Is the Term Useful or Harmful?" The Conversation. 21 September 2022.
http://theconversation.com/toxic-masculinity-what-does-it-mean-where-did-
it-come-from-and-is-the-term-useful-or-harmful-189298. Last accessed 31 July
2023.

Fonseca, Claudia. "Philanderers, Cuckolds, and Wily Women: A Reexamination
of Gender Relations in a Brazilian Working-Class Neighborhood". *Men and
Masculinities* vol. 3, no. 3 (2001): 261–77.

For Britain. "For Britain Manifesto". 2017. https://d3n8a8pro7vhmx.cloudfront.
net/forbritain/pages/113/attachments/original/1519030879/Manfiesto_2.
pdf?1519030879. Last accessed 20 March 2018.

———. "For Britain Priorities". January 2019. https://www.forbritain.uk/
priorities. Last accessed 26 January 2019.

Ford, Robert, and Matthew J. Goodwin. "Angry White Men: Individual and Contextual
Predictors of Support for the British National Party". *Political Studies* vol. 58, no.
1 (2010): 1–25.

———. *Revolt on the Right: Explaining Support for the Radical Right in Britain*. Abingdon;
New York, NY: Routledge, 2014.

Forrest, Ray, and Ade Kearns. "Social Cohesion, Social Capital and the Neighbourhood".
Urban Studies vol. 38, no. 12 (2001): 2125–43.

Foster, Victoria, Michael Kimmel and Christine Skelton. "What About the Boys? An

Overview of the Debates". In *What About the Boys? Issues of Masculinity in Schools*. Eds Wayne Martino and Bob Meyenn. Buckingham; Philadelphia, PA: Open University Press, 2001.

Foucault, Michel. *Power/Knowledge: Selected Interviews and Other Writings, 1972–1977*. Ed. Colin Gordon. New York, NY: Vintage, 1980.

———. *The Foucault Reader: An Introduction to Foucault's Thought*. Ed. Paul Rabinow. London: Penguin, 1991.

Frankenberg, Ruth. *White Women, Race Matters: The Social Construction of Whiteness*. Minneapolis, MN: University of Minnesota Press, 1993.

Fransen, Jayda. "Statement from Jayda Fransen". http://jaydafransen.online/. Last accessed 26 January 2019.

———. "The Fake Right and The Whole Truth". Jayda Fransen Online. 28 July 2022. https://www.jaydafransen.online/the_fake_right_and_the_whole_truth. Last accessed 15 August 2022.

Gallaher, Carolyn. "Researching Repellent Groups: Some Methodological Considerations on How to Represent Militants, Radicals, and Other Belligerents". In *Surviving Field Research: Working in Violent and Difficult Situations*. Eds Chandra Lekha Sriram, John C. King, Julie A. Mertus, Olga Martin-Ortega and Johanna Herman. London: Routledge, 2009.

Garland, Jon, and James Treadwell. "'No Surrender to the Taliban': Football Hooliganism, Islamophobia and the Rise of the English Defence League". In *Papers from the British Criminology Conference* vol. 10 (2010): 19–35. https://www.britsoccrim.org/volume10/2010_Garland_Treadwell.pdf. Last accessed 11 August 2023.

Gartenstein-Ross, Daveed, and Laura Grossman. *Homegrown Terrorists in the US and UK: An Empirical Examination of the Radicalization Process*. Washington, DC: FDD Press, 2009.

Gattinara, Pietro Castelli. "Research Overview of Far Right Narratives". Radicalisation Awareness Network, 2016.

Gear Rich, Camille. "Marginal Whiteness". *California Law Review* vol. 98, no. 5 (2010): 1497–593.

Gentry, Caron. "The Relationship Between New Social Movement Theory and Terrorism Studies: The Role of Leadership, Membership, Ideology and Gender". *Terrorism and Political Violence* vol. 16, no. 2 (2004): 274–93.

Gentry, Caron E. *Disordered Violence: How Gender, Race and Heteronormativity Structure Terrorism*. Edinburgh: Edinburgh University Press, 2020.

———. "Misogynistic Terrorism: It Has Always Been Here". *Critical Studies on Terrorism* vol. 15, no. 1 (2022): 209–24.

Gentry, Caron E., and Laura Sjoberg. *Mothers, Monsters, Whores: Women's Violence in Global Politics*. New York, NY: Zed Books, 2007.

Gerami, Shahin. "Islamist Masculinity and Muslim Masculinities". In *Handbook of Studies on Men and Masculinities*. Eds Michael S. Kimmel, Jeff R. Hearn and Raewyn W. Connell. Thousand Oaks, CA; London: SAGE Publications, 2004. 448–56.

Giardini, Federica. "Public Affects Clues Towards a Political Practice of Singularity". *European Journal of Women's Studies* vol. 6, no. 2 (1999): 149–59.

Giddens, Anthony. *Modernity and Self-Identity: Self and Society in the Late Modern Age.* Stanford, CA: Stanford University Press, 1991.

Gill, Paul, and Emily Corner. "There and Back Again: The Study of Mental Disorder and Terrorist Involvement". *American Psychologist* vol. 72, no. 3 (2017): 231–41.

Giscard d'Estaing, Sophie. "Engaging Women in Countering Violent Extremism: Avoiding Instrumentalisation and Furthering Agency". *Gender & Development* vol. 25, no. 1 (2017): 103–18.

Giulianotti, Richard, and Gary Armstrong. "Avenues of Contestation: Football Hooligans Running and Ruling Urban Spaces". *Social Anthropology* vol. 10, no. 2 (2002): 211–38.

Glynn, Sarah. "Bengali Muslims: The New East End Radicals?" *Ethnic and Racial Studies* vol. 25, no. 6 (2002): 969–88.

Goffman, Erving. *Frame Analysis.* New York, NY: Harper and Row, 1974.

———. *The Presentation of Self in Everyday Life.* London: Penguin, 1990.

Goldstein, Joshua S. *War and Gender: How Gender Shapes the War System and Vice Versa.* Cambridge: Cambridge University Press, 2003.

Goodwin, Jeff. "The Libidinal Constitution of a High-Risk Social Movement: Affectual Ties and Solidarity in the Huk Rebellion, 1946 to 1954". *American Sociological Review* vol. 62, no. 1 (1997): 53–69.

Goodwin, Matthew. "The Roots of Extremism: The English Defence League and the Counter-Jihad Challenge". Chatham House. 2013. https://www.chathamhouse. org/sites/default/files/public/Research/Europe/0313bp_goodwin.pdf. Last accessed 28 July 2023.

Gowrinathan, Nimmi. "The Women of ISIS: Understanding and Combating Female Extremism". *Foreign Affairs.* 21 August 2014. http://www.foreignaffairs.com/ articles/141926/nimmi-gowrinathan/the-women-of-isis. Last accessed 16 August 2023.

———. *Radicalizing Her: Why Women Choose Violence.* London: Penguin Random House, 2022.

Gregory, Andy. "Who Is Behind GB News and What Is Channel's Agenda?" *The Independent.* 15 June 2021. https://www.independent.co.uk/news/uk/home-news/gb-news-channel-launch-andrew-neil-b1864268.html. Last accessed 13 August 2023.

Griffin, Roger. *The Nature of Fascism.* London: Psychology Press, 1991.

Groen, Janny and Annieke Kranenberg. *Women Warriors for Allah: An Islamist Network in the Netherlands.* Trans. Robert Naborn. Philadelphia, PA: University of Pennsylvania Press, 2010.

Gye, Hugo. "Outrage After Irish Bar in Luton Refuses to Serve People Wearing Poppies". *Daily Mail.* 9 November 2015. http://www.dailymail.co.uk/news/ article-3310209/Outrage-Irish-bar-refuses-serve-people-wearing-poppies.html. Last accessed 12 August 2023.

Haider, Syed. "The Shooting in Orlando, Terrorism or Toxic Masculinity (or Both?)". *Men and Masculinities* vol. 19, no. 5 (2016): 555–65.

Halberstam, Jack. *Female Masculinity*. Durham, NC: Duke University Press, 1998.

Hall, Steve. "Daubing the Drudges of Fury: Men, Violence and the Piety of the 'Hegemonic Masculinity' Thesis". *Theoretical Criminology* vol. 6, no. 1 (2002): 35–61.

Hamm, Mark. "Apocalyptic Violence: The Seduction of Terrorist Subcultures". *Theoretical Criminology* vol. 8, no. 3 (2004): 323–39.

Harding, Sandra. "Introduction: Is There a Feminist Method?". In *Feminism & Methodology*. Ed. Sandra Harding. Bloomington, IN: Indiana University Press, 1987. 1–14.

Hardisty, Jean, ed. *Kitchen Table Backlash: The Antifeminist Women's Movement*. Boulder, CO: Westview, 2001.

Harteveld, Eelco, and Elisabeth Ivarsflaten. "Why Women Avoid the Radical Right: Internalized Norms and Party Reputations". *British Journal of Political Science* vol. 48, no. 2 (2016): 1–16.

Haute, Emilie van, and Teun Pauwels. "Caught Between Mainstreaming and Radicalisation: Tensions Inside the Populist Vlaams Belang in Belgium". EUROPP (blog). 11 January 2017. http://blogs.lse.ac.uk/europpblog/2017/01/11/tensions-inside-vlaams-belang-belgium/. Last accessed 15 August 2023.

Heath-Kelly, Charlotte. "Counter-Terrorism and the Counterfactual: Producing the 'Radicalisation' Discourse and the UK PREVENT Strategy". *The British Journal of Politics & International Relations* vol. 15, no. 3 (2013): 394–415.

Hegghammer, Thomas. *Jihad in Saudi Arabia: Violence and Pan-Islamism since 1979*. Cambridge; New York, NY: Cambridge University Press, 2011.

———. "Introduction: What Is Jihadi Culture and Why Should We Study It?". In *Jihadi Culture: The Art and Social Practices of Militant Islamists*. Ed. Thomas Hegghammer. Cambridge: Cambridge University Press, 2017. 1–21.

———. "Non-Military Practices in Jihadi Groups". In *Jihadi Culture: The Art and Social Practices of Militant Islamists*. Ed. Thomas Hegghammer. Cambridge: Cambridge University Press, 2017. 171–220.

Hemmings, Clare. "Invoking Affect". *Cultural Studies* vol. 19, no. 5 (2005): 548–67.

Hewitt, Roger. *White Backlash and the Politics of Multiculturalism*. Cambridge: Cambridge University Press, 2005.

Higate, Paul. "'Cowboys and Professionals': The Politics of Identity Work in the Private and Military Security Company". *Millennium – Journal of International Studies* vol. 40, no. 2 (2012): 321–41.

HM Government. "CONTEST: The United Kingdom's Strategy for Countering Terrorism". The Home Office, 2009.

———. "CONTEST: The United Kingdom's Strategy for Countering Terrorism Annual Report 2012". Home Office. March 2013. https://www.gov.uk/government/uploads/system/uploads/attachment_data/file/170644/28307_Cm_8583_v0_20.pdf. Last accessed 26 July 2023.

———. "Counter-Extremism Strategy". 19 October 2015. https://www.gov.uk/government/publications/counter-extremism-strategy. Last accessed 26 July 2023.

―――. "CONTEST 2023". July 2023. https://assets.publishing.service.gov. uk/government/uploads/system/uploads/attachment_data/file/1171084/ CONTEST_2023.pdf. Last accessed 26 July 2023.

HM Inspector of Prisons. "Muslim Prisoners' Experiences: A Thematic Review". HM Government. 2010. https://www.justiceinspectorates.gov.uk/hmiprisons/ wp-content/uploads/sites/4/2014/04/Muslim_prisoners_2010_rps.pdf. Last accessed 16 August 2023.

Hoffman, Bruce. *Inside Terrorism*. New York, NY: Columbia University Press, 2006.

Hoffman, Bruce, Jacob Ware and Ezra Shapiro. "Assessing the Threat of Incel Violence". *Studies in Conflict & Terrorism* vol. 43, no. 7 (2020): 565–87.

Holbrook, Donald, and Max Taylor. "Introduction". In *Extreme Right Wing Political Violence and Terrorism*. Eds Donald Holbrook, Max Taylor and P. M. Currie. London; New York, NY: Bloomsbury, 2013. 1–13.

Holmes, Mary. "The Emotionalization of Reflexivity". *Sociology* vol. 44, no. 1 (2010): 139–54.

Home Affairs Select Committee. "Radicalisation: The Counter-Narrative and Identifying the Tipping Point". House of Commons Home Affairs Select Committee. August 2016. http://www.publications.parliament.uk/pa/cm201617/cmselect/ cmhaff/135/135.pdf. Last accessed 16 August 2023.

Home Office. "Prevent Strategy". 2011. https://www.gov.uk/government/uploads/ system/uploads/attachment_data/file/97976/prevent-strategy-review.pdf. Last accessed 26 July 2023.

―――. "CONTEST: The United Kingdom's Strategy for Countering Terrorism". London: The Home Office. June 2018. https://assets.publishing.service.gov.uk/ government/uploads/system/uploads/attachment_data/file/716907/140618_ CCS207_CCS0218929798-1_CONTEST_3.0_WEB.pdf. Last accessed 26 July 2023.

―――. "Home | ENOUGH". https://enough.campaign.gov.uk/. Last accessed 16 August 2023.

Hooper, Charlotte. *Manly States: Masculinities, International Relations, and Gender Politics*. New York, NY: Columbia University Press, 2001.

Hope Not Hate. "Al-Muhajiroun Network". The Hate Files. Hope Not Hate, 2013. http://www.hopenothate.org.uk/research/the-hate-files/al-muhajiroun-network/. Last accessed 15 August 2023.

―――. "International Counter-Jihad Organisations". 11 January 2018. https:// hopenothate.org.uk/2018/01/11/what-is-counter-jihadism/. Last accessed 7 August 2023.

―――. "State of Hate 2019: People Vs the Elite?". February 2019. https:// hopenothate.org.uk/wp-content/uploads/2019/02/state-of-hate-2019-final-1. pdf. Last accessed 13 August 2023.

―――. "State of Hate 2022: On the March Again". 9 March 2022. https:// hopenothate.org.uk/2022/03/09/state-of-hate-2022-on-the-march-again/. Last accessed 27 July 2023.

―――. "State of Hate Report 2023". February 2023. https://hopenothate.org.uk/

BIBLIOGRAPHY

wp-content/uploads/2023/02/state-of-hate-2023-v7-1.pdf. Last accessed 23 July 2023.

—————. "Briefing: National Action". https://hopenothate.org.uk/research-old/investigations/briefing-national-action/. Last accessed 11 August 2023.

—————. "Britain First: Army of the Right". https://hopenothate.org.uk/wp-content/uploads/2017/11/Britain-First-Army-of-the-Right.pdf. Last accessed 31 July 2023.

Hopkins, Peter. *The Issue of Masculine Identities for British Muslims After 9/11: A Social Analysis*. Lewiston, NY: Edwin Mellen Press Ltd, 2008.

Hopkins, Steven. "Tommy Robinson Claims He Was Paid Thousands to Leave EDL". HuffPost UK. 4 December 2015. http://www.huffingtonpost.co.uk/2015/12/03/tommy-robinson-claims-quilliam-paid-him-to-leave-edl_n_8710834.html. Last accessed 13 August 2023.

Horgan, John. *The Psychology of Terrorism*. London; New York, NY: Routledge, 2002.

—————. "The Case for First Hand Research". In *Research on Terrorism: Trends, Achievements and Failures*. Ed. Andrew Silke. London; Portland, OR: Routledge, 2004. 30–57.

—————. "Discussion Point: The End of Radicalization?". START: National Consortium for the Study of Terrorism and Responses to Terrorism. 28 September 2012. http://www.start.umd.edu/news/discussion-point-end-radicalization. Last accessed 31 July 2023.

—————. "Interviewing the Terrorists: Reflections on Fieldwork and Implications for Psychological Research". *Behavioral Sciences of Terrorism and Political Aggression* vol. 4, no. 3 (2012): 195–211.

Horgan, John G., Max Taylor, Mia Bloom and Charlie Winter. "From Cubs to Lions: A Six Stage Model of Child Socialization into the Islamic State". *Studies in Conflict & Terrorism* vol. 40, no. 7 (2017): 645–64.

Hosein, Imran Nazar. "Ten Major Signs of the Last Day – Has One Just Occurred?". 10 Rajab 1428. http://www.imranhosein.org/articles/signs-of-the-last-day/76-ten-major-signs-of-the-last-day-has-one-just-occurred.html. Last accessed 3 August 2017.

Huckerby, Jayne. "Women and Preventing Violent Extremism: The U.S. and U.K. Experiences". NYU School of Law, Center for Human Rights and Global Justice. 2011. http://chrgj.org/wp-content/uploads/2012/10/Women-and-Violent-Extremism-The-US-and-UK-Experiences.pdf. Last accessed 11 August 2023.

—————. "Women, Gender and the U.K. Government's CVE Efforts: Looking Back and Forward". In *A Man's World? Exploring the Roles of Women in Countering Terrorism and Violent Extremism*. Eds Naureen Chowdhury Fink, Sara Zeiger and Rafia Bhulai. Hedayah and The Global Center on Cooperative Security, 2016. 76–99.

—————. "In Harm's Way: Gender and Human Rights in National Security". *Duke Journal of Gender Law & Policy* vol. 27, no. 1 (2020): 179–202.

Hugman, Richard, Eileen Pittaway and Linda Bartolomei. "When 'Do No Harm' Is Not Enough: The Ethics of Research with Refugees and Other Vulnerable Groups". *The British Journal of Social Work* vol. 41, no. 7 (2011): 1271–87.

Hussain, Ghaffar, and Erin Marie Saltman. "Jihad Trending: A Comprehensive Analysis of Online Extremism and How to Counter It". The Quilliam Foundation. 2014. https://preventviolentextremism.info/sites/default/files/Jihad%20 Trending-%20A%20Comprehensive%20Analysis%20of%20Online%20 Extremism%20and%20How%20to%20Counter%20it.pdf. Last accessed 16 August 2023.

Hussain, Yasmin, and Paul Bagguley. "Reflexive Ethnicities: Crisis, Diversity and Re-Composition". *Sociological Research Online* vol. 20, no. 3 (2015): 18.

Hutchings, Kimberly. "Making Sense of Masculinity and War". *Men and Masculinities* vol. 10, no. 4 (2007): 389–404.

Hutton, Alice. "Don't Vote, Radical Cleric Anjem Choudary Tells Muslims". *The Times.* 3 April 2015. https://www.thetimes.co.uk/article/dont-vote-radical-cleric-anjem-choudary-tells-muslims-vfsp57z5jzh. Last accessed 16 August 2023.

Hymas, Charles. "Efforts to Combat Extremism Failing Because of Way Government Has Defined It, Commissioner Says". *The Telegraph.* 6 October 2019. https://www.telegraph.co.uk/politics/2019/10/06/efforts-combat-terrorism-failing-governments-definition-extremism/. Last accessed 27 July 2023.

ICHOR Trust Team. "I.C.H.O.R. Trust Home". http://www.ichortrust.co.uk/index.php. Last accessed 17 April 2017.

Ignazi, Piero. "The Silent Counter-Revolution". *European Journal of Political Research* vol. 22, no. 1 (1992): 3–34.

Ilan, Jonathan, and Sveinung Sandberg. "How 'Gangsters' Become Jihadists: Bourdieu, Criminology and the Crime-Terrorism Nexus". *European Journal of Criminology* vol. 16, no. 3 (2019): 278–94.

Ilyas, Mohammed. "Islamist Groups in the UK and Recruitment". *Journal of Terrorism Research* vol. 4, no. 2 (2013). http://ojs.st-andrews.ac.uk/index.php/jtr/article/view/631. Last accessed 16 August 2023.

———. "The 'Al-Muhajiroun Brand' of Islamism". *Interface: A Journal for and about Social Movements* vol. 6, no. 1 (2014): 441–53.

Ingram, Nicola. "Working-Class Boys, Educational Success and the Misrecognition of Working-Class Culture". *British Journal of Sociology of Education* vol. 30, no. 4 (2009): 421–34.

Inhorn, Marcia. *The New Arab Man.* Princeton, NJ: Princeton University Press, 2012.

Jackson, Paul, Matthew Feldman, Mark Pitchford and Trevor Preston. *The EDL: Britain's 'New Far Right' Social Movement.* Northampton: University of Northampton, 2011.

Jacques, Karen, and Paul J. Taylor. "Female Terrorism: A Review". *Terrorism and Political Violence* vol. 21, no. 3 (2009): 499–515.

James, Osamudia R. "White Like Me: The Negative Impact of the Diversity Rationale on White Identity Formation". *New York University Law Review* vol. 89, no. 2 (2014): 425–512.

Jasper, James M. "The Emotions of Protest: Affective and Reactive Emotions in and Around Social Movements". *Sociological Forum* vol. 13, no. 3 (1998): 397–424.

Jayda Fransen Online. https://www.jaydafransen.online/. Last accessed 15 August 2023.

"JAYDA FRANSEN EPIC RANT ON LONDON TERROR ATTACK!". YouTube.

2017. https://www.youtube.com/watch?v=flX11KVNj5Y. Last accessed 14 August 2023.

Jensen, Sune Qvotrup, and Jeppe Fuglsang Larsen. "Sociological Perspectives on Islamist Radicalization – Bridging the Micro/Macro Gap". *European Journal of Criminology* vol. 18, no. 3 (2019): 426–43.

Jereza, Rae. "Inheritance as Alternative to Ethnographic Empathy with the Far Right". C-REX – Center for Research on Extremism. RightNow! (blog). November 2022. https://www.sv.uio.no/c-rex/english/news-and-events/right-now/2022/inheritance-as-alternative-to-ethnographic-empathy.html. Last accessed 3 August 2023.

Jewkes, Rachel, Robert Morrell, Jeff Hearn, Emma Lundqvist, David Blackbeard, Graham Lindegger, Michael Quayle, Yandisa Sikweyiya and Lucas Gottzén. "Hegemonic Masculinity: Combining Theory and Practice in Gender Interventions". *Culture, Health & Sexuality* vol. 17, no. sup2 (2015): 112–27.

Jones, Adam. "Does 'Gender' Make the World Go Round? Feminist Critiques of International Relations". *Review of International Studies* vol. 22, no. 4 (1996): 405–29.

Jones, Owen. *Chavs: The Demonization of the Working Class*. London: Verso Books, 2012.

Juris, Jeffrey S. "Performing Politics: Image, Embodiment, and Affective Solidarity During Anti-Corporate Globalization Protests". *Ethnography* vol. 9, no. 1 (2008): 61–97.

Kaiser, Susanne. *Political Masculinity: How Incels, Fundamentalists and Authoritarians Mobilise for Patriarchy*. Trans. Valentine A. Pakis. Cambridge; Medford, MA: Polity Press, 2022.

Kalra, Virinder S., and Nisha Kapoor. "Interrogating Segregation, Integration and the Community Cohesion Agenda". *Journal of Ethnic and Migration Studies* vol. 35, no. 9 (2009): 1397–415.

Kandiyoti, Deniz. "Bargaining with Patriarchy". *Gender and Society* vol. 2, no. 3 (1988): 274–90.

Karner, Christian. *Ethnicity and Everyday Life*. London; New York, NY: Routledge, 2007.

Katz, Jack. *Seductions Of Crime: Moral and Sensual Attractions in Doing Evil*. New York, NY: Basic Books, 1988.

Kellen, Konrad. "Origins of Terrorism: Psychologies, Ideologies, Theologies, States of Mind". In *Origins of Terrorism: Psychologies, Ideologies, Theologies, States of Mind*. Eds Walter Reich and Walter Laquer. Washington, DC; Baltimore, MD; London: Woodrow Wilson Center Press, 1998. 43–58.

Kennedy, Dominic. "Hate Preacher Abu Haleema Flees After Far-Right Fanatic Tommy Robinson Finds Him". *The Times*. 7 June 2017. https://www.thetimes.co.uk/article/hate-preacher-abu-haleema-flees-after-far-right-fanatic-tommy-robinson-finds-him-bjh0csdbf. Last accessed 16 August 2023.

Kenney, Michael. *The Islamic State in Britain: Radicalization and Resilience in an Activist Network*. Cambridge: Cambridge University Press, 2018.

Kenney, Michael, Stephen Coulthart and Dominick Wright. "Structure and

Performance in a Violent Extremist Network: The Small-World Solution". *Journal of Conflict Resolution* vol. 61, no. 10 (2016): 2208–34.

Khan, Sara, and Tony McMahon. *The Battle for British Islam: Reclaiming Muslim Identity from Extremism.* London: Saqi Books, 2016.

Khelghat-Doost, Hamoon. "The Strategic Logic of Women in Jihadi Organizations". *Studies in Conflict & Terrorism* vol. 42, no. 10 (2019): 853–77.

Khosrokhavar, Farhad. "Terrorism in Europe". Centre for Studies in Islamism and Radicalisation at the Department of Political Science, University of Aarhus. 2008. https://ps.au.dk/fileadmin/site_files/filer_statskundskab/subsites/cir/pdf-filer/khosrokhavar.pdf. Last accessed 16 August 2023.

Kimmel, Michael. "Integrating Men into the Curriculum". *Duke Journal of Gender Law & Policy* vol. 4, no. 1 (1997): 181–96.

———. "Racism as Adolescent Male Rite of Passage: Ex-Nazis in Scandinavia". *Journal of Contemporary Ethnography* vol. 36, no. 2 (2007): 202–18.

———. *Angry White Men: American Masculinity at the End of an Era.* New York, NY: Bold Type Books, 2017.

———. *Healing from Hate: How Young Men Get Into—and Out of—Violent Extremism.* Oakland, CA: University of California Press, 2018.

Kimmel, Michael S. "Globalization and Its Mal(e)Contents: The Gendered Moral and Political Economy of Terrorism". *International Sociology* vol. 18, no. 3 (2003): 603–20.

Kimmel, Michael, and Abby L. Ferber. "'White Men Are This Nation': Right-Wing Militias and the Restoration of Rural American Masculinity" vol. 65, no. 4 (2000): 582–604.

Kimmel, Michael S., Jeff R. Hearn and Raewyn W. Connell, eds. *Handbook of Studies on Men and Masculinities.* Thousand Oaks, CA; London: SAGE Publications, 2004.

King, Anthony. "Thinking with Bourdieu Against Bourdieu: A 'Practical' Critique of the Habitus". *Sociological Theory* vol. 18, no. 3 (2000): 417–33.

King, Michael, and Donald M. Taylor. "The Radicalization of Homegrown Jihadists: A Review of Theoretical Models and Social Psychological Evidence". *Terrorism and Political Violence* vol. 23, no. 4 (2011): 602–22.

Kirby, Paul. "Refusing to Be a Man? Men's Responsibility for War Rape and the Problem of Social Structures in Feminist and Gender Theory". *Men and Masculinities* vol. 16, no. 1 (2013): 93–114.

Kirby, Paul, and Marsha Henry. "Rethinking Masculinity and Practices of Violence in Conflict Settings". *International Feminist Journal of Politics* vol. 14, no. 4 (2012): 115–49.

Klausen, Jytte, Eliane Tschaen Barbieri, Aaron Reichlin-Melnick and Aaron Y. Zelin. "The YouTube Jihadists: A Social Network Analysis of Al-Muhajiroun's Propaganda Campaign". *Perspectives on Terrorism* vol. 6, no. 1 (2012): 36–53.

Klausen, Jytte, Rosanne Libretti, Benjamin W. K. Hung and Anura P. Jayasumana. "Radicalization Trajectories: An Evidence-Based Computational Approach to Dynamic Risk Assessment of 'Homegrown' Jihadists". *Studies in Conflict & Terrorism* vol. 43, no. 7 (2020): 588–615.

Kontos, Louis, and David Brotherton. *Encyclopedia of Gangs*. Westport, CT; Oxford: Greenwood Press, 2008.

Kronsell, Annica. "Gendered Practices in Institutions of Hegemonic Masculinity". *International Feminist Journal of Politics* vol. 7, no. 2 (2005): 280–98.

Kundnani, Arun. *Spooked! How Not to Prevent Violent Extremism*. London: Institute of Race Relations, 2009.

———. "Radicalisation: The Journey of a Concept". *Race & Class* vol. 54, no. 2 (2012): 3–25.

Kupers, Terry A. "Toxic Masculinity as a Barrier to Mental Health Treatment in Prison". *Journal of Clinical Psychology* vol. 61, no. 6 (2005): 713–24.

Kyle, Jordan, and Limor Gultchin. "Populists in Power Around the World". Tony Blair Institute for Global Change. November 2018. https://institute.global/policy/populists-power-around-world. Last accessed 6 August 2023.

Lahoud, Nelly. "The Neglected Sex: The Jihadis' Exclusion of Women From Jihad". *Terrorism and Political Violence* vol. 26, no. 5 (2014): 780–802.

———. "Can Women Be Soldiers of the Islamic State?". *Survival* vol. 59, no. 1 (2017): 61–78.

———. "Empowerment or Subjugation: An Analysis of ISIL's Gendered Messaging". UN Women. 2018. https://arabstates.unwomen.org/sites/default/files/Field%20Office%20Arab%20States/Attachments/Publications/Lahoud-Fin-Web-rev.pdf. Last accessed 2 August 2023.

Lammy, David. "Islamists, Gangs, the EDL – All Target Alienated Young Men". *The Guardian*. 24 May 2013. http://www.theguardian.com/uk/2013/may/24/islamists-gangs-edl-target-young-men. Last accessed 31 July 2023.

Lange, Sarah L. de, and Liza M. Mügge. "Gender and Right-Wing Populism in the Low Countries: Ideological Variations across Parties and Time". *Patterns of Prejudice* vol. 49, no. 1–2 (2015): 61–80.

Lash, Scott. "Reflexive Modernization: The Aesthetic Dimension". *Theory, Culture & Society* vol. 10, no. 1 (1993): 1–23.

Lawler, Stephanie. "Disgusted Subjects: The Making of Middle-Class Identities". *The Sociological Review* vol. 53, no. 3 (2005): 429–46.

Leek, Cliff, and Michael Kimmel. "Conceptualizing Intersectionality in Superordination: Masculinities, Whitenesses, and Dominant Classes". In *Routledge International Handbook of Race, Class, and Gender*. Ed. Shirley A. Jackson. Oxford; New York, NY: Routledge, 2014. 3–9.

Lefebvre, Henri. *The Production of Space*. Trans. Donald Nicholson-Smith. Malden, MA: Wiley-Blackwell, 1991.

Lohlker, Rüdiger. "Jihadi Masculinities: Another Masculinity in Crisis". In *Jihadi Thought and Ideology*. Eds Rüdiger Lohlker and Tamara Abu-Hamdeh. Berlin: Logos, 2013. 138–64.

Lowles, Nick. "Racist Terrorism on Rise, Businessman Bankrolls 'Street Army'". Turkish Forum English (blog). 19 November 2009. https://www.turkishnews.com/en/content/2009/11/19/racist-terrorism-on-rise-businessman-bankrolls-%e2%80%98street-army%e2%80%99/. Last accessed 14 August 2023.

————. "State of Hate 2018". Hope Not Hate. February 2018. https://www. hopenothate.org.uk/research/state-of-hate-2018/overview/. Last accessed 11 August 2023.

Lugones, María C., and Elizabeth V. Spelman. "Have We Got a Theory for You! Feminist Theory, Cultural Imperialism and the Demand for 'the Woman's Voice'". *Women's Studies International Forum* vol. 6, no. 6 (1983): 573–81.

Mac an Ghaill, Mairtin, and Chris Haywood. "British-Born Pakistani and Bangladeshi Young Men: Exploring Unstable Concepts of Muslim, Islamophobia and Racialization". *Critical Sociology* vol. 41, no. 1 (2015): 97–114.

Macey, Marie. "Class, Gender and Religious Influences on Changing Patterns of Pakistani Muslim Male Violence in Bradford". *Ethnic and Racial Studies* vol. 22, no. 5 (1999): 845–66.

MacInnes, John. "The Crisis of Masculinity and the Politics of Identity". In *The Masculinities Reader*. Eds Stephen M. Whitehead and Frank J. Barrett. Cambridge: Polity Press, 2001. 311–29.

MacKay, Finn. *Female Masculinities and the Gender Wars: The Politics of Sex*. London: IB Tauris Bloomsbury, 2021.

MacKinnon, Catharine A. "Feminism, Marxism, Method, and the State: An Agenda for Theory". *Feminist Theory* vol. 7, no. 3 (1982): 515–44.

Macklin, Graham, and Joel Busher. "The Missing Spirals of Violence: Four Waves of Movement–Countermovement Contest in Post-War Britain". *Behavioral Sciences of Terrorism and Political Aggression* vol. 7, no. 1 (2015): 53–68.

Maddox, David. "'Defund the BBC!' New Prime Minister Told to Abolish Licence Fee as Fury Grows at Broadcaster". *Daily Express*. 14 July 2022. https://www.express. co.uk/news/politics/1639932/BBC-licence-fee-Tory-leadership-hopefuls-campaign-group-defund-update. Last accessed 13 August 2023.

Maher, Shiraz. *Salafi-Jihadism: The History of an Idea*. London: C. Hurst & Co., 2016.

Malik, Maleiha. "'The Branch on Which We Sit': Multiculturalism, Minority Women and Family Law". In *Feminist Perspectives on Family Law*. Eds Alison Diduck and Katherine O'Donovan. Abingdon; New York, NY: Routledge-Cavendish, 2006. 211–31.

Malthaner, Stefan. "Radicalization: The Evolution of an Analytical Paradigm". *European Journal of Sociology / Archives Européennes de Sociologie* vol. 58, no. 3 (2017): 369–401.

Malthaner, Stefan, and Peter Waldmann. "The Radical Milieu: Conceptualizing the Supportive Social Environment of Terrorist Groups". *Studies in Conflict & Terrorism* vol. 37, no. 12 (2014): 979–98.

Mandel, David R. "Radicalisation – What Does It Mean?" In *Home-Grown Terrorism: Understanding and Addressing the Root Causes of Radicalisation among Groups with an Immigrant Heritage in Europe*. Eds Thomas M. Pick, Anne Speckhard and Beatrice Jacuch, 2009.

Mann, Arshy. "The Misogynist Ideology Behind Toronto's Incel Terror Attack Must Be Confronted". Xtra. 26 April 2018. https://www.dailyxtra.com/the-misogynist-ideology-behind-torontos-incel-terror-attack-must-be-confronted-86222. Last accessed 8 August 2023.

Manne, Kate. *Down Girl: The Logic of Misogyny*. London: Penguin, 2019.

March, Luke. "Contemporary Far Left Parties in Europe: From Marxism to the Mainstream?". Friedrich Ebert Stiftung. 2009. https://library.fes.de/pdf-files/id/ipa/05818.pdf. Last accessed 27 July 2023.

Margolin, Devorah. "Neither Feminists nor Victims: How Women's Agency Has Shaped Palestinian Violence". Tony Blair Institute for Global Change. 2018. https://institute.global/policy/neither-feminists-nor-victims-how-womens-agency-has-shaped-palestinian-violence. Last accessed 1 August 2023.

Marston, Sallie A. "The Social Construction of Scale". *Progress in Human Geography* vol. 24, no. 2 (2000): 219–42.

Matfess, Hilary. *Women and the War on Boko Haram: Wives, Weapons, Witnesses*. London: Zed Books, 2017.

Mattheis, Ashley. "Shieldmaidens of Whiteness: (Alt) Maternalism and Women Recruiting for the Far/Alt-Right". *Journal for Deradicalization* no. 17 (2018): 128–62.

———. "Women and the Alt-Right". VOX – Pol Conference, Amsterdam. 2018.

Mattheis, Ashley A, and Charlie Winter. "'The Greatness of Her Position': Comparing Identitarian and Jihadi Discourses on Women". International Centre for the Study of Radicalisation and Political Violence. 2019. https://icsr.info/wp-content/uploads/2019/05/ICSR-Report-'The-Greatness-of-Her-Position'-Comparing-Identitarian-and-Jihadi-Discourses-on-Women.pdf. Last accessed 29 July 2023.

McClintock, Anne. "'No Longer in a Future Heaven': Woman and Nationalism in South Africa". *Transition* vol. 51 (1991): 104–23.

McDonald, Hannah. "Hate Preacher Anjem Choudary Arrested on Suspicion of Terrorism". Mail Online. 18 July 2023. https://www.dailymail.co.uk/news/article-12308877/Hate-preacher-Anjem-Choudary-arrested-suspicion-terrorism-offences-dawn-police-raid-home.html. Last accessed 27 July 2023.

McDowell, Linda. *Redundant Masculinities? Employment Change and White Working-Class Youth*. New York, NY: John Wiley & Sons, 2011.

McGhee, Derek. *The End of Multiculturalism? Terrorism, Integration and Human Rights*. Maidenhead: Open University Press, 2008.

McIntosh, Peggy. "White Privilege and Male Privilege: A Personal Account of Coming to See Correspondences Through Work in Women's Studies (1988)". In *On Privilege, Fraudulence, and Teaching as Learning: Selected Essays 1981–2019*. New York, NY: Routledge, 2019. 17–28.

———. "White Privilege: Unpacking the Invisible Knapsack (1989)". In *On Privilege, Fraudulence, and Teaching as Learning: Selected Essays 1981–2019*. New York, NY: Routledge, 2019. 29–34.

McLaughlin, Peter, and Tommy Robinson. *Mohammed's Koran: Why Muslims Kill for Islam*. Peter McLaughlin, 2017.

McVeigh, Stephen, and Nicola Cooper. "Introduction". In *Men After War*. Eds Stephen McVeigh and Nicola Cooper. London: Routledge, 2013. 1–17.

Meadowcroft, John, and Elizabeth A. Morrow. "Violence, Self-Worth, Solidarity and

Stigma: How a Dissident, Far-Right Group Solves the Collective Action Problem". *Political Studies* vol. 65, no. 2 (2017): 373–90.

Mearns, Dave, Brian Thorne and John McLeod. *Person-Centred Counselling in Action*. London: SAGE Publications, 2013.

Mehta, Akanksha. "The Aesthetics of 'Everyday' Violence: Narratives of Violence and Hindu Right-Wing Women". *Critical Studies on Terrorism* vol. 8, no. 3 (2015): 416–38.

Meier, Anna A. "The Idea of Terror: Institutional Reproduction in Government Responses to Political Violence". *International Studies Quarterly* vol. 64, no. 3 (2020): 499–509.

Meleagrou-Hitchens, Alexander, and Hans Brun. "A Neo-Nationalist Network: The English Defence League and Europe's Counter-Jihad Movement". London: International Centre for the Study of Radicalisation and Political Violence, 2013. https://www.diva-portal.org/smash/get/diva2:1235939/FULLTEXT01.pdf. Last accessed 7 August 2023.

Memmi, Albert. *Racism*. Minneapolis, MN: University of Minnesota Press, 1999.

Messerschmidt, James W. *Masculinities and Crime: Critique and Reconceptualization of Theory*. Lanham, MD: Rowman & Littlefield, 1993.

———. "Becoming 'Real Men': Adolescent Masculinity Challenges and Sexual Violence". *Men and Masculinities* vol. 2, no. 3 (2000): 286–307.

Messerschmidt, James W., and Achim Rohde. "Osama Bin Laden and His Jihadist Global Hegemonic Masculinity". *Gender & Society* vol. 32, no. 5 (2018): 663–85.

Michel, Sonya. "Maternalism and Beyond". In *Maternalism Reconsidered: Motherhood, Welfare and Social Policy in the Twentieth Century*. Eds Marian Van Der Klein, Rebecca Jo Plant and Nichole Sanders. New York, NY: Berghahn Books, 2012.

Miller, Jody. "The Strengths and Limits of 'Doing Gender' for Understanding Street Crime". *Theoretical Criminology* vol. 6, no. 4 (2002): 433–60.

Miller, William Ian. *The Anatomy of Disgust*. Cambridge, MA: Harvard University Press, 1997.

Miller-Idriss, Cynthia. *The Extreme Gone Mainstream: Commercialization and Far Right Youth Culture in Germany*. Princeton, NJ: Princeton University Press, 2017.

Modleski, Tania. *Feminism Without Women: Culture and Criticism in a 'Postfeminist' Age*. New York, NY: Routledge, 1991.

Modood, Tariq. "British Asian Muslims and the Rushdie Affair". *"Race", Culture and Difference*. Eds James Donald and Au Rattansi. London: SAGE Publications, 1992. 260–77.

———. "A Defence of Multiculturalism". *Soundings* vol. 29, no. 29 (2005): 62–71.

Moghadam, Assaf. "Motives for Martyrdom: Al-Qaida, Salafi Jihad, and the Spread of Suicide Attacks". *International Security* vol. 33, no. 3 (2008): 46–78.

Moghaddam, Fathali M. "The Staircase to Terrorism: A Psychological Exploration". *American Psychologist* vol. 60, no. 2 (2005): 161–69.

Mohanty, Chandra T., and Satya P. Mohanty. "Contradictions of Colonialism". *Women's Review of Books* (1990): 19–21.

Mondon, Aurelien, and Aaron Winter. *Reactionary Democracy: How Racism and the Populist Far Right Became Mainstream.* London: Verso Books, 2020.

Morrison, John, Andrew Silke and Eke Bont. "The Development of the Framework for Research Ethics in Terrorism Studies (FRETS)". *Terrorism and Political Violence* vol. 33, no. 2 (2021): 271–89.

Mudde, Cas. "Right-Wing Extremism Analyzed: A Comparative Analysis of the Ideologies of Three Alleged Right-Wing Extremist Parties (NPD, NDP, CP'86)". *European Journal of Political Research* vol. 27, no. 2 (1995): 203–24.

———. "The War of Words Defining the Extreme Right Party Family". *West European Politics* vol. 19, no. 2 (1996): 225–48.

Mullins, Christopher. *Holding Your Square: Masculinities, Streetlife and Violence.* Cullompton: Willan, 2006.

Murphy, Paul Austin. "Counter-Jihad: Beyond The EDL: The EDL's Tommy Robinson in Amsterdam [Video]". 2010. http://theenglishdefenceleagueextra.blogspot. co.uk/2010/10/edls-tommy-robinson-in-amsterdam-video.html. Last accessed 2 July 2015.

Muslim Council of Britain. "Finsbury Park Terror Attack: Five Years On". 18 June 2022. https://mcb.org.uk/finsbury-park-terror-attack-five-years-on/. Last accessed 13 August 2023.

Myles, John. "From Habitus to Mouth: Language and Class in Bourdieu's Sociology of Language". *Theory and Society* vol. 28, no. 6 (1999): 879–901.

Mythen, Gabe, Sandra Walklate, and Fatima Khan. "'I'm a Muslim, but I'm Not a Terrorist': Victimization, Risky Identities and the Performance of Safety". *British Journal of Criminology* vol. 49, no. 6 (2009): 736–54.

Nagel, Joane. "Masculinity and Nationalism: Gender and Sexuality in the Making of Nations". *Ethnic and Racial Studies* vol. 21, no. 2 (1998): 242–69.

Naraghi-Anderlini, Sanam. "Challenging Conventional Wisdom, Transforming Current Practices: A Gendered Lens on PVE". Berghof Foundation. May 2018. https://berghof-foundation.org/library/challenging-conventional-wisdom-transforming-current-practices-a-gendered-lens-on-pve. Last accessed 31 July 2023.

Narayan, Kirin. "How Native Is a 'Native' Anthropologist?". *American Anthropologist* vol. 95, no. 3 (1993): 671–86.

Nayak, Anoop. "White Lives". In *Racialization: Studies in Theory and Practice.* Eds Karim Murjil and John Solomos. Oxford: Oxford University Press, 2005.

———. "After Race: Ethnography, Race and Post-Race Theory". *Ethnic and Racial Studies* vol. 29, no. 3 (2006): 411–30.

———. "Displaced Masculinities: Chavs, Youth and Class in the Post-Industrial City". *Sociology* vol. 40, no. 5 (2006): 813–31.

Nesser, Petter. *Islamist Terrorism in Europe: A History.* London: C. Hurst & Co., 2016.

Neumann, Peter, and Scott Kleinmann. "How Rigorous Is Radicalization Research?". *Democracy and Security* vol. 9, no. 4 (2013): 360–82.

Neumann, Peter R. "Chapter Two: Recruitment Grounds". *The Adelphi Papers* vol. 48, no. 399 (2008): 21–30.

————. "The Trouble with Radicalization". *International Affairs* vol. 89, no. 4 (2013): 873–93.

Nguyen, Athena. "Patriarchy, Power, and Female Masculinity". *Journal of Homosexuality* vol. 55, no. 4 (2008): 665–83.

O'Driscoll, Sean. "Ukip Reject Anne Marie Waters Founds Own Far-Right Party". *The Times.* 10 October 2017. https://www.thetimes.co.uk/article/ukip-reject-anne-marie-waters-founds-own-far-right-party-95wmr6wrh. Last accessed 31 July 2023.

OSCE. "Women and Terrorist Radicalization". 2011. https://www.osce.org/files/f/documents/4/a/99919.pdf. Last accessed 27 July 2023.

Ouzgane, Lahoucine, ed. *Islamic Masculinities.* London: Bloomsbury, 2006.

Pai, Hsiao-Hung. *Angry White People: Coming Face-to-Face With the British Far Right.* London: Zed Books, 2016.

Pantucci, Raffaello. *"We Love Death as You Love Life": Britain's Suburban Terrorists.* London: C. Hurst & Co., 2015.

Parashar, Swati. "Gender, Jihad, and Jingoism: Women as Perpetrators, Planners, and Patrons of Militancy in Kashmir". *Studies in Conflict & Terrorism* vol. 34, no. 4 (2011): 295–317.

Parpart, Jane L., and Marysia Zalewski. "Introduction: Rethinking the Man Question". In *Rethinking the Man Question: Sex, Gender and Violence in International Relations.* Eds Jane L. Parpart and Marysia Zalewski. London; New York, NY: Zed Books, 2008. 1–22.

Peachey, Paul, Jonathan Brown and Kim Sengupta. "Lee Rigby Murder: How Killers Michael Adebolajo and Michael Adebowale Became Ultra-Violent Radicals". *The Independent.* 19 December 2013. https://www.independent.co.uk/news/uk/crime/lee-rigby-murder-how-killers-michael-adebolajo-and-michael-adebowale-became-ultraviolent-radicals-9015743.html. Last accessed 16 August 2023.

Pearson, Elizabeth. "The Case of Roshonara Choudhry: Implications for Theory on Online Radicalization, ISIS Women, and the Gendered Jihad". *Policy & Internet* vol. 8, no. 1 (2015): 5–33.

————. "Online as the New Frontline: Affect, Gender, and ISIS-Take-Down on Social Media". *Studies in Conflict & Terrorism* vol. 49, no. 11 (2017): 850–74.

————. "Why Men Fight and Women Don't: Masculinity and Extremist Violence". Tony Blair Institute for Global Change. September 2018. http://institute.global/insight/co-existence/why-men-fight-and-women-dont-masculinity-and-extremist-violence. Last accessed 31 July 2023.

————. "Wīlayat Shahīdat: Boko Haram, the Islamic State, and the Question of the Female Suicide Bomber". In *Boko Haram: Behind the Headlines.* Eds Jason Warner and Jacob Zenn. West Point, NY: CTC Sentinel, 2018. 33–52.

————. "Extremism and Toxic Masculinity: The Man Question Re-Posed". *International Affairs* vol. 95, no. 6 (2019): 1251–70.

————. "Gendered Reflections? Extremism in the UK's Radical Right and al-Muhajiroun Networks". *Studies in Conflict & Terrorism* vol. 46, no. 4 (2023): 489–512.

Pearson, Elizabeth, and Chitra Nagarajan. "Gendered Security Harms: State Policy and the Counterinsurgency Against Boko Haram". *African Conflict and Peacebuilding Review* vol. 10, no. 2 (2020): 108–40.

Pearson, Elizabeth, and Emily Winterbotham. "Women, Gender and Daesh Radicalisation: A Milieu Approach". *The RUSI Journal* vol. 162, no. 3 (28 July 2017): 60–72.

Pearson, Elizabeth, Emily Winterbotham and Katherine E. Brown. *Countering Violent Extremism: Making Gender Matter*. Basingstoke: Palgrave Macmillan, 2020.

Pearson, Elizabeth, and Jacob Zenn. "#BringBackOurGirls? Two Years After the Chibok Girls Were Taken, What Do We Know?". War on the Rocks. 14 April 2016. http://warontherocks.com/2016/04/bringbackourgirls-two-years-after-the-chibok-girls-were-taken-what-do-we-know/. Last accessed 31 July 2023.

Pedahzur, Ami, Arie Perliger and Leonard Weinberg. "Altruism and Fatalism: The Characteristics of Palestinian Suicide Terrorists". *Deviant Behavior* vol. 24, no. 4 (2003): 405–23.

Perry, Barbara, and Ryan Scrivens. "Uneasy Alliances: A Look at the Right-Wing Extremist Movement in Canada". *Studies in Conflict & Terrorism* vol. 39, no. 9 (2016): 819–41.

Peter, Marshall. "EDL Women Tell Cameron We're Not Sick". Demotix. 8 October 2011. https://web.archive.org/web/20111011144736/http://www.demotix.com/news/863998/edl-women-tell-cameron-were-not-sick. Last accessed 15 August 2023.

Peterson, Spike V. "How (the Meaning of) Gender Matters in Political Economy". *New Political Economy* vol. 10, no. 4 (2005): 499–521.

Peterson, V. Spike. "Introduction". *Gendered States: Feminist (Re)visions of International Relations Theory*. Ed. V. Spike Peterson. Boulder, CO; London: Lynne Rienner, 1992. 1–30.

———. "Gendered Nationalism". *Peace Review* vol. 6, no. 1 (1994): 77–83.

Pfeil, Fred. *White Guys: Studies in Postmodern Domination and Difference*. London: Verso Books, 1995.

Pilkington, Hilary. *Loud and Proud: Passion and Politics in the English Defence League*. Manchester: Manchester University Press, 2016.

———. "'EDL Angels Stand Beside Their Men… Not Behind Them': The Politics of Gender and Sexuality in an Anti-Islam(Ist) Movement". *Gender and Education* vol. 29, no. 2 (2017): 238–57.

Pin-Fat, Véronique, and Maria Stern. "The Scripting of Private Jessica Lynch". *Alternatives: Global, Local, Political* vol. 30, no. 1 (2005): 25–53.

Polletta, Francesca, James M. Jasper and Jeff Goodwin. "Introduction: Why Emotions Matter." *Passionate Politics: Emotions and Social Movements*. Chicago, IL: University of Chicago Press, 2001. 1–26.

Poloni-Staudinger, Lori, and Candice D. Ortbals. *Terrorism and Violent Conflict: Women's Agency, Leadership, and Responses*. New York, NY: Springer, 2012.

Porta, Donatella della, and Mario Diani. *Social Movements: An Introduction*. Malden, MA: Wiley-Blackwell, 2005.

Porta, Donatella della, and Heinz-Gerhard Haupt. "Patterns of Radicalization in Political Activism: An Introduction". *Social Science History* vol. 36, no. 3 (2012): 311–20.

Poulter, James. "The English Far-Right's War on Anti-Fascist Football Ultras". Vice. 13 February 2015. https://www.vice.com/en/article/4wm3jb/is-english-far-right-hooligans-war-on-left-wing-football-ultras-spreading-to-the-premier-league-181. Last accessed 14 August 2023.

Powell, Tom. "Hundreds of Protesters Descend on Whitehall after Tommy Robinson Arrested for 'Breaching the Peace'". *Evening Standard*. 26 May 2018. https://www.standard.co.uk/news/london/hundreds-of-protesters-descend-on-whitehall-after-tommy-robinson-arrested-for-breaching-the-peace-a3849046.html. Last accessed 31 August 2023.

Puar, Jasbir K., and Amit S. Rai. "Monster, Terrorist, Fag: The War on Terrorism and the Production of Docile Patriots". *Social Text* vol. 20, no. 3 (2002): 117–48.

Pyke, Karen D., and Denise L. Johnson. "Asian American Women and Racialized Femininities: 'Doing' Gender Across Cultural Worlds". *Gender and Society* vol. 17, no. 1 (2003): 33–53.

Quilliam. "Quilliam Briefing Paper: The Threat of Radicalisation on British University Campuses". London: Quilliam, 2010.

Quinn, Ben. "Tommy Robinson Link With Quilliam Foundation Raises Questions". *The Guardian*. 12 October 2013. https://www.theguardian.com/uk-news/2013/oct/12/tommy-robinson-quilliam-foundation-questions-motivation. Last accessed 13 August 2023.

———. "French Police Make Woman Remove Clothing on Nice Beach Following Burkini Ban. *The Guardian*. 24 August 2016. https://www.theguardian.com/world/2016/aug/24/french-police-make-woman-remove-burkini-on-nice-beach. Last accessed 10 August 2023.

Qutb, Sayyid. *Milestones*. London: Islamic Book Service, 2006.

Rajan, V. G. Julie. *Women Suicide Bombers: Narratives of Violence*. London: Routledge, 2012.

Ralph-Morrow, Elizabeth. "Vigilantism in the United Kingdom: Britain First and 'Operation Fightback'". In *Vigilantism Against Migrants and Minorities*. Eds Tore Bjørgo and Miroslav Mareš. Abingdon; New York, NY: Routledge, 2019.

Ramalingam, Vidhya. "Old Threat, New Approach: Tackling the Far Right Across Europe". London: Institute for Strategic Dialogue, 2014. https://www.isdglobal.org/wp-content/uploads/2016/03/OldThreatNewApproach_2014.pdf. Last accessed 6 August 2023.

Ranstorp, Magnus. "Introduction: Mapping Terrorism Research – Challenges and Priorities". In *Mapping Terrorism Research: State of the Art, Gaps and Future Direction*. Ed. Magnus Ranstorp. London; New York, NY: Routledge, 2007. 1–28.

Rapoport, David. "The Fourth Wave: September 11 in the History of Terrorism". *Current History* vol. 100, no. 650 (2001): 419–24.

Rashid, Naaz. *Veiled Threats: Representing the Muslim Woman in Public Policy Discourses*. Bristol: Policy Press, 2008.

BIBLIOGRAPHY

————. "Giving the Silent Majority a Stronger Voice? Initiatives to Empower Muslim Women as Part of the UK's 'War on Terror'". *Ethnic and Racial Studies* vol. 37, no. 4 (2014): 589–604.

Raymond, Catherine Zara. "Al Muhajiroun and Islam4UK: The Group Behind the Ban". King's College London: International Centre for the Study of Radicalisation and Political Violence. May 2010. https://icsr.info/wp-content/uploads/2010/06/ICSR-Feature-Al-Muhajiroun-and-Islam4UK-The-group-behind-the-ban.pdf. Last accessed 16 August 2023.

Rensmann, Lars. "The New Politics of Prejudice: Comparative Perspectives on Extreme Right Parties in European Democracies". *German Politics & Society* vol. 21, no. 4 (2003): 93–123.

Richards, Anthony. "Conceptualizing Terrorism". *Studies in Conflict & Terrorism* vol. 37, no. 3 (2014): 213–36.

————. "From Terrorism to 'Radicalization' to 'Extremism': Counterterrorism Imperative or Loss of Focus?". *International Affairs* vol. 91, no. 2 (2015): 371–80.

Roberts, Mary Louise. "Beyond 'Crisis' in Understanding Gender Transformation". *Gender & History* vol. 28, no. 2 (2016): 358–66.

Robinson, Fiona. "Stop Talking and Listen: Discourse Ethics and Feminist Care Ethics in International Political Theory". *Millennium – Journal of International Studies* vol. 39, no. 3 (2011): 845–60.

Robinson, Sally. "Pedagogy of the Opaque: Teaching Masculinity Studies". In *Masculinity Studies and Feminist Theory*. Ed. Judith Kegan Gardiner. New York, NY: Columbia University Press, 2002.

Robinson, Tommy. *MIG Crew. The Story of Luton's MIG Crew As Told From the Sharp End of Football's Frontline*. Hove: Pennant Books Ltd, 2007.

Robinson, Tommy. *Enemy of the State*. Batley: The Press News Ltd, 2015.

Rogers, Brooke, and Peter R. Neumann. "Recruitment and Mobilisation for the Islamist Militant Movement in Europe". King's College London, International Centre for the Study of Radicalisation and Political Violence. 2007. https://icsr.info/wp-content/uploads/2008/10/1234516791ICSREUResearchReport_Proof1.pdf. Last accessed 16 August 2023.

Rolin, Kristina. "Standpoint Theory as a Methodology for the Study of Power Relations". *Hypatia* vol. 24, no. 4 (2009): 218–26.

Roose, Joshua M., and Joana Cook. "Supreme Men, Subjected Women: Gender Inequality and Violence in Jihadist, Far Right and Male Supremacist Ideologies". *Studies in Conflict & Terrorism* (2022): 1–29.

Roose, Joshua M., Michael Flood, Alan Greig, Mark Alfano and Simon Copland. *Masculinity and Violent Extremism*. Basingstoke: Palgrave Macmillan, 2022.

Roy, Olivier. "Islamic Terrorist Radicalisation in Europe". In *European Islam: The Challenges for Society and Public Policy*. Eds Samir Amghar, Amel Boubekeur and Michael Emerson. Brussels: Centre for European Policy Studies, 2007. https://www.ceps.eu/wp-content/uploads/2013/02/1556.pdf. Last accessed 1 August 2023.

BIBLIOGRAPHY

————. *Jihad and Death: The Global Appeal of Islamic State*. London: C. Hurst & Co., 2017.

Rubin, Gayle S. "Thinking Sex: Notes for a Radical Theory of the Politics of Sexuality". In *Deviations: A Gayle Rubin Reader*. Durham, NC: Duke University Press, 2011. 137–81.

Rutherford, Adam. *How to Argue With a Racist: History, Science, Race and Reality*. London: Weidenfeld & Nicolson, 2020.

Sageman, Marc. *Understanding Terror Networks*. Philadelphia, PA: University of Pennsylvania Press, 2004.

————. *Leaderless Jihad: Terror Networks in the Twenty-First Century*. Philadelphia, PA: University of Pennsylvania Press, 2008.

————. "The Stagnation in Terrorism Research". *Terrorism and Political Violence*, vol. 26, no. 4 (2014): 565–80.

————. *Misunderstanding Terrorism*. Philadelphia, PA: University of Pennsylvania Press, 2016.

Salter, Michael. "The Problem With a Fight Against Toxic Masculinity". *The Atlantic*. 27 February 2019. https://www.theatlantic.com/health/archive/2019/02/toxic-masculinity-history/583411/. Last accessed 31 July 2023.

Sandberg, Sveinung. "How Gangsters Become Jihadists (And Why Most Don't): Bourdieu, Criminology, and the Crime–Terror Nexus". Faculty of Law Blogs, University of Oxford. 5 November 2018. https://blogs.law.ox.ac.uk/centres-institutes/centre-criminology/blog/2018/11/how-gangsters-become-jihadists-and-why-most-dont. Last accessed 16 August 2023.

Sarnoff, Daniella. "Domesticating Fascism: Family and Gender in French Fascist Leagues". In *Women of the Right: Comparisons and Interplay Across Borders*. Eds Kathleen M. Blee and Sandra McGee Deutsch. University Park, PA: Penn State University Press, 2012. 163–76.

Schippers, Mimi. "Recovering the Feminine Other: Masculinity, Femininity, and Gender Hegemony". *Theory and Society* vol. 36, no. 1 (2007): 85–102.

Schmid, Alex P. "Radicalisation, De-Radicalisation, Counter-Radicalisation: A Conceptual Discussion and Literature Review". International Centre for Counter-Terrorism, The Hague. 2013. https://www.icct.nl/sites/default/files/import/publication/ICCT-Schmid-Radicalisation-De-Radicalisation-Counter-Radicalisation-March-2013_2.pdf. Last accessed 26 July 2023.

Schull, Joseph. "What Is Ideology? Theoretical Problems and Lessons from Soviet-Type Societies". *Political Studies* vol. 40, no. 4 (1992): 728–41.

Scott, Joan. "Gender: A Useful Category of Historical Analysis". *The American Historical Review* vol. 91, no. 5 (1986): 1053–75.

Scrinzi, Francesca. "Caring for the Nation: Men and Women Activists in Radical Right Populist Parties". Final Research Report, European Research Council. 2014. https://www.gla.ac.uk/media/Media_383799_smxx.pdf. Last accessed 15 August 2023.

Searchlight Team. "Anne-Marie Waters Announces that For Britain Has Folded". 13 July

2022. https://www.searchlightmagazine.com/2022/07/anne-marie-waters-announces-that-for-britain-has-folded/#. Last accessed 19 September 2023.

Sedgwick, Eve Kosofsky. "Gosh, Boy George, You Must Be Awfully Secure in Your Masculinity". In *Constructing Masculinity*. Eds Maurice Berger, Brian Wallis and Simon Watson. London; New York, NY: Routledge, 1995. 11–20.

Seghal, Meera. "Mothering the Nation: Maternalist Frames in the Hindu Nationalist Movement in India". In *Women of the Right: Comparisons and Interplay Across Borders*. Eds Kathleen M. Blee and Sandra McGee Deutsch. University Park, PA: Penn State University Press, 2012. 192–207.

Segun, Mausi and Samer Muscati. "'Those Terrible Weeks in Their Camp': Boko Haram Violence Against Women and Girls in Northeast Nigeria". Human Rights Watch, 2014. http://www.hrw.org/sites/default/files/reports/nigeria1014web.pdf. Last accessed 27 July 2023.

Seierstad, Asne. *One of Us: The Story of Anders Breivik and the Massacre in Norway*. Trans. Sarah Death. London: Virago, 2015.

Sharia Watch Team and Anne Marie Waters. "Introduction To Sharia Watch". Sharia Watch UK. http://www.shariawatch.org.uk/?q=content/introduction-sharia-watch. Last accessed 20 March 2018.

Shepherd, Laura J. "Veiled References: Constructions of Gender in the Bush Administration Discourse on the Attacks on Afghanistan Post-9/11". *International Feminist Journal of Politics* vol. 8, no. 1 (2006): 19–41.

———. "White Feminism and the Governance of Violent Extremism". *Critical Studies on Terrorism* vol. 15, no. 3 (2022): 727–49.

Silber, Mitchell D., and Arvin Bhatt. "Radicalization in the West: The Homegrown Threat". New York Police Department. 2007. https://info.publicintelligence.net/NYPDradicalization.pdf. Last accessed 12 August 2023.

Silke, Andrew. "Cheshire-Cat Logic: The Recurring Theme of Terrorist Abnormality in Psychological Research". *Psychology, Crime & Law* vol. 4, no. 1 (1998): 51–69.

———. "The Devil You Know: Continuing Problems with Research on Terrorism". *Terrorism and Political Violence* vol. 13, no. 4 (2001): 1–14.

———, ed. *Terrorists, Victims and Society: Psychological Perspectives on Terrorism and Its Consequences*. Chichester; Hoboken, NJ: Wiley-Blackwell, 2003.

Sjoberg, Laura. *Gendering Global Conflict: Toward a Feminist Theory of War*. New York, NY: Columbia University Press, 2013.

Sjoberg, Laura, Grace D. Cooke and Stacy Reiter Neal. "Introduction". In *Women, Gender, and Terrorism*. Eds Laura Sjoberg and Caron E. Gentry. Athens, GA: University of Georgia Press, 2011. 1–26.

Skeggs, Bev. "The Making of Class and Gender Through Visualizing Moral Subject Formation". *Sociology* vol. 39, no. 5 (2005): 965–82.

Slack, James. "Banned Terror Group Al Muhajiroun Exploits Government Loophole to Reform Under New Hate-Filled Guise". *Daily Mail*. 17 June 2009. http://www.dailymail.co.uk/news/article-1193706/Banned-terror-group-Al-Muhajiroun-exploits-government-loophole-reform-new-hate-filled-guise.html. Last accessed 31 July 2023.

Slater, Philip. "On Social Regression". *American Sociological Review* vol. 28, no. 3 (1963): 339–64.

Smith, Joan. *Home Grown: How Domestic Violence Turns Men Into Terrorists*. London: riverrun, 2019.

————. "How Toxic Masculinity Is Tied to Terrorism". UnHerd. 16 May 2019. https://unherd.com/2019/05/how-toxic-masculinity-is-tied-to-terrorism/. Last accessed 31 July 2023.

Somers, Margaret R. "The Narrative Constitution of Identity: A Relational and Network Approach". *Theory and Society* vol. 23, no. 5 (1994): 605–49.

Sommers, Jack. "Dover Protest Turns Violent as Far Right Clashes With Anti-Fascist Demonstrators". HuffPost UK. 30 January 2016. https://www.huffingtonpost.co.uk/2016/01/30/dover-protest-turns-violent-demonstrator-bloodied_n_9119604.html. Last accessed 15 August 2023.

Spaaij, Ramón. "Men Like Us, Boys Like Them: Violence, Masculinity, and Collective Identity in Football Hooliganism". *Journal of Sport and Social Issues* vol. 32, no. 4 (2008): 369–92.

Speckhard, Anne. *Talking to Terrorists: Understanding the Psycho-Social Motivations of Militant Jihadi Terrorists, Mass Hostage Takers, Suicide Bombers &"Martyrs"*. McLean, VA: Advances Press, 2012.

Spierings, Niels, and Andrej Zaslove. "Gendering the Vote for Populist Radical-Right Parties". *Patterns of Prejudice* vol. 49, no. 1–2 (2015): 135–62.

Stampnitzky, Lisa. *Disciplining Terror: How Experts Invented "Terrorism"*. Cambridge; New York, NY: Cambridge University Press, 2013.

Stand Up To Racism. "Football Lads Alliance (FLA) Founder Quits, but FLA Is Still a Growing Danger". 17 April 2018. http://www.standuptoracism.org.uk/football-lads-alliance-fla-founder-quits-but-fla-is-still-a-growing-danger/. Last accessed 11 August 2023.

Statham, Paul, Ruud Koopmans, Marco Giugni and Florence Passy. "Resilient or Adaptable Islam? Multiculturalism, Religion and Migrants' Claims-Making for Group Demands in Britain, the Netherlands and France". *Ethnicities* vol. 5, no. 4 (2005): 427–59.

Stearns, Peter. "History of Emotions: Issues of Change and Impact". In *Handbook of Emotions,* 3rd edition. Eds Michael Lewis, Jeannette M. Haviland-Jones and Lisa Feldman Barrett. London: Guilford Press, 2008. 17–31.

Stern, Maria. "Security Outsourcing and Critical Feminist Inquiry: Taking Stock and Looking Forward". In *The Routledge Research Companion to Security Outsourcing.* Eds Joakim Berndtsson and Christopher Kinsey London: Routledge, 2016. 283–90.

Stern, Maria, and Marysia Zalewski. "Feminist Fatigue(s): Reflections on Feminism and Familiar Fables of Militarisation". *Review of International Studies* vol. 35, no. 3 (2009): 611–30.

Stewart, Stephen. "Football Hooligan Heads to Scotland in Recruitment Drive for Far-Right Group". *Daily Record*. 28 October 2017. http://www.dailyrecord.co.uk/news/scottish-news/football-hooligan-heads-scotland-recruitment-11422487. Last accessed 14 August 2023.

Stoltenberg, John. "Andrea Dworkin Was a Trans Ally". *Boston Review*. 8 April 2020. https://www.bostonreview.net/articles/john-stoltenberg-andrew-dworkin-was-trans-ally/. Last accessed 16 August 2023.

Stone, Jennie, and Katherine Pattillo. "Al-Qaeda's Use of Female Suicide Bombers in Iraq: A Case Study". In *Women, Gender, and Terrorism*. Eds Laura Sjoberg and Caron E. Gentry. Athens, GA: University of Georgia Press, 2011.

Sutton, Rupert. "Preventing Prevent? Challenges to Counter-Radicalisaton Policy on Campus". London: Henry Jackson Society, 2015. https://henryjacksonsociety.org/wp-content/uploads/2015/10/Preventing-Prevent_webversion3.pdf. Last accessed 16 August 2023.

Sweney, Mark. "'Proud to Be a Disruptor': GB News Faces Growing Pains as It Tries to Clean Up Image". *The Guardian*. 17 January 2023. https://www.theguardian.com/media/2023/jan/17/gb-news-rightwing-tv-channel. Last accessed 13 August 2023.

Sylvester, Christine. "Empathetic Cooperation: A Feminist Method For IR". *Millennium – Journal of International Studies* vol. 23, no. 2 (1994): 315–34.

Tajfel, Henri, ed. *Differentiation Between Social Groups: Studies in the Social Psychology of Intergroup Relations*. London; New York, NY: Academic Press, 1979.

Telegraph Reporting Team. "Britain First Leader and Deputy Jailed for Religiously-Aggravated Harassment Over 'Hostility' Towards Muslims". *The Telegraph*. 7 March 2018. https://www.telegraph.co.uk/news/2018/03/07/britain-first-leader-deputy-guilty-religiously-aggravated-harassment/. Last accessed 30 July 2023.

Tellmama. "Understanding Hate Incident Patterns After the Westminster Terrorist Attack of the 22nd of March 2017. Building a Pattern of Community Resilience Against Hate – What Worked?". TellMAMA (blog). 4 December 2018. https://tellmamauk.org/understanding-hate-incident-patterns-after-the-westminster-terrorist-attack-of-the-22nd-of-march-2017-building-a-pattern-of-community-resilience-against-hate-what-worked/. Last accessed 16 August 2023.

Tickner, J. Ann. "You Just Don't Understand: Troubled Engagements Between Feminists and IR Theorists". *International Studies Quarterly* vol. 41, no. 4 (1997): 611–32.

Todd, Selina. *The People: The Rise and Fall of the Working Class, 1910–2010*. London: John Murray, 2014.

"Tommy Robinson: 'I Left the EDL to Work With Muslims and Defeat Islamist Ideology'". *Daily Express*. 8 October 2013. http://www.express.co.uk/news/uk/435321/Tommy-Robinson-I-left-the-EDL-to-work-with-Muslims-and-defeat-Islamist-ideology. Last accessed 13 August 2023.

Toros, Harmonie. "Better Researchers, Better People? The Dangers of Empathetic Research on the Extreme Right". *Critical Studies on Terrorism* vol. 15, no. 1 (2022): 225–31.

Travis, Alan. "Extremist Islamist Groups to Be Banned Under New Terror Laws". *The Guardian*. 11 January 2010. http://www.theguardian.com/politics/2010/jan/11/islam4uk-al-muhajiroun-ban-laws. Last accessed 30 July 2023.

BIBLIOGRAPHY

Treadwell, James. "White Riot: The English Defence League and the 2011 English Riots". *Criminal Justice Matters* vol. 87, no. 1 (2012): 36–37.

Treadwell, James, and John Garland. "Masculinity, Marginalization and Violence: A Case Study of the English Defence League". *British Journal of Criminology* vol. 51, no. 4 (2011): 621–34.

True, Jacqui. "Setting the Scene for Preventing Violent Extremism in South East and South Asia: A Way Forward for Women's Engagement in Indonesia and Bangladesh". Monash Gender, Peace and Security Centre. 2019. https://asiapacific.unwomen.org/sites/default/files/2023-03/ap-Monash-Policy-Brief_WEB-re.PDF. Last accessed 31 July 2023.

True, Jacqui, and Melissa Johnston. "Misogyny & Violent Extremism: Implications for Preventing Violent Extremism". UN Women. September 2019. https://asiapacific.unwomen.org/en/digital-library/publications/2019/10/misogyny-violent-extremism. Last accessed 31 July 2023.

Tsukayama, Hayley, and Craig Timberg. "'Twitter Purge' Suspends Account of Far-Right Leader Who Was Retweeted by Trump". *Washington Post*. 5 December 2021. https://www.washingtonpost.com/news/the-switch/wp/2017/12/18/twitter-purge-suspends-account-of-far-right-leader-who-was-retweeted-by-trump/. Last accessed 8 August 2023.

Tyler, Imogen. "'Chav Mum Chav Scum': Class Disgust in Contemporary Britain". *Feminist Media Studies* vol. 8, no. 1 (2008): 17–34.

UN News. "UN Human Rights Panel Concludes ISIL Is Committing Genocide Against Yazidis". 16 June 2016. https://news.un.org/en/story/2016/06/532312. Last accessed 23 July 2023.

UN Women. "Concepts and Definitions". https://www.un.org/womenwatch/osagi/conceptsandefinitions.htm. Last accessed 22 August 2023.

United States Department of State. "Country Reports on Human Rights Practices for 2016: Iraq". Bureau of Democracy, Human Rights and Labor. 7 March 2017. https://web.archive.org/web/20170307090250/https://www.state.gov/documents/organization/265710.pdf. Last accessed 29 July 2023.

Urquhart, Conal, and Mark Townsend. "EDL Marchers Scuffle with Anti-Racist Protesters Near East London Mosque". *The Guardian*. 7 September 2013. https://www.theguardian.com/uk-news/2013/sep/07/edl-marchers-east-london-mosque. Last accessed 14 August 2023.

Urry, John. "The Global Complexities of September 11th". *Theory, Culture & Society* vol. 19, no. 4 (2002): 57–69.

USAID. "Guide to the Drivers of Violent Extremism". 2009. https://www.cvereferenceguide.org/sites/default/files/resources/USAID%20Guide%20to%20the%20Drivers%20of%20Violent%20Extremism%20%281%29.pdf. Last accessed 16 August 2023.

Vale, Gina. "Liberated, Not Free: Yazidi Women after Islamic State Captivity". *Small Wars & Insurgencies* vol. 31, no. 3 (2020): 511–39.

Victoroff, Jeff. "The Mind of the Terrorist: A Review and Critique of Psychological Approaches". *Journal of Conflict Resolution* vol. 49, no. 1 (2005): 3–42.

BIBLIOGRAPHY

Vidino, Lorenzo. "Islamism in Europe". World Watch Research Unit of Open Doors International. 2015. http://opendoorsanalytical.org/wp-content/uploads/2014/10/Islamism-in-Europe-2015.pdf. Last accessed 16 August 2023.

———. "Sharia4: From Confrontational Activism to Militancy". *Perspectives on Terrorism* vol. 9, no. 2 (2015): 2–16.

Virchow, Fabian. "Performance, Emotion, and Ideology: On the Creation of 'Collectives of Emotion' and Worldview in the Contemporary German Far Right". *Journal of Contemporary Ethnography* vol. 36, no. 2 (2007): 147–64.

Walby, Sylvia. "Theorising Patriarchy". *Sociology* vol. 23, no. 2 (1989): 213–34.

———. *Theorising Patriarchy*. Oxford: Basil Blackwell, 1990.

Walton, Chris, Adrian Coyle and Evanthia Lyons. "Death and Football: An Analysis of Men's Talk About Emotions". *The British Journal of Social Psychology* vol. 43, no. 3 (2004): 401–16.

Ward, Albert. "Parliament and Government Have a Class Problem". British Politics and Policy at LSE (blog). 27 October 2022. https://blogs.lse.ac.uk/politicsandpolicy/parliament-and-government-have-a-class-problem/. Last accessed 13 August 2023.

Ware, Vron. "Whiteness in the Glare of War: Soldiers, Migrants and Citizenship". *Ethnicities* vol. 10, no. 3 (2010). 313–30.

Waters, Anne Marie. "Announcement From Anne Marie Waters". For Britain (blog). 13 July 2022. https://www.forbritain.uk/2022/07/13/announcement-from-anne-marie-waters/. Last accessed 13 July 2022.

Weber, Cynthia. *International Relations Theory: A Critical Introduction*. New York, NY: Routledge, 2004.

Wedgwood, Nikki. "Connell's Theory of Masculinity – Its Origins and Influences on the Study of Gender". *Journal of Gender Studies* vol. 18, no. 4 (2009): 329–39.

Weeks, Douglas. "Doing Derad: An Analysis of the U.K. System". *Studies in Conflict & Terrorism* vol. 41, no. 7 (2017): 523–40.

———. *Al Muhajiroun: A Case Study in Contemporary Islamic Activism*. Basingstoke: Palgrave Macmillan, 2020.

West, Candace and Sarah Fenstermaker. "Doing Difference". *Gender & Society* vol. 9, no. 1 (1995): 8–37.

Wetherell, Margaret. *Affect and Emotion: A New Social Science Understanding*. Los Angeles, CA; London: SAGE Publications, 2012.

Wheeler, Nicholas J. "Investigating Diplomatic Transformations". *International Affairs* vol. 89, no. 2 (2013): 477–96.

Whitehead, Antony. "Man to Man Violence: How Masculinity May Work as a Dynamic Risk Factor". *The Howard Journal of Criminal Justice* vol. 44, no. 4 (2005): 411–22.

Whitehead, Stephen M., and Frank J. Barrett. "The Sociology of Masculinity". In *The Masculinities Reader*. Eds Stephen M. Whitehead and Frank J. Barrett. Cambridge: Polity Press, 2001. 1–26.

Wiktorowicz, Quintan. *Radical Islam Rising: Muslim Extremism in the West*. Lanham, MD: Rowman & Littlefield, 2005.

BIBLIOGRAPHY

————. "Anatomy of the Salafi Movement". *Studies in Conflict & Terrorism* vol. 29, no. 3 (2006): 207–39.

Wilson, Helen, and Annette Huntington. "Deviant (M)others: The Construction of Teenage Motherhood in Contemporary Discourse". *Journal of Social Policy* vol. 35, no. 1 (2006): 59–76.

Windisch, Beth. "A Downward Spiral: The Role of Hegemonic Masculinity in Lone Actor Terrorism". *Studies in Conflict & Terrorism* (2021): 1–18.

Winter, Charlie. "Women of the Islamic State: A Manifesto on Women by the Al-Khanssaa Brigade". London: The Quilliam Foundation, 2015.

Winterbotham, Emily, and Elizabeth Pearson. "Different Cities, Shared Stories: A Five-Country Study Challenging Assumptions Around Muslim Women and CVE Interventions". *RUSI Journal* vol. 161, no. 5 (2016): 54–65.

Wright, Lawrence. *The Looming Tower: Al Qaeda's Road to 9/11*. London: Penguin, 2007.

York, Chris. "EDL in Birmingham Shown Where to Go by Mosque and Residents". *The Huffington Post*. 6 April 2017. http://www.huffingtonpost.co.uk/entry/edl-in-birmingham_uk_58e93ffee4b05413bfe36c87. Last accessed 14 August 2023.

Yuval-Davis, Nira. "Women and the Biological Reproduction of 'The Nation'". *Women's Studies International Forum* vol. 19, no. 1/2 (1996): 17–24.

Yuval-Davis, Nira, Floya Anthias and Eleonore Kofman. "Secure Borders and Safe Haven and the Gendered Politics of Belonging: Beyond Social Cohesion". *Ethnic and Racial Studies* vol. 28, no. 3 (2005): 513–35.

Zalewski, Marysia. "Introduction". In *The 'Man' Question in International Relations*. Eds Marysia Zalewski and Jane L. Parpart. Boulder, CO: Routledge, 1997. 1–13.

Zenn, Jacob, and Elizabeth Pearson. "Women, Gender and the Evolving Tactics of Boko Haram". *Journal of Terrorism Research* vol. 5, no. 1 (2014): 46–57.

Zerbisias, Antonia. "Canada Hijab Row Is All About the Anti-Terror Act". Al Jazeera. 5 March 2015. http://www.aljazeera.com/indepth/opinion/2015/03/canada-hijab-row-anti-terror-act-150303085632396.html. Last accessed 11 August 2023.

Zimmerman, Shannon, Luisa Ryan and David Duriesmith. "Recognizing the Violent Extremist Ideology of 'Incels'". Women in International Security. 2018. https://www.wiisglobal.org/wp-content/uploads/2018/09/Policybrief-Violent-Extremists-Incels.pdf. Last accessed 31 July 2023.

INDEX

INDEX

Wahhabism, 191
Walby, Sylvia, 150
Waldmann, Peter, 33
'War on Terror' (WOT), 30–1, 56,
    183, 184, 185, 258, 265
Warner, Bill, 117
Waters, Anne Marie, 19, 25, 60,
    71, 77, 78, 79, 92–3, 110, 129,
    257, 259
  feminine exclusion, 168–78
  masculinity, 140–1
  media, leaders on, 119–22
  racism, 104–5
  radical right, women in, 155–68
Wedgwood, Nikki, 265
Weeks, Doug, 11
Western Europe, 36
Western liberalism, 106
Wetherell, Margaret, 129–30,
    141–2
White Lives Matter, 79, 128, 142,
    145–6
Whitehall, 123
whiteness, 56-8, 89, 143-4, 255
  radical right masculinities 100-7
Wiktorowicz, Quintan, 11, 106,
    183, 211
'Wokewatch', 120
Women and War (Elshtain), 151
Women, Peace and Security (WPS)
    agenda, 13, 28
women
  ALM women, 259–60
  ALM, patriarchal model, 259
  class-based exclusion, 192–4
  and extremism, 36–41
  extremism, gender neglecting,
    44–7
  female group, importance of,
    246–7

feminine exclusion, 168–78
gender inequalities and
    education, 88–99
gender values, 222–9
gendered approach, 261–5
group's gendered ideology,
    229–34
importance, 256
jihadist masculinities, 217–22
masculinities, complex function
    of, 41–4
masculinity studies, 267–71
patriarchal community norms,
    201–4
patriarchal structures, 198–200
racism and discrimination,
    204–11
radical right, women in, 155–68
radical-right participants, 77–9
secular behaviour and gendered
    norms, 195–8
terrorism studies, interviewees
    approaches, 59–68
women's rights, 153–4, 178–9
See also feminism; misogyny
World War II, 117, 143

'X', 2

Yaxley-Lennon, Stephen. See
    Robinson, Tommy
Yezidi women, 5, 28
Yuval-Davis, Nira, 152, 208

Zainab, 241
Zakir (ALM participant), 186, 188,
    192–3, 204, 207, 208, 233–4,
    239–40, 241
Zalewski, Marysia, 38, 263, 267
Zaslove, Andrej, 153